Vulnerability in developing countries

The UNU World Institute for Development Economics Research (UNU-WIDER) was established by the United Nations University as its first research and training centre and started work in Helsinki, Finland, in 1985. The purpose of the institute is to undertake applied research and policy analysis on structural changes affecting developing and transitional economies, to provide a forum for the advocacy of policies leading to robust, equitable and environmentally sustainable growth and to promote capacity-strengthening and training in the field of economic and social policy-making. Its work is carried out by staff researchers and visiting scholars in Helsinki and via networks of collaborating scholars and institutions around the world.

World Institute for Development Economics Research (UNU-WIDER)
Katajanokanlaituri 6 B, FIN-00160 Helsinki, Finland
www.wider.unu.edu

**UNITED NATIONS
UNIVERSITY**

UNU-WIDER

World Institute for Development
Economics Research

Vulnerability in developing countries

Edited by Wim Naudé, Amelia U. Santos-Paulino and Mark McGillivray

United Nations
University Press

TOKYO · NEW YORK · PARIS

United Nations University Press
United Nations University, 53-70, Jingumae 5-chome,
Shibuya-ku, Tokyo 150-8925, Japan
Tel: +81-3-5467-1212   Fax: +81-3-3406-7345
E-mail: sales@hq.unu.edu   general enquiries: press@hq.unu.edu
http://www.unu.edu

United Nations University Office at the United Nations, New York
2 United Nations Plaza, Room DC2-2062, New York, NY 10017, USA
Tel: +1-212-963-6387   Fax: +1-212-371-9454
E-mail: unuona@ony.unu.edu

United Nations University Press is the publishing division of the United Nations University.

Cover design by Mea Rhee
Cover photograph by Ami Vitale/Panos Pictures

Printed in Hong Kong

ISBN 978-92-808-1171-1

Library of Congress Cataloging-in-Publication Data

Vulnerability in developing countries / edited by Wim Naudé, Amelia U. Santos-Paulino and Mark McGillivray.
  p. ; cm.
  Includes bibliographical references and index.
  ISBN 978-9280811711 (pbk.)
  1. Poverty—Developing countries. 2. Public health—Developing countries.
3. Natural disasters—Developing countries. I. Naudé, Wim A. II. Santos
Paulino, Amelia Uliafnova. III. McGillivray, Mark.
  [DNLM: 1. Developing Countries—economics. 2. Poverty. 3. Socioeconomic
Factors. 4. Vulnerable Populations. HC 59.7 V991 2009]
  HC59.7.V83   2009
  362.509172′4—dc22   2009018539

Contents

Figures

Tables

Boxes

Contributors

Colin Andrews is a research analyst within the World Bank's Social Safety Net Team. He previously worked at the UN Food and Agriculture Organization (FAO) within the Agricultural Economics Division. His areas of interest include food policy, vulnerability assessment and supply chain analysis. He holds a Master's degree in Economics from Trinity College, Dublin.

Marlene Attzs is a lecturer in the Department of Economics, University of the West Indies, Trinidad and Tobago. Her primary research interests are in the economics of disaster risk management and climate change adaptation; in gender mainstreaming in disaster risk management and climate change adaptation; and in sustainable tourism development, all with particular reference to small and island developing states.

Ma. Cynthia Serquiña Bantilan is Principal Economist and the Global Theme Leader of the International Crops Research Institute for the Semi-Arid Tropics (ICRISAT) Global Theme on Institutions, Markets, Policy and Impacts. She has a PhD degree in economics and statistics, and has over 30 years' expertise in strategic analysis, research evaluation and impact assessments, monitoring and impact evaluation, poverty and income distribution analysis, econometrics, science policy and research on agriculture–health linkages.

Kate Bird is a socio-economist whose research and advisory work focuses largely on poverty analysis and the tracing of policy impacts to the household and sub-household level. She led the Chronic Poverty Research Centre's research into spatial poverty traps and now leads the Centre's work on the intergenerational transmission of poverty; she is also Programme Leader of the Growth and Equity Programme of the Overseas Development Institute (ODI).

Anis Chowdhury is Professor of Economics, University of Western Sydney (Australia), having obtained his PhD from the University of Manitoba, Canada, and taught at the University of Manitoba, the National University of Singapore and the University of New England (Australia). Founder co-editor of the *Journal of the Asia Pacific Economy*, he has published extensively on East and Southeast Asia. He is currently working at the Department of Economic and Social Affairs of the United Nations (UN-DESA) in New York as Senior Economic Affairs Officer, and has been a consultant to the United Nations Development Programme and the International Labour Organization, and a visiting fellow at UNU-WIDER, the Research Bank of San Francisco and the Institute of Southeast Asian Studies (Singapore).

Margarita Flores is the FAO Representative in Chile. An economist, she holds a PhD from Paris I University. She has worked in the field with peasants' organizations and occupied a Director's post within the Mexican government. She joined the UN system in 1986, first at the Economic Commission for Latin America and the Caribbean. Her areas of interest are rural development and food policy and food security.

Raghav Gaiha is Professor of Public Policy, Faculty of Management Studies, University of Delhi. He has held visiting fellowships at Harvard University, Yale University, MIT, Stanford University, the University of Pennsylvania, the University of Cambridge and the World Bank. He has served as a consultant with the FAO, the International Fund for Agricultural Development, the Asian Development Bank, the Department for International Development and UNU-WIDER. His research interests include poverty, nutrition, institutions and natural disasters in developing countries.

B. Valentine Joseph Gandhi is a consultant for the Social Protection Unit of the World Bank. He is also a Visiting Scientist (Applied Sociology) at ICRISAT. He has a PhD in Economics and Sociology from the Indian Institute of Technology (IIT) Bombay. He specializes in livelihoods analysis, risk and vulnerability, poverty assessments, social protection, HIV/AIDS, agriculture and health, gender, development economics, rural and urban sociology, and qualitative research methodology.

Martin Philipp Heger is a Fulbright Scholar at the University of Hawai'i. His research focuses on natural resource economics and policy, ecosystem valuation and disaster management. He holds a Master's degree in Economics from the University of Vienna and a Master's in Natural Resources and Environmental Management from the University of Hawai'i.

Katsushi Imai is Assistant Professor in Development Economics at the Department of Economics, School of Social Sciences, University of

Manchester. He graduated with an MSc from the London School of Economics and Political Science (LSE) and a PhD from the University of Oxford, and previously taught at Oxford and the University of London. His main research area is poverty and the vulnerability of households in developing countries.

Oleksiy Ivaschenko is an economist in the Europe and Central Asia region of the World Bank. His main research focuses on the analysis of poverty and inequality; international migration; labour markets and health issues in the developing countries.

Alex Julca holds a PhD from the New School for Social Research (New York), having previously followed undergraduate studies in Lima, Peru. He has written on immigration and inequalities and the effects on developing and developed countries. Lately, he has begun writing on the links between structural vulnerabilities and climate change. For the past 10 years he has been working for the United Nations in New York on development and demographic issues.

Rong Kong is Associate Professor in the College of Economics and Management, Northwest Agriculture and Forestry University, China. She has intensive research interests in agribusiness management, agriculture finance, and mid–small enterprises clusters. Currently she is examining the role of trust as it relates to informal, formal and micro-credit lending in China. She obtained her PhD from Northwest

Agriculture and Forestry University in 2002.

Mark McGillivray is Chief Economist of the Australian Agency for International Development. He was previously Deputy Director of UNU-WIDER. He is also an honorary Professor of Development Economics at the University of Glasgow, an External Fellow of the Centre for Economic Development and International Trade at the University of Nottingham, and an Inaugural Fellow of the Human Development and Capability Association.

Cem Mete is Senior Economist at the South Asia region of the World Bank. His current research focuses on the functioning of labour markets in transition countries; the role of changing educational and family circumstances for children's grade progression in Pakistan; and the linkages between socioeconomic status and health outcomes in developing countries.

Wim Naudé is Senior Research Fellow and project director at UNU-WIDER. Previously he was a research director at North-West University, South Africa, and a research officer at the Centre for the Study of African Economies, University of Oxford. He specializes in regional and urban development, entrepreneurship and African development.

Oliver Paddison works in economic affairs at the United Nations in New York. His research interests focus on small-island developing states and least developed countries, relating specifically to natural disasters and climate change, and on social security. He has previously worked for the United Nations in Ethiopia and in Trinidad and Tobago. He obtained his PhD from the Université Catholique de Louvain, Belgium.

Devanathan Parthasarathy is Professor of Sociology at the Department of Humanities and Social Sciences, IIT Bombay, on sabbatical as visiting senior research fellow at the Asia Research Institute, Singapore. A PhD in Sociology, he has taught and researched in interdisciplinary areas in development studies, vulnerability and adaptation to climate change, livelihoods, agriculture and health, caste/ethnic conflicts, gender, law and governance.

Martin Prowse has a background in development studies, and completed his PhD at the University of Manchester on the reform of burley tobacco production and marketing in Malawi. He has worked at the Overseas Development Institute since August 2006, mainly as the managing editor of *The Chronic Poverty Report 2008/09*. His

research interests include poverty and vulnerability, climate change, food security, Q-squared research methodologies and impact evaluation.

Amelia U. Santos-Paulino is Research Fellow and project director at UNU-WIDER. Previously she was a Research Fellow at the University of Sussex's Institute of Development Studies. She holds a PhD in economics from the University of Kent, UK. She has contributed to World Bank and UNCTAD research and publications. She specializes in trade, macroeconomics and development issues.

Calum G. Turvey is the W.I. Myers Professor of Agricultural Finance in the Department of Applied Economics and Management at Cornell University. His research interests include agricultural finance, risk management and rural credit in developing countries. His BSc(Agr) and MSc degrees are in agricultural economics from the University of Guelph in Canada. He holds a PhD in agricultural economics from Purdue University in 1988.

Foreword

Anthony Shorrocks
Director, UNU-WIDER

Vulnerability refers to the risk that some future event will negatively affect the wellbeing of people in a given place. Many people feel that vulnerability is on the increase as population growth and globalization combine to raise humanity's exposure to risk via climate change, natural disasters, disease, conflict and financial crises. Furthermore, it is generally accepted that, although these risks affect everyone, residents of developing countries are more susceptible owing to the higher incidence of poverty. More than a billion people living in extreme poverty have limited opportunities to insure against future setbacks and limited means of coping if adverse events occur. Better understanding of the link between vulnerability and poverty is therefore one of the most pressing issues in development economics.

The purpose of this book is to contribute to this better understanding. It is based on papers by leading scholars in their fields, originally presented at the UNU-WIDER Conference on Fragile States – Fragile Groups, held in Helsinki in June 2007. It offers fresh perspectives on vulnerability in developing countries. In particular, the authors explore the relation between poverty and vulnerability in different contexts – for example, in populous and fast-growing countries such as China and India, in small, landlocked countries in crisis such as Zimbabwe, and in transition countries such as Tajikistan. Various sources of vulnerability are studied such as HIV-AIDS, natural disasters and macroeconomic shocks. This broad scope allows a variety of methodological approaches to be explored.

In scrutinizing the lives of the poor and vulnerable, the book makes clear that poverty and vulnerability are distinct concepts. This has important implications for policy. The book further documents the fact that poor households are frequently unable to avoid many of the sources of risk or to evade the full brunt of the consequences. Indeed, as is stressed in a number of chapters, households' coping strategies may often have adverse implications for vulnerability and poverty. Consequently, as the book concludes, households should not be left alone to deal with the hazards they face, even though they are remarkably inventive and resilient. Their efforts at reducing vulnerability need to be complemented by community and government actions, aided by international players.

This book illustrates well the recent progress made in understanding and elaborating the notion of vulnerability. It also offers a timely reminder that much remains to be done to tackle vulnerability through strengthening household resilience, building appropriate bulwarks against risk, and creating and maintaining quality institutions.

Acknowledgements

A book such as this is the outcome of a complex and delicate process. It would not exist if it were not for the fortunate convergence of the efforts of at least five groups of people. The first is our academic colleagues at UNU-WIDER under the perceptive leadership of Anthony Shorrocks. They provided the intellectual and moral support which saw the genesis of this book during the UNU-WIDER Conference on Fragile States – Fragile Groups, which was held in Helsinki in June 2007. The conference was strengthened by the collaboration of the United Nations Department of Economic and Social Affairs.

The second group is the scholars who participated in the conference and whose papers, following revisions, are included in this book. It has been both a formative and an enjoyable experience working with them.

The third group who made this book possible is the incomparable administrative staff at UNU-WIDER in Helsinki, who worked as a well-oiled machine to ensure a successful conference and a smooth, painless publication process. In particular, Anne Ruohonen and Lisa Winkler deserve credit for meeting the challenges and frustrations of the conference – challenges and frustrations that are inevitable whenever academics embark on a collaborative effort. Barbara Fagerman ensured that the many administrative requirements of such an effort were always met. Lorraine Telfer-Taivainen took meticulous care to prepare the manuscript. And then there is Adam Swallow. Adam, your guiding hand has been indispensable during each stage of the publication process. Thanks.

A fourth group of people whose actions resulted in an improved and timely publication is the staff at UNU Press, including three anonymous referees who provided excellent comments on an earlier version.

Last, but not least, UNU-WIDER gratefully acknowledges the financial contribution to the Conference on Fragile States – Fragile Groups by the Finnish Ministry for Foreign Affairs and the financial contributions to the research programme by the governments of Denmark (Royal Ministry of Foreign Affairs), Finland (Ministry for Foreign Affairs), Norway (Royal Ministry of Foreign Affairs), Sweden (Swedish International Development Cooperation Agency – Sida), and the United Kingdom (Department for International Development).

Wim Naudé, Amelia U. Santos-Paulino and Mark McGillivray
Helsinki and Canberra
December 2008

Abbreviations

CARICOM	Caribbean Community
CCS	Caribbean Community Secretariat
CRED	Centre for Research on the Epidemiology of Disasters
CSW	commercial sex worker
DF	damaging fluctuation
DFID	Department for International Development [UK]
EM-DAT	Emergency events database
FAO	Food and Agriculture Organization of the United Nations
FEWSNET	Famine Early Warning Systems Network
FGLS	feasible generalized least squares
FSAU	Food Security Analysis Unit [FAO]
GDP	gross domestic product
GLCs	government-linked companies
HH	household
ICRISAT	International Crops Research Institute for the Semi-Arid Tropics
IMF	International Monetary Fund
IPC	Integrated Food Security Phase Classification [FAO]
IV	instrumental variable
LAF	Livelihood Analysis Forum
MDC	Movement for Democratic Change [Zimbabwe]
MFIs	micro-finance institutions
NGO	non-governmental organization
ODI	Overseas Development Institute [UK]

PPP	purchasing power parity
PVI	Prevalent Vulnerability Index
RCC	rural credit cooperative
SAT	semi-arid tropics
SIDS	small-island developing states
UNDP	United Nations Development Programme
UN-ISDR	United Nations International Strategy for Disaster Reduction
VCC	village credit committee
VCTC	Voluntary Counseling and Testing Centre
VEP	vulnerability as expected poverty
VEU	vulnerability as low expected utility
VER	vulnerability as uninsured exposure to risk
VLS	village-level studies [by ICRISAT]
WFP	World Food Programme
ZANU-PF	Zimbabwe African National Union-Patriotic Front

1

Vulnerability in developing countries: An introduction

Wim Naudé, Amelia U. Santos-Paulino and Mark McGillivray

1 Introduction

The dawn of the twenty-first century has seen, perhaps more than any other time, a growing concern about the inherent vulnerability of humankind. Indeed, few other concepts summarize as aptly the *zeitgeist* two decades after the end of the Cold War as the concept of vulnerability. Unparalleled advances in living standards and wealth for larger numbers of people than at any time in history have ironically been accompanied by greater awareness of the full panoply of risks that human societies face. While the advanced economies, despite having overcome absolute poverty to a large extent, have in recent times been reeling from the shocks of terrorism, natural disasters, climate change and financial market turbulence, the situation facing billions of people in developing countries is much worse. Here, vulnerability to poverty, vulnerability to ill health, vulnerability to natural hazards and vulnerability to macroeconomic shocks continue to exact a significant toll on people's welfare. What makes the situation in developing countries of greater concern is that here many people lack the assets, infrastructure and institutions that citizens in advanced economies employ, albeit imperfectly, as bulwarks against vulnerability. Also, owing to the globalization of the world economy, continued and even worsening vulnerability in developing countries means increased vulnerability also for citizens in advanced economies. Without addressing their own sources of vulnerability, developing countries cannot make progress in development, including

Vulnerability in developing countries, Naudé, Santos-Paulino and McGillivray (eds),
United Nations University Press, 2009, ISBN 978-92-808-1171-1

achieving the Millennium Development Goals. And, without giving attention to the challenges faced by developing countries in this regard, the advanced economies cannot ultimately reduce their own vulnerability. Addressing vulnerability in developing countries is therefore of immediate global concern.

This book is a modest contribution to further our understanding of vulnerability in developing countries in light of these concerns. In recent years, there has been notable progress in the conceptualization and measurement of vulnerability. The chapters in this book exemplify these advances and illustrate, from various case studies, country experiences and research methodologies, how a better conceptualization and measurement of vulnerability can inform development policy.

2 The concept and measurement of vulnerability

What do we understand by the term "vulnerability" in this book? Vulnerability, we need to note, is a multidisciplinary phenomenon studied within many different scientific fields. These different fields each have their own definitions of vulnerability because they focus on different components of risk (Alwang et al. 2001). Some of the chapters in this book approach vulnerability from a microeconomic point of view. In this view, vulnerability can be defined as the risk of households falling into or remaining in poverty owing either to idiosyncratic hazards (because of the characteristics of the individual household) or to covariate/aggregate hazards (external to the household) (e.g. Dercon 2005: 10). Other chapters take a macro-level view and see vulnerability as the risk that a "system" (such as a country) will be adversely affected by a shock or "perturbation" (Gallopin 2006: 294). These "shocks" or "perturbations" can include natural hazards or macroeconomic shocks. Thus, in general in this book, vulnerability will always be related to an undesirable outcome – for example, vulnerability *to* poverty, vulnerability *to* food insecurity, vulnerability *to* natural hazards or vulnerability *to* macroeconomic shocks. A household's or a country's exposure to hazards and its coping mechanisms (or resilience) will determine how vulnerable it is. The various chapters in this book consider different kinds of hazards: household demographics, geographical location, institutional features, illness, famine, economic specialization, natural hazards, soil degradation and global market fluctuations, to name but a few. They also study various aspects of resilience or coping at both the level of the household and the level of a country, including adverse coping. Some chapters explore ways of distinguishing which types of hazard contribute most to vulnerability; others consider the dynamics of becoming more or less vulnerable.

From a microeconomic perspective, vulnerability to poverty can be measured as either (a) uninsured exposure to risk, (b) expected poverty, or (c) low expected utility (Günther and Harttgen 2006: 3–4). These methods all express vulnerability as being determined by the expected mean and variance of a household's income or consumption. Thus, how vulnerable households are to idiosyncratic or covariate shocks can be measured by the extent to which these shocks may affect their income or consumption. Recent overviews of these methods are explored in Hoddinott and Quisumbing (2003), Ligon and Schechter (2003), Dercon (2005) and Günther and Harttgen (2006). Chapter 2 in this book, by Raghav Gaiha and Katsushi Imai, contains an overview and application of these methods to the case of India.

From a macro-level perspective, a common approach is to analyse vulnerability together with the potential of hazards (such as natural hazards or macroeconomic shocks), resulting in an indicator of how at risk a particular household/population/region/country is. Thus risk is seen as a function of hazard and vulnerability. Various indicators are used to measure hazard potential (such as the occurrence of droughts, fires, earthquakes, floods, price rises, financial crises) and vulnerability (such as gross domestic product, population density, sensitive environments). Often indicators of community resilience are added, such as levels of education, infrastructure and assets. The selection of appropriate indicators depends on the spatial level under consideration, as well as the availability of appropriate data. Briguglio (2001) discusses a number of methods for compiling a macro-level vulnerability "index": these range from normalizing variables and taking their averages, to mapping variables on a categorical scale, to using regression methods to estimate predicted values for an index. Various vulnerability indexes at the country level have been proposed since the United Nations Department of Economic and Social Affairs initiated work on the vulnerability of small island states in the early 1990s. For instance, the Commonwealth Vulnerability Index (CVI) consists of three indicators: export dependency, export diversification and susceptibility to natural disasters (Easter 1998). The Inter-American Bank developed a Prevalent Vulnerability Index (PVI), consisting of the averages of three composite indicators for exposure or physical susceptibility, fragility and resilience. One of the most extensive vulnerability indexes is the Environmental Vulnerability Index (EVI) developed by the United Nations Environment Programme and the South Pacific Applied Geoscience Commission, which uses over 50 indicators covering a large number of dimensions of vulnerability and resilience.

How exposed a household or a country is to a shock, and how resilient it is when exposed to such shocks, are influenced by its institutional environment. In developing countries a large number of people live in states with inadequate willingness or capacity to assist households in reducing risks, mitigating risks and coping with risks, and with weak capacity to manage macroeconomic shocks and natural hazards. Many of these states have in recent years been described as "fragile states". Such state fragility is an important (covariate) source of household and country vulnerability. In fragile states, households are clearly more vulnerable to hazards. A number of chapters in this book explore the consequences of state fragility; for instance in Chapter 7 Margarita Flores and Colin Andrews point to the role of state fragility in vulnerability to hunger, and in Chapters 8 and 10 the role of states in reducing, mitigating and coping with risks associated with natural hazards and macroeconomic shocks is discussed.

Having pointed to the importance of understanding vulnerability in developing countries and having given a short description of the way in which vulnerability is to be understood in this book, we will now provide an introduction to the individual chapters.

3 Overview of the book

3.1 Broad structure

Part I of this book focuses broadly on vulnerability with respect to income and health. It contains six chapters that investigate vulnerability and poverty in the context of the most populous countries in the world – China and India – as well as smaller countries. For instance, Tajikistan is noted for being a country in transition (economic, social, political) and Zimbabwe is, at the time of writing, still in crisis and will be suffering from the consequences of this for some time to come. Part I also considers two pertinent contemporary challenges that impinge on household vulnerability in a dramatic way: HIV/AIDS and food insecurity. What clearly emerges from Part I is that vulnerability is an important way to view poverty, with important implications for policy.

Part II picks up on the point made in various chapters in Part I that much of the source of the risk facing poor households lies beyond their capability to prevent shocks, and that often their coping strategies have adverse consequences for their future vulnerability and poverty status. In particular, the impacts of natural hazards and the increasing openness of small economies in the global economy are important. Part II also extends the discussion towards the macro level and considers vulnerability to natural hazards and to macroeconomic shocks.

Part III contains a conclusion. In Chapter 11, we take stock of the preceding chapters. We ask two broad questions that we hope will guide policy initiatives as well as future research: How can the concept and measurement of vulnerability be even further extended? And what policy lessons can be generalized from the various country case studies offered here?

3.2 Individual chapters

In Chapter 2, **Raghav Gaiha** and **Katsushi Imai** construct various vulnerability measures for households in the Maharashtra and Andhra Pradesh regions of India, predominantly rural areas. They use a unique panel data set spanning 1975–1984 and taken from the village-level studies of the International Crops Research Institute for the Semi-Arid Tropics (ICRISAT). The three types of vulnerability measure from the household-level data constructed in this study are: vulnerability as expected poverty (VEP), vulnerability as low expected utility (VEU) and vulnerability as uninsured exposure to risk (VER). The authors try to combine measures of *ex ante* vulnerability (such as VEP and VEU) with *ex post* measures of vulnerability (such as VER). These measures are also decomposed, and this dissection demonstrates that idiosyncratic risk contributed the most to vulnerability in India (37 per cent) followed by poverty (35 per cent) and covariate (or aggregate) risk (22 per cent). In the context of rural India, the chapter concludes that traditional responses to household vulnerability, which consist of risk reduction, risk mitigation and risk coping, need to be used with caution since there exist many trade-offs between policy measures.

Calum G. Turvey and **Rong Kong** in Chapter 3 study poverty in rural China, pointing out that poverty is rising, households are subject to food insecurity and income inequality is worsening. They argue that a major reason for the high poverty and vulnerability faced by hundreds of millions of rural poor in China is not constraints on physical resources as such, but a lack of access to finance and credit. Elsewhere in the world, most notably Bangladesh, Indonesia and Latin America, micro-credit has played an important role in reducing vulnerability. Turvey and Kong see micro-credit as of vital importance for China too, but point out that suitable micro-finance institutions (MFIs) are still largely lacking (microfinance has only recently become available in China, introduced by the People's Bank of China in 2005). In arguing their case for MFIs in China, Turvey and Kong provide a formal theoretical framework for microcredit, noting that the gap in the literature in this regard may be constraining thinking on the relationship between credit and development. The theoretical model shows that a non-collateral-based micro-credit market based on trust can exist, separate and distinct from commercial lending.

In Chapter 4, **Oleksiy Ivaschenko** and **Cem Mete** consider the dynamics of poverty in Tajikistan. The country, a member of the former Soviet Union, is for various reasons a highly instructive case study on the dynamics of poverty and vulnerability. It is making noteworthy transitions from a centrally planned to a market-based economy, from civil war (which ended in 1998) to post-conflict reconstruction, from economic collapse to growth, and from a predominantly rural country to a more urban-dominated economy. How these transitions affect the dynamics of poverty is investigated by using panel data from a rural household survey from 2003 and 2004. The authors consider various dimensions of the dynamics of poverty. First, an asset-based approach is used to make a distinction between transitory and chronic poverty. Second, both community-level and household-level determinants of poverty are considered. A major finding is that, in Tajikistan, there is a high degree of mobility of households in and out of poverty. In particular, 19 per cent of households moved out of poverty during this period while 15 per cent fell back into poverty. Moreover, the determinants of movements out of and into poverty are analysed, confirming that the geographical location of households matters – households in an area with a high poverty headcount are less likely to escape from poverty. The educational and health status of the household head are further significant factors determining whether a household can climb out of poverty. The study also infers that the factors that allow households to escape from poverty may be distinct from those that allow households to fall back into poverty. Among the latter, household size, the share of working-age individuals in the household, the type of employment the household members are engaged in, and agricultural conditions (such as rainfall) are found to be important.

In Chapter 5, **Kate Bird** and **Martin Prowse** study vulnerability and poverty in the tragic case of Zimbabwe, a country in economic, social and political crisis. Over the period 2005–2007 its economy was the fastest-shrinking economy in the world. The growing destitution and emigration of its population, its hyperinflation and one of the highest rates of HIV/AIDS infection in the world made global headlines over this period. As the authors argue, it is important to understand how vulnerability and poverty affect individual lives below the headlines. In Zimbabwe, given the high incidence of covariate risk affecting households, it is clear that household and individual responses to deal with risk should mainly be focused on coping. Whereas other chapters in this volume take a quantitative approach, or in some cases a theoretical approach, this chapter is a good demonstration of the application of qualitative research methods to understand vulnerability and coping. The authors present five contextualized life histories to illustrate the "current processes of impoverishment and adverse coping" in Zimbabwe. What stands out from their chapter is how adverse forms of coping can exacerbate household poverty and vulnerability and can push households into chronic poverty. These adverse forms of coping noted in the Zimbabwean case include children dropping out of school, soil degradation as a result of desperate but unsustainable farming methods, cutting down on healthcare, and engagement in criminal activities.

In the final two chapters in Part I attention turns to the relationship between ill health and vulnerability. This is because good health is a desirable development outcome in its own right, but also because the health status of a household head is a significant determinant of whether or not a household can climb out of poverty. The health status of individuals in developing countries is influenced both by their own behaviour and by external shocks (such as climatic conditions and natural hazards). In the former, education plays an important role in equipping individuals to make sensible lifestyle choices. In the latter, broader and coordinated public sector intervention is most often required.

In Chapter 6, we return to India, and specifically the semi-arid region of Andhra Pradesh. **B. Valentine Joseph Gandhi**, **Ma. Cynthia Serquiña Bantilan** and **Devanathan Parthasarathy** show that HIV/AIDS poses a significant and growing risk to household livelihood strategies in this environmentally challenging region. It is the region with the highest (2 per cent) HIV infection rate in India. Although this rate may be low compared with infection rates in southern Africa (for example Zimbabwe, as discussed in Chapter 5), the rate of infection has been growing and the sheer number of people infected is significant. India has the highest number of HIV-infected people in the world. Therefore, Gandhi et al. attempt to determine who is most vulnerable to HIV and to identify the reasons. They present a theoretical framework to guide their attempts to link vulnerability and HIV, a framework that may be adopted in future by other researchers. A key insight emphasized in this chapter is that, as in the case of Zimbabwe, adverse forms of coping can raise household vulnerability and contribute towards chronic poverty. In the case of Andhra Pradesh, a fragile agricultural region, a well-recognized covariate risk is drought. A traditional coping response to drought is migration. However, as the authors observe, migration exposes migrants to a higher risk of contracting HIV. To make matters worse, migrants are most often not reached by government programmes to combat HIV, owing to their migratory behaviour.

The effects of illness, such as caused by HIV, are often exacerbated by poor nutrition. This is not limited to areas ravaged by illness. Globally it has been estimated that more than 800 million people are undernourished. Food crises are a growing source of covariate risk for millions of people in a large, and growing, number of countries. In Chapter 7, **Colin**

Andrews and **Margarita Flores** indicate that in 2007 a total of 34 countries faced food crises and required emergency food assistance. Tackling this requires first and foremost that the causes of food insecurity be addressed and its impact mitigated.[1] It also requires that international efforts at emergency responses to food crises be scaled up. This response is a vital requirement in reducing household vulnerability in countries that are prone to food crises. The core of Chapter 7 is therefore an evaluation of the Food and Agriculture Organization's "Integrated Food Security and Humanitarian Phase Classification", a tool to assist international agencies with a consistent framework for the flow of information for the early analysis and correct identification of food crises. As Andrews and Flores indicate, international responses to food crises are often hampered by the difficulty of distinguishing the symptoms of chronic destitution from those of a critically unstable situation.

Part II of this volume commences with Chapter 8 by **Martin Philipp Heger**, **Alex Julca** and **Oliver Paddison**. The focus of the paper is the Caribbean region, which has been described as one of the areas in the world where people are most vulnerable to natural hazards. As also shown in Chapter 9 by Marlene Attzs, more than 4 million people in the Caribbean were affected by natural disasters between 1990 and 1996, mostly in the form of hurricanes. The authors report that in the 2004 hurricane season direct damage of US$3.1 billion was caused, with extensive indirect damage in the form of the breakup of families, the increased risk of disease and lack of access to education and health facilities, to name but a few. The region is also seriously exposed to macroeconomic shocks, owing to the high concentration of the countries' productive and foreign trade structures (see also Chapter 10 by Anis Chowdhury in this volume). The resilience of the islands is hampered by their small physical and economic size and economic specialization, so that repeated setbacks from natural disasters perpetuate poverty, which in turn further increases vulnerability in a vicious circle of underdevelopment. Various ways to mitigate the impact of disasters are discussed, with the authors arguing the case for greater emphasis on *ex ante* mitigation strategies such as diversification of the islands' production and export structures.

Chapter 9 continues the focus on vulnerability to natural hazards and its impact on poverty. In this chapter, **Marlene Attzs** discusses how the economic, social and environmental conditions facing many Caribbean small island developing states exacerbate the impact of natural hazards, and often cause them to result in natural disasters. Attzs emphasizes the difference between natural hazards and natural disasters, pointing out that "disasters are not simply extreme events created entirely by natural forces; rather, they are sometimes manifestations of unresolved problems of development". In the case of the Caribbean, she points to poverty, which, as we have seen in other contexts, leads to adverse coping. In the Caribbean this includes hillside farming and slash-and-burn agriculture, which result in flooding and mudslides during heavy rains. A further unresolved problem of development that has implications for household coping with natural hazards is the role of women. Attzs calls for a "gendered" approach to disaster risk management, based on two observations. The first is that women often make up a disproportionate share of the poor, and the second is that women's traditional roles of caregivers and their often more extensive social networks make them important agents in the identification and mitigation of risks and in post-disaster assistance. In the Caribbean, as Attzs points out, women may play a catalysing role in the channelling of financial support for post-disaster reconstruction, because they tend to receive the greatest proportion of remittances. Remittances are identified in this chapter as a vital, and rapidly rising, source of foreign financial assistance in the Caribbean. In the case of Jamaica, one of the most vulnerable countries in the Caribbean, remittances contribute up to 87 per cent of total financial support received by the poorest households. The growing importance of remittances for households in the Caribbean reflects in part the continued out-migration of people from the area. As we have seen in other contexts in this volume, a frequent response of people to vulnerability, in particular covariate risk, is to migrate. In dealing with natural hazards, and their possible greater frequency in an era of climate change, this is a message well worth remembering when designing cross-country mitigation and adaptation strategies.

In Chapter 10, **Anis Chowdhury** focuses on the vulnerability of all small island economies to macroeconomic shocks. He notes that small island economies, such as the Caribbean and Pacific islands, are characterized by vulnerability owing to their natural environment, such as smallness, remoteness and exposure to natural hazards. He adds to these sources of vulnerability yet another: vulnerability to global markets because of the openness of these economies and their narrow export base. He proceeds to discuss the nature of this macroeconomic vulnerability and to argue for the importance of stabilizing macroeconomic policies. The analysis is based on the view that volatility in GDP and growth is a source of vulnerability for poor households. As he argues, the poor have less human capital to adapt to adverse labour market developments, fewer assets and less access to credit to smooth consumption. The real danger exists that negative macroeconomic shocks could lead to irreversible losses in nutritional and educational status: even if GDP recovers, the level and incidence of poverty may persist. With volatility of output as a source of vulnerability, Chowdhury argues that macroeconomic policies should aim not only at price stability but also at output and

employment stabilization. Although his focus is on small island economies, his analysis is also relevant for the large number of small, fragmented but increasingly internationally integrated and open developing
economies in Africa and Latin America. Using the example of Singapore,
Chowdhury shows that, contrary to conventional wisdom, macroeconomic policies can both be stabilizing and promote growth. The preconditions are that countries build and strengthen appropriate labour
market, financial and governance institutions.

Note

1. A full discussion of these issues falls outside the scope of the present volume, but the interested reader is referred to a recent UNU-WIDER volume on food security (Guha-
Khasnobis et al. 2007).

REFERENCES

Alwang, J., P. B. Siegel and S. Jorgenson (2001). "Vulnerability: A View from
    Different Disciplines". Social Protection Discussion Paper 0115, World Bank,
    Washington DC.
Briguglio, L. (2001). "The Vulnerability Index". Paper presented at the AOSIS
    Workshop on Trade, Sustainable Development and SIDS, Montego Bay,
    Jamaica, 12–15 December.
Dercon, S., ed. (2005). *Insurance against Poverty*. Oxford: Oxford University
    Press UNU-WIDER Studies in Development Economics.
Easter, C. (1998). "Small States and Development: A Composite Index of Vul-
    nerability". In *Small States: Economic Review and Basic Statistics. Annual
    Series 4*. London: Commonwealth Secretariat.
Gallopin, G. C. (2006). "Linkages between Vulnerability, Resilience, and Adap-
    tive Capacity". *Global Environmental Change* 16: 293–303.
Guha-Khasnobis, B., S. S. Acharya and B. Davis (2007). *Food Insecurity, Vulner-
    ability and Human Rights Failure*. Basingstoke: Palgrave Macmillan Studies in
    Development Economics and Policy.
Günther, J. and K. Harttgen (2006). "Estimating Vulnerability to Covariate and
    Idiosyncratic Shocks". University of Göttingen, Department of Economics.
Hoddinott, J. and A. Quisumbing (2003). "Methods for Microeconometric Risk
    and Vulnerability Assessment". Social Protection Discussion Paper 0324,
    World Bank, Washington DC.
Ligon, E. and L. Schechter (2003). "Measuring Vulnerability". *Economic Journal*
    113: C95–C102.

Part I

Income and health

2

Measuring vulnerability and poverty: Estimates for rural India

Raghav Gaiha and Katsushi Imai

1 Introduction

The objective of this chapter is to quantify the vulnerability of rural households in the semi-arid region of south India to aggregate and idiosyncratic risks (crop and weather risks and illness and unemployment risks, respectively). Vulnerability is distinguishable from "poverty"[1] in the sense that there exist those who are non-poor but vulnerable and those who are non-vulnerable but poor. As a measure of deprivation, vulnerability is more appealing because it takes into account not just fluctuating levels of living but also the resilience of subsets of households (e.g. the landless, smallholders) against aggregate and idiosyncratic shocks. It is, however, more difficult to identify the vulnerable, not only because there are different measures (e.g. *ex ante* versus *ex post* vulnerability) but also because tracking the wellbeing of a particular household over many years, or before and after a shock, requires reliable panel data that are seldom available.

There has been a surge of interest in measuring vulnerability (e.g. Hoddinott and Quisumbing 2003a,b; Ligon 2005; Ligon and Schechter 2003; Gaiha and Imai 2004; Dercon 2005). So one objective of the present chapter is to review different measures of vulnerability and to apply them to the panel data for semi-arid rural south India. These studies also point to the need for designing anti-poverty policies to address vulnerability, especially in rural areas, where agricultural yields and

Vulnerability in developing countries, Naudé, Santos-Paulino and McGillivray (eds),
United Nations University Press, 2009, ISBN 978-92-808-1171-1

revenues fluctuate a great deal owing to changes in weather, floods, pest infestation and market forces. Besides, different segments of the rural population are exposed to various risks – especially idiosyncratic risks – in the absence of easy access to medical care or drinking water, in un-hygienic living conditions and in limited opportunities for diversifying income sources. These difficulties are compounded by the lack of finan-cial intermediation and formal insurance, by credit market imperfections and by weak infrastructure (e.g. physical isolation because of limited transportation facilities). More specifically, if policymakers design pov-erty alleviation policies in the current year on the basis of a poverty threshold of income in the previous year, the "poor" who receive income support may have already escaped from poverty and the "non-poor" who do not receive income support may have slipped into poverty owing to various unanticipated shocks (e.g. changes in relative crop prices). One approach would be to focus on poverty dynamics (e.g. Gaiha and Deolalikar 1993; Baulch and Hoddinott 2000) or chronic poverty (e.g. Hulme et al. 2001), taking into account poverty transition or the long-term poverty status *ex post*. Another and more challenging approach would be to combine both *ex ante* and *ex post* measures of vulnerability. This, however, presupposes that many of the risks – both aggregate and idiosyncratic – and the resilience of subsets of households against such shocks can be anticipated. This is, of course, easier said than done. It is nevertheless arguable that, to the extent that *ex post* measures of vulner-ability can be combined with *ex ante* measures, this would help in the design of a more effective strategy to deal with vulnerability.

As a case study, we will construct vulnerability measures of households in semi-arid rural India, drawing upon the panel household data from the International Crops Research Institute for the Semi-Arid Tropics (ICRI-SAT) for 1975–1984. Although several recent studies analyse vulnerabil-ity using the ICRISAT data, few have employed the various measures proposed and focus on identifying who the vulnerable are and whether they are distinguishable from the poor in a static sense.[2] So our analysis is designed to be more comprehensive and richer from a policy perspec-tive. The rest of the chapter is organized as follows. In section 2, a review of salient features of the ICRISAT panel survey is followed by a discus-sion of measurement errors in the consumption expenditure data and their implications for insurance. Section 3 gives an exposition of three different empirical methodologies used here to measure the vulnerability of households. Econometric results and findings are summarized in sec-tion 4. The final section offers concluding observations.

2 Data

2.1 Salient features

The analysis is based on (a subset of) the ICRISAT village-level studies (VLS) data sets that cover the semi-arid tract (SAT) in Maharashtra and Andhra Pradesh. Agro-climatologically, the SAT includes those tropical regions where rainfall exceeds potential evaporation for four to six months in a year. Mean annual rainfall ranges from about 400 mm to 1,200 mm. India's SAT is vast and covers about 15 to 20 large regions, each embracing several districts. Based on cropping, soil and climatic criteria, three contrasting dryland agricultural regions were selected by ICRISAT: the Telengana region in Andhra Pradesh, the Bombay Deccan in Maharashtra, and the Vidarbha region, also in Maharashtra. Three representative districts – namely Mahbubnagar in the Telengana region, Sholapur in the Bombay Deccan and Akola in the Vidarbha region – were selected on rainfall, soil and cropping criteria. Next, typical *talukas* (smaller administrative units) within these districts were selected, followed by the selection of six representative villages from these *talukas*. Finally, a random stratified sample of 40 households was selected in each village. This comprised a sample of 30 cultivator and 10 landless labour households. To ensure equal representation of different farm size groups, the cultivating households were first divided into three strata, each having an equal number of households. A random sample of 10 households was drawn from each tercile; the 10 landless labour households were also randomly selected. Landless labour households were defined as those operating less than half an acre (0.2 ha) and whose main source of income was agricultural wage earnings. All households were interviewed by investigators who resided in the sample villages, had a university degree in agricultural economics, came from rural backgrounds and spoke the local language.

A fixed sample size of cultivator and landless labour households in each village means that the sampling fractions and relative farm sizes that demarcate the cultivator terciles vary from village to village. The likelihood that a village household was in the sample ranged from about 1 in 4 in the smaller Akola villages to about 1 in 10 in the larger Mahbubnagar villages. Landless labour households are somewhat under-represented in the sample. On average, across the six villages, they comprise about one-third of the households in the household population of interest, but their share in the sample is only one-quarter. However, since their mean household size is less than that of cultivator households, a one-quarter representation is a fair reflection of their presence in the individual population of interest (Walker and Ryan 1990).

The data collected are based on panel surveys carried out at regular intervals from 1975 to 1984 covering production, expenditure, time allocation, prices, wages and socioeconomic characteristics of the 240 households in the sample villages representing three agro-climatic zones in the semi-arid region in south India. A description of the agro-climatic and other characteristics of the sample villages is given in Table 2A.1 in Appendix 1. Given the agro-climatic conditions and purposive selection of the villages, the VLS data are not representative of all of rural south India or even, for that matter, of its semi-arid region. Nevertheless, the longitudinal nature and the richness in terms of variables included are what make the ICRISAT VLS data unique.

The present analysis is based on data for 183 households belonging to five sample villages (excluding Kinkheda) because continuous data over the period 1975–1984 are available only on this subset of households. This subsample is used to construct one measure of vulnerability, i.e. vulnerability as expected poverty (VEP).[3] However, given the measurement errors in the consumption expenditure data, measures of vulnerability based on both consumption expenditure and income vulnerability as low expected utility (VEU) and vulnerability as uninsured exposure to risk (VER) are problematic. We shall therefore use expenditure data provided by Gautam (1991) for three villages, namely Aurepalle, Shirapur and Kanzara, to derive estimates of VEU and VER measures.[4]

2.2 Risks and insurance in India

Jacoby and Skoufias (1998) estimate the household response to anticipated and unanticipated income changes, using the ICRISAT data. In their analysis, if the permanent income hypothesis holds, the consumption change is affected positively by unanticipated income changes and not by anticipated income changes. Using the data for Aurepalle and Kanzara, their analysis does not reject the permanent income hypothesis.

Rosenzweig and Wolpin (1993) focus on the role of bullocks as buffer stock for consumption by credit-constrained households in rural India. They find that the sale of bullocks increases when incomes are low, and purchases increase when incomes are high. On the other hand, Lim and Townsend (1998), through a detailed investigation of how rural farming households financed their monthly deficit, reach the conclusion that livestock, including bullocks and other capital assets, play little part in smoothing intertemporal shocks. Instead, buffer stocks of crop inventory and currency, together with credit or insurance, are much more important. Chaudhuri and Paxson (1994), also using the monthly ICRISAT data, investigate the impact of seasonality on income and consumption. They conclude that seasonal patterns in consumption are common across households within villages but are unrelated to income seasonality.

On risk-sharing, Townsend (1994) tests the perfect risk-sharing hypothesis that household consumption is fully insured against idiosyncratic shocks and thus depends only on the aggregate risk. Although this hypothesis is rejected, he shows that the model provides a surprisingly good benchmark in that household consumption co-moves with average village consumption, implying risk-sharing among households. Ravallion and Chaudhuri (1997) point to a weaker result if an allowance is made for measurement errors in own consumption and alternative specifications and estimation procedures are considered. They also draw attention to the possibility that common signals about future income, rather than consumption insurance, would generate co-movements in consumption under the permanent income hypothesis. Lim and Townsend (1998), however, disagree on the grounds that there is non-negligible social interaction among households, as credit/insurance/gifts account for a large part of the difference between expenditure and revenue.

Responses to aggregate and idiosyncratic risks take other forms, too. Changes in child school attendance (Jacoby and Skoufias 1997) and in labour hours in off-farm markets (Kochar 1995, 1999), for example, have been reported. Another recent study by Gaiha and Imai (2004) examines the vulnerability of rural households to poverty when a negative crop shock occurs, using a dynamic panel data model that takes into account effects of crop shocks of varying intensity and duration. They show that even sections of relatively affluent households are highly vulnerable to long spells of poverty when severe crop shocks occur in consecutive years.

Although conclusions differ depending on the questions asked and methodologies used, some of the major findings are summarized below:

 (i) Both poor and relatively affluent households are vulnerable to aggregate shocks such as crop shocks.
(ii) The ability to cope with shocks is generally limited owing to limited consumption insurance or risk-sharing and credit constraints.
(iii) Risk-coping ability is likely to differ among households because of differences in assets, such as livestock, crop inventory and currency. As a result, the poor (mostly assetless) are more likely to increase child or adult labour hours.
(iv) Existing policy interventions, such as the employment guarantee scheme, do not necessarily reach the poor despite their potential risk-reducing roles. So there is a case for more effective risk-reducing, mitigating and coping interventions alongside income-augmenting policies.

3 Methodology

Hoddinott and Quisumbing (2003a,b) provide a comprehensive review of recent approaches and a "toolkit" to quantify the vulnerability of households and data requirements, identifying the following three major approaches used in the empirical literature on vulnerability.[5]

3.1 Vulnerability as expected poverty (VEP)

VEP as an *ex ante* vulnerability measure, proposed by Chaudhuri et al. (2002), was applied by them to the Indonesian household data. Consider, first, an example of VEP. This is the case of vulnerability defined as the probability that a household will fall into poverty in the future

$$V_{it} = \Pr(c_{i,t+1} \leq z), \tag{1}$$

where the vulnerability of a household at time t, V_{it}, is the probability that the i'th household's level of consumption at time $t+1$, $c_{i,t+1}$, will be below the poverty line, z.[6]

In a variant that allows for the degree of vulnerability to rise with the length of the time horizon, the vulnerability of household h for n periods, denoted as $R(\cdot)$ for risk, is the probability of observing at least one spell of poverty for n periods, which, as shown below, is one minus the probability of no episodes of poverty:

$$R_i(n, z) = 1 - [(1 - (\Pr(c_{i,t+1}) < z)), \ldots, (1 - (\Pr(c_{i,t+n}) < z))]. \tag{2}$$

Following this definition and using $I(\cdot)$ as an indicator equalling 1 if the condition is true and 0 otherwise, an alternative measure of vulnerability is that a household is vulnerable if the risk in n periods is greater than a threshold probability, p.[7]

$$V_i(p, n, z) = I\{R_{it}(n, z) > p\}. \tag{3}$$

Neither (1) nor (3) takes into account other dimensions of poverty (e.g. depth of poverty). This limitation is easily overcome by rewriting Equation (1) as

$$V_{it} = \sum_s^S p_S \cdot P(c_{i,t+1}, z) = \sum_s^S p_S \cdot I[c_{i,t+1} \leq z] \cdot [(z - c_{i,t+1})/z]^\alpha, \tag{1'}$$

where $\sum_s^S p_S$ is the sum of the probability of all possible "states of the world", s, in period $t+1$ and α is the welfare weight attached to the gap between the benchmark and the welfare measure – as in the Foster–Greer–Thorbecke (FGT) poverty measure (Foster et al. 1984). In principle, this welfare weight could take values 0, 1, 2.[8] Aggregating across N households,[9]

$$VEP_t = (1/N) \sum_{i}^{N} \sum_{s}^{S} p_S \cdot I[c_{h,t+1} \leq z] \cdot [(z - c_{h,t+1})/z]^{\alpha}. \tag{4}$$

A vulnerability measure such as (4) has considerable relevance. In Indonesia, for example, the headcount index of poverty was low before the financial crisis of 1998 but rose sharply in its wake. This implies that a large proportion of those above the poverty line were vulnerable to shocks. There are two risks in such a context. If the headcount index is low, governments/donors might become complacent. If negative shocks are frequent and severe, such complacency would be misplaced. Besides, if the characteristics of those above the poverty line but vulnerable to shocks differ from those of the poor, targeting the latter may miss a significant proportion of those whose living standards may decline sharply when a shock occurs.

Empirically, a variant of VEP is derived by the following procedure, as in Chaudhuri et al. (2002). The consumption function is estimated as:

$$\ln c_i = X_i \beta + e_i, \tag{5}$$

where c_i is per capita consumption expenditure for the i'th household, X_i represents a bundle of observable household characteristics, β is a vector of coefficients of household characteristics, and e_i is a mean-zero disturbance term that captures idiosyncratic shocks that contribute to different per capita consumption levels. It is assumed that the structure of the economy is relatively stable over time and, hence, future consumption stems solely from the uncertainty about the idiosyncratic shocks, e_i. It is also assumed that the variance of the disturbance term depends on:

$$\sigma_{e,i}^2 = X_i \theta. \tag{6}$$

The estimates of β and θ could be obtained using a three-step feasible generalized least squares (FGLS). Using the estimates $\hat{\beta}$ and $\hat{\theta}$, we can compute the expected log consumption and the variance of log consumption for each household as follows:

$$E[\ln C_i | X_i] = X_i \hat{\beta} \tag{7}$$

$$V[\ln C_i | X_i] = X_i \hat{\theta} \tag{8}$$

By assuming $\ln c_h$ as normally distributed, the estimated probability that a household will be poor in the future (say, at time $t + 1$), is given by:

$$\hat{v}_i = \hat{\Pr}(\ln c_i < \ln z | X_i) = \Phi\left(\frac{\ln z - X_i\hat{\beta}}{\sqrt{X_i\hat{\theta}}}\right). \tag{9}$$

This is an *ex ante* vulnerability measure that can be estimated by cross-sectional data. Equation (9) will provide the probability of a household at time t becoming poor at $t + 1$ given the distribution of consumption at t.

A merit of this vulnerability measure is that it can be estimated by cross-sectional data. However, the measure correctly reflects a household's vulnerability only if the distribution of consumption across households, given the household characteristics at one time, represents the time-series variation of consumption of the household. Hence this measure requires a large sample in which some households experience a good period and others suffer from negative shocks. Also, the measure is unlikely to reflect unexpected large negative shocks (e.g. the Asian financial crisis) if we use the cross-section data for a normal year.

The sample size of the ICRISAT data is not large enough for estimating VEP measures. So we have included all households in the five sample villages. Also, to make our results comparable with some earlier studies (e.g. Gaiha and Deolalikar 1993; Gaiha and Imai 2004), we replace log consumption with log income per capita in the above specification. The VEP simply assumes that consumption vulnerability derives from the stochastic property of the intertemporal consumption stream it faces (Chaudhuri et al. 2002). Since the time-series variation of log income per capita with particular household characteristics can be approximated by the cross-sectional variation of the households with similar characteristics, consumption in the above specification can be replaced by income. Also, nothing precludes us from extending it to the panel data. So we will use both annual cross-section components and panel data in the ICRISAT data to construct VEP measures. Our specification of VEP can be written as follows, based on two earlier studies (Gaiha and Deolalikar 1993; Gaiha and Imai 2004):

$$\ln Y_i = X_i'\beta_1 + L_i'\beta_2 + H_i'\beta_3 + e_i \tag{10}$$

$$\sigma_{e,i}^2 = X_i'\theta_1 + L_i'\theta_2 + H_i'\theta_3 \tag{11}$$

where i indexes the household; Y_i is per capita annual household income from all sources (in constant prices) in a particular crop year; X_i is a vector of household characteristics (e.g. age of household head and its square, household size and its square, and caste); L_i is a vector of owned land area and its square, the share of irrigated land in the total, and non-land assets (i.e. production assets) and its square; H_i is a vector of human capital, such as schooling years of household head; $\sigma_{e,i}^2$ is the variance of the disturbance term, which is affected by various household characteristics. This can be estimated by a three-step FGLS.[10]

3.2 Vulnerability as expected low utility (VEU)

There is a problematic or perverse feature of VEP. In case $\alpha > 1$, the FGT poverty index attributes risk aversion to households. Consider two scenarios. In the first, the risk-averse household is certain that expected consumption in period $t + 1$ will be just below the poverty line so that the probability of poverty (or vulnerability) is 1.0. In the second scenario, although expected mean consumption is unchanged, there is a 0.5 probability that this household's consumption will be just above the poverty line (and above the mean) and a 0.5 probability that the consumption will be just below the mean. Since the household is risk averse, it would prefer the certain consumption in the first scenario to the expected in the second, but the vulnerability is lower in the second (it drops from 1.0 to 0.5). Moreover, even when $\alpha > 1$, the FGT index implies increasing absolute risk aversion, contrary to empirical evidence. This weakness is sought to be overcome by Ligon and Schechter (2003). A brief exposition of this measure is given below.

In this measure of VEU, vulnerability is defined as the difference between the utility derived from some level of certainty-equivalent consumption, z_{ce}, at and above which the household is not considered vulnerable, and the expected utility of consumption. In other words, this certainty-equivalent consumption is akin to a poverty line. Consumption of a household, c_i, has a distribution in different states of the world, so this measure takes the form:

$$V_i = U_i(z_{ce}) - EU_i(c_i), \tag{12}$$

where U_i is a (weakly) concave, strictly increasing function. Equation (12) can be rewritten as:

$$V_i = [U_i(z_{ce}) - U_i(Ec_i)] + [U_i(Ec_i) - EU_i(c_i)]. \tag{13}$$

The first bracketed term on the right is a measure of poverty in terms of the difference in utility between z and c. The second term measures the risk that household h faces. The latter can be decomposed into aggregate or covariate and idiosyncratic risk, as shown below.

$$V_i = [U_i(z_{ce}) - U_i(Ec_i)] \qquad\qquad \text{(poverty)}$$

$$+ \{U_i(Ec_i) - EU_i[E(c_i|x_t)]\} \quad \text{(covariate or aggregate risk)}$$

$$+ \{EU_i[E(c_i|x_t)] - EU_i(c_i)\} \quad \text{(idiosyncratic risk)} \qquad (14)$$

where $E(c_i|x_t)$ is an expected value of consumption conditional on a vector of covariant variables, x_t.

Aggregating across households, an estimate of aggregate vulnerability is obtained:

$$VEU = (1/N) \sum_i^N \left([U_i(z_{ce}) - U_i(Ec_i)] + \{U_i(Ec_i) - EU_i[E(c_i|x_t)]\} \right.$$

$$\left. + \{EU_i[E(c_i|x_t)] - EU_i(c_i)\} \right). \qquad (15)$$

This decomposition is useful because it allows an assessment of whether vulnerability is largely a result of factors underlying poverty (e.g. low assets and/or low returns from them) or of aggregate and idiosyncratic shocks and the inability to cope with them. However, two limitations must be noted. One is that the results may differ depending on the form of the utility function assumed.[11] The second is that the measurement is in terms of utility (i.e. utils).

Ligon and Schechter (2003) assume a particular form of utility function:

$$U(c) = \frac{c^{1-\gamma}}{1-\gamma}, \qquad (16)$$

where γ denotes a household's sensitivity to risk and inequality. They set $\gamma = 2$, following the microeconometric literature. We have accordingly set $\gamma = 2$ in the present study.

They assume:

$$E(c_{it}|\overline{X}_t, X_{it}) = \alpha_i + \eta_t + X_{it}\beta. \qquad (17)$$

With the panel data, one can estimate α_i, unobservable time-invariant individual effects, η_i, time effects same across households, and β, effects of household characteristics or other observable factors on consumption. Using a two-way error component model (Baltagi 2005), Equation (17) can be estimated as:

$$c_{it} = X_{it}\beta_i + \eta_t + \alpha_i + v_{it}, \qquad (18)$$

where v_{it} is an error term that is independent and identically distributed ($\sim$IID $(0, \sigma_v^2)$).

Our purpose is to decompose the total vulnerability arising from poverty and risk into four components using the estimation results for (18). Equation (14) can be rewritten as (14′) by assuming that z, the poverty line, is the mean consumption and by including in it the unexplained risk and measurement error.

$$V_i = [U_i(E_c) - U_i(Ec_i)] \qquad \text{(poverty)}$$

$$+ \{U_i(Ec_{it}) - EU_i[E(c_i|x_t)]\} \qquad \text{(covariate or aggregate risk)}$$

$$+ \{EU_i[E(c_i|x_t)] - EU(c_i|x_t, x_{it})\} \quad \text{(idiosyncratic risk)}$$

$$+ \{EU_i[E(c_i|x_t, x_{it})] - EU_i(c_i)\} \qquad \begin{array}{l}\text{(unexplained risk and} \\ \text{measurement error)}\end{array} \qquad (14')$$

We can derive various conditional expectations in (14′) to decompose the entire vulnerability measure (or VEU measure) for each household by applying restricted least squares to Equation (18) and then substituting each conditional expectation of consumption into (16).

As noted earlier, we use the expenditure data including food and non-food components created by Gautam (1991) and used by Ravallion and Chaudhuri (1997), since substitution of consumption by income in (16) is problematic and idiosyncratic income risks in (14) may be insured. The consumption equation, as in (18), should have income on the right-hand side if the income data are available, as in our case. However, income, if used as the explanatory variable of consumption, is likely to be endogenous for various reasons. For example, savings and liquidation of various household assets (e.g. livestock) are likely to influence not only consumption but also income, since a part of the assets is *typically* used for production purposes. Food consumption affects the productivity of workers and thus increases income through improvements in nutritional status. Hence, in estimating Equation (18), we use the instrumental variable (IV) specification where income is treated as endogenous. As in Ligon and Schechter (2003), the average consumption of all households is normalized to be unity. As a consequence, if resources are allocated in such a way that there is no vulnerability (i.e. no inequality or poverty and no risk), then each household's utility would be 1. Also, if V_i in (14′) is 0.25, then the utility of the average household is 25 per cent less than it would be if resources could be distributed so as to eliminate inequality among households and risk in consumption.

The IV estimation for VEU can be carried out in the same way as for VEP.

First stage:

$$y_{it} = X'_{it}\beta_1 + L'_{it}\beta_2 + H'_{it}\beta_3 + D'_t\beta_4 + \mu_i + e_{it}. \tag{19}$$

Second stage:

$$c_{it} = \gamma_1 y_{it} + X'_{it}\gamma_2 + H'_{it}\gamma_3 + D'_t\gamma_4 + \alpha_i + v_{it}, \tag{20}$$

where time effects are replaced by a vector of year dummies, D'_t, for simplicity.

L_i, a vector of owned land area, the share of irrigated land and non-land assets, are used as instruments; μ_i and α_i are unobserved individual effects. One cannot deny the possibility of the effects of L_i on consumption, but it seems natural to assume that these variables first affect income. Random effects specification is chosen over fixed effects, following the Hausmann specification test. We then compute vulnerability by various conditional expectations of consumption, as in (14').

3.3 Vulnerability as uninsured exposure to risk (VER)

In the absence of effective risk management strategy, shocks result in welfare loss to the extent that they lead to reduction of consumption. In this sense, it is a consequence of uninsured exposure to risk. VER is designed to assess *ex post* welfare loss from a negative shock (e.g. a flood), as opposed to an *ex ante* assessment of future poverty in VEP.

Consider a household, i, residing in a village, v, at time t. Let $\Delta \ln c_{itv}$ denote change in log consumption or the growth rate of consumption per capita of household i between t and $t-1$ and $S(i)_{tv}$ aggregate/covariate shocks and $S(i)_{itv}$ idiosyncratic shocks. Further, let D_v be a set of binary variables identifying each community/village separately and X be a vector of household characteristics. An estimate of VER could then be obtained as:

$$\Delta \ln c_{itv} = \sum_i \lambda_i S_{tv} + \sum_i \beta_i S_{itv} + \sum_{tv} \delta_v(D_v) + \eta X_{itv} + \Delta\varepsilon_{itv}. \tag{21}$$

In the present context, λ and β are of particular interest because they seek to capture the effects of covariate, S_{tv}, and idiosyncratic shocks, S_{itv}, respectively. Note that these effects are net of coping strategies and public responses.

A variant of (21) that has figured prominently in recent studies involves replacing $\sum_i \lambda_i S_{tv}$ and $\sum_i \beta_i S_{itv}$ with $\Delta(\overline{\ln y_{vt}})$ – the growth rate of average community/village income – and $\Delta \ln y_{itv}$ – the growth rate of household income, respectively. These variables are supposed to represent the combined effect of all covariate and idiosyncratic shocks.

$$\Delta \ln c_{itv} = \alpha + \beta \ln y_{itv} + \gamma \Delta(\overline{\ln y_{vt}}) + \delta X_{itv} + \Delta \varepsilon_{itv}. \qquad (22)$$

Much of the empirical literature has concentrated on verifying whether $\beta = 0$, consistent with complete risk-sharing. Although complete risk-sharing is rejected, estimates of β are generally low, suggesting that growth of consumption is related to the growth rate of income but less so than under the alternative hypothesis of no risk-sharing. The higher the estimate of β, the greater the vulnerability of consumption to income risk. In our specification we include schooling years of household head and their squares, caste, household size and their squares, and the first differences of household size and their squares in X_{itv}.

One limitation of measures of vulnerability based on Equations (21) and (22) is the presumption that positive and negative income shocks have symmetric effects. Ability to deal with such shocks, however, differs in general and between different groups of households. So to interpret β in (22) as a measure of vulnerability, as opposed to a measure of consumption insurance, may be misleading. This could be overcome by replacing $\Delta \ln y_{itv}$ with two measures of positive and negative income changes (Hoddinott and Quisumbing 2003b).

In the present study, we use $\Delta(\overline{\ln y_{vt}})$ as a proxy for the aggregate shock, as in Townsend (1994) and Ravallion and Chaudhuri (1997). We also use the crop shock measure for S_{tv}, following Gaiha and Imai (2004). The production shock for each household in the village is measured in terms of a deviation from a semi-logarithmic trend in crop production at the village level *minus* the household's own crop income. Village crop income (minus own crop income) at time t, C_{it}, is:

$$C_{it} = \sum_{j=1}^{n, j \neq 1} c_{jt},$$

where c_{jt} is crop income of household j at t, and n is the number of households in each village. A time trend is fitted to $\ln(C_{it})$, as shown below.

$$\ln(C_{it}) = b_0 + b_1 T. \qquad (23)$$

A measure of crop shock is then the deviation of the $\ln(C_{it})$ from its trend value, $\ln(\hat{C}_{it})$, as shown in Equation (24).[12]

$$S_{it} = \ln(C_{it}) - \ln(\hat{C}_{it}). \qquad (24)$$

Table 2.1 Results for VEP (vulnerability as expected poverty) measure, 1975–1977

	1975				1976				1977			
	Log (income/capita) (β)		Variance (θ)		Log (income/capita) (β)		Variance (θ)		Log (income/capita) (β)		Variance (θ)	
	Coeff.	t-value	Coeff.	t-value	Coeff.	t-value	Coeff.	t-value	Coeff.	t-value	Coeff.	t-value
X_i												
Age of household head	0.0135	(0.82)	−0.0151	(−0.20)	0.0149	(0.68)	0.0740	(0.89)	0.0050	(0.24)	−0.0380	(−0.41)
Age of household head squared	−0.0001	(−0.80)	0.0001	(0.12)	−0.0002	(−0.75)	−0.0007	(−0.78)	0.0000	(0.11)	0.0004	(0.41)
Household size	−0.1767	(−3.54)**	−0.3035	(−1.64)	−0.2606	(−4.50)**	−0.2096	(−1.12)	−0.2686	(−6.31)**	0.0506	(0.25)
Household size squared	0.0060	(1.75)+	0.0136	(1.15)	0.0117	(3.30)**	0.0112	(1.00)	0.0105	(3.98)**	−0.0010	(−0.09)
Caste dummies (high)	0.1909	(1.85)+	0.6303	(1.30)	0.3880	(2.65)**	−0.3037	(−0.57)	−0.0491	(−0.40)	0.3082	(0.53)
(middle high)	0.3610	(3.88)**	0.2954	(0.62)	0.4097	(2.96)**	−0.2134	(−0.42)	0.2630	(2.41)*	−0.1341	(−0.24)
(middle low)	0.1531	(1.57)	0.8427	(1.87)+	0.1167	(0.79)	0.3488	(0.71)	−0.0329	(−0.30)	0.0248	(0.05)

L_i											
Owned area of land	0.0848	(4.56)**	0.0102	(0.14)	0.0202	(0.73)	0.0398	(0.47)	0.0798	(4.30)**	−0.1109	(−1.22)
Owned area squared	−0.0016	(−2.48)*	−0.0002	(−0.08)	−0.0009	(−0.84)	0.0001	(0.04)	−0.0019	(−3.07)**	0.0016	(0.53)
Share of irrigated land	0.0037	(4.08)**	−0.0050	(−1.03)	0.0042	(2.66)**	−0.0012	(−0.21)	0.0048	(3.16)**	0.0022	(0.34)
Non-land production assets	0.0000	(2.32)*	0.0001	(1.69)+	0.0001	(2.85)**	0.0001	(1.06)	0.0001	(3.22)**	0.0001	(1.59)
Non-land assets squared	0.0000	(−1.28)	0.0000	(−1.71)+	0.0000	(−0.81)	0.0000	(−1.76)+	0.0000	(−1.00)	0.0000	(−1.28)
H_i											
Schooling yrs of household head	−0.0006	(−0.02)	0.2595	(2.16)*	0.0275	(0.61)	0.0484	(0.36)	0.0551	(1.56)	−0.0645	(−0.44)
Schooling yrs squared	0.0030	(1.80)+	−0.0283	(−2.46)*	−0.0028	(−0.56)	0.0029	(0.23)	−0.0045	(−1.12)	0.0079	(0.58)
Constant	6.0888	(13.90)	−1.8822	(−1.03)	6.6271	(12.71)	−4.0175	(−2.04)	7.0189	(14.01)	−2.5422	(−1.12)
No. of observations	198		198		200		200		198		198	
F	21.74**		1.53		11.96**		0.63		16.31		0.45	
R^2	.6245		.1045		.4695		.0454		.5551		.0340	

Source: See text.

Notes: ** indicates the coefficient is significant at 1% level; * = significant at 5% level; + = significant at 10% level.

Table 2.2 Results for VEP (vulnerability as expected poverty) measure, 1978–1980

	1978				1979				1980			
	Log (income p.c.) (β)		Variance (θ)		Log (income p.c.) (β)		Variance (θ)		Log (income p.c.) (β)		Variance (θ)	
	Coeff.	t-value	Coeff.	t-value	Coeff.	t-value	Coeff.	t-value	Coeff.	t-value	Coeff.	t-value
X_i												
Age of household head	0.0108 (0.54)		0.0172 (0.19)		0.0053 (0.27)		0.0303 (0.35)		0.0338 (1.15)		−0.1168 (−1.22)	
Age of household head squared	0.0000 (−0.07)		−0.0001 (−0.16)		0.0000 (0.20)		−0.0003 (−0.37)		−0.0002 (−0.84)		0.0012 (1.34)	
Household size	−0.2135 (−4.47)**		0.0109 (0.05)		−0.2194 (−4.77)**		−0.3899 (−2.09)*		−0.0816 (−1.87)+		−0.0877 (−0.47)	
Household size squared	0.0070 (2.33)*		0.0002 (0.01)		0.0076 (2.82)**		0.0150 (1.33)		0.0011 (0.47)		0.0016 (0.15)	
Caste dummies (high)	0.1976 (1.61)		0.5528 (1.01)		0.3507 (2.94)**		0.5456 (1.07)		0.2084 (1.62)		−0.0990 (−0.18)	
(middle high)	0.2552 (2.32)*		0.1801 (0.34)		0.2695 (2.64)**		−0.2810 (−0.56)		0.2052 (1.73)+		0.0626 (0.12)	
(middle low)	0.2439 (2.21)*		0.3591 (0.71)		0.1069 (0.99)		0.0477 (0.10)		−0.0468 (−0.38)		0.1696 (0.34)	

L_i											
Owned area of land	0.0519	(2.85)**	0.0155	(0.18)	0.0819	(4.04)**	0.0620	(0.70)	0.0203	(0.82)	−0.0486	(−0.56)
Owned area squared	−0.0009	(−1.78)+	−0.0014	(−0.50)	−0.0020	(−2.89)**	−0.0030	(−0.94)	−0.0003	(−0.32)	0.0015	(0.44)
Share of irrigated land	0.0068	(4.36)**	0.0042	(0.67)	0.0069	(5.97)**	−0.0001	(−0.02)	0.0038	(1.98)*	0.0136	(2.73)**
Non-land production assets	0.0001	(3.57)**	0.0000	(−0.26)	0.0000	(2.78)**	0.0001	(1.39)	0.0000	(2.27)*	0.0001	(2.05)*
Non-land assets squared	0.0000	(−1.91)+	0.0000	(−0.48)	0.0000	(−2.21)*	0.0000	(−1.85)+	0.0000	(−0.89)	0.0000	(−1.70)+
H_i												
Schooling yrs of household head	0.0239	(0.68)	−0.1193	(−0.87)	0.0285	(0.79)	−0.1661	(−1.25)	−0.0334	(−1.09)	−0.1071	(−0.80)
Schooling yrs squared	−0.0032	(−0.81)	0.0150	(1.16)	−0.0034	(−0.80)	0.0184	(1.47)	0.0018	(0.63)	0.0054	(0.42)
Constant	6.6375	(13.32)	−3.4747	(−1.56)	6.7105	(13.10)	−2.2948	(−1.02)	5.6488	(7.49)	−0.1237	(−0.05)
No. of observations	197		197		196		196		196		196	
F	24.25**		0.41		28.61**		1.31		4.50**		1.45	
R^2	.6510		.0400		.6888		.0922		.2583		.2182	

Source: See text.

Note: ** indicates the coefficient is significant at 1% level; * = significant at 5% level; + = significant at 10% level.

29

Table 2.3 Results for VEP (vulnerability as expected poverty) measure, 1981–1983

	1981				1982				1983			
	Log (income p.c.) (β)		Variance (θ)		Log (income p.c.) (β)		Variance (θ)		Log (income p.c.) (β)		Variance (θ)	
	Coeff.	t-value	Coeff.	t-value	Coeff.	t-value	Coeff.	t-value	Coeff.	t-value	Coeff.	t-value
X_i												
Age of household head	0.0466	(1.44)	−0.2015	(−2.27)*	0.0788	(2.75)**	−0.2454	(−2.23)*	0.0346	(1.51)	0.0487	(0.48)
Age of household head squared	−0.0004	(−1.34)	0.0018	(2.17)*	−0.0007	(−2.68)**	0.0024	(2.37)*	−0.0003	(−1.59)	−0.0005	(−0.57)
Household size	−0.1218	(−3.45)**	0.2270	(1.47)	−0.1872	(−6.84)**	0.2534	(1.34)	−0.1334	(−4.58)**	0.1538	(1.08)
Household size squared	0.0026	(1.69)+	−0.0197	(−2.28)*	0.0059	(5.18)**	−0.0182	(−1.70)+	0.0023	(1.92)+	−0.0074	(−1.03)
Caste dummies (high)	0.0299	(0.24)	−0.2172	(−0.46)	0.2699	(2.46)*	−0.3503	(−0.62)	0.0542	(0.49)	0.1073	(0.21)
(middle high)	0.1070	(0.88)	−0.1174	(−0.26)	0.2664	(2.64)**	−0.7467	(−1.34)	0.2909	(2.52)*	0.3196	(0.63)
(middle low)	−0.1632	(−1.18)	0.5152	(1.15)	−0.0093	(−0.08)	−0.1218	(−0.23)	−0.0408	(−0.34)	0.6130	(1.24)

L_i						
Owned area of land	0.0482 (2.03)*	−0.0019 (−0.02)	0.0533 (2.68)**	−0.0888 (−0.88)	0.1132 (4.97)**	0.0072 (0.08)
Owned area squared	−0.0018 (−2.32)*	−0.0013 (−0.41)	−0.0020 (−2.01)*	0.0032 (0.85)	−0.0026 (−3.30)**	−0.0009 (−0.25)
Share of irrigated land	0.0055 (4.03)**	0.0014 (0.30)	0.0032 (3.51)**	−0.0066 (−1.23)	0.0042 (2.94)**	0.0018 (0.33)
Non-land production assets	0.0000 (4.13)**	0.0001 (2.10)*	0.0000 (4.99)**	0.0001 (2.54)*	0.0000 (0.12)	0.0000 (0.72)
Non-land assets squared	0.0000 (−3.68)**	0.0000 (−0.96)	0.0000 (−5.11)**	0.0000 (−2.09)*	0.0000 (1.63)	0.0000 (−0.99)
H_i						
Schooling yrs of household head	0.0267 (0.80)	−0.1195 (−1.03)	0.0526 (1.76)+	−0.2586 (−1.79)+	0.0539 (1.75)+	−0.0487 (−0.38)
Schooling yrs squared	−0.0036 (−0.98)	0.0071 (0.63)	−0.0037 (−1.00)	0.0206 (1.48)	−0.0025 (−0.78)	0.0014 (0.11)
Constant	5.4574 (6.33)	2.0132 (0.84)	5.0376 (6.73)	2.5040 (0.82)	6.1234 (9.34)	−4.6948 (−1.64)
No. of observations	197	197	197	197	198	198
F	7.72**	1.81	22.89**	1.98	12.29**	0.51
R^2	.3726	.1219	.6378	.1321	.4846	.0378

Source: See text.
Note: ** indicates the coefficient is significant at 1% level; * = significant at 5% level; + = significant at 10% level.

31

4 Results

We carried out econometric estimation based on the specification in the previous section and obtained vulnerability measures. In this section, we will first briefly discuss the estimation results and then summarize vulnerability measures across different household groups, classified by land-holding, educational attainment of household head and caste.

4.1 Vulnerability as expected poverty (VEP)

We applied Equations (10) and (11) to each annual cross-sectional component of the 10-year panel data along the lines of Chaudhuri et al. (2002). The cross-sectional results are given in Tables 2.1–2.4. Results based on GLS panel data, where cross-sectional heteroscedasticity is modelled as in Equation (6), are shown in the last column of Table 2.4.

The results for log income per capita are generally plausible except that the coefficient of schooling years of household head is not significant in most cases. Only in 1982 and 1983 (in Table 2.3) are the coefficients of schooling years positive and significant at the 10 per cent level. Age of household head has a positive and significant effect and its square has a negative and significant effect, reflecting that households with older heads tend to have higher incomes per capita, but this positive effect weakens with age. Caste dummies have significant coefficients in the panel regression. In particular, "high caste" and "middle-high castes" have generally positive and significant coefficients in cross-sectional regressions except in a few years. Owned area of land has a positive and significant effect, while its square has a negative and significant effect in both cross-sectional regressions (except in 1976, 1980 and 1984) and GLS panel results. As expected, both the share of irrigated area and non-land production assets have positive and significant effects.

The regression results on variance of log income per capita are not stable over time. However, it is noted that variance is influenced by some household characteristics, such as household size and its square (e.g. the effect of the former is negative and significant in 1976 while that of the latter is positive and significant), non-land production assets (e.g. the former has a positive and significant coefficient in 1982, but the value is small) and schooling years of household head and its square (e.g. the former has a positive and significant effect in 1975 and the latter has a negative and significant effect). Thus the Chaudhuri–Jalan–Suryahadi specification (2002) yields plausible results.

The VEP measure is then constructed for each household by the cross-sectional regression for each year and also by the panel regression. We

Table 2.4 Results for VEP (vulnerability as expected poverty) measure, 1984, and panel estimation for 1976–1984

| | 1984 | | | | GLS panel estimation | |
| | Log (income p.c.) (β) | | Variance (θ) | | Log (income p.c.) (β) | |
	Coeff.	t-value	Coeff.	t-value	Coeff.	t-value
X_i						
Age of household head	0.0509	(2.05)*	0.0889	(0.73)	0.0209	(3.75)**
Age of household head squared	−0.0005	(−2.43)*	−0.0010	(−0.93)	−0.0002	(−2.97)**
Household size	−0.1493	(−4.23)**	−0.0241	(−0.13)	−0.1841	(−17.56)**
Household size squared	0.0039	(2.57)*	−0.0048	(−0.50)	0.0056	(9.23)**
Caste dummies (high)	−0.0138	(−0.10)	0.5582	(0.92)	0.2223	(7.03)**
(middle high)	0.2728	(2.19)*	0.0638	(0.10)	0.2894	(9.96)**
(middle low)	0.1067	(0.78)	0.6775	(1.16)	0.0689	(2.24)*
L_i						
Owned area of land	0.0455	(1.32)	0.0119	(0.09)	0.0694	(12.71)**
Owned area squared	−0.0013	(−1.19)	0.0015	(0.33)	−0.0015	(7.14)**
Share of irrigated land	0.0019	(0.53)	0.0172	(1.72)+	0.0031	(9.02)**
Non-land production assets	0.0000	(3.39)**	0.0000	(0.79)	0.0000	(14.49)**
Non-land assets squared	0.0000	(−2.05)*	0.0000	(−1.62)	0.0000	(−8.47)**
H_i						
Schooling yrs of household head	−0.0282	(−0.79)	−0.2595	(−1.77)+	0.0083	(1.05)
Schooling yrs squared	0.0056	(1.37)	0.0222	(1.62)	0.0000	(0.00)
Constant	5.7466	(7.85)	−4.6059	(−1.33)	6.3717	(45.03)
No. of observations	119		119		1,896	
F	17.68**		1.39		Wald χ^2 (13)	
R^2	.7042		.1575		Log likelihood	−1,285

Source: See text.
Notes: ** indicates the coefficient is significant at 1% level; * = significant at 5% level; + = significant at 10% level. In 1984 the data are available for only three villages, Aurepalle, Shirapur and Kanzara. Estimation results for variance in the case of panel regressions are not provided by the programme.

compare VEP measures with VEU measures across different groups of households later in this section.

4.2 Vulnerability as low expected utility (VEU)

Table 2.5 provides results of IV estimation for Equations (19) and (20). Since differences between coefficients of the fixed effects IV and the random effects specifications are *not* systematic at the 5 per cent level when using the Hausmann test, the random effects IV specification is preferred (Baltagi 2005). The first-stage regression on the normalized household income yields results similar to the panel regression in Table 2.4 except that the high-caste dummy does not have a significant positive coefficient.[13] In the second stage, normalized household consumption (i.e. consumption that is normalized so that the mean is unity) is estimated by normalized household income. The coefficient of household income is positive and highly significant, implying that if income increases by one unit, consumption will increase by 0.5524. High-caste households tend to consume more than the rest. These results are used to derive various expectations of consumption in (14'), using restricted least squares, and then these expectations are converted into utility (16).

Table 2.6 shows the decomposition of the VEU measure; 0.7476 at the head of the second column is our estimate of the vulnerability of all the households. It is not necessarily easy to give it an intuitive interpretation, but this implies that the utility of the average household is 75 per cent less than the hypothetical situation without any risk or inequality in consumption. In other words, vulnerability so defined is high. Of course, the results presume a specific form of utility function (16) that may not necessarily reflect individual preferences. However, our estimate suggests a potentially very large effect of inequality and poverty on household utility. Our estimate of VEU = 0.7476 is much larger than the Bulgarian estimate of 0.1972, reported by Ligon and Schechter (2003). It is surmised that this large difference is due to the larger magnitudes of risk and inequality of consumption in rural India, and the fact that we use annual consumption data in a rural area for 10 years and Ligon and Schechter (2003) use monthly consumption data for 12 months.

An important finding is that the vulnerability arising from risk (0.4426; 59 per cent of total vulnerability), as the sum of aggregate risks, 0.1671 (22 per cent), and idiosyncratic risks, 0.2750 (37 per cent), is very large. Indeed, it is even larger than the vulnerability associated with poverty, 0.2586 (35 per cent). This is in sharp contrast with Ligon and Schechter's (2003) finding where the corresponding risk component is 0.0279 (14 per cent of the total vulnerability), as the sum of the aggregate (0.0264; 13 per cent) and idiosyncratic risks (0.0014; 1 per cent). The vulnerability

Table 2.5 Results for VEU (vulnerability as expected low utility) measure: G2SLS random effects IV regression for panel data, 1975–1984

Variable	First stage — Normalized HH income		Second stage — Normalized HH income	
	Coeff. (β)	t-value	Coeff. (γ)	t-value
Y_{it}				
Normalized income per capita	–	–	0.5524	(8.31)**
X_{it}				
Age of household head	0.0526	(4.39)**	0.0068	(0.30)
Age of household head squared	−0.0005	(−4.56)**	−0.0001	(−0.27)
Household size	−0.1671	(−7.66)**	−0.0414	(−1.04)
Household size squared	0.0038	(3.11)**	0.0011	(0.51)
Caste dummies (high)	−0.0398	(−0.55)	0.2450	(1.96)+
(middle high)	0.2801	(3.90)**	0.0237	(0.18)
(middle low)	0.0910	(1.36)	0.0528	(0.43)
L_i				
Owned area of land	0.0791	(6.49)**	–	–
Owned area squared	−0.0020	(−5.26)**	–	–
Share of irrigated land	0.0045	(3.59)**	–	–
Non-land production assets	0.0000	(11.39)**	–	–
Non-land assets squared	0.0000	(−3.15)**	–	–
H_i				
Schooling yrs of household head	0.0176	(1.07)	0.0053	(0.18)
Schooling yrs squared	−0.0011	(−0.79)	−0.0007	(−0.26)
D_t				
Whether in the crop year 1976	0.0733	(0.93)	−0.1375	(−0.95)
1977	0.2848	(3.62)**	0.0937	(0.64)
1978	0.1692	(2.14)*	−0.2052	(−1.41)
1979	0.2704	(3.38)**	−0.1324	(−0.89)
1980	0.2136	(2.64)**	−0.1285	(−0.86)
1981	0.5263	(6.37)**	−0.1676	(−1.07)
1982	0.6914	(8.26)**	−0.8669	(−5.32)**
1983	0.8348	(9.79)**	−0.7004	(−4.08)**
1984	0.7745	(8.70)**	−0.6574	(−3.77)**
Constant	−0.4726	(−1.53)	0.6220	(1.09)
No. of observations	1184		1184	
Wald χ^2 (22)	Wald χ^2 (22) 1020		Wald χ^2 (13) 142	
Hausmann test for the choice between fixed effects IV model and random effects IV model	$\chi^2 = 19.57$ Prob $> \chi^2 = 0.297$			

Source: See text.

Note: ** indicates the coefficient is significant at 1% level; * = significant at 5% level; + = significant at 10% level.

Table 2.6 Decomposition of VEU (vulnerability as expected low utility) measure and its determinants: Regression of each vulnerability measure on time series means of household variables (between estimator)

Average value X_i	VEU 0.7476		= Poverty (inequality) 0.2586		+ Aggregate risk 0.1671		+ Idiosyncratic risk 0.2750		+ Unexpected risk 0.0470	
	Coeff.	t-value	Coeff.	t-value	Coeff.	t-value	Coeff.	t-value	Coeff.	t-value
Age of household head	-0.1903	(-2.31)*	-0.0876	(-2.50)*	0.0361	(0.68)	-0.0128	(-0.09)	-0.1260	(-1.18)
Age of household head squared	0.0017	(2.11)*	0.0008	(2.28)*	-0.0003	(-0.52)	0.0000	(-0.02)	0.0012	(1.17)
Household size	0.3246	(1.81)+	0.2291	(3.00)**	0.0024	(0.02)	0.1460	(0.49)	-0.0529	(-0.23)
Household size squared	-0.0019	(-0.18)	-0.0081	(-1.75)+	-0.0006	(-0.08)	0.0036	(0.20)	0.0031	(0.22)
Caste dummies (high)	0.0357	(0.07)	-0.2194	(-1.07)	-0.5049	(-1.62)	0.8656	(1.07)	-0.1056	(-0.17)
(middle high)	-0.0721	(-0.15)	-0.2305	(-1.13)	-0.0643	(-0.21)	-0.0208	(-0.03)	0.2435	(0.39)
(middle low)	0.5487	(1.27)	-0.0123	(-0.07)	-0.4380	(-1.58)	1.5197	(2.11)*	-0.5207	(-0.94)

L_i									
Owned area of land	-0.1570	(-1.53)	-0.0411	(-0.94)	0.0666	(1.01)	-0.2983	(-1.74)+	0.1158	(0.87)
Owned area squared	0.0040	(1.35)	0.0013	(1.05)	-0.0015	(-0.78)	0.0071	(1.44)	-0.0030	(-0.78)
Share of irrigated land	-0.0006	(-0.04)	-0.0029	(-0.48)	-0.0023	(-0.25)	0.0034	(0.15)	0.0012	(0.06)
Non-land production assets	-0.0001	(-1.19)	-0.0001	(-2.69)**	0.0000	(-0.33)	0.0000	(0.17)	0.0000	(-0.09)
Non-land assets squared	0.0000	(1.20)	0.0000	(2.16)*	0.0000	(0.23)	0.0000	(0.19)	0.0000	(-0.15)
H_i									
Schooling yrs of household head	-0.1259	(-0.95)	-0.0293	(-0.52)	0.0478	(0.56)	-0.1844	(-0.83)	0.0401	(0.23)
Schooling yrs squared	0.0063	(0.57)	0.0017	(0.37)	-0.0057	(-0.81)	0.0128	(0.69)	-0.0024	(-0.17)
Constant	4.7809	(2.25)	2.2663	(2.51)	-0.7829	(-0.57)	0.1343	(0.04)	3.1633	(1.15)
No. of observations	1184		1184		1184		1184		1184	
Joint significance: $F(14, 117) =$	2.73**		4.23**		0.64		0.91		0.38	
R^2	.1874		.3358		.0542		.0758		.0381	

Source: See text.

Note: ** indicates the coefficient is significant at 1% level; * = significant at 5% level; + = significant at 10% level.

associated with poverty is also large in our case (0.2586; 35 per cent), much larger than that in Bulgaria, 0.1079 (31 per cent of the total vulnerability).

Our results are different from Ligon's (2005), based on the ICRISAT data for three villages, Aurepalle, Shirapur and Kanzara, for 1976–1981. The latter show that:

- Idiosyncratic risk for consumption is generally small, as it ranged from 2 to 4 per cent of the total risk (i.e. the sum of aggregate and idiosyncratic risks and unexplained risk and measurement errors).
- Aggregate risk is large except in Shirapur (58 per cent of total risk in Aurepalle, 5 per cent in Shirapur and 26 per cent in Kanzara).
- Unexplained risk is large in all three villages (38 per cent of the total risk in Aurepalle, 88 per cent in Shirapur and 60 per cent in Kanzara). These results are different for the following reasons:
- We have used adjusted consumption data, corrected for measurement errors, whereas Ligon (2005) uses unadjusted data.
- Our specifications differ from Ligon's (2005).[14]
- All three villages are considered together for 1975–1984 in our analysis, whereas Ligon (2005) considers each village separately for 1976–1981. Although the sum of idiosyncratic and unexplained risks in the total risk is similar (66 per cent in our case and 70 per cent in Ligon's 2005), it is surmised that some unexplained risks and measurement errors in Ligon's analysis are, in fact, idiosyncratic risks, as reported in our study.

Although generalizations of our findings to different settings are not straightforward, our analysis suggests that vulnerability associated with idiosyncratic and aggregate shocks has a significant negative impact on a household's wellbeing. Our analysis also suggests that completely insuring against idiosyncratic risks has a larger impact on the average utility of households than completely eliminating inequality.

In another exercise, we regress each component of vulnerability on time series means of various household characteristics to explore the determinants of vulnerability in Table 2.6. A household headed by an older member has a lower (total) VEU measure because of lower vulnerability associated with poverty. On the other hand, a larger household tends to have a higher VEU measure because of the higher poverty measure. Also, the more non-land production assets a household has, the lower the VEU measure of poverty is. Turning to aggregate shocks, households in a high caste and middle-low caste tend to be less vulnerable to them. Households in a middle-low caste and those with less owned land are more vulnerable to idiosyncratic shocks. This suggests that the landless or small farmers tend to be vulnerable to idiosyncratic shocks resulting in reduced consumption.

We have carried out regressions for estimated VEP measures and a static poverty measure using the same specification to do comparisons of determinants of different vulnerability measures and static poverty (Table 2.7). Static poverty can be simply defined by comparing log household income per capita with a poverty threshold of Rs 180 per capita of income per year at 1960–1961 prices. Static poverty is estimated by a fixed effects probit model by fitting it to those below the poverty cut-off point.

It is noted that determinants of poverty and those of VEP measures are quite similar. In particular, landholding is crucial in both poverty reduction and reduction of vulnerability. Non-land assets also reduce poverty and vulnerability. However, having an older person as a household head is significant in reducing the cross-sectional VEP measure and VEU measure, but it is not significant in poverty reduction. On the other hand, caste is one of the significant determinants of poverty but not of vulnerability (i.e. VEU and cross-sectional VEP). Surprisingly, variables on schooling years of head are not significant.

4.3 Vulnerability as uninsured exposure to risk (VER)

The results for VER are presented in Table 2.8. We estimate Equations (21) and (22) by applying random effects GLS[15] to the annual data for three sample villages, Aurepalle, Shirapur and Kanzara. The specification in Case A of each column is the same as in Ravallion and Chaudhuri (1997) except that we have added household characteristics.

The results in Case A are generally consistent with Ravallion and Chaudhuri (1997). The complete risk-sharing hypothesis (i.e. $\beta = 0$ where β is the coefficient of $\Delta(\overline{\ln y_{vy}})$) is not rejected in Aurepalle (which implies that risk is shared among households in this village). In Shirapur and Kanzara, β is negative and significant. That is, in bad periods, consumption is well (or over) insured in these villages.

In Case B, where we use the crop shock measure instead of $\Delta(\overline{\ln y_{vy}})$, in Aurepalle consumption is significantly reduced in the event of a negative shock and vice versa. Hence there is no insurance against a crop shock. In both Shirapur and Kanzara, however, β is negative and significant, implying that some sort of risk-insurance mechanism was in place, and that the risk was shared among households during a crop shock in these two villages. This raises the issue of why VEU arising from idiosyncratic risks is so high *despite* risk-sharing mechanisms. One possibility is that income risk is so large that risk-sharing can reduce only a part of the idiosyncratic shocks. Even if there is constant consumption over the years to completely eliminate the idiosyncratic VEU, consumption will still vary because risk-sharing ceases to be effective when aggregate shocks occur.

Table 2.7 Determinants of VEP (vulnerability as expected poverty) measure and static poverty

| | VEP | | | | Poverty | |
| | (based on cross-sectional data) | | (based on panel data) | | (static binary variable) | |
	Coeff.	t-value	Coeff.	t-value	Coeff.	t-value
X_i						
Age of household head	-0.0456	(-4.11)**	-0.0108	(-1.10)	-0.0595	(-1.42)
Age of household head squared	0.0002	(1.57)	0.0000	(-0.45)	0.0005	(1.31)
Household size	0.1687	(11.09)**	0.2038	(15.13)**	0.3140	(5.25)**
Household size squared	-0.0063	(-7.97)**	-0.0073	(-10.48)**	-0.0078	(-2.69)**
Caste dummies						
(high)	-0.1513	(-1.07)	-0.4644	(-3.69)**	-0.4637	(-2.05)*
(middle high)	0.1243	(1.00)	-0.2384	(-2.17)*	-0.5790	(-2.55)*
(middle low)	–		–		-0.3556	(-1.70)+
L_i						
Owned area of land	-0.0426	(-4.46)**	-0.0607	(-7.18)**	-0.1444	(-3.74)**
Owned area squared	0.0006	(1.89)+	0.0009	(3.07)**	0.0027	(2.21)*
Share of irrigated land	-0.0024	(-3.94)**	-0.0026	(-4.76)**	-0.0052	(-1.19)
Non-land production assets	0.0000	(-3.33)**	0.0000	(-7.04)**	0.0000	(-2.26)*
Non-land assets squared	0.0000	(3.80)**	0.0000	(6.76)**	0.0000	(-0.35)

H_i						
Schooling yrs of household head	−0.0126	(−1.14)	0.0071	(0.72)	0.0215	(0.37)
Schooling yrs squared	0.0011	(1.07)	−0.0015	(−1.67)	−0.0034	(−0.67)
Constant	1.7697	(6.00)	0.7258	(2.78)	1.1602	(1.08)
No. of observations	1181		1181		1181	
Joint significance test	$F(13, 1036) = 36.04**$		$F(13, 1036) = 51.51**$		Wald $\chi^2(14) = 118.01**$	
Hausmann test for the choice between random effects model and fixed effects model	$\chi^2(11) = 86.03**$		$\chi^2(11) = 21.01**$		N/A	
R^2	.2799		.5942		.2488	(Pseudo R^2)

Source: See text.

Note: ** indicates the coefficient is significant at 1% level; * = significant at 5% level; + = significant at 10% level.

Table 2.8 Results for VER (vulnerability as uninsured exposure to risk) measure: GLS random effects, GLS for panel data, 1975–1984

	Aurepalle				Shirapur				Kanzara			
	Case A		Case B		Case A		Case B		Case A		Case B	
	Coeff.	t-value	Coeff.	t-value	Coeff.	t-value	Coeff.	t-value	Coeff.	t-value	Coeff.	t-value
$\Delta\ln y_{it}$: First difference of log income	0.2065	(5.34)**	0.2185	(5.32)**	0.0974	(2.39)*	0.0717	(1.83)+	0.5383	(4.91)**	0.3999	(3.63)**
$\Delta\ln y_{it}$: First difference of village mean of log income	0.0887	(0.94)	–	–	-0.4539	(-3.86)**	–	–	-1.3910	(-4.46)**	–	–
Crop shock variable	–	–	0.1753	(3.02)**	–	–	-0.7198	(-3.40)**	–	–	-0.3234	(-1.30)
Schooling yrs of HH head	0.0361	(0.85)	0.0311	(0.74)	0.0153	(0.62)	0.0204	(0.82)	0.0046	(0.14)	0.0032	(0.09)
Schooling yrs squared	-0.0012	(-0.27)	-0.0008	(-0.20)	-0.0013	(-0.71)	-0.0018	(-0.95)	0.0002	(0.07)	0.0004	(0.11)
Household size	-0.0131	(-0.31)	-0.0104	(-0.25)	-0.0266	(-0.55)	-0.0299	(-0.61)	-0.0146	(-0.38)	-0.0129	(-0.32)
Household size squared	0.0003	(0.10)	0.0002	(0.08)	0.0012	(0.43)	0.0014	(0.48)	0.0010	(0.48)	0.0009	(0.41)
ΔHousehold size	-0.2162	(-2.83)**	-0.2066	(-2.73)**	-0.2568	(-2.20)*	-0.2683	(-2.29)*	0.0513	(0.43)	-0.0222	(-0.18)
ΔHousehold size squared	0.0046	(0.87)	0.0034	(0.66)	0.0101	(1.70)+	0.0104	(1.74)+	-0.0060	(-0.85)	-0.0039	(-0.54)
Caste dummies (high)	-0.1695	(-1.31)	-0.1650	(-1.30)	0.0228	(0.21)	0.0196	(0.18)	-0.0752	(-0.48)	-0.0797	(-0.47)
(middle high)	-0.2521	(-1.57)	-0.2358	(-1.50)	0.1025	(0.54)	0.1081	(0.57)	-0.0516	(-0.48)	-0.0472	(-0.42)
(middle low)	-0.0228	(-0.34)	-0.0180	(-0.27)	-0.0340	(-0.28)	-0.0490	(-0.40)	-0.0667	(-0.43)	-0.0546	(-0.34)
Constant	0.1121	(0.78)	0.0998	(0.70)	0.1265	(0.63)	0.1501	(0.74)	0.1124	(0.77)	0.0097	(0.06)

No. of observations	351	347	349	345	351	346
Joint significance: Wald $\chi^2(11) =$	110.29**	117.41	28.17**	25.66**	41.91**	23.57*
Hausmann test for the choice between random & fixed effects Model: $\chi^2(11) =$	4.68	4.47	3.31	3.30	1.74	1.97
R^2	.2455	.2595	.0771	.0715	.1100	.0695

Source: See text.

Notes: Case A: village mean of log income used; Case B: Crop shock measure used; ** indicates the coefficient is significant at 1% level; * = significant at 5% level; + = significant at 10% level.

Table 2.9 Descriptive statistics of vulnerability measure

Variable	Obs	Mean	Std dev.	Min.	Max.
VEP (based on cross-sectional data)	1181	0.498	0.429	0.000	1.000
VEP_GLS (based on panel data)	1181	0.479	0.480	0.000	1.000
POVERTY (static measure of poverty)	1181	0.477	0.500	0.000	1.000
VEU	1181	0.748	1.739	−0.547	18.050
VEU_POVERTY	1181	0.259	0.556	−0.801	6.917
VEU_AGGREGATE	1181	0.167	0.828	−6.425	4.397
VEU_IDIOSYNCRATIC	1181	0.275	2.749	−6.380	21.051
VEU_UNEXPLAINED	1181	0.047	2.095	−20.344	3.533

Source: See text.

Moreover, some aggregate shocks (e.g. earthquakes) cannot be insured against.

4.4 Vulnerability across different groups

Tables 2.9 and 2.10 contain descriptive statistics and a correlation matrix of vulnerability measures. *POVERTY* denotes static poverty measured by the headcount index (i.e. the proportion of households with per capita income below a cut-off point, z). It is not surprising that the correlation between *POVERTY* and *VEU_POVERTY* is high (the coefficient being 0.52), but it must be noted that *POVERTY* is not highly correlated with *VEU_AGGREGATE* or *VEU_IDIOSYNCRATIC*. However, the *VEP* measure (an *ex ante* measure), obtained from a cross-section regression as well as from a panel using GLS, is highly correlated with *POVERTY* (with correlation coefficients of 0.57 and 0.48, respectively). A valid inference, therefore, is that poverty is *related* to but *distinct* from vulnerability. So also are *ex ante* (VEP) and *ex post* measures (VEU) of vulnerability *related* but *distinct* concepts. Their correlations (i.e. 0.25 to 0.26) are not high but non-negligible.

Tables 2.11 and 2.12 summarize means of various vulnerability measures by landholding class, household head's schooling years and caste. Here are some observations.

- The landless or small farmers are more vulnerable than larger farmers. In particular, small farmers face large idiosyncratic consumption risks.
- A household headed by a person without education is much more vulnerable and much poorer than one headed by a person with some education. However, higher schooling years do not have a dramatic effect on vulnerability.

Table 2.10 Correlation matrix of vulnerability and other household characteristics

	VEP	VEP_GLS	POVERTY	VEU	VEU_POVERTY	VEU_AGGREGATE	VEU_IDIOSYNCRATIC	VEU_UNEXPLAINED	school	ownarea	lowcast	midlcast	midhcast	highcast
VEP	1.00													
VEP_GLS	0.80	1.00												
POVERTY	0.57	0.48	1.00											
VEU	0.26	0.25	0.27	1.00										
VEU_POVERTY	0.54	0.54	0.52	0.41	1.00									
VEU_AGGREGATE	0.11	0.12	0.08	−0.24	−0.10	1.00								
VEU_IDIOSYNCRATIC	0.10	0.10	0.09	0.59	0.19	−0.42	1.00							
VEU_UNEXPLAINED	−0.10	−0.12	−0.06	0.04	−0.13	−0.01	−0.71	1.00						
School	−0.31	−0.30	−0.21	−0.14	−0.25	−0.10	−0.08	0.09	1.00					
Ownarea	−0.42	−0.42	−0.32	−0.17	−0.43	−0.03	−0.08	0.08	0.44	1.00				
Lowcast	0.36	0.39	0.25	0.04	0.32	0.14	−0.06	−0.02	−0.29	−0.29	1.00			
Midlcast	0.12	0.09	0.02	0.16	0.04	−0.04	0.19	−0.12	−0.21	−0.16	−0.30	1.00		
Midhcast	−0.06	−0.04	0.00	−0.05	−0.03	0.12	−0.10	0.05	0.04	−0.07	−0.27	−0.26	1.00	
Highcast	−0.37	−0.40	−0.24	−0.14	−0.30	−0.19	−0.03	0.09	0.42	0.46	−0.41	−0.39	−0.35	1.00

Source: See text.

Table 2.11 Comparisons of vulnerability across different groups

| | Land-holding status | | | |
Variable	Landless	Small farmers	Middle farmers	Large farmers
VEP (based on cross-sectional data)	0.643	0.632	0.511	0.195
VEP_GLS (based on panel data)	0.604	0.631	0.513	0.163
POVERTY (static measure of poverty)	0.671	0.571	0.498	0.156
VEU	0.905	1.213	0.615	0.208
VEU_POVERTY	0.559	0.363	0.229	−0.150
VEU_AGGREGATE	0.267	0.023	0.371	0.052
VEU_IDIOSYNCRATIC	0.264	0.965	−0.343	0.051
VEU_UNEXPLAINED	−0.186	−0.138	0.358	0.254

| | Household head's years of schooling | | |
Variable	0	<= 5	> 5
VEP (based on cross-sectional data)	0.622	0.362	0.293
VEP_GLS (based on panel data)	0.597	0.373	0.250
POVERTY (static measure of poverty)	0.569	0.351	0.359
VEU	1.010	0.396	0.407
VEU_POVERTY	0.396	0.060	0.100
VEU_AGGREGATE	0.204	0.106	0.137
VEU_IDIOSYNCRATIC	0.543	−0.026	−0.157
VEU_UNEXPLAINED	−0.133	0.257	0.327

| | Caste | | | |
Variable	Low	Middle–low	Middle–high	High
VEP (based on cross-sectional data)	0.769	0.591	0.442	0.280
VEP_GLS (based on panel data)	0.815	0.560	0.434	0.216
POVERTY (static measure of poverty)	0.701	0.496	0.476	0.309
VEU	0.881	1.250	0.579	0.423
VEU_POVERTY	0.574	0.303	0.225	0.029
VEU_AGGREGATE	0.367	0.109	0.376	−0.049
VEU_IDIOSYNCRATIC	−0.039	1.272	−0.268	0.148
VEU_UNEXPLAINED	−0.020	−0.433	0.245	0.295

Source: See text.

- Households in lower castes are more vulnerable than those in higher/ upper castes.
- If households are landless and at the same time without education or in low castes, they are highly vulnerable to aggregate shocks.

Table 2.12 Cross-tabulation by different categories

Variable	Landless and no schooling	Landless and low caste	Landless, no schooling and low caste	Small farmers and no schooling	Small farmers and low caste	Small farmers, no schooling and low caste
VEP (based on cross-sectional data)	0.694	0.811	0.771	0.716	0.834	0.839
VEP_GLS (based on panel data)	0.658	0.847	0.805	0.721	0.896	0.884
POVERTY (static measure of poverty)	0.698	0.755	0.726	0.637	0.728	0.784
VEU	0.965	0.976	0.877	1.543	0.869	0.907
VEU_POVERTY	0.604	0.679	0.580	0.427	0.599	0.636
VEU_AGGREGATE	0.356	0.509	0.435	0.019	0.117	0.115
VEU_IDIOSYNCRATIC	0.331	−0.223	0.032	1.365	0.373	0.523
VEU_UNEXPLAINED	−0.326	0.011	−0.170	−0.268	−0.221	−0.368

Source: See text.

5 Concluding observations

Some important findings are summarized from a larger policy perspective. An attempt was made to assess the vulnerability of rural households in the semi-arid tract of south India, based upon the ICRISAT panel survey. Both *ex ante* and *ex post* measures of vulnerability were computed. The latter were decomposed into aggregate and idiosyncratic risk and poverty components. Our decomposition shows that idiosyncratic risks account for the largest share (37 per cent), followed by poverty (35 per cent) and aggregate risk (22 per cent). It is somewhat surprising that idiosyncratic risks (e.g. illness or unemployment) contribute more than poverty to vulnerability. Despite some degree of risk-sharing at the village level, the landless or small farmers are vulnerable to idiosyncratic risks, forcing them to reduce consumption. Subsets comprising the landless without education or members of lower castes are highly vulnerable to idiosyncratic and aggregate risks.[16]

An important conclusion that emerges from the empirical analysis is that, although poverty and vulnerability are related and overlap to some extent, these are distinct concepts and vulnerability broadens the area of intervention. Deprivation must be viewed from a larger perspective that goes beyond poverty status in a specific year or month, allowing for frequent and large changes in income, sources of income and prices, as a consequence of changes in the policy regime, natural disasters, conflicts, seasonality of agricultural production and personal misfortunes. If credit and insurance markets were complete and worked efficiently, the case for a shift in anti-poverty policies would be weak. A feature, however, of rural areas, especially in the semi-arid regions, is that such markets not only are incomplete but also are subject to imperfections. So a broader area of intervention is consistent with a deeper concern for poverty reduction. Briefly, careful attention must be given to combining income-augmenting policies with those that not only reduce aggregate and idiosyncratic risks but also build resilience against them, as elaborated below.

Responses to risks are usually classified into: (i) risk reducing; (ii) risk mitigating; and (iii) risk coping. This classification must, however, be used with some caution because of overlapping categories. Income diversification at the household level, for example, could be interpreted both as a risk-reducing and as a risk-mitigating measure. Similarly, workfare could be viewed both as a risk-mitigating and as a risk-coping measure. Finally, nothing is implied about the workability and/or effectiveness of these measures because they are context-specific. Whether smallholders sell bullocks when a crop fails, or borrow more frequently or simply participate more in public works programmes depends largely on the context. A related issue is that, whereas some of the responses at different levels may be mutually reinforcing (e.g. income diversification, micro-finance and agricultural research and extension), others may undermine the role of some (e.g. social security may adversely affect precautionary savings, social assistance may erode informal networks of support, work-fare may discourage job search and income diversification).

In conclusion, although there is a case for broadening the area of intervention, it is far from obvious what the trade-offs are between income diversification, savings and different forms of insurance. The challenge of poverty reduction lies, therefore, not so much in a standard menu of policies but in a clearer and deeper understanding of the risks that vast segments of the rural population are exposed to and in building their resilience against them.

Appendix 1: Characteristics of study regions and villages

Table 2A.1 Characteristics of study regions and villages

Mahbubnagar	Sholapur	Akola
Aurepalle and Dokur	Shirapur and Kalman	Kanzara and Kinkheda
Rainfall unassured	Rainfall unassured; frequent crop failure	Rainfall assured
Pronounced rainfall; uncertainty at sowing	Deep black soils in lowlands; shallower lighter soils in uplands	Black soils; fairly homogeneous
Red soil; marked soil heterogeneity	*Rabi*, or post-rainy season, cropping	*Kharif* cropping
Kharif, or rainy season, cropping	*Rabi* sorghum	Upland cotton, mung bean and hybrid sorghum
Paddy, castor, local *kharif* sorghum, pearl millet and pigeon pea	Some dug wells	Limited irrigation sources in 1970s and early 1980s
Agricultural intensification around dug wells and tanks	Technologically stagnant	Sustained technical change in dryland agriculture
Neglect of dryland agriculture	Tenancy; dearth of bullocks; more equitable distribution of land	More educated
Harijans and caste rigidities; inequitable distribution of land ownership		

Source: Walker and Ryan (1990).

Appendix 2: Trend of crop shocks in sample villages

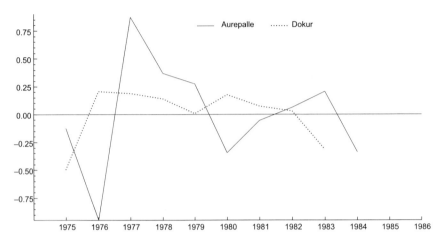

Figure 2A.1 Crop shock in Aurepalle and Dokur in Andhra Pradesh.
Source: Gaiha and Imai (2004).
Note: Crop shock is averaged for each village.

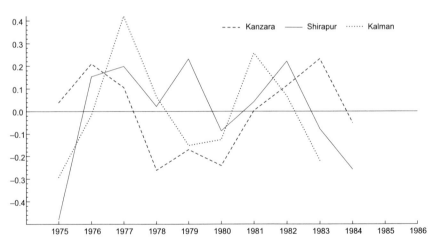

Figure 2A.2 Crop shock in Shirapur, Kalman and Kanzara in Maharashtra.
Source: Gaiha and Imai (2004).
Note: Crop shock is averaged for each village.

Acknowledgements

We would like to acknowledge helpful comments from Partha Dasgupta, P. L. Scandizzo, David Newbery, C. J. Bliss, G. Thapa and participants in the 13th International Conference on Panel Data at the University of Cambridge, July 2006, at the UNU-WIDER conference on "Fragile States – Fragile Groups", Helsinki, June 2007, and at seminars at the University of Manchester, the University of Rome "Tor Vergata", the University of Rome "La Sapienza", Doshisha University and Osaka University. This study was funded and supported by the Asia and the Pacific Division of the International Fund for Agricultural Development (IFAD). The views expressed, however, are ours and we are responsible for any errors or deficiencies.

Notes

1. See, for example, Hoddinott and Quisumbing (2003a,b) and World Bank (2000).
2. Examples include Rosenzweig and Wolpin (1993), Chaudhuri and Paxson (1994), Townsend (1994), Ravallion and Chaudhuri (1997), Jacoby and Skoufias (1998), Lim and Townsend (1998) and Gaiha and Imai (2004).
3. An exposition of different measures of vulnerability is given in a subsequent section.
4. Even though it is widely believed that the ICRISAT data are rich and reliable, they are, of course, not free from some measurement problems. Some doubts, for example, have been raised about own consumption of home production and grain stocks. Ravallion and Chaudhuri (1997) report a systematic under-reporting of own consumption of crop outputs produced. Without an appropriate adjustment, Townsend (1994) overestimates the degree of risk-sharing in the village. See Gautam (1991) for details of sources for the measurement errors.
5. This section provides a summary of the methodological sections of Hoddinott and Quisumbing (2003b). See Hoddinott and Quisumbing (2003b) for more details.
6. The poverty cut-off point we use represents the minimum cost of a nutritionally adequate diet, i.e. Rs 180 per capita per year (at 1960–1961 prices), which has been widely used in the literature; see Gaiha and Imai (2004) for more details.
7. See, for example, Pritchett et al. (2000).
8. These three values of α represent the headcount, depth of poverty and distributionally sensitive measures of poverty in the Foster–Greer–Thorbecke class of poverty indices.
9. In a related measure, Kamanou and Morduch (2002) define vulnerability as expected change in poverty, as opposed to expected poverty per se. Specifically, they define vulnerability in a population as the difference between the expected value of a poverty measure in the future and its current value.
10. See Chaudhuri et al. (2002) and Hoddinott and Quisumbing (2003b) for technical details.
11. It is, however, arguable that, although the results may be sensitive to the functional form assumed, the relative components of the decomposition are not likely to be affected much (Hoddinott and Quisumbing 2003b).
12. Crop shocks occur at different times in a year, given the diversity of cropping systems in the sample villages. As shown in Appendix 1, traditional cropping systems embrace the rainy season cereal/pulse intercrop in Aurepalle and the post-rainy season sorghum systems in Shirapur and Kalman. What is also observed is irrigated paddy production

in Dokur and Aurepalle and hybrid sorghum in Kanzara and Kinkheda (Gaiha and Imai 2004). As shown in Figures 2A.1 and 2A.2 in Appendix 2, the crop shocks in the sample villages in Andhra Pradesh and Maharashtra over the period 1975–1984 were frequent and large. What is also striking is that, whereas these shocks were similar in the Maharashtra villages, this was not the case in the Andhra Pradesh villages. In the latter, not just the intensity but also the pattern varied significantly. For example, a large negative shock in one village coincided with a large positive shock in another. Considering that large fractions of households depend on agriculture as the main source of livelihood, such shocks are bound to have significant effects on household incomes (Gaiha and Imai 2004).

13. It is because the significant coefficient of "high caste" in the second stage in turn has affected the first stage in the iterative estimation.
14. We have used IV estimates of household income, whereas Ligon (2005) employs the Newey–West estimator whereby the cross-sectional correlation is adjusted but does not instrument income in the consumption function.
15. The Hausmann test favours random effects over fixed effects in all cases in Table 2.4.
16. A limitation of the present study is that our econometric results are based on panel data which are not so recent. However, since poverty rates are still high in backward states (e.g. Himanshu 2007) and in socially disadvantaged groups such as scheduled castes or tribes (e.g. Gaiha et al. 2008) – particularly in rural India – most of our findings are likely to have considerable validity for those state/regions and disadvantaged groups that have characteristics similar to those of the ICRISAT sample. The relatively small sample size is another limitation that has been partly overcome by using the panel data. While reliable panel data sets – especially for both rural and urban areas – are few and far between, the ICRISAT panel continues to be researched because of its richness. In any case, many of our results are robust to different specifications. The policy implications, however, could differ given the expansion of personal and weather insurance in rural areas in recent years and the expansion of job opportunities. Of particular significance is the two-year-old National Rural Employment Guarantee Scheme. If implemented better, besides reducing the risk of poverty, it could serve the insurance function more effectively during periods of catastrophic events (e.g. droughts). So, although the disaggregation of vulnerability into the three components may change, it is far from self-evident that their ranking or relative shares would change significantly. We are grateful to an anonymous reviewer for raising this issue.

REFERENCES

Baltagi, B. (2005). *Econometric Analysis of Panel Data*. Chichester: John Wiley & Sons.
Baulch, B. and J. Hoddinott (2000). "Economic Mobility and Poverty Dynamics in Developing Countries". *Journal of Development Studies* 36(6): 1–24.
Chaudhuri, S. and C. Paxson (1994). "Consumption Smoothing and Income Seasonality in Rural India". Discussion Paper 173, Princeton University.
Chaudhuri, S., J. Jalan and A. Suryahadi (2002). "Assessing Household Vulnerability to Poverty from Cross-Sectional Data: A Methodology and Estimates from Indonesia". Discussion Paper 0102-52, Columbia University.
Dercon, S. (2005). "Risk, Insurance and Poverty". In S. Dercon (ed.), *Insurance against Poverty*. Oxford: Oxford University Press for UNU-WIDER.

Foster, J., J. Greer and E. Thorbecke (1984). "A Class of Decomposable Poverty Measures". *Econometrica* 52(3): 761–766.

Gaiha, R. and A. Deolalikar (1993). "Persistent, Expected and Innate Poverty: Estimates for Semi Arid Rural India, 1974–1984". *Cambridge Journal of Economics* 17(4): 409–421.

Gaiha, R. and K. Imai (2004). "Vulnerability, Persistence of Poverty, and Shocks – Estimates for Semi-Arid Rural India". *Oxford Development Studies* 32(2): 261–281.

Gaiha, R., G. Thapa, K. Imai and V. Kulkarni (2008). "Has Anything Changed? Disparity, Deprivation and Discrimination in Rural India". *Brown Journal of World Affairs* 14(2): 113–125.

Gautam, M. (1991). "Measurement Errors and Consumption Analysis: A Case on Indian Panel Data". Mimeo, World Bank, Washington DC.

Himanshu (2007). "Recent Trends in Poverty and Inequality: Some Preliminary Results". *Economic and Political Weekly* 42: 497–508.

Hoddinott, J. and A. Quisumbing (2003a). "Data Sources for Microeconometric Risk and Vulnerability Assessments". World Bank Social Protection Discussion Paper 0323, Washington DC.

Hoddinott, J. and A. Quisumbing (2003b). "Methods for Microeconometric Risk and Vulnerability Assessments". World Bank Social Protection Discussion Paper 0324, Washington DC.

Hulme, D., K. Moore and A. Shepherd (2001). "Chronic Poverty: Meaning and Analytical Frameworks". CPRC Working Paper 2, Chronic Poverty Research Centre, University of Manchester.

Jacoby, H. and E. Skoufias (1997). "Risk, Financial Markets, and Human Capital in a Developing Country". *Review of Economic Studies* 64(3): 311–335.

Jacoby, H. and E. Skoufias (1998). "Testing Theories of Consumption Behavior Using Information on Aggregate Shocks". *American Journal of Agricultural Economics* 80(1): 1–14.

Kamanou, G. and J. Morduch (2002). "Measuring Vulnerability to Poverty". UNU-WIDER Discussion Paper 2002/58, Helsinki.

Kochar, A. (1995). "Explaining Household Vulnerability to Idiosyncratic Income Shocks". *American Economic Review* 85(2): 159–164.

Kochar, A. (1999). "Smoothing Consumption by Smoothing Income: Hours-of-Work Responses to Idiosyncratic Agricultural Shocks in Rural India". *Review of Economics and Statistics* 81(1): 50–61.

Ligon, E. (2005). "Targeting and Informal Insurance". In S. Dercon (ed.), *Insurance against Poverty*. Oxford: Oxford University Press for UNU-WIDER.

Ligon, E. and L. Schechter (2003). "Measuring Vulnerability". *Economic Journal* 113(486): C95–C102.

Lim, Y. and R. M. Townsend (1998). "General Equilibrium Models of Financial Systems: Theory and Measurement in Village Economies". *Review of Economics Dynamics* 1(1): 59–118.

Pritchett, L., A. Suryahadi and S. Sumarto (2000). "Quantifying Vulnerability to Poverty: A Proposed Measure Applied to Indonesia". World Bank Policy Research Working Paper 2437, Washington DC.

Ravallion, M. and S. Chaudhuri (1997). "Risk and Village India: Comment". *Econometrica* 65(1): 171–184.

Rosenzweig, M. R. and K. I. Wolpin (1993). "Credit Market Constraints, Consumption Smoothing, and the Accumulation of Durable Production Assets in Low-Income Countries: Investments in Bullocks in India". *Journal of Political Economy* 101(2): 223–244.

Townsend, M. R. (1994). "Risk and Insurance in Village India". *Econometrica* 62(3): 539–591.

Walker, T. S. and J. G. Ryan (1990). *Village and Household Economies in India's Semi Arid Tropics.* Baltimore, MD: Johns Hopkins University Press.

World Bank (2000). *World Development Report 2000/01: Attacking Poverty.* Washington DC: World Bank.

3

Vulnerability, trust and micro-credit: The case of China's rural poor

Calum G. Turvey and Rong Kong

1 Introduction

The vulnerabilities of peoples in developing countries to economic re-pression are both persistent and degrading. The direct consequence is that hundreds of millions of households, mostly in rural areas, suffer from chronic economic hardship and languish in a perpetual state of pov-erty and food insecurity. The root causes of economic suffering are many but it is well understood that the most vulnerable of populations, those in a persistent poverty trap, are those who lack physical and financial resources. Physical resources imply the economic resources – land, build-ings, inputs, etc. – from which livelihoods are derived, and financial re-sources imply the capital with which to acquire the physical resources. The stock of physical resources and the financial wherewithal to acquire those resources are inextricably linked. To many, the root cause of the poverty trap is not the constraint on physical resources but the financial constraints or credit constraints that prohibit the acquisition of sufficient resources to escape poverty.

This is particularly true in China, where rural poverty is endemic, food insecurity is widespread and the income gap between rural and urban households is increasing. Table 3.1 and Figure 3.1 provide a summary of income class frequencies between 1995 and 2004. The actual frequencies are found in the first three columns and the cumulative frequencies in the last three columns. In 2004, 12.54 per cent of rural households had net (disposable) income of less than 1,200 yuan per year and nearly 50 per

Vulnerability in developing countries, Naudé, Santos-Paulino and McGillivray (eds),
United Nations University Press, 2009, ISBN 978-92-808-1171-1

Table 3.1 Distribution of rural household income in China, 1995–2004

Income (yuan)	Frequency				Cumulative frequency			
	1995	2000	2003	2004	1995	2000	2003	2004
<100	0.21	0.31	0.49	0.40	0.21	0.31	0.49	0.40
100–200	0.36	0.20	0.18	0.13	0.57	0.51	0.67	0.53
200–300	0.78	0.43	0.31	0.21	1.35	0.94	0.99	0.74
300–400	1.47	0.69	0.52	0.31	2.82	1.63	1.51	1.05
400–500	2.30	1.01	0.78	0.53	5.12	2.64	2.29	1.58
500–600	3.37	1.37	1.19	0.85	8.49	4.01	3.48	2.43
600–800	9.54	4.44	3.25	2.43	18.03	8.45	6.73	4.86
800–1,000	11.63	5.72	4.87	3.64	29.66	14.17	11.60	8.50
1,000–1,200	11.83	6.75	5.52	4.04	41.49	20.92	17.13	12.54
1,200–1,300	5.38	3.75	2.97	2.51	46.87	24.67	20.10	15.05
1,300–1,500	9.74	7.42	6.39	5.11	56.61	32.09	26.49	20.16
1,500–1,700	7.92	7.48	6.45	5.69	64.53	39.56	32.93	25.85
1,700–2,000	9.39	10.45	9.39	8.57	73.92	50.01	42.32	34.42
2,000–2,500	10.29	14.54	13.79	13.69	84.21	64.56	56.11	48.11
2,500–3,000	5.89	10.29	10.81	11.76	90.10	74.85	66.92	59.87
3,000–3,500	3.49	7.11	8.02	8.85	93.59	81.95	74.95	68.72
3,500–4,000	1.95	4.76	5.84	7.09	95.54	86.71	80.79	75.81
4,000–4,500	1.34	3.44	4.20	5.25	96.88	90.15	84.99	81.06
>4,500	3.12	9.85	15.01	18.94	100.00	100.00	100.00	100.00

Source: China   Statistics   1995–2005   (http://www.stats.gov.cn/tjsj/ndsj/2007/indexeh.htm) and authors' calculations.

cent had net income of less than 2,500 yuan per year. Only 19 per cent of households had net income in excess of 4,500 yuan in 2004. Figure 3.1 illustrates the cumulative effect. The figure shows that significant improvements in rural household income have taken place over the past few years, but despite these gains poverty and insecurity are still widespread.

Table 3.2 refines the breakdown between various groups in terms of household income. Note that the first column for low-income households refers to about 80 per cent of all households (as per Table 3.1), with the remaining four categories representing only about 20 per cent of households.

Income is heavily skewed towards poverty. Net income is measured by household income less household expenses including production inputs. The values under consumption expenditures indicate a discrepancy between expenditures made and expenditures in cash, indicating that in all classes there is a deficit in cash available for consumption purposes. Deficits range from −1,747.77 to −1,376.63. Even the high-income households face food consumption shortfalls. In the absence of a pure measure

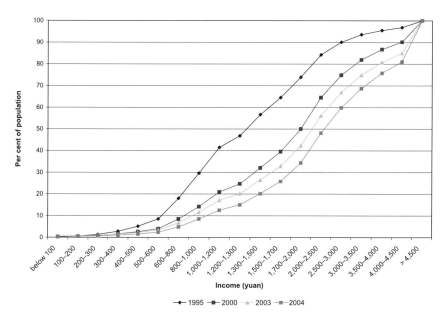

Figure 3.1 Cumulative index of rural household net income.

of food insecurity, the total deficit is also provided as the difference between cash and total consumption expenditures. The second last row in
the table indicates that the deficit in consumption expenditures related
to food purchases is about 94 per cent. In other words, although rural
households are able to cover fixed costs and general household/farm expenditures, there is insufficient income remaining to meet food consumption requirements. Food insecurity to this extent will result in a persistent
poverty trap, from which farm households are unlikely to escape in the
absence of growth opportunities.

   Table 3.3 provides a historical summary of the urban rural income gap
in China. Of importance is the last column, which provides the ratio of
rural to urban household income. In 1978 rural households had only
38.9 per cent of urban household income. This improved substantially between 1980 and 1990, but since reforms in 1991 the gap has widened
again. By 2004 rural income was only 31.2 per cent of urban income.
The widening gap is indicative of the rapid growth found in China's industrial sectors. As indicated by Table 3.3, rural poverty in China is widespread. Not only do rural households experience food insecurity, but
their position relative to urban households is rapidly deteriorating. This
chapter examines the potential role of micro-credit as a means to reduce
income and food vulnerabilities by providing the means for production

Table 3.2 Household consumption expenditure of rural households by level of income, 2004

	Household level of income:				
	Low	Lower middle	Middle	Upper middle	High
Persons per household	4.60	4.34	4.10	3.86	3.50
Per capita annual income (yuan)	8,182.71	11,576.04	14,494.61	18,469.91	31,114.69
Per capita annual net income (yuan)	4,631.60	7,994.24	10,571.81	13,925.61	24,257.28
Consumption expenditure	5,742.14	6,861.51	8,000.97	9,493.87	14,451.91
Food	3,194.11	3,650.44	4,043.05	4,506.68	5,652.06
All other goods and services	2,548.03	3,211.07	3,957.93	4,987.19	8,799.84
Cash consumption expenditure	3,935.56	4,991.19	6,147.24	7,713.41	12,986.94
Food	1,501.88	1,902.67	2,314.40	2,850.31	4,275.44
All other goods and services	2,433.68	3,088.52	3,832.84	4,863.09	8,711.50
Food consumption deficit (cash expenditures on food minus food expenditures)	−1,692.23	−1,747.77	−1,728.65	−1,656.37	−1,376.63
Total deficit (cash minus consumption expenditure)	−1,806.58	−1,870.32	−1,853.73	−1,780.47	−1,464.97
% deficit on food	94	93	93	93	94
Approximate % of population	80		20		

Source: China Statistics 2005 (http://www.stats.gov.cn/tjsj/ndsj/2007/indexeh.htm) and authors' calculations.

expansion, income enhancement, a reduction in the poverty gap and a step towards sustainability. However, it is also noted in this chapter that, unlike other nations, China does not have a well-established mechanism for micro-credit and there is a general unwillingness by traditional lenders such as the rural credit cooperatives (RCCs) to lend in the absence of collateral. From an implementation and policy point of view, the chapter argues for micro-lending on the basis of trust, and, indeed, through various modelling approaches we show that lending on trust is not only viable with suitable incentives but also consistent with micro-lending in other jurisdictions such as in Bangladesh, India, South America and Southeast Asia.

Table 3.3 Per capita annual income of urban and rural households, 1978–2004

Year	Annual net income of rural households (per capita)		Annual disposable income of urban households (per capita)		Rural/urban household income ratio
	Value (yuan)	Index	Value (yuan)	Index	
1978	133.6	100.0	343.4	100.0	0.389
1980	191.3	139.0	477.6	127.0	0.401
1985	397.6	268.9	739.1	160.4	0.538
1989	601.5	305.7	1373.9	182.5	0.438
1990	686.3	311.2	1510.2	198.1	0.454
1991	708.6	317.4	1700.6	212.4	0.417
1992	784.0	336.2	2026.6	232.9	0.387
1993	921.6	346.9	2577.4	255.1	0.358
1994	1221.0	364.4	3496.2	276.8	0.349
1995	1577.7	383.7	4283.0	290.3	0.368
1996	1926.1	418.2	4838.9	301.6	0.398
1997	2090.1	437.4	5160.3	311.9	0.405
1998	2162.0	456.2	5425.1	329.9	0.399
1999	2210.3	473.5	5854.0	360.6	0.378
2000	2253.4	483.5	6280.0	383.7	0.359
2001	2366.4	503.8	6859.6	416.3	0.345
2002	2475.6	528.0	7702.8	472.1	0.321
2003	2622.2	550.7	8472.2	514.6	0.310
2004	2936.4	588.1	9421.6	554.2	0.312

Source: China Statistics 1978–2005   (http://www.stats.gov.cn/tjsj/ndsj/2007/indexeh.htm) and authors' calculations.

2 Micro-lending and economic development

Until the past 20 or so years credit has been rationed to the poor because it is believed that the poor are not creditworthy, have limited or no collateral, and do not generate sufficient income with which to repay a loan. This applies not only to the acquisition of fixed resources such as land and buildings that could contribute to economies of size, but to the purchase of variable inputs (seed, feed, fertilizer) that could enhance economies of scale. Given the ill-effects of credit constraints, it is no wonder that these constraints above all hold the greatest shadow price, and the more vulnerable the household the greater this shadow price will be. More recently, the traditional view of creditworthiness has been challenged. Nowhere has this been more apparent than in the activities of Bangladesh's Grameen Bank, which in 1978 started providing micro-credit to poor households in rural areas. The escalation of micro-credit and micro-finance institutions (MFIs) throughout the developing world has resulted in a burst of growth in some rural communities, providing benefits in terms of rural entrepreneurship, growth, income enhancement, poverty reduction and increased food security and livelihoods (see reviews by Hartarska and Holtmann 2006; Meyer and Nagarajan 2006; Zeller 2006). Although it is understood that micro-credit provides a counter-model for a non-collateral economy that is juxtaposed to the collateral-based credit rationing model of, say, Stiglitz and Weiss (1981: 393), little formality has been given to micro-credit.

The purpose of this chapter is to provide such a framework, using as a starting point the principles of Grameen-type lending. This type of no-collateral lending, together with incentive mechanisms such as self-help groups that bolster trust, has in many instances proved to be successful.

3 Economics and trust

Yunus (1999) argues that the poor are creditworthy because they are trustworthy (see also Turvey and Kong 2006). Yet the role of trust in an economic system is not well understood, and the idea that trust can substitute for the conventional metrics of profitability, liquidity, leverage and repayment capacity found in conventional credit-scoring or risk-rating models (e.g. Turvey 1991; Turvey and Brown 1990) is foreign to the conventional lender. For this reason the conventional economic models, including the lending models of Stiglitz and Weiss, have excluded vulnerable populations. But why should trust-based micro-lending work? Is trust induced by economic circumstance, or are incentives to make one trustworthy required to induce trust, or is trust simply innate? Consider the rational description provided by James (2002: 291). In deciding on whether agent A should trust another agent B, the economic approach is for A to investigate the incentives that B has either to honour or to dishonour the trust offered by A. If B has an incentive to be trustworthy, then A will trust B. Rabin (1993) considers a "fairness equilibrium" in which people like to help those who are helping them but are willing to hurt those who do not, even if the cost of the latter exceeds all possible benefits. James (2002) argues that such thinking assumes that all agents are rational utility maximizers, and that people are honest only to the extent that the appearance of honesty or honesty itself pays more than dishonesty. In other words, one is trustworthy if one does not have the incentive to exploit others.

This is, of course, a depressing view of human behaviour, but it is endemic. The use of credit-scoring models, for example, assumes dishonesty first; only experience brings about trust. And the economic justification for this presumption is that it is inherent in any economy that a number of unidentifiable individuals are, for whatever reason, dishonest. There is also evidence that trust-based economies outperform other economies in terms of economic growth (Fukuyama 1995; Beugelsdijk et al. 2004) and trust plays an integral part in the reduction of transactions costs (Chiles and McMackin 1996). In terms of credit, the number of loan defaults or arrears will far exceed the number of dishonest players because it is true that an honest person, by circumstance rather than laziness, may at one time or another be unable to meet the obligation. The problem is that what is ultimately observed is the default *ex post* rather than the probability of default *ex ante*. Yet in repeated experiments (such as the Grameen Bank), lending based on trust appears to work. To a large extent this may be owing to the use of self-help groups, which act as a collective to enforce trust. The recurring question, from an economic point of view, is how and why this works. It appears perhaps that there are two separate but not mutually exclusive games at play. First, if the borrower is a group, then there is a game of mutual enforcement within the group to ensure equal effort. Thus the group becomes trustworthy. Second, there is the game between the borrower (individual or group) and the lender (a non-governmental organization or a micro-finance institution).

The game within the group is a simple one based loosely on the prisoner's dilemma. Here a group member can take action to reduce effort (the free-rider effect) but must consciously absorb the fact that the remaining members can individually or as a group take an opposing action against him. Kandel and Lazear (1992) introduce a "peer pressure" function that integrates with utility to affect behaviour. Here the function $P(e_i; e_j, e_k, \ldots, e_n, a_i, a_j, a_k, \ldots, a_n)$ captures the pressure that is felt by participant i, which depends on his own effort, e_i, and the efforts of others, $e_j, \ldots, e_n$, as well as the joint actions that he and group members can take $a_i, a_j, a_k, \ldots, a_n$. There are n separate games played out, each with imperfect information about the actions of the remaining members of the group or the collective action of the group itself. If agent i is dishonest, the collective response of the group could do more harm than good. The same applies to all agents. Consequently none will reveal themselves and the group will act as one. In other words, it may be the case that all group members are dishonest and would enjoy a free ride but, in the absence of information about other members' intentions, all individuals behave with honesty and the group becomes trustworthy (James 2002).

Now consider the game between a lender and a borrower. Unless the group members conspire, the lender will look upon the group more favourably than on an individual. Consider a lender–borrower version of the trust–honour game (Figure 3.2). If the lender trusts the borrower and the borrower is honourable then a loan is made, raising the consumption of the borrower by $C(D) - (1 + i)D$ and returning revenue

		Borrower	
		Honour	Exploit
Lender	Trust	$iD, C(D) - (1+i)D$	$-D(1+i), C(D)$
	Distrust	$0, C(0) - C(D) < 0$	$0, 0$

Figure 3.2 Prisoner's dilemma payoff matrix to trust–honesty game.

to the lender of iD. If the borrower is dishonest and wants to exploit the trust and not repay the loan, then the lender loses principal plus interest, $D(1 + i)$, while the borrower benefits to the gross value of $C(D)$. If the lender distrusts the borrower then no loan is offered, resulting in no gain or loss to the lender but an opportunity cost to the borrower of $C(0) - C(D) < 0$. (The pair $0, C(0) - C(D) < 0$ can also be considered as a 0,0 pair.) The final pair is 0,0 for the distrust–exploit pair.

The borrower has a dominating strategy trust–exploit. If $[(C(D))/D] - 1 = i$, then gains in trust–honour are equal and the lender then has no dominant strategy. In this situation, the lender, having knowledge of the borrower's exploitive possibility, will make no loan and a Nash equilibrium occurs at distrust–exploit. If $[C(D)/D] - 1 < i$, then the lender has a dominating strategy in honour–trust. But this also means that, if the borrower exploits the trust, the lender has more to lose. Again, the Nash equilibrium is distrust–exploit. Ultimately, what this suggests is that, in the presence of an exploitive nature by a borrower, no loans would be made.

Yet, in micro-credit, loans are made, which suggests that, to many pairs, trust–honour is a Nash equilibrium. How can this be? The trust–honour game provides no incentive for good behaviour. For example, if the lender knows that the borrower would not default, then clearly trust–honour is an equilibrium. But borrowers represent an adversely selected group so there is no way that an exploiter can be identified a priori. Consequently the lender will provide the incentive that, if the borrower honours the obligation, then there will be a second opportunity to borrow, but if there is default then all opportunity for future borrowing cedes. In this case the trust–honour cell will accumulate over two periods as $(2iD, C(2D) - (1 + i)2D)$, whereas the remaining cells will remain as is. The borrower's exploit choice will dominate the honour choice under the lender's trust only if $i > [(C(2D) - C(D))/2D] - 1$. In other words, if the lender is non-exploitative in interest rates then the likelihood of default diminishes and trust–honour is a Nash equilibrium. Obviously if the borrower incorporates the loss of all future borrowings then for some T it will be true that $i < [(C(TD) - C(D))/TD] - 1$ and again trust–honour becomes a Nash equilibrium. Interestingly, if we consider two individuals such that $C_i(D) > C_j(D)$, then the incentives for i to exploit the trust of the lender will be lower than j. It is on this basis that we proceed with the model of the micro-credit market.

4 A micro-credit equilibrium

To keep the model simple we stick to the two major assumptions implied by the Grameen model. These are (i) that the poor place a higher value on money than do the rich and (ii) that the poor have a higher probability of loan repayment than do the rich. We define the loan value function as a measure of utility $V(\omega)$, where the dependent variable is measured as a percentage and the independent variable is measured as income, ω. The value function can be viewed as a schedule representing a willingness to pay for credit and it is assumed, quite reasonably, that $V'(\omega) < 0$; that is, the value placed on the next dollar available, and hence the willingness to pay for that next dollar, is decreasing in income. In other words, the poor are willing to pay a higher interest rate than the rich. The supply of funds is measured by the loan default function $L(\omega)$ as an increasing function of income (e.g. $L'(\omega) > 0$), with the dependent variable representing a percentage cost (expectation) of loss and the independent variable is again income. This function is unusual and is based on the premise, as expressed by Yunus, that the poor are more trustworthy than the rich. However, since most applications of micro-credit involve the poor with little or no collateral, much of the lending decision in micro-credit revolves around trust. Hence, $L(\omega)$ can be viewed as a schedule for the trust in repayment and assumes that, in the absence of collateral, the rich are more likely to default than the poor.

The general form of welfare is given by:

$$W = \max \int_0^{\omega^*} [V(\omega) - L(\omega)]\, d\omega, \tag{1}$$

where ω^* represents the barrier between $[V(\omega) - L(\omega)] \geq 0$ and $[V(\omega) - L(\omega)] < 0$. We further define:

$$V(\omega) = A\omega^{-\beta_1} \tag{2}$$

and

$$L(\omega) = B\omega^{-\beta_2}, \tag{3}$$

where β_1 is the marginal value of the next dollar of income and β_2 is the marginal propensity to default. Equation (2) can be viewed as a *vulnerability* schedule in that it places a much higher value on the marginal dollar for the poor, whereas a low value is given to the rich. Equation (3) in contrast might be viewed as a *corruptibility* schedule which associates greater moral hazard of loan default and bad debts with the rich rather than with the poor.

The slopes of $V(\ )$ and $L(\ )$ measure the rate of change in V or L as income increases. Thus:

$$\frac{\partial V(\omega)}{\partial \omega} = -\beta_1 A \omega^{-\beta_1 - 1} < 0$$

$$\frac{\partial^2 V(\omega)}{\partial \omega^2} = \beta_1 (\beta_1 + 1) A \omega^{-\beta_1 - 2} > 0$$

and

$$\frac{\partial L(\omega)}{\partial \omega} = B \beta_2 \omega^{\beta_2 - 1} > 0$$

$$\frac{\partial^2 L(\omega)}{\partial \omega^2} = B(\beta_2 - 1)\beta_2 \omega^{\beta_2 - 2} \begin{matrix} > 0 \\ = 0 \\ < 0 \end{matrix} \left. \begin{matrix} \beta_2 > 1 \\ \beta_2 = 1 \\ \beta_2 < 1 \end{matrix} \right|$$

In other words, we characterize vulnerability as a decreasing function of income that decreases at an increasing rate. This suggests that the poorer one becomes in terms of income, the greater the value of money.

The $L(\ )$ function is always increasing. In other words, the model assumes a corruptible population in which higher income leads to a lower value of money and hence, with less "respect" for money, a higher chance of default. This is of course a broad generalization and should not suggest that the wealthy will default as a matter of course; rather the propensity to default will be higher for the wealthy. The slope of the default curve is determined by the elasticity. If $\beta_2 > 1$, then the function increases at an increasing rate. In the figures we present, this is the assumption made. If, however, $\beta_2 = 1$, the default function is constant, indicating that the propensity to default is linearly related to income. Finally, if $\beta_2 < 1$, the propensity to default is, on the margin, higher for lower-income people than for higher-income people. Higher-income people will still default more than lower-income people, but the increase in the propensity to default gets incrementally smaller as income rises.

The coefficients β_1 and β_2 represent the respective elasticities, or the percentage change in $V(\ )$ or $L(\ )$ with respect to a percentage change in income. In other words, if β_1 is 0.5 then a 1 per cent increase in income will reduce the utility value of money by 0.5 per cent, and if β_2 is 0.5 then a 1 per cent increase in income will increase the propensity to default by 0.5 per cent.

The welfare-maximizing level of income is given by the intersection of the value and loan default curves $V(\omega) = L(\omega)$ or

$$A\omega^{-\beta_1} = B\omega^{\beta_2}. \tag{4}$$

From (4) the level of income that maximizes welfare is given by:

$$\omega^* = \left[\frac{A}{B}\right]^{\frac{1}{\beta_1+\beta_2}}. \tag{5}$$

According to the rule, any loans below ω^* will be made using micro-credit, while loans above ω^* will be denied and the borrower will be required to seek credit elsewhere.

Comparative statics yield

$$\frac{\partial\omega^*}{\partial\beta_1} = \frac{\partial\omega^*}{\partial\beta_2} = -\frac{\omega^* \ln\left(\frac{A}{B}\right)}{(\beta_1 + \beta_2)^2} < 0. \tag{6}$$

In other words, if the marginal value of money increases, the wealth threshold decreases. Likewise, if the marginal propensity to default increases, the wealth threshold decreases. The results in (6) hold because the derivatives are anchored by A and B. However, if A changes then:

$$\frac{\partial\omega^*}{\partial A} = \frac{\omega^*}{(\beta_1 + \beta_2)A} > 0. \tag{7}$$

And if B changes:

$$\frac{\partial\omega^*}{\partial B} = -\frac{\omega^*}{(\beta_1 + \beta_2)B} < 0. \tag{8}$$

The welfare-maximizing interest rate to be charged on loans is found by substituting (5) into (2).

$$V^* = V(\omega^*) = A\left[\frac{A}{B}\right]^{\frac{-\beta_1}{\beta_1+\beta_2}}. \tag{9}$$

We refer to this rate, at least theoretically, as the Grameen rate because it applies to all loan applicants below ω^*. However, there are a number of variants of this model. The interest rate charged in (9) is determined not by market rates but by the value to the holder, so it may well be that $V^* > r$, where r is the commercial loan rate. Suppose further that a government observing the spread between the micro-credit rate and the commercial rate decides to impose by fiat a maximum rate on micro-loans so that $V^* > r^* \geq r$. At r^*,

$$\omega(r^*) = \left[\frac{r^*}{A}\right]^{-\frac{1}{\beta_1}} > \omega^*. \tag{10}$$

Thus, the threshold for loans widens, more loans are accepted and loan risks increase. That is,

$$L(\omega(r^*)) = B\left[\frac{r^*}{A}\right]^{-\frac{\beta_2}{\beta_1}} > L(\omega^*). \tag{11}$$

The basic structure is illustrated in Figure 3.3, with the borrower's valuation curve $V(\ )$ downward sloping and the lender's loss curve $L(\ )$ increasing. The equilibrium is at ω^* and V^*. To the right of ω^*, $L(\ ) > V(\ )$, indicating that losses exceed the willingness to pay. Hence loans to the right of ω^* are denied micro-credit loans and forced into the commercial market. Loans to the left of ω^* are considered for micro-credit at the rate V^*. In this model, V^* applies to all micro-credit loans regardless of how poor the borrowers are. The social benefits to the poor are defined by the area above V^* and below the $V(\ )$ schedule,

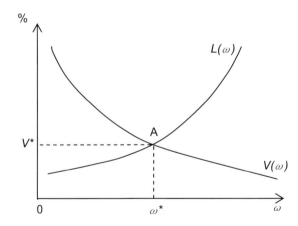

Figure 3.3 General model of micro-credit market showing equilibrium below which micro-credit loans will be made based on trust, and above which loans will be made based on collateral.

while benefits to the non-governmental organization (NGO) or MFI that provides these loans is measured by the area below V^* and above $L(\ )$.

There are three artefacts of the model that require theoretical foundation. First, the value function $V(\omega)$ is decreasing in ω; second, $L(\omega)$ is increasing in ω; and, third, an equilibrium at ω^* exists below which micro-credit is made and above which micro-credit is denied.

For the first proposition we apply expected utility defined over the variables C, D, ω; $U[C(\omega(D))]$ and applying the quotient rule get

$$\frac{\partial U(\ )}{\partial C(\ )}\frac{\partial C(\ )}{\partial \omega(\ )}\frac{\partial \omega(\ )}{\partial D(\ )} > 0 \rightarrow \frac{\partial V(\ )}{\partial \omega(\ )}\frac{\partial \omega(\ )}{\partial D(\ )} < 0. \tag{12}$$

The first part of (12) holds by monotonicity of the utility function, whereas the second part emerges from the convexity of utility. Here, $\partial V(\ )/\partial \omega(\ ) < 0$ represents the change in the marginal utility $[\partial U(\ )/\partial C(\ )][\partial C(\ )/\partial \omega(\ )] > 0$, and $\partial \omega(\ )/\partial D(\ ) > 0$ by assumption of the leveraging effect of credit.

The second proposition is more difficult. First assume two individuals with different income endowments such that $\omega_i < \omega_j$. We further assume that a point of satiation in consumption exists such that the marginal benefit of additional consumption units leveraged by an additional unit of debt is zero, i.e.

$$\frac{\partial C_k(D^*)}{\partial D} = 0 \rightarrow C_{\max}.$$

A consumption relation $(\partial C_i(D))/\partial D > (\partial C_j(D))/\partial D$ states that the marginal increase in consumption of a poor individual will be higher than the marginal increase in consumption of the wealthier individual. By concavity of the consumption function it must be true that $C_j > C_i$ and $C_{\max} - C_j < C_{\max} - C_i$. We introduce the concept of a reneging temptation and define the following function $\Gamma(C_{\max} - C_k)$ and its shape by

$$\frac{\partial \Gamma(\ )}{\partial (C_{\max} - C_k)} < 0.$$

In other words, the smaller the value of $C_{\max} - C_k$, the greater will be the temptation to default. Thus, when considering the dominating trust–exploit strategy in Figure 3.2 (e.g. $(-D(1+i), C(D)))$, then we can state that, because $C_j > C_i$, then the rich agent j will have a greater propensity to exploit than the poorer agent i.

We can take this a step further by assuming that T, the number of periods for which future micro-loans will be desired, decreases as ω increases. In other words,

$$T = T(\omega), \quad \frac{\partial T}{\partial \omega} \leq 0$$

and

$$\frac{\partial^2 T}{\partial \omega^2} \begin{cases} < 0 \\ = 0 \\ > 0 \end{cases}$$

are reasonable properties of the game that suggest not only the existence of a reneging temptation but also its various forms. In terms of Figure 3.3, as ω increases, the welfare benefits from micro-credit decrease quite rapidly, i.e.,

$$\lim_{\omega \to \omega^*} V(\omega) - L(\omega) \to 0$$

and

$$T(\omega) \to 0.$$

Interestingly, if there is no information passed between the micro-credit market and the commercial market (beyond ω^*) then most surely the reneging temptation will be high. If, however, credit reports are passed from the micro-credit market to the commercial market, then most likely the reneging temptation will be diminished.

Finally, if the value function $V(\omega)$ is decreasing in ω and $L(\omega)$ is increasing in ω, then an equilibrium at ω^* exists below which micro-credit is made and above which micro-credit is denied.

5 Preliminary assessment of rural credit cooperatives in China

In this section we examine rural credit in China as it relates to efforts by the rural credit cooperatives (RCCs) to provide micro-credit to rural farms and households. RCCs in China are formal regulated financial institutions which provide micro-credit to farmers. Basically RCCs classify farmers in their area firstly by different credit levels and then according to the credit level to decide upon the sum of loans given to farmers in the range 1,000 to 20,000 yuan. Considering sustainability and profitability, RCCs usually prefer to choose as principal clients those farmers who are in the middle class in terms of income. Farmers with lower incomes have great difficulty in obtaining loans from RCCs. Moreover, loans can be used only for producing rather than for consuming. More generally, the Chinese central government sets a regulated policy for micro-credit lending, and the interest rate on RCC loans is considerably lower than the rate offered by MFIs or NGOs and it cannot be exceeded. A ceiling

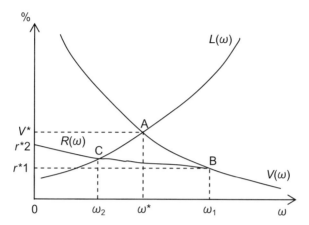

Figure 3.4 Conceptual model of rural micro-credit market in China, showing the loan rate schedule of a rural credit cooperative.

is set on the legislated lending rate but RCC rates can fluctuate within a scale below the ceiling limitation.

This is illustrated in Figure 3.4, which maps the RCC rate schedule $(R(\omega))$ onto Figure 3.3. Note that the RCC discriminates between borrowers, with higher rates (r^*2) charged to the poor. Note also that the RCC rate everywhere is below the MFI rate defined by point A. Several things are suggested by this market. First, because the RCC offers a lower rate, it is attractive to borrowers between ω^* and ω_1. If the RCC views income as a metric, it will prefer these loans and incur losses. In fact, under the model assumptions the RCC will profit only for loans below ω_2. The policy implications are important. First, by offering low-interest micro-credit loans, the RCC is crowding out micro-credit from NGOs or MFIs, which, by recognizing risk, will charge a higher rate.

A variant of Figure 3.4 is provided in Figure 3.5. Here, the upper end of the allowed flexible rates exceeds the equilibrium rate of the MFI/NGO. Here we find incomplete crowding out. The RCC crowds out the MFI to the right of ω_3. To the left of ω_3, borrowers would prefer the lower MFI rate, suggesting that, even in the presence of a central credit policy in China, there is some room for MFIs and NGOs to make micro-credit loans. Unfortunately, this is not what is observed in China. An examination of the history of micro-credit suggests a market more closely represented by Figure 3.6.

In Figure 3.6 the $L(\ )$ curve bends back at lower income levels. This need not be associated with trust, but may simply be a consequence of farmers not having the economic wherewithal to repay loans according to a conventional schedule. As a result, neither MFIs nor NGOs will lend below ω_4 and the RCC will not provide micro-credit below ω_3. The

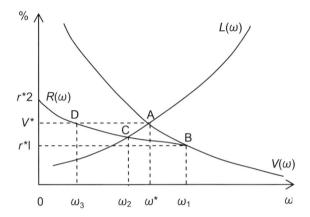

Figure 3.5 Conceptual model of rural micro-credit market in China when RCC loan rates rise above micro-credit loan rate.

market for MFI loans is limited to only the range of income between ω_3 and ω_4. Borrowers below ω_4 are in fact credit rationed. In the absence of credit below ω_4, there exists a market for informal lending through moneylenders who are more willing through usurious rates to exploit the willingness of the poor to pay high rates. The moneylender schedule is described in Figure 3.6 by the curve $M(\omega)$ and rates to the poor will exceed r_m. Moneylenders are crowded out of the market by either the RCC or the MFI/NGO at incomes to the right of ω_4.

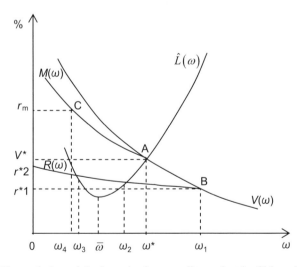

Figure 3.6 Expanded model of rural micro-credit market in China showing RCC and moneylender loan schedules and how micro-credit can crowd out usury rates.

6 Rural credit in China

Much has been written in recent years regarding rural credit in China, but no formality has been placed on the results as we have done in this model. In this section we review the current state of rural finance in China to determine how accurately our theoretical model fits the reality of rural credit. First, Grameen-type lending is not foreign to China and has been in place for about 30 years, but its impact and application have been limited. One observation that appears to bear this out is the fact that the rural credit market is not in equilibrium. That is, research suggests that the effective money demand of Chinese farmers is not being met by the effective money supply through formal markets. Consequently farmers are highly reliant on informal types of finance.

6.1 Micro-credit and credit rationing in China

Our theoretical model argues that there exists a non-collateral-based micro-credit market that is separate and distinct from conventional commercial lending. Its existence depends on a number of agents. First, in the absence of micro-credit the poor are excluded from credit markets except through family, friends and moneylenders. Here, moneylenders refer to agents of usury. In our model we distinguish between a separate entity called a micro-finance institution or NGO and a conventional lender such as the RCC. We argue that micro-loans can and should be offered at a higher rate to compensate the lender for high transaction costs and credit risk. However, the existence of a commercial institution subject to central party policy such as the RCC can crowd out MFIs and NGOs from offering micro-credit.

Micro-finance in China is relatively new. It was not until 2003 that the Chinese government encouraged the use of foreign and private capital to establish MFIs to provide capital to agriculture. The People's Bank of China started to pilot credit-only MFIs in May 2005 (He 2006a). Interest rates charged on MFI loans were unregulated and ranged from 9.396 per cent to 23.40 per cent for one MFI, and from 15.66 to 22.30 per cent (with an average of 20.05 per cent) for another. In comparison, informal credit ranged from 3.5 per cent to 21.6 per cent, with a weighted average of 10.53 per cent, while interest rates on RCC loans ranged from 8.0 to 12.0 per cent. It is likely that in He's (2006a) case study the informal rate was between friends and family, for he observes that the effective rate for pawnshops averaged 42.0 per cent, with a high of 60.0 per cent.

In He's case study, 60.8 per cent of loans were unsecured. The MFI was also involved in Grameen-style group lending, which, as discussed earlier, could lead to reduced risk; nonetheless, the bulk of the activity was in the non-collateral market. Furthermore, as suggested by the model, there is a built-in incentive that, as long as the loan is repaid, the borrower will have the opportunity to borrow further higher amounts. The majority of MFI unsecured loans are small and are offered at the higher interest rates. However, in the period between the initiation of the MFI in April 2006 and August 2006, He's case study showed that 100 per cent of 183 loans made were current.

He (2006b) also conducted a study of farm household micro-lending by RCCs. The role of RCCs is fast increasing in rural China and these are the primary suppliers of micro-credit to farm households. As of 2002, 92.64 per cent of RCCs across China provided micro-credit facilities and 49.98 per cent had developed group lending activities. The micro-lending facility is based upon the creditworthiness of the borrower but the micro-loans are made without mortgage or security. The system of credit rating is based upon past credit history and trust. The credit history is based first on the concept of a credit village or a credit township. These are referred to as financial safety zones where each village is rated on any recorded history of payment and default (above 80 per cent of households in a village), public order and control of usury. The trust element is based upon a village or county review panel called the village credit committee (VCC). Once creditworthiness is established, the borrower is provided with a letter of credit which states the creditworthiness and the allowable credit limit. This letter is tender at any RCC. The VCC provides input (screens) into individuals' creditworthiness, works to ensure that the loans are used for the intended purposes and that borrower households follow best management practices, and encourages repayment of loans. The VCC is an integral part of the system, for it is on the basis of the judgement of the VCC whether any individual receives a loan. Since collateral and security are not at issue with RCC micro-loans, the VCC individual recommendation is largely based on trust. Furthermore, although not explicitly mimicking the role of group lending, the VCC screening and monitoring activities provide the requisite social encouragement to repay loans in a timely fashion.

He's (2006b) commentary is in agreement with the specific utility–trust argument developed above. In particular, the VCC activities promote social responsibility in lending, while the incentives for further borrowings encourage repayment. Indeed, He shows for Hongze and Laozishan counties in Jiangsu province that the RCC micro-credit model is working reasonably well: non-performing loans fell from 24.6 per cent and 17.2 per cent, respectively, in 2001 to 3.4 per cent and 2.9 per cent in 2006. Interestingly, prior to initiating micro-credit loans in 2001, around 50 per cent of RCCs incurred operating losses from loan portfolios. After 2001, the losses fell considerably as micro-lending increased. For example, prior to 2001, lending to the poor on an unsecured basis was virtually non-existent among RCCs. By 2006, unsecured loans exceeded 90 per cent in He's study area, operating profits increased from 1.4 per cent to 37.4 per cent of business income, and the cost ratio fell from 96.2 per cent to 59.4 per cent. In terms of this chapter's thesis it is suggested that lending to the poor on an unsecured basis will result in lower costs of default and higher profit margins. This seems to be consistent with He's (2006b) findings. He's results are by no means universal and, as he suggests, not all RCCs are profitable or efficient. Huang and Wen (2006) report on RCCs in Xinyu city that reveal substantial micro-credit losses, with default rates increasing from 2.3 per cent in 2001 to 16.4 per cent in 2005.

6.2 Credit rationing

Although micro-credit through RCCs increased substantially between 2001 and 2006, and overall loan performance and profitability improved, there is still substantial evidence of credit rationing of the poor. In a study of farm household demand for credit in Tongren/Guizhou provinces, He and Li (2005) found that 84 per cent of surveyed households ($N = 720$) indicated that they needed loans. Demand increased inversely with income, with 87.8 per cent of poor households, 83.9 per cent of middle-income households and 77.1 per cent of high-income ones demanding credit. Approximately one-third of households (34.5 per cent) had never received a formal loan. Of this group, 22.0 per cent of high-income, 31.2 per cent of middle-income and 47.5 per cent of lower-income households had not received loans. In other words, nearly 50 per cent of the poorer farm households appear to be credit constrained. It is unclear, however, if the credit constraints are always linked with household income, for He and Li provide evidence for RCCs that seems to indicate a bias in awarding loans to cooperative members over non-cooperative members. Nonetheless, He and Li provide evidence not only that large numbers of farm households are excluded from formal credit markets entirely but that, of those that received loans, nearly 59 per cent stated that the loan award was insufficient to meet their total credit needs. It is unclear whether this is a result of biased lending by the RCCs or just prudent lending behaviour for unsecured credit. The credit constraints imposed by formal lenders are most likely prudential in that only 47 per cent of total credit needs was for agricultural or other productive uses and 53 per cent was for private use such as tuition fees, medical charges, and the cost of weddings and funerals.

The role of guarantees is critical to the model. In the model it is argued that utility and trust are sufficient to encourage repayment of loans and that collateral may not be important when lending to the poor. Only 8.3 per cent of the households surveyed by He and Li were required to place a mortgage on property, leaving 91.7 per cent of loans without collateral. Of the group without collateral, nearly all (95 per cent) provided no guarantee at all. About 27 per cent of all loans (RCC, family and friends, moneylenders) to respondents were not repaid at maturity. The major reason was that the farm households simply did not have the cash on hand at the time the loan was due. But such results are masked. That a loan was not repaid at maturity does not mean that it was not repaid at all. For example, 19.6 per cent of RCC loans were not repaid at maturity, yet the default rate on RCC loans in 2006 was only about 3 per cent. In other words, because of the sequencing, timing and risk of cash flow in farm households, the inflexibility of terms may be more of a contributing factor than unwillingness to repay.

The theoretical proposition holds that the marginal utility of money for the poor is higher than for the rich and, as a consequence, in a repeated game of borrowing the poor will be more creditworthy than the rich. This proposition has not been empirically examined but Shan (2003) argues that RCC lending on micro-credit is actually less risky than commercial lending because RCCs impose more restrictive covenants on farmer borrowing than on non-farm borrowing. Importantly, Shan maintains that the RCCs are very much aware of the high utility value of money and the need for repeated, cyclical borrowing by farmers. Thus the long-term sustainability of trade is sufficient reason for farmers to accept whatever restrictions the RCCs impose, including prompt repayment.

According to a survey in Gaozhou city, Guangzhou province, farm households were sorted by credit class into four groups, namely excellent, good, normal and bad. Certificates were delivered to all groups except the bad group, with maximum credit of 8,000 yuan to the excellent group, 5,000 yuan to the good group, and 1,000–3,000 yuan to the normal group. Credit risk was generally very low, with no evidence of differences between the groups. An investigation by Gaozhou RCC in August 2002 showed that over 31 per cent of borrowers (out of 61,929 farmer households) repaid loans initially and more than 22 per cent of borrowers returned loans ahead of the due date. This suggests that about 47 per cent of borrowers from across the various classes did not repay the loans on schedule However, by the end of 2002 the rate of repayment of micro-credit loans in all RCCs in Gaozhou city was as high as 94.5 per cent; the rate of default was only 5.5 per cent, but it did not indicate which of these loans could not be repaid in the future.

Huang and Wen (2006) argue that much of this is owing to inefficiencies among the RCCs themselves, including in relation to collections. They do not seem to imply any dishonesty on the part of borrowers. Huang and Wen provide an interesting anecdote about borrower behaviour and RCC risk rating. They report a situation in which 40.20 per cent of total farmer households (79,687) in Xinyu city received credit certificates whereas only 9.44 per cent of households were actually entitled to. An error in lending was no doubt made, perhaps owing to insufficient monitoring, but 20–30 per cent of farmer households repaid their loans and interest initially, and about 45 per cent of farmer households returned the principal and interest on time. About 15 per cent of households altered the original borrowing conditions (restructured the loans), and only 5 per cent of households cheated the RCCs and deliberately defaulted. Although Huang and Wen were using this story to illustrate inefficiencies in RCC management, it can also be used to illustrate how a Type II error (refusing a loan when the borrower is a good credit risk – see Turvey 1991) can be made. In this case, thousands of farm households were provided with loans when according to the risk rating they should not have been. Yet, despite the negative credit rating, the vast majority ultimately repaid the loan.

6.3 Informal lending in China

According to our proposition, the absence of credit results from (i) central policies affecting RCC lending policies, which crowd out MFIs through low-rate lending policies; and (ii) MFIs and NGOs being cognizant of agrarian price and yield risks and, in the absence of collateral, not lending to the very or ultra poor as a matter of course, even where there is limited access to MFI or NGO credit.

The extent of informal lending in China cannot be so easily measured since many transactions are between friends or relatives rather than through moneylenders. Guo and He (2006) would agree with this assessment, stating that the absence of adequate formal finance would lead to an increase in informal finance. The two are imperfect substitutes, but the inadequacy of the supply of formal financing no doubt gives rise to informal financing out of necessity. As Guo and He state (2006: 3), "the shackle of rural economic development is the scarcity of capital". Informal financing includes free credit (amongst friends), illegal private banks (moneylenders), rotating savings and credit associations, pawn-broking, private pooling of funds, and private discount.

In fact the prevalence of informal finance is not in dispute. Guo and He cite a number of studies indicating that informal finance for farm households in some provinces ranges from 24 per cent to 95 per cent of loans outstanding and that in some districts the percentage of informal borrowing is around 70 per cent of farm households' total debt. Guo and He's calculations suggest that the monetary intensity of informal lending to farmers ranges between 1.89 and 2.60 times formal lending, which is about the same as for self-employed labour or privately run enterprises in rural areas. These proportions were higher, in aggregate, than for all loans in China, including those in urban areas. Indeed, so prevalent is informal credit in China that Guo and He call for its legitimization and recommend that formal credit to rural areas should recognize the realities of agriculture.

China has designated 592 state-level counties as being in poverty. These counties receive loans at approximately 2.88 per cent, in comparison with RCC rates of 5.31 per cent plus (40–50 per cent). Survey data, however, indicate that informal lending involves average rates in excess of 45 per cent. The repayment rates on informal lending are not known; however, Guo and He (2006) found that poverty loans issued by the Agricultural Bank of China have a repayment rate of only 30 per cent.

He and Li (2005) provide survey data on informal credit in Tongren/ Guizhou provinces. Noting that the break point between "legal" and usurious interest rates is 40 per cent, only 19.33 per cent of borrowers from informal lenders knew of rates that were below 40 per cent whereas 80.67 per cent knew of rates above 40 per cent and 23.1 per cent knew of usury rates above 100 per cent. These seem to be extreme rates and are perhaps linked to local economies. In fact, only 13.5 per cent of farm households actually used informal lending at usurious rates above 40 per cent, but across the various counties in He and Li's study the variance was high, ranging from 1.67 per cent to 34.17 per cent of farm households. The main reason for accepting loans at usurious rates was because no alternative formal finance was available or awarded at the amounts required.

Informal lending by family and friends is far more important than lending through moneylenders. While nearly 55 per cent of respondents obtained one or more loans from the RCC, nearly 41 per cent obtained non-usurious loans from family and friends. All told, only 5 per cent of loans taken by He and Li's respondents had rates in excess of 22.3 per cent, which indicates that that for the most part moneylenders have been crowded out by RCC lending practices and rates and by benevolent friends and relatives.

The change in credit use before and after the micro-credit reform in 2001 has also been noted by Huo and Qu (2005), who conducted a longitudinal survey of farmers between 2000 and 2004. They found that in 2000 only 31.0 per cent of households in their sample $(N = 102)$ held commercial debt but, by 2003, 61.2 per cent held debt. They also confirm some other findings regarding borrowing activity: borrowing from the

Agricultural Bank is minimal (1.29 per cent) and from rural credit cooperatives moderate (17.2 per cent), whereas non-usurious informal loans between individuals account for 76.6 per cent of all loans. In fact, Huo and Qu found that 92.3 per cent of informal loans required no interest at all; the remaining loans had interest rates ranging from 39.13 per cent to 60.87 per cent. Interestingly the authors are quite explicit in acknowledging that amongst this group of surveyed households disputes among friends were virtually non-existent and moneylending was too rare to have social consequences. These results seem to suggest, at least through 2003, that there exists an excess demand for credit that is satisfied by neither the commercial lenders nor the RCCs. In this community, informal lending between friends and family is very common, and this level of activity crowds out the moneylenders. It is not entirely clear, however, whether the borrowing from friends at no or little interest is the cultural norm or whether it is a consequence of credit rationing. If it is a cultural norm, then our model may be missing a critical element in that the curve for informal lending, which we have rising above the $V(\ )$ curve for the RCC, actually lies below it. In this case, it is cultural lending that crowds out RCC and other commercial lending activity. In actuality it appears that informal loans result from an inadequate supply of capital for agricultural and rural investment use. Furthermore, it may not be so much that the farmers are credit constrained in the usual sense of credit being awarded according to a credit score or evaluation, as that many of the RCCs in the study area are inefficient and loan repayment is poor. The authors found that, in 25 counties in the north area of Wei River, 65.48 per cent of the county-level credit cooperatives had non-performing loans, exceeding 45.50 per cent of the loan portfolio, and a large proportion of the credit cooperatives were already insolvent (in 2003; recall the recovery of the RCCs by 2006 discussed above).

Similar results have also been reported by Lei and Li (2006) from a survey in Taian city, Shandong province, which showed that 107 out of 135 farm households obtained money from informal channels such as borrowing from relatives, friends and moneylenders, while only 47 farm households received loans from the RCC. A survey of 140 farmer households in Xinyu city revealed that 82.6 per cent used informal lending, most of which occurred between relatives with no interest or lower interest (Huang and Wen 2006).

7 Conclusions and further work

Guo and He (2006) suggest that the rural banking system is irrational from a number of points of view. One of the more obvious functional deficiencies is the reliance on Western-style credit rating and intermediary accounting when the majority of borrowers have no property rights over collective land. Such a system does not work and, in the context of this chapter, it is divisive, splitting the credit market between one that is collateral-based and receives the bulk of formal financing and one that is non-collateral and based on trust, usury or both. He calls for a more diversified system of credit that is less reliant on state-owned enterprises and more inclusive of specialized institutions that address the vagaries of the agricultural economy. It is unclear whether, as reported by the Agricultural Development Bank of China, the fact that only 30 per cent of poverty alleviation loans are repaid is due to abuse or inability. If it is inability, then all that needs to be done is to re-engineer repayment terms to meet the temporal needs of borrowers. However, trust may also come into play. Recall the proposition that the rural poor will have higher repayment rates because they place such a high utility on the money borrowed that it is unlikely that they would willingly default on such a loan and give up the option to borrow more money in the future. That is, if a loan is provided at 2.88 per cent when the next best alternative is 36 per cent or 45 per cent, it is highly unlikely that default would take place as a matter of course unless there was no alternative. In other words, farmers might very well be willing to default if by doing so it did not affect future borrowing, or if renewal of the low-interest poverty alleviation loan was not possible regardless of whether the borrower repaid or not. For a trust-based economy to work, there must be flexibility.

Our approach is pedagogical but the model provides an economic structure to micro-credit that is fundamentally different from the collateral-based models of lending. For example, Figure 3.3 can be used to illustrate how the Grameen Bank operates its micro-loans in Bangladesh. In other jurisdictions, such as in China, the central policy is to offer micro-credit to farmers at low interest rates. This we show in Figure 3.4. These rates are below the MFI rate. The consequence is that the rural credit cooperatives that administer the loans accept some loans that would otherwise be untrustworthy and hence the default rate in many credit cooperatives in China is high (lower-trust loans). In addition, the central rate is below the MFI rate, so the number of NGOs or MFIs in China is lower than in other countries. China's cooperative banking system has not fully endorsed either the self-help group model or the notion of trust as a form of capital. Thus, in China, the very poor are credit constrained from the micro-credit market. In India, MFIs such as BASIX have made headway into micro-credit and other forms of finance. However, commercial banks are also involved in micro-credit and both are largely promoted by rural development NGOs. Unlike in China, the micro-credit lenders in India lend fundamentally on trust, mostly through the use of self-help groups, and are focused largely on the poor in rural areas. One variant of the model explains how an MFI can coexist with subsidized credit from government banks. Here, the MFI does not micro-lend to the very poor. This created a void which was filled by government bank lending. The model also shows how the emergence of micro-credit has affected informal lending and usury rates from money-lenders.

We believe that a credit framework based on trust rather than assets can be used to explain, from an economic point of view, much of what is observed in micro-credit lending in agriculture. The pedagogy of the model should be of broad interest to development economists studying micro-credit and to agricultural finance scholars studying alternative lending models.

Acknowledgements

We would like to thank Jaclyn Kropp, David Just and Jianchao Luo for helpful comments on this research. This research has been partially supported by the National Natural Science Fund (PRC), ratification number 70873096, and the Education Humanities and Social Science Fund (PRC), ratification number 07JA790027.

REFERENCES

Beugelsdijk, S., H. L. F de Groot and A. B. T. M van Schaik (2004). "Trust and Economic Growth: A Robustness Analysis". *Oxford Economic Papers* 56(1): 118–134.

Chiles, T. H. and J. F. McMackin (1996). "Integrating Variable Risk Preferences, Trust and Transactions Cost Economics". *Academy of Management Review* 21(1): 73–99.

Fukuyama, G. (1995). *Trust: The Social Virtues and the Creation of Prosperity.* New York: The Free Press.

Guo, P. and G. He (2006). "Estimation of the Aggregate of China's Rural Informal Finance". CRFIR Working Paper, China Agricultural University, Beijing.

Hartarska, V. M. and M. Holtmann (2006). "An Overview of Recent Developments in the Microfinance Literature". *Agricultural Finance Review* 66(2): 147–166.

He, G. (2006a). "Credit-only Commercial Micro Credit: Pilots in China – Case Analysis of Quan Li Microcredit Ltd Co.: Guangyuan, Sichuan, PR China". CRFIR Working Paper, China Agricultural University, Beijing.

He, G. (2006b). "Farm Household Micro Lending of RCCs: Case Study of Hongze County, Jiangsu Province". CRFIR Working Paper, China Agricultural University, Beijing.

He, G. and L. Li (2005). "People's Republic of China: Financial Demand Study of Farm Households in Tongre, Guizhou of PRC". ADB Technical Assistance Consultant's Report, Project 35412, Asian Development Bank, Manila.

Huang, C. and Z. Wen (2006). "Study on Rural Financial System Arrangements Based on Farmers' Financing". *Wuhan Finance* 12: 47–48.

Huo, X. and X. Qu (2005). "Analysis on Farmers' Loan Demand and Supply in Traditional Agriculture Areas in West China". *China Rural Economy* 8: 58–67.

James, H. S., Jr (2002). "The Trust Paradox: A Survey of Economic Inquiries into the Nature of Trust and Trustworthiness". *Journal of Economic Behaviour and Organization* 47(3): 291.

Kandel, E. and E. P. Lazear (1992). "Peer Pressure and Partnerships". *Journal of Political Economy* 100(4): 801–817.

Lei, S. and J. Li (2006). "An Imbalanced Situation between Farm Household Demand for Credit and the Rural Financial Market: An Empirical Study in Tai'an City, Shandong Province". *Agricultural Economy Issues* 7: 55–61.

Meyer, R. L. and G. Nagarajan (2006). "Microfinance in Developing Countries: Accomplishments, Debates and Future Directions". *Agricultural Finance Review* 66(2): 167–194.

Rabin, M. (1993). "Incorporating Fairness into Game Theory and Economics". *American Economic Review* 83(5): 1281–1302.

Shan L. (2003). "Empirical Analysis on Farmer Households' Loan Demands, Safety, Profitability and Credit Situation of Micro Credit". *Journal of Financial Research* 6: 128–134.

Stiglitz, J. E. and J. Weiss (1981). "Credit Rationing in Markets with Imperfect Information". *American Economic Review* 71(3): 393–410.

Turvey, C. G. (1991). "Credit Scoring for Agricultural Loans: A Review with Applications". *Agricultural Finance Review* 51: 43–54.

Turvey, C. G. and R. Brown (1990). "Credit Scoring for a Federal Lending Institution: The Case of Canada's Farm Credit Corporation". *Agricultural Finance Review* 50(July): 47–57.

Turvey, C. G. and R. Kong (2006). "Muhammad Yunus: A Biography". *Agricultural Finance Review* (Fall).

Yunus, M. (1999). *Banker to the Poor: Micro Lending and the Battle against World Poverty*. New York: Public Affairs.

Zeller, M. (2006). "A Comparative Review of Major Types of Rural Microfinance Institutions in Developing Countries". *Agricultural Finance Review* 66(2): 195–214.

4

Assets, poverty dynamics and vulnerability: Evidence from rural Tajikistan

Oleksiy Ivaschenko and Cem Mete

1 Introduction

This chapter exploits an asset-based approach to study the (asset-based) poverty dynamics of rural households in Tajikistan. We use a panel of rural households that were observed during two time periods: June–July 2003 and July–November 2004. Analysing the dynamics of rural poverty in Tajikistan during this time period is particularly interesting in view of the drastic changes that have occurred in the country over the last several years. Emerging in 1999 from civil war and a prolonged period of economic collapse,[1] the country's economic performance has been impressive since the year 2000, with sustained real annual growth rates in gross domestic product (GDP) of 7–9 per cent.[2]

Economic growth has been accompanied by a substantial reduction in poverty, from 81 per cent of the population living below the poverty line (US$2.15 per day) in 1999 to 64 per cent in 2003 (World Bank 2006). Although the poverty headcount fell during this period by 19 percentage points in rural areas compared with 14 percentage points in urban centres, it remains higher in the rural regions: 65 per cent versus 59 per cent. As 73 per cent of the population live in the countryside, poverty in Tajikistan continues to be an overwhelmingly rural phenomenon. Economic growth and the resultant poverty reduction are explained by three major factors: (i) the cessation of conflict, which allowed economic activity to resume and markets to develop; (ii) the initial impact of the macroeconomic stability and agricultural reforms in the non-cotton sector,

Vulnerability in developing countries, Naudé, Santos-Paulino and McGillivray (eds),
United Nations University Press, 2009, ISBN 978-92-808-1171-1

which enabled farmers to diversify production and increase productivity; and (iii) a large increase in migrant workers leaving Tajikistan for Russia and other countries. However, there have been concerns that, once the initial benefits of these "special" factors dry up, Tajikistan's poverty reduction trends may not be sustainable (World Bank 2006).

In view of the sound economic growth rates, markedly reduced but still very high rural poverty, and concerns over the sustainability of the country's poverty reduction trend, it is important from a policy perspective to understand the key factors at the micro (household/community) level that explain the transition of rural households into and out of poverty. This is the main objective of this chapter. The chapter contributes to the literature on welfare dynamics in general, and to studies of poverty in Tajikistan in particular, on several fronts:

- utilizing an assets-based approach to better capture the permanent (as opposed to transitory) component of welfare changes for rural households;
- investigating explicitly the importance of community/local factors versus household/individual-level characteristics to explain movements into and out of (asset-based) poverty.

It is worth noting that a study of the general factors affecting poverty transition in Tajikistan was undertaken by Angel-Urdinola et al. (2008). We expand on this work by focusing specifically on the determinants of welfare dynamics in rural areas. More specifically, we combine household survey data with data on the district (*rayon*) level to take into account the poverty impact of community-level factors such as the share of private (*dekhan*) farms per hectare of land under cotton cultivation, the level of debt and distance to the market or district centre.[3]

The chapter is structured as follows. Section 2 discusses the main developments in Tajikistan's rural sector since 1999, as well as the correlates of rural poverty at the district (*rayon*) level. Section 3 provides the theoretical and empirical framework for the analysis of (asset-based) poverty mobility at the household level. It also describes the data and the constructed asset index. Section 4 presents the empirical results, and Section 5 concludes with a summary of the main findings and their policy implications.

2 Tajikistan's rural sector developments since 1999, and the correlates of rural poverty at the district level

2.1 Rural sector developments since 1999

Tajikistan's rural sector has witnessed substantial changes since the country emerged from civil conflict in 1999. These include agricultural reform,

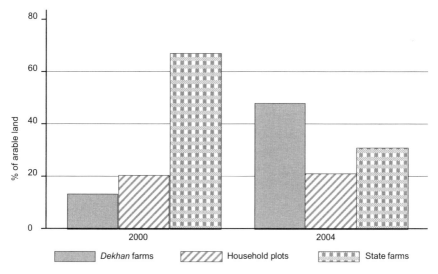

Figure 4.1 Change in land ownership structure, 2000–2004.
Source: Authors' estimates.

and specifically the rapidly changing structure of land ownership; significant output growth owing to increased yields; and unfavourable developments in the price of cotton, the dominant cash crop of Tajikistan.

In terms of the ownership structure, the country's agricultural sector had been fairly unreformed until the late 1990s, but experienced considerable transformation thereafter. In 2000, the agricultural sector was still dominated by the old state farms inherited from the Soviet system.[4] These farms accounted for more than 60 per cent of the arable land (Figure 4.1) but contributed only about 30 per cent of total agricultural sector output because of low efficiency (Figure 4.2). The ownership structure changed radically during 1999–2004, as old state farms were dismantled and private ownership (*dekhan*) farms were created.[5] As a result, the share of land cultivated by the state farms declined to approximately 30 per cent, while that cultivated by the newly created *dekhan*s increased to almost 50 per cent (Figure 4.1). A fourfold increase in the output of the *dekhan*s during 1999–2003 raised their contribution to sector output from 10 to 24 per cent. The share of land cultivated as household plots remained stable, at about 20 per cent, but these plots contributed about half of agricultural output (Figure 4.2).

After a period of prolonged decline, Tajikistan's agriculture sector enjoyed noticeable growth after 1999: over the period 1999–2003, gross output increased by 64 per cent, with most of this expansion occurring during 2001–2003. The crop sector, which accounts for 81 per cent of output, grew by 65 per cent during 1999–2003, while livestock, accounting

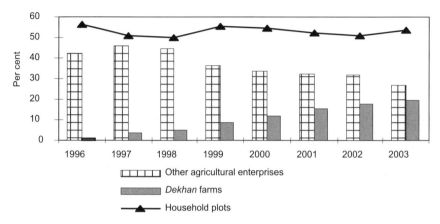

Figure 4.2 Composition of gross agricultural output, 1996–2003.
Source: Ukaeva (2005).

for 19 per cent of sector output, expanded by 61 per cent.[6] The agricultural production developments of this period can be well illustrated with data on cotton production. Cotton traditionally has been a major agricultural commodity, and continues to account for about two-thirds of total crop output value (Ukaeva 2005). The cotton sector has experienced substantial output fluctuations during periods of civil conflict and economic transition. Between 1991 and 1999, cotton output declined 62 per cent, from 820,000 tons to 313,000 tons, but it then increased 73 per cent between 1999 and 2003, although still accounting for only 65 per cent of the 1991 level. The increase in output is mostly a reflection of improved yields (1.1 tons per hectare in 1999 to 1.8 tons per hectare in 2003; Figure 4.3) as well as an increase in the cultivation area.

The cotton sector in Tajikistan has been severely hit by declining global prices. Despite output increasing by more than two-thirds between 1999 and 2003, the declining global prices reduced the real value of output by 7 per cent during the same period (Figure 4.3).[7] Adverse developments in international cotton prices, coupled with the farmers' ill-advised pricing arrangements with investors, have resulted in dubious "debts" that the producers are struggling to repay.[8] These developments are expected to have an impact on the standards of living of Tajikistan's rural population.

2.2 The correlates of rural poverty at the district level

How are the developments of the rural sector, as outlined above, correlated with poverty? To gain some insights into this issue, we look at the correlation of selected key variables of the rural section at the *rayon* level

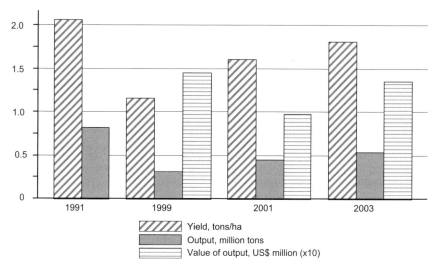

Figure 4.3 Trends in cotton output, yield and value, 1991–2003.
Source: Computed by the authors using official data on cotton production.

with the poverty headcount at a similar level, as obtained from the poverty mapping conducted in Tajikistan (Baschieri and Falkingham 2005). Some of the variables will be used later to explain poverty mobility at the household level. A number of interesting findings emerge from simple scatter plots of the district-level data (Figures 4.4 and 4.5).

A U-curve relationship exists between the share of land under cultivation in mountainous terrain and the poverty headcount, whereas the share of pastoral land is not correlated with poverty. Overall, about 60 per cent of Tajikistan is covered by mountainous terrain, with significant differences across the *rayons*. The data suggest that both territories with an insignificant percentage of mountainous terrain and territories with a significant percentage are likely to be very poor, with a poverty headcount of about 80 per cent (Panel A, Figure 4.4). The share of pastoral land does not seem to be a factor (Panel C, Figure 4.4).

A higher share of irrigated farming land is associated with somewhat lower levels of poverty. However, the level of irrigation is a very weak correlate of poverty. The data indicate that even well-irrigated areas are likely to have huge variations in the level of poverty, ranging from a high of 80 per cent to a low of 40 per cent (Panel B, Figure 4.4). A larger portion of land under *dekhan* cultivation is correlated with lower poverty levels. However, the increase in *dekhan* farming land between 2000 and 2004 shows no correlation with poverty. The level of *dekhan* farming in 2000 (prior to its substantial increase in the structure of land ownership) seems to be negatively correlated with the poverty headcount (Panel D,

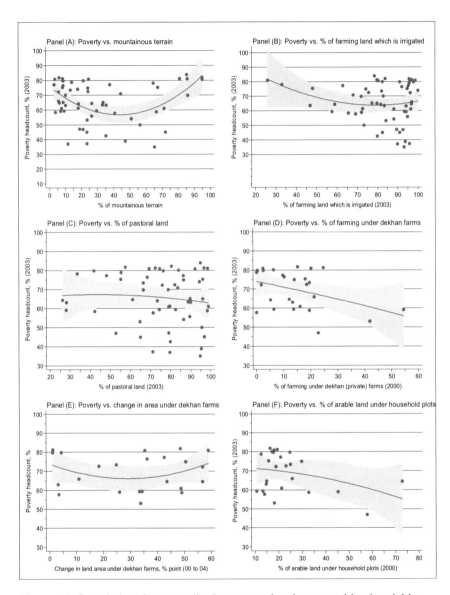

Figure 4.4 Correlations between district poverty headcount and land variables.
Source: Authors' calculations based on Tajikistan Living Standard Survey data.
Note: Poverty headcount = percentage of the population living on less than US$2.15 per day.

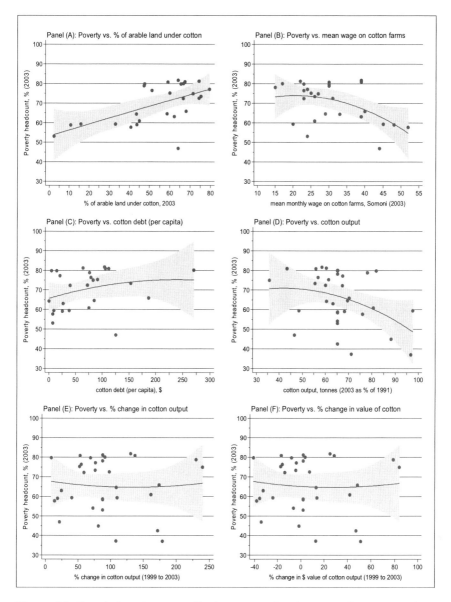

Figure 4.5 Correlations between district poverty headcount and cotton production.
Source: Authors' calculations based on Tajikistan Living Standard Survey data.
Note: Poverty headcount = percentage of the population living on less than US$2.15 per day.

Figure 4.4). However, additional *dekhan* cultivation has not been re-flected in poverty levels (Panel E, Figure 4.4). This finding is consistent with other evidence that suggests that the increasing ratio of *dekhan* cul-tivation has not been accompanied by improved productivity on these farms (World Bank 2005). Moreover, many of these *dekhan* farms are in cotton production, and have thus been affected by the sector's adverse development. A larger share of arable land under household plots is weakly associated with lower poverty levels. The share of this type of land has remained quite stable over time at about 20 per cent. It would appear that districts with a somewhat higher than average share of land under household plots exhibit lower levels of poverty (Panel F, Figure 4.4). The importance of this type of farming to overall agricultural pro-duction is, however, unlikely to change.

The districts with more extensive cotton cultivation are likely to have higher poverty levels (Panel A, Figure 4.5). As might be expected, there is a negative correlation between a district's average cotton farm wages and poverty levels (Panel B, Figure 4.5). However, this relationship is at least partly driven by the fact that, in poorer districts, cotton farm workers are paid lower wages. We also find that the average wage arrears per person are higher in the poorer areas than elsewhere.[9] These findings suggest that in poorer areas cotton farm labourers receive lower wages and they are less likely to be paid on time. We find a very weak correla-tion between the level of the cotton farm debt (per capita) and poverty at the district level (Panel C, Figure 4.5).

The extent of decline in output during the 1990s is strongly (positively) associated with poverty. Based on cotton output data, we find that dis-tricts with greater output gaps between 1991 (the peak output year be-fore economic collapse) and 2003 are much more likely to be poorer. The changes in cotton output and its value between 1999 and 2003 are not correlated with levels of poverty at the district level (Panels E and F, Figure 4.5).

The above examination of the key correlates of poverty at the district level provides a solid basis for analysing (asset-based) poverty mobility at the household level in the next section.

3 Theoretical and empirical framework for an asset-based analysis of poverty mobility

3.1 Using an asset-based poverty line to identify poverty transitions

The literature on poverty dynamics has increasingly recognized the importance of adopting an asset-based approach to study changes in well-

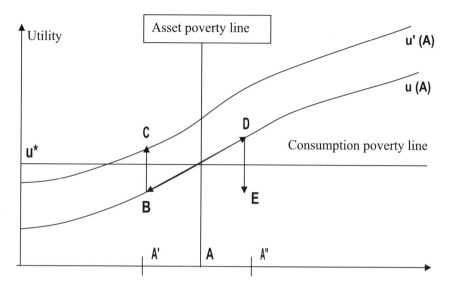

Figure 4.6 Poverty transitions: Consumption poverty line vs. asset poverty line. *Source*: Carter and Barrett (2006).

being, especially in response to a wide range of different (climatic, health, political and other) shocks.[10] Differentiating between stochastic and structural poverty transitions implies the availability of information on assets and expected levels of wellbeing. To illustrate the importance of the asset-based approach in capturing welfare status changes, we use the conceptual framework advocated by Carter and May (2001) and Carter and Barrett (2006). This framework is presented in Figure 4.6.

In essence, in any time period a household can be regarded as *structurally poor* if household consumption falls below the consumption poverty line **u*** and its stock of assets falls below the asset poverty line **A**.[11] Such a state is described by point **B** in Figure 4.6. A household can be regarded as *stochastically poor* if it holds assets above level **A**, yet its level of consumption is below the poverty line **u*** (described by point **E**). A household that has over time moved from below to above the consumption poverty line **u*** could be regarded as having made a *stochastic transition out* of poverty if its assets are still mapped below the asset poverty line **A.** This case is represented by the shift from point **B** to point **C**, which may occur because of increased crops in a given year owing to favourable weather conditions. As a result, the livelihood function shifts upwards from **u(A)** to **u'(A)**, reflecting the increased returns on existing assets.

The *stochastic transition into* poverty is represented here by the shift from point **D** to point **E,** whereby household consumption drops below the poverty line, as returns to existing assets temporarily diminish but the level of asset holdings stays above the asset poverty line. This is exemplified by the household that has experienced a temporary consumption decline because of a negative shock (e.g. drought) but is expected to bounce back to a level of consumption above the poverty line. A household that has shifted over time across the consumption poverty line u^* could be regarded as having made a *structural transition out* of poverty if it has also accumulated sufficient additional assets to move above the asset poverty line **A** (represented here by the shift from point **B** to point **D**). Conversely, the shift from point **D** to point **B** would represent a *structural transition into* poverty. As Figure 4.6 indicates, there could be multiple options for poverty transition paths, but the main point here is that changes in consumption that are not accompanied by changes in the assets base can be regarded as stochastic rather than structural transitions.

3.2 Data

This study uses panel components from two surveys: the 2003 Tajikistan Living Standard Survey (TLLS) and the 2004 Energy Household Survey (EHS). To our knowledge, these are the only nationally representative surveys that contain comparable questions over time and a panel component. One restriction that these survey data impose, however, is the time period under consideration: 2003 and 2004. Thus we are not able to compare the findings with trends in poverty dynamics that prevailed before the transition to a market economy (or even with trends during the first phase of transition, when the economy contracted and poverty increased).

The 2003 TLLS provides a nationally representative sample of households stratified by *oblast* (region) and rural/urban settlements based on a selection of households recorded in the 2000 census. The survey was conducted during June–July 2003. The sample size is 4,156 households representing 26,141 individuals. The 2004 EHS survey was conducted between July and November of 2004. The sample, also representative of the overall population, includes 2,600 households and 15,339 individuals. The panel component consists of 1,396 households representing 8,368 individuals; 589 of the households are rural.[12] The 2004 EHS used the same sample frame (list of clusters) as the 2003 TLLS. A comparison of the distribution of the basic variables from the panel sample against the 2003 cross-section indicates that the panel sample is fairly representative of the overall population, at both rural and urban levels. Both surveys collected information on such household attributes as demographics, education and health, income and expenditures, assets, and consumption.

The analysis of poverty dynamics here uses the panel component of the two surveys, and is based on an asset index. Construction of the asset index is described below.

In addition to utilizing household-level data, the empirical analysis at the micro (household) level exploits a few key district-level variables to capture agricultural reform and various policy changes (discussed earlier). The analysis also uses community survey data from the 2003 TLLS, to allow us to identify whether cotton was grown in a particular community, whether rainfall during the survey year was better or worse relative to the previous year, as well as certain other important community-level characteristics that are likely to be associated with a household's mobility out of or into poverty.

3.3 Constructing the asset index and asset-based poverty line

In order to construct an asset index, we rely on principal component analysis (Lawley and Maxwell 1971).[13] The principal component constitutes a linear index capturing most of the information (variance) common to all the variables – denoted by A_{ij}, the observation for household i and asset j (for example, whether or not a household has a television). Principal component analysis finds a small number of n factors, denoted by the letter f, which can be used to reconstruct the original variables (in this case original information on assets) as linear functions of the q factors, so that:

$$A_{ij} = f_{i1}\beta_{1j} + f_{i2}\beta_{2j} + \cdots + f_{iq}\beta_{qj} + \varepsilon_{ij}.$$

A_{ij} is known since it is one of the values describing whether or not household i has asset j. The term f_{ik} represents the observation for household i of the value of factor k, which needs to be estimated. The term β_{kj} is the coefficient indicating the dependence of the observed asset variable j upon the factor k, this coefficient being also estimated. The residual, ε_{ij}, is the error term. In other words, factor analysis produces an index representing (through the vector of common factors $\mathbf{F}$) the data-generating process underlying the actual observations A_{ij}. This is done by finding the one dimension of the space in which the original observations are represented with the largest variance, from

$$j = 1, \ldots, p \quad \text{to} \quad k = 1, \ldots, n \quad \text{with} \quad n < p.$$

Only assets found to be fully comparable in both surveys were used for the analysis. These included the number of such items as: kerosene stoves, wood-burning stoves, refrigerators, generators, freezers, washing machines, microwave ovens, black and white TVs, colour TVs, video players, CD/tape recorders, video cameras, electric radiators, air conditioning units, water boilers, computers, satellite dishes, motorcycles or scooters, cars, trucks, and tractors.

Asset indexes typically also include housing characteristics, such as the type of floor and walls of the dwelling. However, given that the analysis is based on a one-year panel, housing variables remained largely unchanged and were thus excluded. We also excluded variables related to the ownership of agricultural assets and livestock. If the accumulation of assets in the rural areas takes place largely through the acquisition of agricultural assets, the omission of these variables from the asset index is likely to underestimate welfare changes. However, as discussed in greater detail later, according to the data, significant changes in rural households concern the possession of durable goods (which make up the asset index).[14] In fact, rural households accumulated major durable goods faster than did urban households (Table 4.1).

Moreover, as our attempt is to understand the determinants of rural households moving into and out of asset-based poverty, the exclusion of agricultural assets and livestock from the asset index may even be advisable. This is because household agricultural assets and community agricultural characteristics (explanatory variables in our regression model) are likely to be determined simultaneously by such factors as agricultural reform, thus representing an endogeneity problem.

Analysing changes in the possession of the durables making up our asset index, we find that the average (per household) number of colour TVs, video players, refrigerators, cars and other goods increased noticeably between 2003 and 2004, particularly in the rural regions. The average number of wood-burning stoves and black and white TVs declined during the same period. There was also a noticeable decline in the number of electric radiators, presumably because of rising electricity costs. The last column in Table 4.1 presents the asset scoring coefficient (from the factor analysis) for the major assets owned by households. The scoring coefficient effectively indicates the weight of a specific variable in estimating the total asset score. A positive coefficient suggests a positive association between having the particular asset and the overall welfare index. A higher value of the scoring coefficient suggests a stronger association. Note that most of the assets for which possession increased between 2003 and 2004 display a positive scoring coefficient with magnitudes between 0.2 and 0.3. Finally, ownership of assets such as wood stoves, usually associated with lower welfare, decreased between 2003 and 2004. The scoring coefficient for wood stoves is close to zero, suggesting a rather flat association between having the asset and household wel-

Table 4.1 Change in average number of main assets possessed by households and scoring coefficients: Tajikistan, 2003–2004 (panel sample)

No. of:	All households			Rural households			Urban households			Asset scoring coefficient
	2003 Mean	2004 Mean	Growth rate, %	2003 Mean	2004 Mean	Growth rate, %	2003 Mean	2004 Mean	Growth rate, %	
Colour TV sets	0.355	0.449	26.3	0.182	0.291	60.1	0.457	0.541	18.4	0.311
Video players	0.137	0.233	70.0	0.087	0.173	100.3	0.167	0.268	60.7	0.297
Refrigerators	0.433	0.473	9.3	0.236	0.264	11.7	0.548	0.596	8.7	0.207
Washing machines	0.159	0.170	6.8	0.117	0.099	−15.8	0.183	0.211	15.1	0.199
Electric radiators	0.179	0.017	−90.6	0.061	0.000	−100.0	0.248	0.027	−89.2	0.158
Cars	0.135	0.153	13.6	0.146	0.163	11.8	0.128	0.147	14.7	0.269
Wood stoves	0.648	0.458	−29.3	1.076	0.827	−23.2	0.398	0.244	−38.8	0.011
Black & white TVs	0.521	0.498	−4.4	0.577	0.585	1.3	0.489	0.448	−8.3	−0.090

Source: Authors' estimates based on the 2003 TLSS and 2004 EHS.
Note: Some high growth rates are the result of the very low base. The scoring coefficient indicates the weight of the particular asset in the calculation of the total asset score.

fare. The scoring coefficient for black and white TVs is even negative. It is important to note that the scoring coefficients are estimated with the pooled 2003 and 2004 samples (panel), which makes the estimated asset indices fully comparable between the two years.

It is worth noting that there was substantial mobility in the ownership of various assets, with households acquiring and disposing of assets. For instance, about 20 per cent of rural households overall acquired a colour TV (Panel A, Figure 4.7), and this figure was almost 60 per cent among the households that had moved out of poverty (Panel C, Figure 4.7). About 15 per cent of rural households bought a video player (Panel A, Figure 4.7), while at the same time about 5 per cent of these households got rid of one (Panel B, Figure 4.7).

About 28 per cent of the households that had exited poverty bought a new refrigerator (Panel C, Figure 4.7), while about 22 per cent had disposed of one (Panel D, Figure 4.7).[15] Households that had become (asset) poor displayed a substantial shedding of assets (Panel F, Figure 4.7). Only wood stoves and black and white TVs were among the goods acquired by this household group (Panel E, Figure 4.7). As mentioned above, the scoring coefficient for a wood stove is close to zero, and it is negative for a black and white TV. The presented data clearly suggest that the ownership of assets by rural households in Tajikistan has been far from a static process, even in a period as short as one year.

We set up an asset-based poverty line at a level equivalent to the 50th percentile of the asset index distribution (using the 2003 distribution). The chosen cut-off level is rather arbitrary, but is consistent with the fact that over half of the population – based on a welfare indicator of per capita consumption and the poverty line of US$2.15 per day – is estimated to be poor. The 50th percentile cut-off level was also used in a previous study of poverty dynamics in urban and rural Tajikistan (Angel-Urdinola et al. 2008).[16]

Given this asset-based poverty line, what was the extent of poverty mobility among rural households in the panel? The poverty mobility matrix is presented in Table 4.2. Out of 322 households qualifying as asset poor in 2003 (base year), 113 households, or 35 per cent, had moved out of poverty a year later. Out of 267 households classified as non-poor in the base year, 91 households, or 34 per cent, had become poor one year later. In terms of the share of the total panel sample, 19 per cent of households had shed poverty and 15 per cent had become impoverished. These findings confirm substantial mobility in asset holdings even over a relatively short period of time. The regression analysis in the following section attempts to explain this mobility with an array of variables at the household, community and district level.

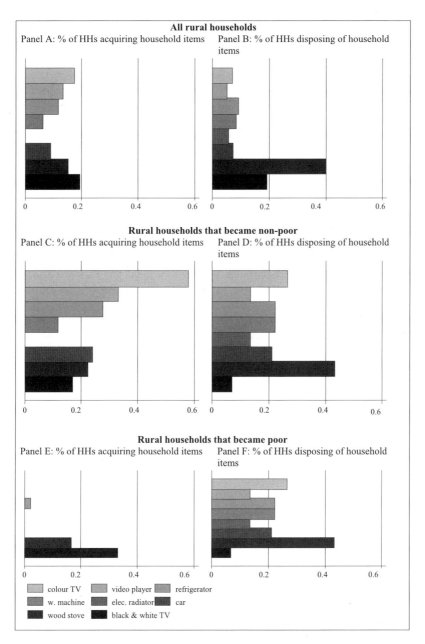

Figure 4.7 Share of rural households that acquired or disposed of assets (panel households).
Source: Authors' estimates, based on 2003 TLSS and 2004 EHS.

Table 4.2 Poverty mobility (based on assets) for rural households

Poverty status, 2003	Retained status, 2004			Changed status, 2004			Total		
	N	% of total	% of row total	N	% of total	% of row total	N	% of total	% of row total
Poor	209	35.5	64.9	113	19.2	35.1	322	54.7	100.0
Non-poor	176	29.9	65.9	91	15.4	34.1	267	45.3	100.0
Total	385	65.4	65.4	204	34.6	34.6	589	100.0	100.0

Source: Authors' estimates, based on 2003 TLSS and 2004 EHS.

3.4 The empirical model

The event of a household transiting out of (or into) (asset-based) poverty is modelled within the probability framework. The (*ex post*) realization of the event (experience of the transit into (out of) poverty between 2003 and 2004) is used to define the samples at risk of leaving (falling into) poverty. The probability of experiencing a transit out of (or into) poverty is modelled as follows:

$$\Pr(P_{i,t}^0 = 0 | P_{i,t-1}^0 = 1; D_{i,t-1}, X_{i,t-1}, X_{R,t-1}, \beta) = \Phi(D_{i,t-1}, X_{i,t-1}, X_{R,t-1}, \beta) \tag{1}$$

$$\Pr(P_{i,t}^0 = 1 | P_{i,t-1}^0 = 0; D_{i,t-1}, X_{i,t-1}, X_{R,t-1}, \beta) = \Phi(D_{i,t-1}, X_{i,t-1}, X_{R,t-1}, \beta) \tag{2}$$

Equation (1) models the probability of a household to be non-poor in period t (2004) conditional on being poor in period $t - 1$ (2003). Equation (2) models the probability of a household to be poor in period t (2004) conditional on being non-poor in period $t - 1$ (2003). As is already clear from the discussion, P^0 is the indicator of being poor based on the asset poverty line. Both equations are modelled conditional on a household's distance from the poverty line in period $t - 1$, which is denoted by $D_{i,t-1}$.[17] $X_{i,t-1}$ denotes various household-level characteristics, and $X_{R,t-1}$ denotes various regional-level characteristics at the region (*oblast*), district (*rayon*) and community (village) level. β denotes the vector of parameters. It is important to note that, although for ease of presentation $X_{R,t-1}$ indicates that the variable is expressed in levels at time $t - 1$, some variables in the model actually capture changes occurring before $t - 1$. For instance, a community reports rainfall shocks between $t - 2$ and $t - 1$. We also investigate the impact on poverty mobility of the share of cultivation under private farming at time $t - 4$, as well as the impact of the change in this variable between $t - 4$ and $t - 2$. In other words, some of the explanatory variables are lagged by more than one year; and some explanatory variables are actually changes rather than levels. These equations are estimated using the maximum-likelihood estimator.

4 Empirical results

Appendix Tables 4A.1–4A.3 present the estimation results for three alternative models exploring the predictors of moving out of and into poverty. Model 1 looks at poverty mobility predictors where community-level characteristics are *not* included among the regressors (Appendix Table 4A.1). It includes household head characteristics such as age, gender, education and self-reported health status; household demographics such as the share of adults; the employment status of household members; and regional (*oblast*) dummies. Model 1 is estimated using two specifications, with and without district (*rayon*) characteristics. For ease of comparison of the coefficients, the estimation results of the moving out of poverty model are presented next to the estimation results of the becoming poor model.

Model 2 extends Model 1 by including community-level characteristics among the explanatory variables (Appendix Table 4A.2). These include the size of the population point, distance to the nearest market, whether cotton is produced in the area, and the reported amount of rain compared with the previous year. Model 2 is also estimated using two specifications. Specification 1 excludes the interaction between the "cotton" variable (a dummy variable indicating if cotton is produced in the community) and various other factors. Specification 2 includes the interactions between the "cotton" variable and such factors as distance to the market, share of household adults working in agriculture, education status and gender of the household head. These interaction terms are designed to gain a better understanding of the importance of the "cotton" variable in explaining the poverty transitions.

Model 3 uses a richer set of district-level characteristics that apply only to cotton-producing districts in order to get a better understanding of poverty mobility in these areas (Appendix Table 4A.3). It is worth noting that two-thirds of the households in the rural panel sample reside in the cotton-producing districts. Here, we investigate a few, very important agricultural policy variables that impact on poverty mobility: the share of total arable land under cotton, cotton farm debt (per hectare of cotton-cultivated land), the share of arable land under *dekhan* (private) farms in 2000 (prior to its significant increase), and the change in the share of *dekhan* land between 2000 and 2004. Again, Model 3 is estimated with two specifications: specification 1 includes the interaction terms for the "cotton" variable, while specification 2 ignores the interaction terms.

Although the main purpose of this exercise is to explore the effects of various additional variables, it also enables us to investigate the robustness of the regression results. Next, we discuss the effects of the variables that had statistically significant coefficient estimates across different specifications.

4.1 The main predictors of moving out of poverty

The sample of all rural households

The probability of climbing out of poverty is significantly affected by both geographical factors and household-level characteristics. The level of poverty in a district is a significant predictor of poverty mobility at the household level. The estimates indicate that, after controlling for other characteristics, for a household located in a district with a 30 per cent poverty headcount (based on the US$2.15 per day poverty line), there is a 70 per cent probability of escaping poverty, whereas the probability is a mere 5 per cent for a household located in a district with a poverty headcount of 90 per cent (Panel A, Figure 4.8).[18] Thus living in a region with weak economic growth significantly reduces the chances of moving out of poverty. Even when the district poverty headcount is controlled for, living in the RRS region is associated with a more than 30 per cent lower chance of shedding poverty than living in Khatlon (the reference region in the regression) (Appendix Table 4A.2). This reflects the fact that, between 1999 and 2003, RRS had the lowest rate of per capita GDP growth, averaging annually only 2 per cent, whereas it was 14 per cent in Khatlon (GBAO and Sugd had comparable rates of growth). Location in neither a cotton-producing district nor a cotton-producing community has no bearing on the odds of moving out of poverty. Controlling for other factors, cotton production in a district is found to have no statistically significant impact on household mobility out of poverty (Appendix Table 4A.1). The same is true with respect to the impact of living in a cotton-producing community (Appendix Table 4A.2).

At the household level, the household head's schooling is related to a significantly higher probability of escaping poverty. The estimates suggest that the probability of shedding poverty increases from the 25 per cent that applies to the household head with less than secondary education to 50 per cent for those with university education (Panel B, Figure 4.8). Better health status also improves the odds of moving out of poverty: the probability of exiting poverty rises from about the 17 per cent

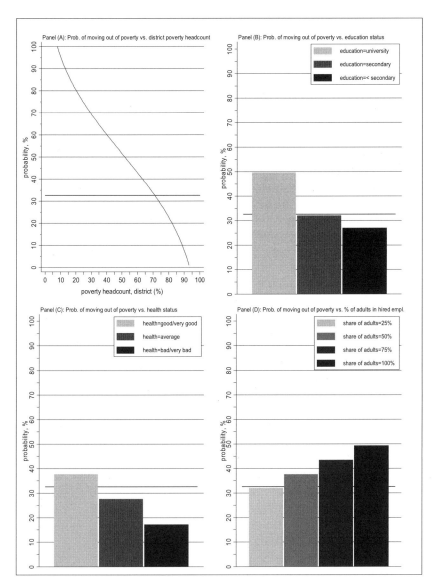

Figure 4.8 Determinants of the probability of moving out of poverty.
Source: Authors' estimates, based on 2003 TLSS and 2004 EHS.

observed for household heads with (self-reported) bad or very bad health to almost 40 per cent for those enjoying good or very good health (Panel C, Figure 4.8). Finally, a larger share of adults in waged employment has a positive impact on the poverty exit probability. This improves from 30 per cent to 50 per cent as the share of adults in hired employment goes up from 25 to 100 per cent (Panel D, Figure 4.8).

The sample of rural households located in cotton-producing communities

Using the sample of households located in cotton-producing districts only, we can explore the impact on poverty mobility of several variables related to the structural (and exogenous) changes that have taken place in the agricultural sector of Tajikistan. The regional factor has a substantial impact on poverty mobility in cotton-producing districts (similar to its impact for all rural households). In the cotton-producing districts of the country, the probability of moving out of poverty ranges from 10 per cent in RRS to 43 per cent Khatlon (Panel A, Figure 4.9). A larger initial fraction of land under private farming (*dekhan*) improves the odds: the chances of exiting poverty increase from 30 per cent when a tenth of the land is *dekhans* (the average level in 2000) to 70 per cent when the share of these farms increases to 30 per cent. However, the rate of increase in the share of *dekhan* farming between 2000 and 2004 shows no association with the chances of shedding poverty. The estimated effect of this variable is not statistically significant (Appendix Table 4A.3). The extent of the cotton farm debt (per hectare of land under cotton cultivation) has a strong impact on poverty mobility. It is estimated that if the debt were to double from US$0.50 to US$1.00 per hectare, the probability of moving out of poverty would drop from 40 per cent to 10 per cent (Panel C, Figure 4.9). Distance to the market in cotton-producing areas also affects poverty mobility. A somewhat counterintuitive finding is the observation that greater distances to the market or the district centre improve the odds of moving out of poverty (Panel D, Figure 4.9). However, one needs to bear in mind that several earlier studies on Tajikistan (World Bank 2006) indicate a high degree of government control and regulation of the cotton market. It may well be that our finding indicates that being in the proximity of the "watchful eye of the state" does not promote the sharing of benefits from cotton production. It would be useful to explore this finding further in future research.

4.2 The main predictors of moving into poverty

The sample of all rural households

The factors that explain a household's likelihood of falling into poverty are different from those that explain moving out of poverty (Appendix Tables 4A.1 and 4A.2). The probability of moving into poverty declines significantly once the share of working-age individuals in a household increases. The estimates suggest that the probability of falling into poverty

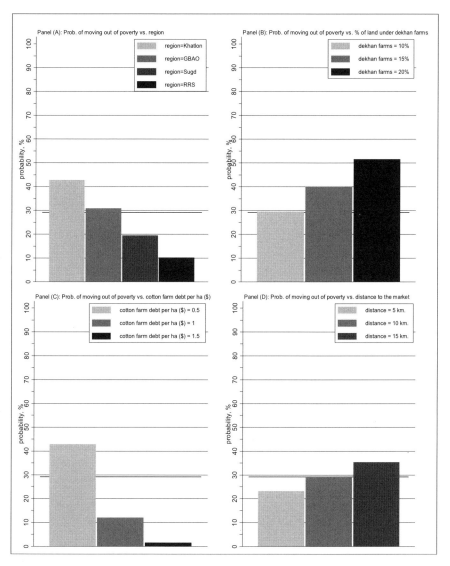

Figure 4.9 Determinants of the probability of moving out of poverty (cotton-producing districts only).
Source: Authors' estimates, based on 2003 TLSS and 2004 EHS.

101

declines from 55 per cent to 10 per cent when the share of adults in-creases from 25 per cent to 100 per cent (Panel A, Figure 4.10). Employ-ment in public administration reduces the risk of impoverishment: the probability of falling into poverty drops from 20 per cent to 3 per cent as the share of adults in administrative employment increases from 25 per cent to 100 per cent (Panel B, Figure 4.10). Household size is also a factor: the estimates suggest a U-shaped relationship between the prob-ability of becoming poor and household size (Appendix Table 4A.2). In other words, small households (elderly people living alone) and very large households (usually households with many children) face a higher risk of falling into poverty than does the average-sized household.

Examining the impact of district/community-level characteristics, we find that variations in rainfall are associated with the risk of becoming poor. Households located in communities with less than the average amount of rain over the previous year face a 55 per cent chance of be-coming poor versus 28 per cent for households in non-drought commun-ities (Panel C, Figure 4.10). Agricultural employment in cotton-producing areas is associated with a *higher* risk of impoverishment compared with similar employment in non-cotton-producing areas.[19] According to esti-mates, if half of the adults in a cotton-producing district work in the agri-cultural sector, the risk of poverty is 55 per cent in the cotton-producing areas but only 25 per cent in non-cotton areas. However, increasing the share of household members employed in agriculture in cotton-producing areas improves the odds of *not* falling into poverty (Panel D, Figure 4.10).

The sample of rural households located in cotton-producing communities

Using the sample of only those households that are located in cotton-producing districts, we note the following major findings. Region of resi-dence has a substantial impact on poverty mobility in cotton-producing districts (similar to its impact on the probability of moving out of pov-erty). Households in the RRS region face a 65 per cent probability of fall-ing into poverty, whereas it is 20 per cent for those living in Khatlon (Panel A, Figure 4.11). A higher share of land under cotton cultivation in the district *increases* the risk of falling into poverty: once the share of cotton-cultivated land increases from 40 per cent to 60 per cent, this com-pounds the odds from 20 per cent to 40 per cent (Panel B, Figure 4.11). Distance to the market is also a factor: the estimates suggest that, as dis-tance increases, the probability of becoming poor generally declines (Panel C, Figure 4.11). The explanation here is likely to be the same as discussed above in the case of moving out of poverty. A larger pro-portion of adults in agricultural employment reduces the probability of

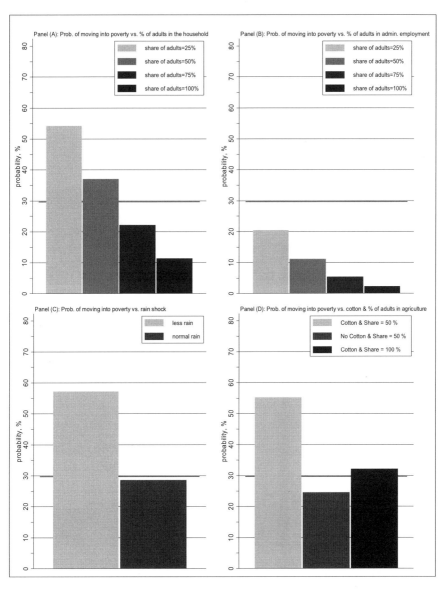

Figure 4.10 Determinants of the probability of moving into poverty.
Source: Authors' estimates, based on 2003 TLSS and 2004 EHS.

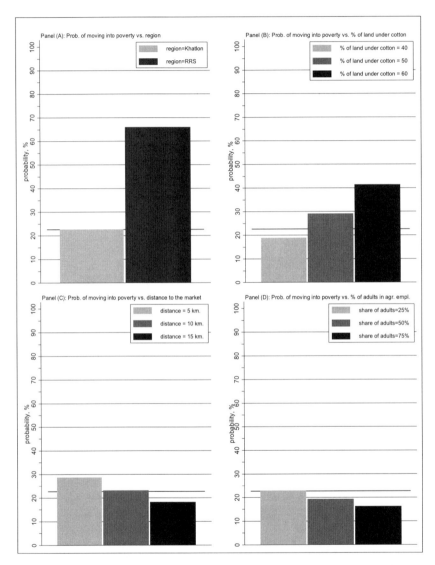

Figure 4.11 Determinants of the probability of moving into poverty (cotton-producing districts only).
Source: Authors' estimates, based on 2003 TLSS and 2004 EHS.

falling into poverty, although the effect is very marginal. As the share of agricultural employees increases from 25 per cent to 75 per cent, the odds of becoming poor decline from 22 per cent to 16 per cent (Panel D, Figure 4.11).

5 Conclusions

Tajikistan's rural sector has witnessed substantial changes since the country emerged from civil conflict in 1999. Gross agricultural output increased 64 per cent from 1999 to 2003, and there were also significant developments in the agricultural reform agenda, including a rapidly changing structure of land ownership as the old Soviet-era farms were dismantled and privately owned *dekhan* farms were created. During this period there was a noticeable increase in crop yields, including cotton, the major agricultural commodity in Tajikistan. However, despite improved cotton yields, output value dropped because of declining international prices for cotton. Moreover, cotton farms accumulated substantial debts to creditors. This period of rapid changes makes the analysis of the process of poverty mobility among rural households very interesting.

This study uses the panel component of two surveys conducted in Tajikistan at an interval of one year to explore the major determinants of the transition of households out of (or into) poverty. Household poverty status is measured in the asset space, which, compared with a welfare measure based on consumption, provides a better indication of structural poverty transition. In addition to analysing the determinants of poverty transitions at the household level, we also look at the correlates of poverty at the district (*rayon*) level. The findings have important implications, which are briefly discussed below.

Several household-level factors emerge as key predictors of poverty transition, suggesting the importance of continued investments to improve human capital outcomes. The odds of exiting poverty increase with a higher level of education and improved health status of the household head, as well as with a higher ratio of adults in waged employment. The risk of falling into poverty declines with a higher share of working-age people in the household and a larger share of adults working in public administration. The district-level data suggest that areas where cotton farming has a more prominent role are likely to have higher levels of poverty. The analysis of poverty mobility at the household level also indicates that households located in cotton-producing areas do *not* enjoy better odds of climbing out of poverty. The analysis actually reveals that having a higher share of land under cotton cultivation in the district increases the probability of falling into poverty. Moreover, there are indications that that living in a cotton-producing area located near to markets (or the district centre) worsens the chances of escaping poverty. Furthermore, the accumulated debt of the cotton farms is estimated to present a substantial drawback to transiting out of poverty. These findings are disheartening, given the importance of cotton in Tajikistan's agricultural production and the number of people employed in the sector. A new critical look at the cotton sector is needed by policymakers in order to understand why cotton production does not broadly benefit the population of the cotton-producing areas.

The rate of increase in the share of *dekhan* (private) farming in a district had little impact on poverty levels and poverty mobility. Examination of the poverty correlates at the district level indicates that lower poverty levels are associated with larger portions of arable land being transferred to *dekhan* farms. However, the increase in this type of farming between 2000 and 2004 showed no positive impact on poverty levels or poverty mobility. The analysis at the household level indicates that larger initial shares of private farming improve the odds of escaping poverty. Nevertheless, the rate of increase in this type of farming has not yet improved the chances of mobility out of poverty. This is likely a reflection of the fact that land ownership transfers are often on paper only, and thus are not accompanied by improvements in farm productivity.

There is strong evidence of geographical poverty mobility traps. A higher level of poverty in a district significantly reduces the chances of a household of moving out of poverty. Living in a region with an overall slow economic growth rate is also found to undermine the odds of escaping poverty and to increase the odds of falling into poverty. The risk of impoverishment significantly increases for households in regions that experienced drought. In other words, everything else being equal, the geographical location of a household matters considerably in terms of its chances of escaping or falling into poverty. It is worth noting that this observation regarding geographical poverty traps in relation to rural households in Tajikistan confirms numerous similar findings in other countries and settings, for example in post-reform China (Jalan and Ravallion 2002).

Appendix

Table 4A.1 Determinants of the transition out of, and into, poverty for rural households (probit model): With no community characteristics

	A		B		C		D	
	Move-out poverty		Move-into poverty		Move-out poverty		Move-into poverty	
Variable	dF/dx	Std. err.	dF/dx	Std. err.	dF/dx	Std. err.	dF/dx	Std. err.
Gap between 2003 asset index and the poverty line	0.288*	0.164	−0.082***	0.026	0.277*	0.167	−0.082***	0.026
Household (HH) head characteristics								
Age of HH head, years	0.012	0.016	0.005	0.018	0.018	0.016	0.006	0.018
Age of HH head squared (/100), years	−0.007	0.015	−0.002	0.017	−0.013	0.015	−0.003	0.017
HH head education = secondary	0.066	0.085	0.072	0.096	0.027	0.088	0.065	0.097
HH head education = university	0.294**	0.128	−0.038	0.122	0.265**	0.132	−0.056	0.121
HH head is female	0.028	0.090	0.049	0.097	0.034	0.091	0.074	0.100
HH head health > average	0.189*	0.102	0.096	0.105	0.210*	0.104	0.104	0.104
HH head health = average	0.111	0.121	−0.028	0.119	0.128	0.125	−0.035	0.119
Demographics and employment of HH members								
HH size	0.075*	0.041	−0.052**	0.027	0.068*	0.042	−0.048*	0.027
HH size squared	−0.004	0.002	0.002***	0.001	−0.003	0.002	0.002*	0.001
Share of adults in the HH	0.018	0.151	−0.576***	0.168	0.003	0.154	−0.550***	0.172
Share of adults in hired (wage) employment	0.148	0.111	0.013	0.138	0.193*	0.115	0.027	0.139
Share of adults working in agriculture	0.038	0.090	0.010	0.097	0.070	0.092	−0.013	0.099

Table 4A.1 (cont.)

Variable	A Move-out poverty		B Move-into poverty		C Move-out poverty		D Move-into poverty	
	dF/dx	Std. err.	dF/dx	Std. err.	dF/dx	Std. err.	dF/dx	Std. err.
Share of adults working in health/education/public admin.	−0.010	0.268	−0.510*	0.304	0.039	0.270	−0.552***	0.308
Region (oblast) dummies								
Oblast = GBAO	0.031	0.095	−0.037	0.095	0.054	0.099	−0.066	0.099
Oblast = Sugd	0.120	0.079	0.062	0.097	−0.067	0.105	0.071	0.154
Oblast = RRS	−0.166*	0.078	0.087	0.093	−0.284**	0.095	0.062	0.124
District (rayon) characteristics								
Poverty headcount in *rayon*, %					−0.008*	0.004	0.001	0.003
% of farming land irrigated					0.008	0.018	−0.008	0.016
% of farming land irrigated (^2/100)					−0.009	0.012	0.006	0.012
Cotton is produced in *rayon*					0.083	0.088	−0.192*	0.105
Number of observations	322		267		322		267	
χ^2	42.264		45.836		51.668		50.474	
Log-likelihood	−187.53		−148.38		−182.83		−146.07	
Pseudo-R^2	.101		.134		.124		.147	

Source: Authors' estimates, based on 2003 TLSS and 2004 EHS.

Notes: *** indicates significance at the .01 level; ** at .05; * at .10; dF/dx indicates the estimated marginal effect (at the mean for continuous variables, and 0/1 change for dummy variables). Note that in the probit model pseudo-R^2 does not have a clear meaning (as opposed to R^2 for the OLS).

108

Table 4A.2 Determinants of the transition out of, and into, poverty for rural households (probit model): With community characteristics and "cotton" variable interactions

	A		B		C		D	
	Move-out poverty		Move-into poverty		Move-out poverty		Move-into poverty	
Variable	dF/dx	Std. err.	dF/dx	Std. err.	dF/dx	Std. err.	dF/dx	Std. err.
Gap between 2003 asset index and the poverty line	0.294*	0.169	−0.084***	0.027	0.296*	0.170	−0.081***	0.027
Household (HH) head characteristics								
Age of HH head, years	0.020	0.017	0.007	0.018	0.021	0.017	0.009	0.018
Age of HH head squared (/100), years	−0.015	0.016	−0.003	0.017	−0.016	0.016	−0.005	0.017
HH head education = secondary	0.036	0.088	0.062	0.098	0.053	0.103	0.129	0.103
HH head education = university	0.248*	0.134	−0.052	0.122	0.232*	0.159	0.063	0.149
HH head is female	0.021	0.092	0.050	0.098	0.052	0.124	0.106	0.113
HH head health > average	0.212*	0.104	0.106	0.104	0.217*	0.109	0.125	0.105
HH head health = average	0.107	0.126	−0.040	0.120	0.129	0.134	−0.009	0.127
Demographics and employment of HH members								
HH size	0.071*	0.042	−0.056**	0.027	0.067	0.042	−0.060**	0.028
HH size squared	−0.003	0.002	0.002**	0.001	−0.003	0.002	0.003**	0.001
Share of adults in the HH	−0.003	0.155	−0.579***	0.171	0.002	0.159	−0.604***	0.171
Share of adults in hired (wage) employment	0.195*	0.115	0.044	0.144	0.216*	0.120	−0.007	0.148
Share of adults working in agriculture	0.065	0.092	0.019	0.100	0.102	0.103	0.094	0.106
Share of adults working in health/education/public admin.	0.067	0.273	−0.586*	0.315	0.093	0.276	−0.539*	0.330

109

Table 4A.2 (cont.)

Variable	A Move-out poverty		B Move-into poverty		C Move-out poverty		D Move-into poverty	
	dF/dx	Std. err.	dF/dx	Std. err.	dF/dx	Std. err.	dF/dx	Std. err.
Region (oblast) dummies								
Oblast = GBAO	0.069	0.105	−0.025	0.114	0.053	0.109	−0.072	0.111
Oblast = Sugd	−0.098	0.102	0.051	0.166	−0.165	0.107	−0.002	0.163
Oblast = RRS	−0.318***	0.084	0.155	0.130	−0.343***	0.080	0.153	0.130
District (rayon) characteristics								
Poverty headcount in *rayon*, %	−0.009**	0.004	0.004	0.004	−0.011**	0.004	0.004	0.004
% of farming land irrigated	0.001	0.018	0.008	0.017	0.005	0.019	−0.000	0.018
% of farming land irrigated (^{2}/100)	−0.003	0.012	−0.006	0.012	−0.007	0.013	−0.001	0.012
Community characteristics								
Size of the population point, '000 people	0.003	0.005	0.001	0.006	0.004	0.005	−0.001	0.006
Less rain compared with last year	−0.028	0.144	0.288*	0.178	−0.030	0.144	0.286*	0.179
Distance to the nearest market, km	−0.002	0.004	−0.001	0.004	−0.002	0.004	−0.001	0.004
Cotton is produced in the area ("cotton" community)	0.071	0.083	−0.004	0.115	0.097	0.177	0.561*	0.257

110

Interactions of the "cotton" community variable

"Cotton" community & distance to market		0.018	0.016	−0.002	0.027
"Cotton" community & share of HH adults working in agriculture		−0.160	0.206	−0.504*	0.306
"Cotton" community & HH head education = secondary		−0.045	0.141	−0.206	0.157
"Cotton" community & HH head education = university		0.203	0.342	−0.300	0.059
"Cotton" community & HH head is female		−0.100	0.167	−0.222	0.121
Number of observations	322	267	322		267
χ^2	53.152	50.251	55.976		56.303
Log-likelihood	−182.09	−146.18	−180.67		−143.15
Pseudo-R^2	.127	.147	.134		.164

Source: Authors' estimates, based on 2003 TLSS and 2004 EHS.

Notes: *** indicates significance at the .01 level; ** at .05; * at .10; dF/dx indicates the estimated marginal effect (at the mean for continuous variables, and 0/1 change for dummy variables).

Table 4A.3 Determinants of the transition out of, and into, poverty for rural households in cotton-producing districts (probit model): With community characteristics and "cotton" variable interactions

	A		B		C		D	
	Move-out poverty		Move-into poverty		Move-out poverty		Move-into poverty	
Variable	dF/dx	Std. err.	dF/dx	Std. err.	dF/dx	Std. err.	dF/dx	Std. err.
Gap between 2003 asset index and the poverty line	0.559**	0.228	−0.148***	0.040	0.623***	0.233	−0.168***	0.042
Household (HH) head characteristics								
Age of HH head, years	0.021	0.021	0.004	0.019	0.022	0.021	0.008	0.019
Age of HH head squared (/100), years	−0.016	0.019	−0.004	0.018	−0.016	0.020	−0.006	0.018
HH head education = secondary	0.164	0.096	−0.093	0.127	0.200*	0.110	−0.016	0.129
HH head education = university	0.437***	0.152	−0.240*	0.089	0.430**	0.196	−0.128	0.135
HH head is female	0.122	0.115	−0.006	0.106	0.080	0.155	0.013	0.122
HH head health > average	0.142	0.122	0.022	0.136	0.125	0.128	0.017	0.138
HH head health = average	−0.020	0.140	−0.105	0.132	−0.014	0.149	−0.074	0.141
Demographics and employment of HH members								
HH size	0.062	0.053	−0.028	0.051	0.061	0.053	−0.039	0.052
HH size squared	−0.003	0.003	0.001	0.003	−0.002	0.003	0.002	0.003
Share of adults in the HH	0.039	0.197	−0.476**	0.218	−0.024	0.207	−0.552**	0.216
Share of adults in hired (wage) employment	0.151	0.142	−0.066	0.198	0.194	0.152	−0.132	0.203
Share of adults working in agriculture	0.125	0.114	0.009	0.135	0.222	0.145	0.128	0.142

Region (oblast) dummies							
Oblast = GBAO	−0.088	0.119	0.113	0.157	−0.104	0.126	0.057	0.155
Oblast = Sugd	0.085	0.201	−0.344	0.102	−0.204	0.190	−0.305	0.115
Oblast = RRS	−0.286**	0.088	0.400**	0.180	−0.274*	0.094	0.410**	0.185
District (rayon) characteristics							
% of farming land irrigated	0.137	0.133	−0.331***	0.128	0.166	0.144	−0.301**	0.127
% of farming land irrigated (^{2}/100)	−0.087	0.083	0.205**	0.080	−0.111	0.091	0.184***	0.080
% of total arable land under cotton	−0.002	0.004	0.010***	0.003	−0.003	0.004	0.010***	0.003
Cotton farm debt (per hectare of land under cotton)	−0.363	0.275	0.348	0.275	−0.681**	0.325	0.199	0.278
% of arable land under *dekhan* farms, 2000	0.011	0.008	0.001	0.010	0.020**	0.009	0.011	0.011
% point change in the share of land under *dekhan* farms, 2000–2004	0.000	0.002	−0.001	0.003	0.000	0.003	0.001	0.003
Community characteristics							
Size of the population point, '000 people	−0.003	0.011	0.032**	0.016	−0.003	0.011	0.031*	0.016
Distance to the nearest market, km	0.003	0.006	−0.013**	0.006	0.005	0.006	−0.014**	0.005

Table 4A.3 (cont.)

	A		B		C		D	
	Move-out poverty		Move-into poverty		Move-out poverty		Move-into poverty	
Variable	dF/dx	Std. err.	dF/dx	Std. err.	dF/dx	Std. err.	dF/dx	Std. err.
Interactions of the "cotton" community variable								
"Cotton" community & distance to market					0.052**	0.024	0.060*	0.033
"Cotton" community & share of HH adults working in agriculture					−0.267	0.242	−0.743*	0.447
"Cotton" community & HH head education = secondary					−0.073	0.153	0.014	0.249
"Cotton" community & HH head education = university					0.123	0.385	−0.23	0.072
"Cotton" community & HH head is female					0.072	0.237	−0.080	0.207
Number of observations	217		167		217		167	
χ^2	44.996		41.685		52.267		46.747	
Log-likelihood	−115.39		−83.51		−111.76		−80.98	
Pseudo-R^2	0.163		0.200		0.190		0.224	

Source: Authors' estimates, based on 2003 TLSS and 2004 EHS.
Notes: *** indicates significance at the .01 level; ** at .05; * at .10; dF/dx indicates the estimated marginal effect (at the mean for continuous variables, and 0/1 change for dummy variables).

114

Notes

The findings, interpretations, and conclusions expressed herein are those of the author(s) and do not necessarily reflect the views of the International Bank for Reconstruction and Development (the World Bank) and its affiliated organizations, or those of the executive directors of the World Bank or the governments they represent.

1. Looking at cotton output across *rayons* (the smallest administrative unit), we observe that between 1991 and 1999 there was an average output decline of 62 per cent. Cotton output has increased since 1999 by an average of 91 per cent, but still remains at about 66 per cent of its 1991 level.

2. Despite solid growth rates, Tajikistan's per capita GDP in 2004 was still merely US$225, making it the poorest country in the Europe and Central Asia region.

3. Angel-Urdinola et al. (2008) differentiate between urban and rural areas by including an urban/rural dummy in their regression, which uses a combined (urban and rural) panel sample, and thus they make no attempt to analyse welfare dynamics determinants that would be specific to the rural areas.

4. State farms encompass both the *sovhoz* (soviet farms) and *kolhoz* (collective farms) ownership forms, which are in effect the same.

5. A thorough overview of agricultural reforms in Tajikistan is provided in World Bank (2005). The major findings of this study are: (i) the process of land restructuring has been rather inequitable; (ii) the reform of state farms, in particular in cotton-producing areas, has resulted in numerous distortions; many state cotton farms were dismantled into a number of smaller units, each with a farm manager and 150–200 workers, with workers having little decision-making power and being paid mostly in kind; (iii) cotton production under current conditions is generally not profitable to the farmers.

6. See Ukaeva (2005) for a detailed discussion based on the decomposition of agricultural growth between 1999 and 2003.

7. Owing to civil conflict and low cotton production, Tajikistan missed the opportunity to benefit from the historically high cotton prices in the mid-1990s. International cotton prices declined from about US$0.90 per pound in 1995/96 (the highest level over the last 30 years) to about US$0.45 per pound in 2003 (one of the lowest levels over the last 30 years). Since then, prices have bounced back somewhat to about US$0.60 per pound. International prices are projected to remain at about the same level for the next few years, or at least not to be likely to go up because of such factors as new technologies (genetically modified cotton), more extensive use of existing technologies, new areas allocated to cotton production (i.e. the increased role of China in the global production of cotton) and government policies (such as direct subsidies to cotton farmers). For a more detailed discussion of the issues, see Becerra (2004).

8. Budgetary pressures in 1997 led the government to sign a partnership with the Swiss cotton trading company, P. Reinhart, which, based on cotton deliveries backed by a government guarantee, was to provide the necessary financing. In 1998, the government guarantee was replaced with a "commercial" financing scheme whereby Reinhart worked with a number of local agents (referred to as financiers, futurists or investors). This framework became the basis of cotton production and marketing. Unwise pricing arrangements squeezed the profit margins of the cotton farmers, putting many in a debt trap. These debts, currently estimated at US$280 million, have paralysed the cotton sector, because indebted farmers are unable to obtain credit elsewhere. Indebted farmers are also reluctant to privatize and invest in their land, adding a further impediment to the growth of the agriculture sector. For further discussion, see World Bank (2005).

9. The graph is not presented here, but is available from the authors on request.
10. See the February 2006 special issue of the *Journal of Development Studies* 42(2) for the set of papers presenting the conceptual framework and empirical evidence for an asset-based approach.
11. The asset poverty line in Figure 4.6 is simply the level of assets corresponding to the level of wellbeing equal to the consumption poverty line.
12. The majority of households in the panel are urban because the 2004 EHS over-sampled these areas.
13. For a comprehensive discussion of the pros and cons of an asset-based welfare analysis, see Filmer and Pritchett (1998) and Sahn and Stifel (2000, 2003). An asset index retains certain properties necessary for proper welfare analysis, such as transparency in construction and ranking individuals credibly in terms of welfare. As argued by Filmer and Pritchett (1998), Carter and May (2001) and Carter and Barrett (2006), an asset index is likely to be a better indicator of long-run household wealth than per capita household consumption. However, a significant limitation of an asset index is that it treats the ownership of assets as giving similar utility without allowing for differences in unobserved quality.
14. Another important consideration is that an asset index that includes only durables may be good at capturing transitions out of structural poverty but not transitions into structural poverty (unless rural households, when faced with hardship, prefer to sell durable goods before selling agricultural assets or livestock). However, application of the asset index to the panel data indicates that in the rural regions the share of households escaping poverty (35.1 per cent) is almost the same as the proportion falling into poverty (34.1 per cent).
15. It is worth noting that, in many cases, when a new asset is purchased the old one will be just discarded unless it has a tradeable value on the market. When a household replaces an old TV, its asset position does not change but, if it merely gets rid of the old set without buying a new one, its wealth position deteriorates.
16. In the study by Angel-Urdinola et al. (2008), the authors have an urban/rural dummy in their panel sample that includes households living in both urban and rural areas. They do not attempt to investigate the determinants of welfare dynamics that would be specific to rural areas.
17. The poverty mobility literature often uses a specification in which the event is conditional on the distance from the poverty line (e.g. Canto 2002). This improves the overall fit of the model and allows one to obtain more accurate parameter estimates on other variables of interest.
18. The horizontal line in the graphs indicates the predicted probability of climbing out of, or falling into, poverty at the means of the variables in the estimation sample. In other words, this line indicates the average odds of poverty transition.
19. The household survey data do not specify how many adults are actually employed on the cotton farm (no cotton is produced on household plots). However, it is safe to assume that agricultural employment in cotton-producing areas consists mostly of employment in the cotton sector.

REFERENCES

Angel-Urdinola, D. F., C. Mete and S. R. Cnobloch (2008). "Poverty Dynamics in Tajikistan". World Bank, Washington DC, manuscript.

Baschieri, A. and J. Falkingham (2005). "Developing a Poverty Map of Tajikistan: A Technical Note". S3RI Applications and Policy Working Papers A05/11, Southampton Statistical Sciences Research Institute, Southampton.

Becerra, C. A. V. (2004). "The World Cotton Market: A Long-Term Outlook". Working Paper presented at the WTO African Regional Workshop on Cotton, 23–24 March, Cotonou.

Canto, O. (2002). "Climbing out of Poverty, Falling back in: Low Income Stability in Spain". *Applied Econometrics* 34(15): 1903–1916.

Carter, M. R. and B. C. Barrett (2006). "The Economics of Poverty Traps and Persistent Poverty: An Asset-Based Approach". *Journal of Development Studies* 42(2): 178–199.

Carter, M. R. and J. May (2001). "Poverty, Livelihood and Class in Rural South Africa". *World Development* 27(1): 1–20.

Filmer, D. and L. Pritchett (1998). "Estimating Wealth Effects without Income or Expenditure Data". WB Policy Research Paper 1994, World Bank, Washington DC.

Jalan, J. and M. Ravallion (2002). "Geographic Poverty Traps? A Micro Model of Consumption Growth in Rural China". *Journal of Applied Econometrics* 17: 329–346.

Lawley, D. and A. Maxwell (1971). *Factor Analysis as a Statistical Method*. London: Butterworth & Co.

Sahn, D. and D. Stifel (2000). "Poverty Comparisons over Time and across Countries in Africa". *World Development* 28(1): 2123–2155.

Sahn, D. and D. Stifel (2003). "Exploring Alternative Measures of Wealth in the Absence of Expenditure Data". *Review of Income and Wealth* 49(4): 463–489.

Ukaeva, U. (2005). "Decomposition of Agricultural Growth in Tajikistan". Mimeo, World Bank, Washington DC.

World Bank (2005). "Priorities for Sustainable Growth: A Strategy for Agriculture Sector Development in Tajikistan". Mimeo, World Bank, Washington DC.

World Bank (2006). "Republic of Tajikistan Poverty Assessment Update". Report No. 30853-TJ, World Bank, Washington DC.

5

Vulnerability, poverty and coping in Zimbabwe

Kate Bird and Martin Prowse

1 Introduction

Statistics and trends are hardly able to convey the magnitude of the current crisis in Zimbabwe. Its economy is shrinking fast, with gross domestic product contracting by 40 per cent between 2000 and 2007. Agricultural production (by volume) has reduced by 50 per cent in the same time period, and as of May 2007 inflation was around 300 per cent per month. An estimated 80 per cent of adults in the economically active age group are unemployed and over 85 per cent of Zimbabweans are now categorized as poor. Moreover, the HIV incidence rate is one of the highest in the world, and life expectancy for women, at 34 years, has declined from 65 years a decade ago.[1] In some parts of the country, 50 per cent of pregnant women are having their children at home, unattended by a trained medical practitioner. Recent bouts of speculation assert that Zimbabwe is now heading for total collapse and perhaps even conflict (Evans 2007).

There have been many attempts to explain how a once relatively prosperous country such as Zimbabwe has experienced such a profound decline. Adverse climatic conditions and the persistence of HIV/AIDS can only partly explain the high levels of poverty and vulnerability. Many analysts agree that politics, poor governance and the weakening of the rule of law are major causes. Harassment by state actors, insecure land and housing tenure, and macroeconomic meltdown have impacted harshly on livelihoods. Declines in wellbeing have been compounded by

Vulnerability in developing countries, Naudé, Santos-Paulino and McGillivray (eds), United Nations University Press, 2009, ISBN 978-92-808-1171-1

declining access to increasingly fragmented local and national markets, to basic agro-inputs and to public services of even a rudimentary standard.

Particular attention has been paid to government policies such as the fast-track land reform programme and Operation Murambatsvina, which have undermined agricultural production and swept away lives and livelihoods, respectively. Although the outcomes of these policies are clear for all to see and judge in media accounts, the reasons for their implementation are harder to discern in populist discourses. Just as politics, in the form of explicit support for the Zimbabwe African National Union-Patriotic Front (ZANU-PF), pervades so many aspects of life in Zimbabwe now, politics underpinned and drove these destructive state interventions.

It is not the purpose of this chapter to catalogue the frighteningly rapid decline of Zimbabwe, or to offer a partial and long-sighted account of the international and domestic politics that contributed to the enactment and implementation of both aforementioned fiascos (although we do touch upon both below). The aim of this chapter is to use five contextualized life history interviews, conducted and written by Kate Bird, to act as a window on current processes of impoverishment and adverse coping in three geographical spheres: peri-urban, urban and rural. The study areas (Mhangtivi, Bulawayo, and Makoni)[2] were selected purposively and were chosen (i) to be representative of both urban and rural Zimbabwe, (ii) to include Shona and Ndebele populations, and (iii) to include a community of mobile and vulnerable people. Three individual study sites were then selected in collaboration with a local non-governmental organization (NGO). These sites were: (i) Plot Shumba, a peri-urban site 30 minutes drive from Mhangtivi, where households live in small, fragile, temporary structures; (ii) Mzilikazi, an inner-city high-density residential area in Bulawayo; and (iii) Zenzele village, Makoni district, a wealthier-than-average communal area village. Each location highlights key aspects of Zimbabwe's recent economic and political turmoil.

First, we offer a brief description of each area's characteristics and the livelihood strategies conducted in this location. Second, we further contextualize the life histories by offering a summary of one or two major drivers of impoverishment and adverse coping in each location, as well as relevant wider details. So, in the case of Plot Shumba, the peri-urban location, we outline the drivers of the fast-track land reform programme and HIV/AIDS, in addition to details on labour markets. In the case of Mzilikazi we outline the drivers of the authoritarian state and Operation Murambatsvina, as well as details on urban poverty and state repression. And in the case of Zenzele village, we outline the drivers of fragmented and imperfect agricultural input markets and distorted agricultural output markets. Third, and most importantly, the study catalogues for each location how current adverse forms of coping appear to be creating irreversible losses of wellbeing. In this respect, the chapter utilizes arguments made by Hoddinott (2006) based on his work on persistent effects of the rainfall shock in 1994–1995 in Zimbabwe.

Hoddinott (2006) assesses the extent to which households at different income levels drew down livestock holdings in the face of a moderate rainfall shock, and the influence of the shock on the body mass index (BMI) of husbands, wives and children. Hoddinott finds that the rainfall shock substantially reduced crop and total household income and increased the sale of livestock, with the extent of sales strongly influenced by pre-shock asset-holding levels. Moreover, Hoddinott notes that, although the rainfall shock did not affect the BMI of husbands, the BMI of wives did fall, although this was mitigated by the sale of livestock, with wives' BMI recovering the following year. Highly significantly, the BMI of children aged 12–24 months was adversely affected by the rainfall shock, and whereas children from wealthy households recovered their lost growth trajectory, children in poorer households did not: they suffered a permanent loss in height, human capital formation and potential earnings.[3]

There are two key points regarding our use of Hoddinott's (2006) findings as a peg on which to hang our arguments – these relate to methods and inference, and the type of shock. First, Hoddinott's conclusions are drawn from detailed panel survey data and in this sense are robust, using quantitative measures. In contrast, this chapter mainly uses life history data, and the small sample size and purposive site selection mean that the conclusions drawn are necessarily tentative and suggestive. This is not to say, however, that qualitative data are necessarily weak or anecdotal. Numerical methods, such as surveys, are good at capturing states or conditions (Ellis 2000), whereas qualitative methods are good at capturing processes (Murray 2002). Although not representative in a strict sense, qualitative research can highlight key themes and processes that may be "typical" of individuals with similar sets of socio-biographical characteristics in similar circumstances. Second, Hoddinott's (2006) findings are based on a "conventional" singular shock, for which risk-sharing and insurance mechanisms have been honed through generations. Current shocks in Zimbabwe are multiple and complex, with conventional shocks overlain by massive governance and macroeconomic failings, which, in our view, are undoubtedly increasing the likelihood of permanent losses of wellbeing. Moreover, Hoddinott's work is restricted to rural resettlement areas in Mashonaland Central Province (which lies to the north of Harare), in Mashonaland East Province (which lies southeast of Harare) and Mutanda in Manicaland Province. Although certain current shocks in Zimbabwe are broadly covariant (such as inflation), many hazards are differentiated across urban and rural spheres, creating different patterns of vulnerability and adverse coping strategies.

The structure of the chapter is as follows. Section 2 outlines how Zimbabwe relates to the fragile states discourse, summarizes who in the development literature constitute fragile groups, introduces some important distinctions within the literature on coping strategies and outlines a simple scheme of coping strategies. Section 3 offers contextualized life histories from the three locations outlined above. In the last section, we argue that the tentative findings from this research surely add weight to arguments that the international community should be more, rather than less, proactive in delivering aid to Zimbabwean people.

2 State fragility and Zimbabwe

To be able to understand how the Zimbabwean case relates to the *fragile* states discourse, we need to understand current definitions of *fragility* and associated terms. Within international development, a common classification of fragile states – used, for example, by the UK's Department for International Development (DFID) and by the Development Assistance Committee of the Organisation for Economic Co-operation and Development (OECD-DAC) – is where the state cannot or will not offer basic services and functions to the majority of the population (Warrener and Loehr 2005). A related but distinct approach is that taken by Torres and Anderson (2004), who recast the notion of fragile states as difficult environments where the state is unable or unwilling to productively direct national or international resources to alleviate poverty. Using this notion of difficult environments, DFID (2005) differentiates developing countries along two axes: (i) political will, and (ii) institutional capacity, creating a four-stage typology:

- *good performers*: sufficient capacity and political desire to maintain relationships with development-related international actors;
- *weak but willing*: limited capacity;
- *strong but unresponsive*: tendency towards repression; and
- *weak-weak*: lacking both capacity and political desire.

As is described through this chapter, the Zimbabwean state currently fits into the third category: strong but unresponsive (and with a tendency towards repression). The state cannot be seen to be failing because it is too pervasive, and in many ways has become parasitic on the populace, crushing dissent with increasingly ruthless vigour. It is not yet clear the extent to which the tentatively constructed power-sharing government will be able to address these governance concerns.

Cammack et al. (2006) argue that DFID's definition of fragility fits only one broad donor approach – that of *functionality*, where the lack of institutional capacity and political desire to reduce poverty reflect a poorly articulated social contract (see Murshed 2006). In addition, state fragility is also variously defined by donors in terms of *outputs*, where the state in question fosters and propagates insecurity and conflict, and *relationships*, where communication and collaboration with other states are fraught and tense (Cammack et al. 2006).

Zimbabwe performs inconsistently across these varied criteria of fragility. In terms of *functionality*, the Zimbabwean state certainly has the institutional capacity to reduce poverty and increase wellbeing across all sections of the population, but it has none of the political desire. Instead, increased repression, militarization and politicization have been the norm since at least 2000. As for *outputs*, and despite fears to the contrary, it appears that Zimbabwe has not directly exported many spillover effects, thus destabilizing neighbours. Its main export has been people, with mass emigration to South Africa and beyond. Moreover, the cloud that has engulfed Zimbabwe has had a silver lining for some regional countries: Zimbabwean tobacco farmers now produce in Zambia, Mozambique, Tanzania and Malawi; some horticultural production has shifted to South Africa; manufacturing has moved to Botswana and South Africa; and tourist receipts from Victoria Falls now accrue to Zambia. State failure in Zimbabwe has certainly led to strained relationships with many development partners (for example, the International Monetary Fund departed in 1997), but not with Southern African Development Community governments (which until recently have been loathe to criticize Mugabe) or trading partners such as Iran, China and Russia (which have increased their involvement in the Zimbabwean economy). In sum, Zimbabwe is certainly fragile, if not failed, in terms of functionality, but in terms of outputs and relationships the picture appears mixed.

2.1 Fragile groups in Zimbabwe

Although the title of the UNU-WIDER conference for which this chapter was prepared refers to *fragile* groups, the development literature more usually refers to *vulnerable* groups. These commonly include children (particularly orphans), the sick, people with physical and mental impairments, widows and widowers, the elderly and the landless (Babirye 1999; Mijumbi and Okidi 2001). Moreover, the Chronic Poverty Research Centre has shown that social marginalization, discrimination and disadvantage are linked with *ascribed status* (e.g. ethnicity, race, religion and caste), oppressive labour relations (e.g. migrant, stigmatized and bonded labourers) and being an *outsider* (e.g. migrant labourers, refugees and internally displaced people, those without the documents necessary to access citizenship rights) (CPRC 2003: 45). People identified as belonging to these groups may be more exposed to risk, owing to their poor capabilities, their low functioning and their failure to accumulate and retain assets.

However, describing a group as fragile or vulnerable masks the fact that individuals and categories of people may be differentially vulnerable to specific risks at particular times (Bird and Shinyekwa 2005: 73). For example, Marcus and Wilkinson (2002: 37) note that not only can "the term 'vulnerable group' be stigmatizing", but it "can be inaccurate, camouflaging the strengths of marginalized and disadvantaged people and their contributions to society, and presenting a falsely homogenous picture of diverse situations".[4] From this viewpoint, the use of the terms *fragile* and *vulnerable* encourages a view of groups and individuals as "passive" and non-responsive, emphasizing weakness, a lack of agency and an inability to cope (Hewitt 1998; Bankoff 2001). In contrast, any attempt at understanding individual or group fragility or vulnerability must focus on actors' capacity and ingenuity to respond, as Moser (1998: 3) states:

> Analysing vulnerability involves identifying not only the threat but also the resilience or responsiveness in exploiting opportunities, and in resisting or recovering from the negative effects of a changing environment. The means of resistance are the assets and entitlements that individuals, households, or communities can mobilize and manage in the face of hardship.

We now turn to the literature on the strategies and activities employed by those under situations of duress, commonly referred to as coping strategies.

2.2 Coping strategies and resilience

The term *coping strategy* emphasizes the ability of households to decide and select appropriate activities in light of their assets and endowments.[5] This is not to deny that coping activities are circumscribed by constraints and the availability of opportunities but to flag up the agency and capacity of individuals, households and communities to strategize. Within the coping strategy literature, there are some straightforward distinctions.

First, there is a difference between idiosyncratic (individual) and covariant shocks. The effect of idiosyncratic shocks – for example, the illness of a family member – can be insured against within a community to a certain degree. It is more difficult to recover from shocks that operate at an aggregate level, affecting entire communities, countries and regions

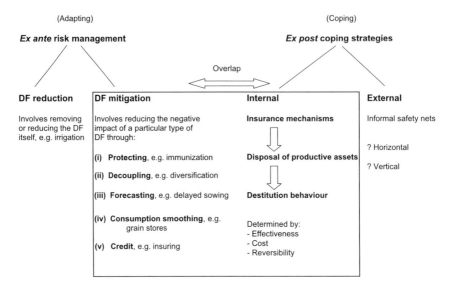

Figure 5.1 *Ex ante* and *ex post* responses to damaging fluctuations.
Source: Taken from Prowse (2003); adapted from Devereux (2001), Sinha and Lipton (1999), Moser (1998) and Ellis (2000).

(covariant shocks), because risk cannot be shared (Dercon 2000). Second, households adopt a range of sequenced coping strategies in order to respond to shocks. These can be divided into two groups: *ex ante* risk management strategies and *ex post* risk-coping strategies. The former can be further divided into strategies that avoid the impact of shock (sometimes termed *shock reduction*) and those that ameliorate the worst effects of a shock (sometimes termed *shock mitigation*). The latter can be divided into strategies internal to the household and those within the wider community (external). These simple distinctions are illustrated in Figure 5.1, which, following Sinha and Lipton (1999), utilizes the term *damaging fluctuation* (DF) instead of shock.

A household's initial conditions (household assets and characteristics, including dependency ratios) influence a household's vulnerability to shocks and the forms of coping open to it. Responses to food insecurity have shown that people adopt coping strategies in a predictable sequence to trade off short-term consumption needs against longer-term economic viability. Strategies with limited long-run costs tend to be adopted first. Once households and individuals have exhausted their less damaging options, they tend to progress to forms of adverse coping and then to survival strategies.

Lack of assets, both private and collective, drives poor people into deeper and more intractable poverty after a shock. Those with few material, financial, natural or social assets are vulnerable to relatively minor shocks, especially if bunched and unpredictable. Without assets to form the basis of effective coping strategies and resilience, people can experience catastrophic declines into persistent poverty and, more to the point, face increased morbidity and reduced life expectancy. Poor people without reserves may adopt forms of adverse coping that may support short-term survival while undermining wellbeing in the medium to long term. Such adverse coping can entail the liquidation of crucial productive assets, the reduction of consumption in ways that have potentially irreversible welfare effects (eating smaller amounts of less nutritious food, avoiding essential medical expenditures, withdrawing children from school) or the adoption of behaviour that undermines trust and social standing (theft and begging, engagement in commercial sex work, abandoning children with their grandparents) (CPRC 2003).

The following life histories illustrate recent processes of impoverishment in Zimbabwe. These demonstrate how such adverse coping not only is leading to tragic loss of life and increased incidence of illbeing, but is impairing future generations through the creation of irreversible outcomes that will scar Zimbabwe for decades.

3 Contextualized life histories

The five simple life histories presented in this section are as follows. From Plot Shumba, the peri-urban area included in our study, we present case studies of two young women living with AIDS. We describe where they live and draw wider observations about life in Zimbabwe from the shocks that have affected their community. To provide some background to key drivers of impoverishment in Plot Shumba, Boxes 5.2 and 5.3 below offer an overview of, respectively, the fast-track land reform programme and changes in rural labour markets. We also offer details on the HIV pandemic in Zimbabwe.

From Mzilikazi, Bulawayo, we discuss the experiences of a young man who was orphaned as a child, got drawn into gang-related crime as a teenager and is now unemployed. Again, we use this example to discuss wider issues facing urban Zimbabwe and to show how the sequenced and composite shocks experienced in his life so far will make an exit from poverty extremely difficult, even when economic recovery occurs in Zimbabwe. To offer some contextual detail, we summarize state repression and Operation Murambatsvina and describe recent urban poverty trends.

Finally we present the stories of two rural households where grandparents are struggling with poverty and ill health to bring up their grandchildren. We use these stories to illustrate how many children are growing up in poverty having been orphaned by AIDS or while their parents seek work in urban areas. To frame this discussion, we offer details on imperfect and distorted agricultural input and output markets in rural Zimbabwe.

3.1 Plot Shumba

Plot Shumba is a privately owned peri-urban site around 30 minutes' drive from Mhangtivi, the main regional town, and easy walking distance from the high-density suburb of Matemba. In Plot Shumba, 58 households live in small, fragile, temporary structures scattered over 3 acres of a 66 acre piece of rain-fed agricultural land. The land is used extensively as grazing for a small herd of cattle, sheep and goats belonging to the plot owner. Plot Shumba developed gradually as a settlement between the early 1970s and the late 1990s, with the owner's permission. Residents tended to move to the Plot because they had nowhere else to go – they had lost their commercial farming or mining job and therefore their home; they were unemployed, had lost contact with their rural home or had work but could not afford urban rents.

In the late 1990s the community came to the attention of "agents of the state" and since 1998 the community has been evicted and its members have had their homes and assets destroyed three times. Community members have suffered various forms of harassment and social, political and economic exclusion, ranging from being refused medical treatment because of community membership through to retailers refusing to sell them food during the 2003 food security crisis. For about 18 months between 2005 and late 2006 the community received food aid (distributed by local NGOs), but distribution to this community was then stopped because of World Food Programme (WFP) shortages. The range of livelihood activities undertaken by women has not changed a great deal since 2000: casual labour (*maricho*) and casual domestic work; small-scale local trading (food, grass brooms, fresh milk, non-timber forest products, firewood); backyard industries (hairdressing, bicycle repair, making doilies, tailoring/needlework); growing horticultural crops; and some informal commercial sex work. Households also engage in gold panning and crushing gold ore (conducted by men) and receive support from NGOs. However, the tighter application of environmental and licensing regulations has limited some of these livelihood strategies (see Box 5.1). Bans on gold panning, the cutting and selling of firewood and vending without a licence are now observed. If caught by members of the Zimbabwe

Box 5.1 Vending licences: Official requirements

Official requirements for obtaining a vending licence are:
- Application forms: application forms should be bought from the council at a cost of ZW$300,000.
- Health screening: a prospective vendor must be screened at his or her own expense for communicable diseases such as TB. At the time of the research the cost of health screening was ZW$2.5 million, which most prospective vendors considered to be too high.
- Police clearance: prospective vendors should be cleared by the police for any criminal record. Those with criminal records are denied licences. This was introduced during operation Murambatsvina (May/June 2005), when the government argued that a number of informal traders were involved in crime and the sale of stolen goods.
- Licences for a particular type of vending are issued on the condition that a certain quota for each category has not been exceeded.

Traders who sell herbs and other traditional medicines must register with the Zimbabwe National Traditional Healers Association. The association charges a fee for registration and an annual membership subscription.

Unofficial requirements for the issuance of a vending licence include:
- Proof of party affiliation and paid-up membership.
- "Money for drinks" for council officials to speed up the process and to ignore official requirements such as health check-ups and criminal records.
- "Gifts" to officials in the form of merchandise to be sold by the vendor.

Each licence stipulates the products a vendor can sell. A licence issued for the sale of fruit and vegetables is not valid for the sale of other products. This limits the vendors' opportunities to identify and occupy niches, which change as the economy collapses.

Republic Police or municipal police – dubbed *tight grip* – community members risk being physically assaulted, having their commodities confiscated or destroyed or having to pay a fine or bribe (in cash or kind). Evading detection takes time and further reduces the viability of a number of livelihood activities.

In contrast to women, men reported that their livelihood activities had altered considerably since 2000. Previously they relied mostly on commercial farm work. However, since 2000 gold panning and small-scale vending have become more significant.[6] Disruption to the agricultural sector, driven by the fast-track land reform, resulted in a marked decline in agricultural activity and employment (see Boxes 5.2 and 5.3). Some are still involved in unlicensed vending and firewood collection but these activities tend to be ad hoc, owing to the risk of arrest.

Overall, people at Plot Shumba were struggling to find work at the time the fieldwork was conducted. This is partly because of widespread unemployment, but their reputation as supporters of the Movement for Democratic Change (MDC) makes finding work more difficult, as does their lack of a ZANU-PF membership card. Many also lack proper ID papers and have "alien" status. In the current political climate, such people are the last to be offered jobs or provided with services. Clearly, the settlement has been strongly affected by the land invasions surrounding fast-track land reform processes. Instead of focusing on those directly displaced by the fast-track land reform, the following life histories of Angel and Linah from Plot Shumba further illustrate the channels of decline in the context of state repression. Both narratives, as well as the further three life histories later in the chapter, are accompanied by a "map" that depicts the trajectory of the wellbeing of respondents through time.[7]

Life history interview with Angel: Young, destitute, and desperately sick

Angel lives alone with her 19-month-old baby in a small tin shack (around 2.2 metres by 1.7 metres) in Plot Shumba. She is very ill with AIDS and tuberculosis and her illness has made her very weak, making it difficult for her to speak or move. Her skin is dry and her hair is thin, brittle and reddish brown rather than black. She is thin and gaunt and her appearance is such that she could be either male or female and almost any age from mid-teens to early forties (although she is actually only 25). Angel's illness was only confirmed in February 2006 when the NGO working in her community offered her HIV testing. She has been diagnosed with TB and cannot start anti-retrovirals until her TB has been successfully treated. Unfortunately, owing to her late diagnosis she started treatment only a month before our interview in July 2006. Angel looked so ill when we met that it seemed unlikely she would survive.

Angel had her first child when she was 12, but carried on going to school until Form 2 (the second class in secondary school). At this stage she had to drop out because her family ran out of money. She left her baby with her mother's family (when he was 21 months old) and as a 14 year old moved to a town in the Midlands near Plot Shumba to look for work. Luckily, she found some and worked as a "house girl" for a middle-class family. But after a year she had to leave – her "madam" was not paying her and she felt exploited. Having nowhere to go, she

Box 5.2 Fast-track land reform

Frequently, media representations of Zimbabwe's crisis depict the "war veteran" movement as a militia arm of ZANU-PF. Although the war veterans were certainly integral to the chaotic appropriation of white-owned farmland from 2000, relations between ZANU-PF and the war veterans (nomenclature that obscures the much broader constituency – including many retrenched workers from urban areas – of this political force) were not always so close-knit. From 1997 the war veterans were a key political threat to the continued hegemony of Mugabe's ZANU-PF. To stave off possible political defeat, Mugabe co-opted the veterans through generous payments including pensions. He also gave them the green light to invade white-owned commercial farms.

Zimbabwe's fast-track land reform is closely linked to the revision of the country's constitution in 2000, which asserted the state's right to seize land from large-scale farmers for redistribution. A national referendum in February 2000 rejected the proposals but, despite this loss, the government amended the constitution and passed a new Land Acquisition Act in April 2000, which legalized compulsory acquisition (Kinsey 2004). In June 2000, Mugabe announced the fast-track land reform programme, stating that it was necessary to correct colonial imbalances in land ownership (*CAJ News*, 6 March 2007). In the meantime, farm invasions began during the early months of 2000 (Chaumba et al. 2003). These may have been spontaneous or orchestrated by the war veterans. They also coincided with a regional rainfall shock and harvest failures that were so severe that they precipitated demands for food aid (Potts 2006).

A study of some of those involved in farm invasions at the peak of the fast-track land reform process shows that they were either young men with a desire for land or female-headed households, often widows and divorcees, fleeing social stigma in communal land areas. Settlers were either the relatively rich or the relatively poor (as proxied by cattle ownership). Wealthier households with large numbers of cattle were found to be able to straddle communal and "invaded" land and create patron–client relations with the poorer settlers through the loaning of cattle for draught power in return for the provision of labour. Poorer households had few assets and had little to lose, and were found to make their living through casual labour, poaching and possibly theft (Chaumba et al. 2003).

In June 2002 around 3,000 white farmers were ordered to leave their farms (Addison and Laakso 2003), and by August 2002 the fast-track land reform was completed. More than 5,000 white-owned

Box 5.2 (cont.)

commercial farms were seized and, by the end of 2002, only 600 white farmers remained in the country (Sachikonye 2003). Over 10 million hectares of land had changed hands, with 300,000 farmers gaining access to plots of 5–10 hectares and over 50,000 farmers gaining access to plots large enough for commercial farming. The process was chaotic and access to plots was mainly organized through ZANU-PF party structures. Instead of an equitable process of redistribution to the landless, it became highly politicized and patronage systems came into play. In the end, a number of members of the black political elite gained large tracts of high-quality land (Scarnecchia 2006), held for speculation rather than productive farming. Importantly, the land reform process has displaced thousands of farm workers, many of whom were first-, second- or third-generation immigrants from Malawi, Zambia and Mozambique and were regarded by many Zimbabweans as "aliens" and outsiders (see Box 5.3).

moved to Plot Shumba in 2002 and built a shack. But in February 2003 the army demolished Plot Shumba as part of the state's drive against squatter settlements and informality (called Operation Mariawanda). Angel was severely beaten and spent a month sleeping in the open at the long-distance bus shelter (along with others from the Plot). The landowner obtained a court order enabling them to move back and the residents rebuilt their homes.

In February 2004, Angel's cousin helped her to get a job at a local small-scale goldmine selling beer. While she was there she met a gold panner and fell in love. But the mine owner went bankrupt in August 2004 and she lost her job and her home and was forced to return to Plot Shumba with her boyfriend. For a while things looked up – Angel made a living selling vegetables. She became pregnant in 2004 and gave birth to their first son in March 2005. However, that same month her boyfriend was killed when the mine he was working in collapsed, killing him and three other men. Angel stayed at Plot Shumba until it was demolished during Operation Murambatsvina. Afterwards she had to rebuild her shack again. Now unable to care effectively for herself or her son (who despite his 19 months does not walk, talk or make eye contact), Angel relies on local networks and the NGO for her and her son's survival. In all likelihood, this support has not been sufficient for either mother or son. See Figure 5.2 charting Angel's history.

Box 5.3 Rural labour markets

In the early 1990s, work on commercial farms was mainly shunned by black Zimbabweans, and demand was filled by migrant Malawians, Mozambicans and Zambians. However, by 2000 this had changed, and around three-quarters of farm labourers were Zimbabwean. Both "alien" and domestic farm workers tended to be the poorest sections of rural communities and they were locked into a patron–client system with estate owners. Although they had weak employment rights and often lacked political rights (for example, "aliens" only gained the right to vote in local elections in 1998) (Sachikonye 2003), they were ensured some security from the estate owner and management.

After the fast-track land reform programme, newly resettled farmers had little ability or willingness to engage non-household labour, and over 100,000 farm workers lost their jobs and were evicted from their homes. Some migrant workers were forcibly relocated by the authorities to marginal areas of the country with little infrastructure (such as the Lower Zambezi valley). Displacement from farms has reduced access to housing, health and education services by workers, who are often forced to move to squatter camps or informal housing in urban or peri-urban areas, such as Plot Shumba. Former farm workers were legally entitled to a severance package from their employers, but only 25 per cent of these employers received timely compensation from the government, which made it difficult for them to provide their workers with severance pay. (Sachikonye 2003)

Life history interview with Linah: Wayward adolescent or victim of child abuse?

Linah is a 16-year-old orphan who is both a figure of fun in Plot Shumba and thoroughly socially integrated into her community. One of her nicknames translates as "the hedonist" or "fun seeker", the other (behind her back) is Moneylink (the system for sending remittances home). Linah was orphaned when she was a toddler and came with her older sister to live with her grandmother in Plot Shumba. Their household also includes two male cousins – her mother's sister's sons – who moved in when her aunt died. Even though Linah is still in her teens, her life has had a number of twists and turns. She has never been to school and ran away at around the age of 11 to live with a 23-year-old man in the local town of Matemba. The relationship broke down and she returned to her grandmother's house at Plot Shumba. Her rebellious, and sometimes promiscuous, behaviour caused her grandmother to throw her out when she was

132

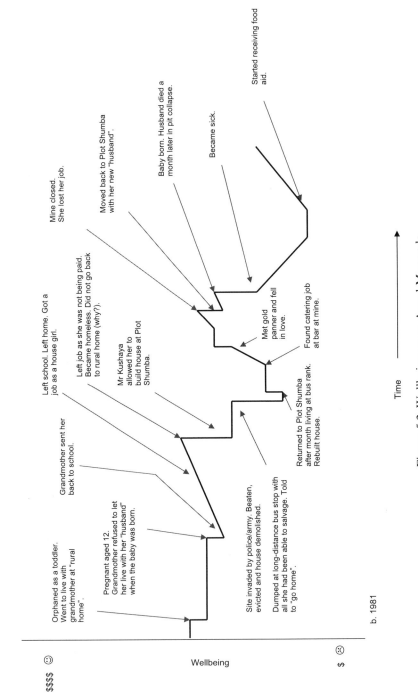

Figure 5.2 Wellbeing map: Angel Muponda.

$$$$

☺

Wellbeing

☹

$

b. 1981

Time

Orphaned as a toddler. Went to live with grandmother at "rural home".

Grandmother sent her back to school.

Pregnant aged 12. Grandmother refused to let her live with her "husband" when the baby was born.

Left school. Left home. Got a job as a house girl.

Mine closed. She lost her job.

Left job as she was not being paid. Became homeless. Did not go back to rural home (why?).

Moved back to Plot Shumba with her new "husband".

Mr Kushaya allowed her to build house at Plot Shumba.

Baby born. Husband died a month later in pit collapse.

Became sick.

Started receiving food aid.

Met gold panner and fell in love.

Found catering job at bar at mine.

Site invaded by police/army. Beaten, evicted and house demolished.

Dumped at long-distance bus stop with all she had been able to salvage. Told to "go home".

Returned to Plot Shumba after month living at bus rank. Rebuilt house.

around 13 years old. Linah found herself on the street in the local town, and to survive she turned to informal commercial sex work.

During this time she met a man at the Matemba Rural Council and he became her regular boyfriend. She moved back in with her grandmother and stopped sleeping with other men. Then she became pregnant. When I met Linah she was around 5 months pregnant. But she was not sure when the baby was due because of her inability to afford the consultation charge (US$2) for a pre-natal check. As she is HIV positive, and without a check-up, it is unlikely that she will be able to have her baby in hospital. Without a hospital birth, it is unlikely that she will receive Nevaraprin during labour to prevent the mother-to-child transmission of HIV or that the baby will get follow-up treatment. It is also unlikely that she will receive formula to be able to feed her baby and will, instead, breastfeed (potentially increasing the risk of transmission). After she was tested and her HIV status confirmed, she told her boyfriend. He told her that he loved her anyway and would stay with her. At the time of the interview, she had not seen him for two weeks. Figure 5.3 charts Linah's history.

Both Linah and Angel are HIV positive and their stories show how poverty and marginality combined to increase their chance of risky behaviour. Angel's story reveals how a series of events has driven her into severe poverty and close to death. Assuming that Angel's TB is cured and her health improves on a sustained ART programme, having dropped out of school at 14 her employment opportunities will be limited, even if the Zimbabwean economy recovers. Having had her home demolished twice, she has almost no household possessions and no productive or physical assets. Although she is well liked by the people in Plot Shumba, they are similarly destitute. She is disconnected from her rural home and marginalized from mainstream society and will thus find it hard to use social or political networks to improve her wellbeing. Angel's son is growing up in destitution and the 19 month old's life chances are very limited, if he manages to survive infancy.

Linah's story illustrates, perhaps, how difficult it is for elderly grandparents to raise children alone. Linah needed more guidance and protection than she received. Once her grandmother had thrown her out, earning alternatives other than commercial sex work were limited. Being HIV positive, with no education and with a baby to support, her options are extremely limited. Like Angel, she has no physical or productive assets and her networks are with other very poor people. In the future, her best hope is to find casual work and accumulate enough to move into livelihood activities with a higher return – opportunities that are extremely circumscribed in the current political climate.

134

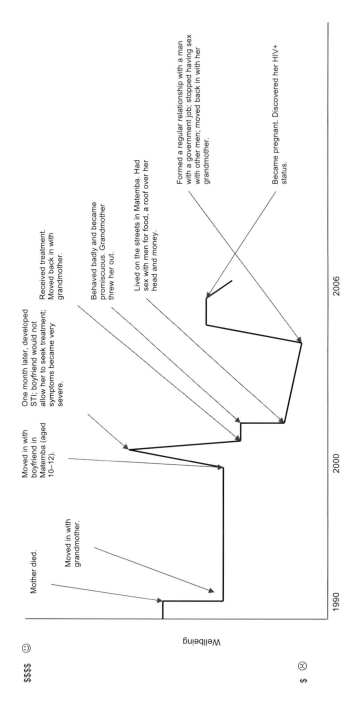

Figure 5.3 Wellbeing map: Linah.

HIV is a key element in both of these life stories. The HIV/AIDS pandemic in Zimbabwe has been a significant factor in poverty trends both before and after 2000. Official UN statistics show that the HIV infection rate is 24.6 per cent, one of the highest in the world. Other studies offer varying statistics. A national statistically significant sample of women applying for pre-natal care found the HIV rate to be 21 per cent in 2004, although the high proportion of women giving birth at home suggests that many of the poorest women were not included in this study (thus lowering the rate). A different assessment, based on a survey of micro-credit recipients, found that around 40 per cent of households displayed signs of being affected by HIV (using chronic illness as a proxy) (Barnes 2003).

Although around 3 million people in Zimbabwe are HIV positive, only 50,000 of them have access to anti-retroviral therapy treatment. Zimbabweans can expect to die younger than anyone else in the world: as mentioned before, the life expectancy of a Zimbabwean woman today is just 34 years, and a Zimbabwean man can expect to live to 37 years. HIV-affected households have a greater proportion of household members who are economically inactive, are less likely to seek medical treatment owing to a lack of funds and have a lower monthly income, indicating the vicious circle of impoverishment and HIV-positive status (Barnes 2003). The impacts of HIV on wellbeing are multiple and interlinked. For example, chronically ill households are more likely to miss meals, eat poorer-quality food, use wild foods and focus food provision to the economically active household members (to the detriment of others). We can see these factors at work in the case of both Angel and Linah, limiting not only their own life expectancies but also those of their children, who are the future for Zimbabwe in years to come.

3.2 Mzilikazi, Bulawayo

Mzilikazi is an old, fairly central and well-established inner-city high-density residential area in Bulawayo that used to house the town's wealthier skilled and semi-skilled black workers. The area is well laid out and spacious, and homes have piped water and electricity. Houses tend to be semi-detached brick bungalows with two or more bedrooms, tin, asbestos or tile roofs and small gardens. However, the appearance of prosperity and calm is misleading. The area has been deeply affected by Zimbabwe's recession and unemployment is high. A number of households depend on sub-letting in order to cover their basic living costs. Overcrowding has intensified following Operation Murambatsvina, because many of the outhouses that residents had constructed in their backyards to provide a source of rental income were demolished. Some of the

Box 5.4 Livelihood activities of selected men and women in Mzilikazi

Men	Women
Decades ago, when their children were young	
Husbands of the key informants were employed as: • city council worker (slashing grass by rivers and roads and spraying for mosquitoes) • domestic workers • post office worker (deliveries) (later a driver for the post office) • salesman/driver for a manufacturing company • selling vegetables from their urban "garden" • vending: buying bread for resale • electrician for the National Railways (later, self-employed electrician) Other men in Mzilikazi at that time: • furniture makers (carpenters) • self-employed builders • cross-border traders • hairdressers • raised and sold poultry	The key informants were employed as: • domestic workers • vending home-made brooms • selling vegetables from their urban "garden" • catering in formal beer halls • vendor selling roasted mealie cobs • vendor selling fruit and sweets • vendor selling second-hand clothes • tailor in a clothing factory • agricultural casual labourer (paid in kind, in clothes)

"landlords" now share their small homes with a second family. Crime is a serious problem, much of it perpetrated by criminal gangs (*tsotsies*).

Only a few residents are still in formal employment, and most rely on income-generating strategies covering illegal, semi-legal and legal activities. Vending is now a key (though risky and unreliable) source of livelihood. "Everyone has become a vendor" is an oft-cited phrase, despite the fact that a vendor without a licence risks harassment (see Box 5.4).

Many older residents in Mzilikazi receive pensions or welfare grants, but they are almost worthless because their purchasing power has been eroded by inflation. Remittances do not provide widespread or reliable support. The average level of wellbeing is reported to have collapsed in

Box 5.4 (cont.)

Ten years ago	
Four out of the six husbands had died, the remaining two were: • electrician • salesman/driver Other men in Mzilikazi at that time: • some ex-council workers became plumbers (to fill a demand that was previously filled by the council) • hairdressers	• domestic workers • vending home-made brooms • vending roasted mealie cobs • vending vegetables • working in an old people's home as a cleaner/orderly • cross-border trading (until her passport expired - her father was Zambian so she is finding it difficult to get a new passport; she has to formally renounce her right to Zambian nationality) Some of the changes in livelihood activity are due to changes in opportunity and others are due to changes in their age.
As of August 2006	
Five out of the six women are now widows. The remaining husband was: • salesman/driver	• vending sweets • vending fruit • horticulture Some people do not have a livelihood. They rely on support from social welfare, which gives them food handouts, or on whatever their children can give them.

Source: Focus group discussion with a group of older women, August 2006, Mzilikazi, Bulawayo.

recent years. Newly poor residents appeared to be stunned by both the rapidity and the depth of their poverty and were being driven into unfamiliar forms of coping. Illegal or adverse coping strategies are increasing: commercial sex work, crime (housebreaking, mugging), illicit beer brewing, gambling and drug dealing. Teenagers and young adults have been drawn into these activities to make a living, deepening the generation gap between the old and the young. Older people report that they live in perpetual fear of the youth. Under-aged prostitution is widespread.

The life story of Blessing illustrates how crime has become a livelihood choice for the unemployed and alienated youth of urban Zimbabwe.

Life history interview with Blessing: The livelihood choice of urban unemployed youth?

Blessing (22) is an orphan and currently lives with his stepfather. He was an only child, never knew his father, and his mother fell ill when he was 9 years old, and died shortly afterwards. He dropped out of school at this age as his stepfather would not pay for his education. He has been unemployed ever since. He can remember nothing good about his childhood after his mother died. During the interview Blessing said he was hungry and had no way of getting food. His clothes were dirty and he had not washed recently. He looked miserable.

Blessing lived for a part of his childhood with his stepfather and for a few years with his paternal grandmother. He was thrown out by his stepparents in 1999 when he was 16 and lived on the streets. The following year, he moved in with his grandmother. After realizing that his grandmother "could not cater for his needs", he joined the *tsotsies* and started going into town with them to steal. Caught by the police, he was sentenced to a two-year prison term (2001–2002). Life in prison was very tough and Blessing turned his back on the gangsters. After his release he moved in with his grandmother, tried to find a job but could not because he lacks a national ID and a birth certificate (his paperwork had not been organized by the time his mother died). To keep himself busy, Blessing joined a youth centre and became part of a dance troupe that tours Bulawayo to put on performances. They make some money from dancing but he would "like to diversify" because he recognizes that as he gets older he will not be able to maintain the quality of his performances. Also, he does not make enough money from dancing and he often goes hungry. He would like to become a vendor, selling fruit and vegetables, but knows the risks involved from police harassment of vendors. He says that, to reduce the risk, he would sell locally in Mzilikazi rather than in the city centre.

Unfortunately, his grandmother died in August 2005 and he moved back in with his stepfather. Until recently Blessing's stepmother was part of this household but she left shortly before I met him. He has a poor relationship with his stepfather and since his stepmother left his stepfather's behaviour has deteriorated. He is a violent man and Blessing is afraid of him. He is locked out of the house while his stepfather is at work and has to spend the day outside. Blessing says that he cannot talk to him and cannot ask him for help.

Figure 5.4 shows how sequential shocks have marred Blessing's life, almost before it began. By the age of 9, both of his parents had died and he had dropped out of school. Now functionally illiterate, long-term unemployed and with a criminal record, he is unlikely to access formal sector employment. It is difficult to see a way out for Blessing. His best hope is that the economy begins to recover soon, generating employment, and that he can pick up unskilled manual work – an unlikely scenario in the short term. Moreover, networks are likely to play an important role in recruitment processes, and Blessing is poorly connected. His story is replicated many times over in places like Mzilikazi. Illegal or adverse coping strategies are increasingly being adopted, limiting future life chances. Until alternative livelihood options present themselves, it is likely that areas such as Mzilikazi, despite its middle-class heritage, will continue to be blighted by crime.

The life story of Blessing, and of those in Mzilikazi more broadly, reflects urban poverty trends in Zimbabwe. Urban poverty in Zimbabwe declined through the 1980s. In 1981, around 30 per cent were below the minimum wage in high-density areas in Harare and by 1991 this had fallen to 10–15 per cent, making urban Zimbabweans amongst the wealthiest and most secure anywhere in Africa (Potts 2006). But during the 1990s urban poverty increased, mainly owing to stabilization policies associated with structural adjustment, and it has mushroomed since 2000 (Potts 2006). By 2006, the vast majority of Zimbabweans were living beneath the poverty line; over 85 per cent of Zimbabweans were defined as poor by the Consumer Council of Zimbabwe (cited in Potts 2006; see also Hawkins 2006).

The experience of those pursuing disparate illegal livelihoods in Mzilikazi gives some indication that the real power brokers in Zimbabwe are the security services: the army, the Central Intelligence Organization (CIO) and the police. Although there are splits within and between these, the soldiers and the CIO ultimately hold power. We close this urban section by showing how the state security sector misuses its power with a summary of Operation Murambatsvina and through cataloguing recent examples of state oppression in Zimbabwe (Box 5.5).

Operation Murambatsvina took place in May/June 2005 and was described by the government as an attempt to control the "economic saboteurs" operating the black market and to improve the quality of the urban housing stock by ensuring that planning permissions and building regulations were obeyed. Three alternative explanations have been suggested: (i) the desire to punish opposition supporters, many of whom are urban based, and to tighten control over the population; (ii) to disperse potential sources of political agitation from urban areas to rural areas (in rural areas people can be "disciplined" more easily and less

140

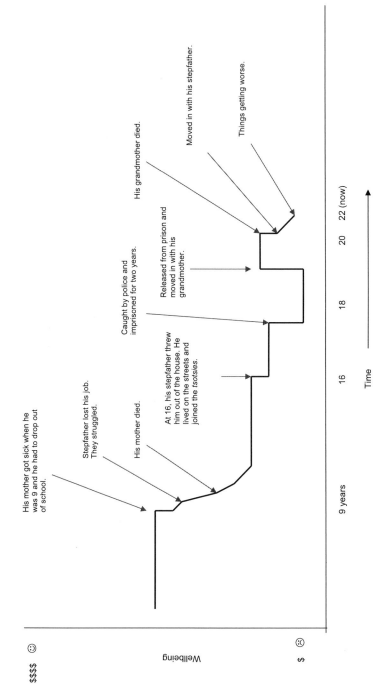

Figure 5.4 Wellbeing map: Blessing Dhlami.

Box 5.5 Recent examples of oppression

Examples of the misuse of state power between January and May 2007 include:

- A crackdown on the opposition in early 2007, following accusations from Mugabe that they were trying to topple the regime on behalf of Zimbabwe's former colonial master, Britain. Violence and repression were used to suppress the independent media, harass human rights defenders and intimidate opposition leaders and peaceful demonstrators.
- In February 2007, in reaction to growing unrest over the economy, police outlawed rallies and demonstrations in Harare and other parts of the country regarded as opposition strongholds. Using teargas, batons and water cannons, police scuttled a rally that Morgan Tsvangirai, leader of the Zimbabwean opposition Movement for Democratic Change (MDC), was to hold at Zimbabwe Grounds in Highfield to launch his 2008 presidential election campaign (*Financial Gazette*, 1 March 2007).
- In March 2007, Morgan Tsvangirai and several other members of his party were detained in a police raid in the capital, Harare. Scores of police officers in riot gear, wielding AK-47 assault rifles, barricaded all the roads around Harvest House, the MDC headquarters in Harare. Police confirmed a crackdown on "perpetrators of violence" (IRIN Africa 2007).
- Four members of the opposition MDC were prevented from leaving Zimbabwe, including one MP, Nelson Chamisa, who was badly beaten when travelling to a meeting in Brussels. A significant number of activists and opposition supporters are still being arrested and tortured throughout Zimbabwe. Trade and student union members have been harassed and arrested.
- Opposition supporters were denied state-supplied food aid. In a public statement, Charumbira, president of Zimbabwe's Council of Chiefs, confirmed that traditional leaders had been ordered to consider only ZANU-PF supporters on programmes initiated by the government. "We cannot afford to continue feeding the enemy because they are sell-outs", he said. ZANU-PF denies using food aid as a political weapon (*ZimOnline*, 31 January 2007).

Source: Proudlock (2007).

transparently); and (iii) with the informal sector crushed, control of the economy returns firmly to the government and the dependence of the population on the state for food increases, reducing the scope for opposition.

Operation Murambatsvina targeted illegal structures and informal businesses, demolishing buildings, vending sites and other informal business premises without planning permission and driving the informal sector underground. The operation resulted in the loss of livelihoods for those previously working in the informal sector. It is estimated that some 650,000–700,000 people were directly affected through the loss of shelter and/or livelihoods (Tibaijuka 2005). Government figures state that almost 95,000 dwelling units were destroyed, displacing some 570,000 people, with a further 98,000 losing their livelihoods in the informal sector (Potts 2006).

The United Nations also estimated that, after Operation Murambatsvina, at least 114,000 were living in the open without shelter and the government curtailed international assistance to internally displaced people (Human Rights Watch 2005). Few were able to access alternative government accommodation (Operation Garikai) owing to strict conditions, including evidence of formal employment and a monthly salary (Human Rights Watch 2005). The police intimidated and beat displaced people and forcibly moved them to transit camps, after which the government assigned them to rural regions on the basis of their identity numbers. These relocations have placed an additional burden on rural areas, which now have additional people to house and feed in place of the remittances they may previously have received. The operation has had a long-run impact. The police have enforced stringent licensing regulations more tightly and the requirement that all vendors sell only from covered premises generates a powerful barrier to entry. Also, new regulations have been introduced to control the informal sector, and those applying for a vending licence now have to obtain police clearance (see Box 5.1). People without IDs (e.g. "aliens") or with a criminal record are denied licences. Many people are still in effect homeless and the large numbers of urban households that depended on renting backyard property in order to cover their basic living costs have lost an important source of income. These factors are reflected in the case of Mzilikazi and in the limited opportunities available to Blessing, whose wellbeing is unlikely to improve in either the short or the long term.

3.3 Zenzele village, Makoni district

Zenzele village is in Mutoro Ward, about 40 kilometres from Rusape town in the relatively rich Shona heartlands. The village is wealthier than the average village in a communal area, despite its sandy soils with very low fertility. For many households, a year-round income and food source are derived from access to several cultivable wetlands, where vegetables, water yam (*madhumbe* or *magogoya*) and small amounts of rice are grown. For others, annual dryland farming is reliant on the unimodal pattern of rainfall. Many households in the village have both small (chickens, goats, rabbits, guinea fowl and pigs) and large livestock (mainly cattle and donkeys). Poor households tend to be limited to a couple of chickens and livestock numbers are dwindling through cattle rustling, disease,[8] distress sales and slaughter for festive occasions or as payment to meet contingencies.[9]

The (group) village headman retains strong control over his community, and governs Zenzele and 48 other villages. Zenzele was selected as one of the three field sites to be visited in August 2006 because the village headman is famous in Zimbabwe for having resurrected the traditional practice of *Zunde ra Mambo*. This is a form of highly localized taxation that, in theory, generates a food store to protect local food security. Zenzele is wealthier than many others in the communal areas and has an active *Zunde* scheme. As a result, it is likely that this village illustrates a better-than-average example of a communal farming area in Zimbabwe. However, despite the *Zunde ra Mambo* scheme and the involvement of WFP and a local NGO, there were a number of food-insecure households.

Until recently, agriculture was the main livelihood strategy in Zenzele, with men and women involved in agriculture throughout much of the year. Agro-processing activities converted some of the local produce for local consumption or sale either within the community or on the local or national market. Although agriculture is still significant, many households are now involved in the collection of natural resources from common lands (Boxes 5.6 and 5.7 on agricultural input and output markets, respectively). These activities include: collecting clay for pottery-making or bricks (large amounts of wood are required to fire kilns for these activities); cutting reeds/grass for roof thatching; cutting and selling firewood (despite being illegal); and gathering and eating/selling wild foods (e.g. mopane worms, wild mushrooms, collecting, roasting and selling termites, and catching, roasting and selling field mice).

Considering the frequency of natural resource collection as a livelihood strategy, a surprisingly large number of households have family members in regular salaried employment working mainly in urban areas (39 people in 22 households). However, remittances from these households were unreliable, mainly because inflation reduced the amount they were able to send to families. Instead, reverse remittances were flowing, with rural relatives sending urban-based family members food (mostly grain).

Casual labour (*maricho*) is an important source of livelihood in Zenzele village, but is associated (by the non-poor) with the "lazy" poor,

Box 5.6 Fragmented and imperfect agricultural input markets

Before the start of the economic collapse, Zimbabwe had considerable success in improving yields in maize through the adoption of green revolution technologies (hybrid seeds and carefully timed fertilizer applications). This resulted in a rapid increase in maize production during the 1980s and 1990s but, as the economy moved into sharp recession, the use of hybrid maize seeds has declined substantially, because they have become scarce and expensive. Over 70 per cent of smallholders are now using open pollinated varieties (OPVs) (Bird et al. 2006). Attempts to support food production have included the distribution of improved OPV seeds and fertilizer by humanitarian programmes (Rohrbach et al. 2004). Unfortunately, these programmes have been marred by poor-quality seed and poor labelling (including a lack of information about whether the seeds are hybrid or OPV) (Rohrbach et al. 2004).

Availability of seed and key agro-chemicals is highly variable, and even farmers with the money to purchase the increasingly expensive inputs have not been able to obtain them during the last four growing seasons. Some inputs are available, but selectively. For example, "new farmers" who benefited from land allocations following the fast-track land reform now receive subsidized fuel and fertilizer from the state. But they commonly sell these inputs on the parallel markets, finding this more profitable than growing price-controlled grains. When seed and agro-chemicals are available on the open market, hyper-inflation puts their cost beyond the reach of many producers.

Without fertilizer, yields are very low, driving many households into a downward spiral of food insecurity, income declines and an inability to purchase the next season's agricultural inputs (Bird et al. 2006: 7). Diesel shortages since 2000 have made transport scarce and increasingly expensive, hampering rural producers' access to markets.

who "don't plan". In addition, a minority of individuals are involved in artisanal activities, including carpentry, blacksmithing and tailoring. Some villagers have other income-generating activities, including beer-brewing and NGO-supported projects such as soap-making, honey-harvesting and oil-pressing. Barter appears increasingly important, and individuals from neighbouring villages come to barter maize for other food products, utensils, soap, matches and new and second-hand clothes. For example, a finished clay pot is bartered in exchange for a bowl full of maize or a chicken. The two life histories below vividly illustrate the negative impact of sequenced and composite shocks on the lives of individual children and older people.

Box 5.7 Distorted agricultural output markets

Maize, wheat and white sorghum are now classified as "restricted crops" in Zimbabwe, meaning that they can be sold only to the state-owned and -administered Grain Marketing Board (GMB) at below export parity. Liquidity problems mean that the GMB does not collect these crops post harvest, requiring farmers, even very poor ones, to pay their own transport to GMB depots. Richer communal farmers club together to hire transport, but this is expensive and is likely to exclude poorer farmers and those with limited marketable surplus. These, and other farmers, rely on illegal "side marketing" and beer-brewing.

The sale of maize by the GMB at subsidized prices further distorts local and national food markets. Anecdotes suggest that trade *within* GMB warehouses creates margins for certain officials (buying maize at the consumer market price, reselling at the higher GMB purchase price), and jokes in circulation during 2006 told of lorries driving round in circles, leaving one exit having bought at the consumer price, entering the facility at another entrance and selling at the GMB purchase price, without unloading.* Despite commercial maize mills functioning at a fraction of their capacity, new mills are apparently being constructed by senior ZANU-PF officials because GMB will prefer party-owned mills rather than go to the private sector.

It could be expected that producers might shift towards the production of uncontrolled small grains such as sorghum and millet. But such grains are labour intensive, are vulnerable to *quelea* attack and do not benefit from substantial consumer demand. For example, local and national markets are poorly integrated and producers struggle to sell surpluses. The effects of decades of promotion of hybrid maize by the Agricultural Research and Extension Trust are difficult to wipe away.

Tobacco used to be Zimbabwe's main national industry and foreign exchange earner, contributing 25–30 per cent of total earnings and at least 6 per cent of total national employment (Woelk et al. 2001). But since 2000 production has collapsed (from 200,000 to less than 50,000 tons per annum), with many of the large-scale white farmers leaving the country to farm elsewhere in the region.

Cotton in many ways mirrors the development of maize production in Zimbabwe, with a highly successful local breeding programme and integrated pest management techniques. At the end of the 1970s, over 90 per cent of Zimbabwe's cotton was produced by large farms. Through the 1980s, government policy supported increased small-holder involvement, and by 1990 smallholders were responsible for over 50 per cent of production (Keeley and Scoones 2003). "Single

Box 5.7 (cont.)

channel" marketing ensured input provision, high-quality produce and competitive prices for growers (Tschirley et al. 2006). This relied on the monopsony enjoyed by the Cotton Marketing Board (CMB), which enabled prices to be fixed through negotiation with the Commercial Farmers Union, and these negotiations delivered farmers the highest prices in the region (Tschirley et al. 2006). During the 1990s, the cotton sector was gradually liberalized but strict quality controls were maintained, and before economic collapse cotton farmers were able to access inputs and seed relatively easily. However, by 2001 out-grower schemes had become increasingly important, because they enabled smallholders to access inputs (Tschirley et al. 2006). Within the context of economic collapse, the conditions of cotton's success – credit, high productivity and excellent-quality cotton exports – have been hard to sustain and there is now a danger that quality control will decline and Zimbabwean cotton will fail to maintain the excellent prices it has enjoyed on world markets.

In the context of market collapse and reduced multinational investment, large-farm to small-farm linkages such as out-grower schemes and conventional contract farming arrangements have taken on a particular significance in Zimbabwe. Cut flowers and horticultural exports dropped to just US$2 million in 2001/2002, but bounced back to US$37.3 million in 2003/2004, at a time when production became increasingly smallholder driven, owing, in part, to the restructuring of the agricultural sector following land reform. In the context of input scarcity, the supply chains of some smallholder horticultural crops have been vertically integrated (Masakure and Henson 2005), and contract farming offers some "islands of normality" in the context of widespread market failure (Shepherd and Prowse 2007).

* In February 2007 the Grain Marketing Board was reportedly buying maize at ZW$52,000 per ton and selling it to politically connected millers at ZW$600 per ton, who then would sell the subsidized maize at exorbitant prices (*Zimbabwe Independent* 2007).

Life history interview with Natalie and Isaac: Reversible ill health and food insecurity?

Natalie (57) and Isaac (66) look after seven grandchildren. Two are orphans, but the others were left with them by their daughters when the children were young because the daughters could not afford to raise them in town. The daughters are having a difficult time and none of them has sent any money for over two years. They do not currently support Natalie and Isaac or even visit their own children, but say they will do so when they have some money. Natalie and Isaac have no money for school fees for the children. Previously one of their sons sent money regularly, but as he has got married he now has other obligations.

In 1999 Isaac lost his job with the dairy board, where he worked as a mechanic. In 2000 Isaac began to have problems with his legs. This illness worsened and he began to have problems walking and now he can walk only very slowly and tentatively, supported with a stick. The local clinic diagnosed high blood pressure, and Isaac received tablets that improved the condition. Unfortunately, the clinic has been unable to supply further tablets, so the condition has deteriorated again. Isaac also has slurred speech, which started in 2002, and a painful shoulder.

Natalie has also been unwell with what she describes as a "sore stomach". Although she received some treatment from the local clinic, this has not cured the symptoms, which are now so severe that she is unable to work. Natalie reported that since they became sick they do not have the strength to farm their land, cultivating only 2 of their 8 acres. This provides them with enough food for only three months of the year. The children are too young to work all the land, but sometimes do casual work for food. The household is regarded as one of the poorest households in their community and over the last couple of years they have received food aid for limited periods from the village headman and the World Food Programme (but this has never been enough to last through to the next harvest and they have had to limit their meals). Figure 5.5 charts Natalie's history.

Growing up in poverty has limited the life chances of Natalie and Isaac's grandchildren. The lack of money for school fees has already resulted in one child dropping out of school. The saddest aspect of this story is that Natalie's and Isaac's health could be easily and cheaply improved through the intervention of a community health worker and the money to pay for transport and treatment. With these simple interventions, the fortunes of the household would be at least partially reversed.

Life history interview with Lovemore and Anna: Raising children in a high-dependency ratio household

Lovemore Samuel Zenzele (74) is the brother of the local chief. Despite this, he was described by others in his village as one of the poorest people they knew. He is very frail and suffers from painful and swollen legs. His wife, Anna (84), has only partial sight in one eye. Between them, they look after five orphaned grandchildren ranging in age from 9 to 20. They struggle to feed the family and to keep the children clothed and in school.

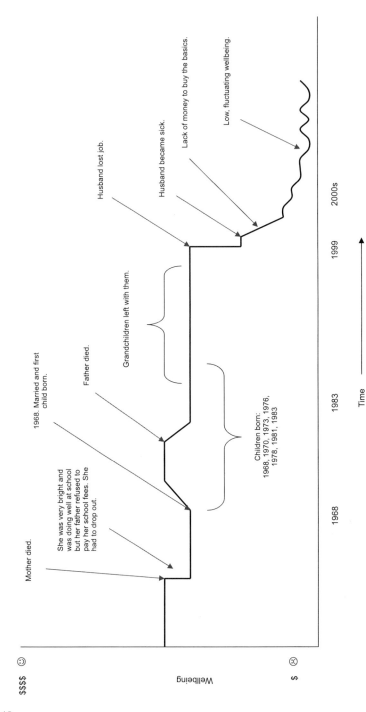

Figure 5.5 Wellbeing map: Natalie Musanhi.

When asked to describe changes in their standard of living over time, Mr and Mrs Zenzele said that they were better off when they were a young couple. During part of their adult life the couple lived in Bulawayo. Their return to Zenzele in 2001 was precipitated by the death of one of their adult daughters. Now responsible for three grandchildren, the couple could not afford to raise them in the city. Soon after, Lovemore lost his job and moved back to the village to join the family. Another daughter died in 2003, leaving two more children to be cared for by the grandparents, who have very limited resources.

The couple have 2–3 acres of land but must rely on others to cultivate it. They depend on the village headman to plough and plant the seeds and on their grandchildren to weed the fields and bring the harvest in. They get support from different people in the community, and have also received food aid from the WFP. Looking to the future, Anna needed treatment for two ailments and has a referral letter from the local clinic, but cannot afford the bus fare to the clinic. Without a more reliable income (or remittances from the children's parents), it is likely the household will continue to be food insecure and that the children will all have to drop out of school, affecting their future life chances. Figure 5.6 charts Lovemore's history.

These two case studies (Natalie and Isaac, and Anna and Lovemore) illustrate how the loss of work in old age can trigger a downward wellbeing trajectory for a whole household. In both cases, wage earners lost jobs at a time when the economy was starting to contract. Without a pension or support from their extended families, the households have had to rely on their limited physical ability to cultivate crops and on the support of members of the community. Moreover, in both cases, the additional needs imparted by an extended household unit have stretched meagre resources, and declining health has limited their ability to maintain the household's food security. The children in these households spend much of each year facing food insecurity and struggle to stay in education. This is likely to have a long-run negative impact on their development. Limited education will be difficult to make up later, and physical stunting and (possible) cognitive impairment caused by long-run malnutrition will be compounded by the absence of energetic and proactive parenting. These children will inherit few, if any, assets, limiting their chances of marriage and future livelihoods. These factors will combine to constrain their chances of escaping poverty.

4 What more can donors do to limit permanent loss of wellbeing?

Should donors provide support to poor people in fragile and failed states? Put bluntly, yes. Without humanitarian intervention and without

150

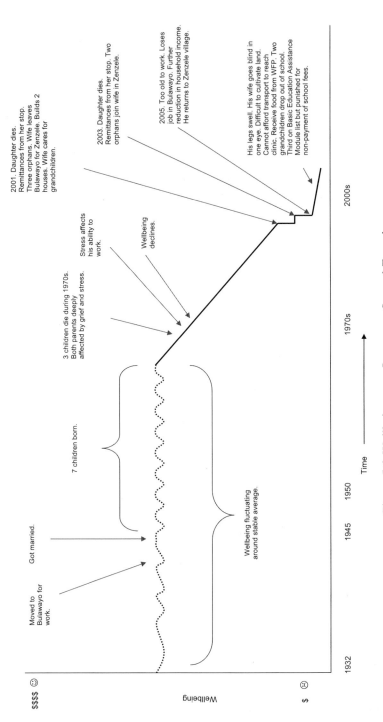

Figure 5.6 Wellbeing map: Lovemore Samuel Zenzele.

the type of intervention that helps to slow the erosion of assets and the decline in livelihoods into adverse forms of coping, the poor and very poor are likely to be driven into long-term poverty that is very difficult to reverse. Therefore, there are strong ethical grounds for providing such support. Many bilateral donors have signed up to the human-rights-based approach to development. For those that have, then "strong but unresponsive" states are just the types of environment in which the key duty bearer (the government) is likely to be abdicating responsibility for delivering the rights of a large proportion of the population. In such a situation, other actors arguably should step in, if they can.

One argument against intervention is that such an act (even through NGO partners and those directly in support of poor communities) will delay regime change. This argument appears to presuppose a route to regime change that, in our opinion, is unproven (i.e. that without humanitarian and development support, the citizenry will rise up to depose despotic leaders and find alternative and more benign leaders to govern the country). Furthermore, evidence suggests that regime change involving violent conflict, rather than broad-based political change, imposes disproportionate costs on the poor, who need longer than other groups in society to rebuild their asset base and to recover pre-conflict levels of wellbeing. Multilateral and bilateral donors need to take great care in thinking through aid modalities for "strong but unresponsive" states. This is particularly so in a country where any external involvement is likely to be interpreted through a politicized and highly partisan lens. As a result, there may be strong arguments for bilateral donors, and in particular DFID, funding interventions to Zimbabwe through the European Union or the UN system.

Notes

1. This figure is based on data collected by the World Health Organization in 2004 and may now be down to 30 years (Howden 2006).
2. The names of all people and many places and organizations have been changed in this chapter to protect anonymity.
3. For further and contrasting approaches to persistent poverty and poverty traps see the Special Issue of the *Journal of Development Studies* (2006: 42(2)) and Bowles et al. (2006).
4. See also Prowse (2003).
5. This section draws in places from Busse (2006).
6. Mining has overtaken agriculture as the main foreign exchange earner in Zimbabwe, with gold contributing half of this. The government plans to take a 51 per cent stake in all new mining investments. For example, Impala Platinum from South Africa has recently invested US$800 million in the attempt to double production at one mine. Whereas formal gold output fell by 30 per cent in 2004, informal mining has seen a boom, with

an estimated 200,000 deriving livelihoods from gold panning. However, the state has clamped down on informal mining to control incomes derived from this livelihood strategy, allegedly arresting over 16,000 informal miners (see *BBC News*, 28 December 2006, at ⟨http://news.bbc.co.uk/1/hi/world/africa/6214431.stm⟩, accessed 22 January 2009).
7. These maps draw on the method of presenting life histories used by Davis (2006).
8. Associated with the suspension of free dipping services and declining access to veterinary services.
9. E.g. to hire transport to take sick family members to hospital or to transport bodies.

References

Addison, T. and L. Laakso (2003). "The Political Economy of Zimbabwe's Descent into Conflict". *Journal of International Development* 15(4): 457–470.

Babirye, D. (1999). *Uganda Participatory Poverty Assessment Progress Report.* Kampala: Ministry of Finance Planning and Economic Development.

Bankoff, G. (2001). "Rendering the World Unsafe: 'Vulnerability' as Western Discourse". *Disasters* 25(1): 19–35.

Barnes, C. (2003). *Microfinance and Households Coping with HIV/AIDS in Zimbabwe: An Exploratory Study.* The Horizon Progam, Management Systems International, University of Zimbabwe, Harare.

Bird, K. and I. Shinyekwa (2005). "Even the 'Rich' Are Vulnerable: Multiple Shocks and Downward Mobility in Rural Uganda". *Development Policy Review* 23(1): 55–85.

Bird, K., P. Hobane and G. Zimbizi (2006). "Community Dynamics and Coping Strategies in Zimbabwe". Synthesis Report, study commissioned by DFID-Zimbabwe.

Bowles, S., S. N. Durlauf and K. Hoff (2006). *Poverty Traps.* New York: Russell Sage Foundation.

Busse, S. (2006) *An Annotated Bibliography on Indigenous Coping Strategies and Community Dynamics in Response to Extreme Poverty and Vulnerability in Zimbabwe.* London: Overseas Development Institute; available at ⟨http://www.odi.org.uk⟩ (accessed 22 January 2009).

Cammack, D., D. McLeod, A. Rocha Menocal, with K. Christiansen (2006). "Donors and the 'Fragile States' Agenda: A Survey of Current Thinking and Practice". ODI Report to JICA, Overseas Development Institute, London.

Chaumba, J., I. Scoones and W. Wolmer (2003). "New Politics, New Livelihoods: Changes in the Zimbabwean Lowveld since the Farm Occupations of 2000". Sustainable Livelihoods in Southern Africa Research Paper 3, Institute of Development Studies, Brighton.

CPRC [Chronic Poverty Research Centre] (2003). *The Chronic Poverty Report 2004/05.* Manchester: Chronic Poverty Research Centre.

Davis, P. (2006). "Poverty in Time: Exploring Poverty Dynamics from Life History Interviews in Bangladesh". CPRC Working Paper 69, Chronic Poverty Research Centre, Manchester.

Dercon, S. (2000). "Income Risk, Coping Strategies and Safety Nets". WPS/2000.26, Centre for the Study of African Economies, Oxford University, Oxford; available at ⟨http://www.csae.ox.ac.uk/workingpapers/pdfs/20-26text.pdf⟩ (accessed 22 January 2009).

Devereux, S. (2001). "Livelihood Insecurity and Social Protection: A Re-emerging Issue in Rural Development". *Development Policy Review* 19(4): 507–519.

DFID [Department for International Development] (2005). "Why We Need to Work More Effectively in Fragile States". Department for International Development, London.

Ellis, F. (2000). *Rural Livelihoods and Diversity in Developing Countries*. Oxford: Oxford University Press.

Evans, G. (2007). "Africa at Risk or Rising? The Role of Europe, North America and Europe on the Continent". Paper presented to the Aspen Atlantic Group/ Stanley Foundation Conference, Berlin, 5 May.

Financial Gazette (2007). 1 March; available at ⟨http://www.fingaz.co.zw/⟩, also available at ⟨http://www.allafrica.com⟩.

Hawkins, T. (2006). "Still Standing: The Economic, Political and Security Situation in Zimbabwe 2006 and Implications for the SADC Region". Paper presented at the Security 2006 conference, The Institute for Strategic Studies, University of Pretoria, Pretoria.

Hewitt, K. (1998). "Excluded Perspectives in the Social Construction of Disaster". In E. L. Quarantelli (ed.), *What Is a Disaster: Perspectives on the Question*. London: Routledge.

Hoddinott, J. (2006). "Shocks and Their Consequences Across and Within Households in Rural Zimbabwe". *Journal of Development Studies* 42(2): 301– 321.

Howden, D. (2006). "Dead by 34: How Aids and Starvation Condemn Zimbabwe's Women to Early Grave". *The Independent*, Online Edition, 17 November; available at ⟨http://www.independent.co.uk/news/world/africa/dead-by-34-how-aids-and-starvation-condemn-zimbabwes-women-to-early-grave-424669. html⟩ (accessed 22 January 2009).

Human Rights Watch (2005). "Zimbabwe: Evicted and Forsaken: Internally Displaced Persons in the Aftermath of Operation Murambatsvina". *Human Rights Watch* 17: 16(A).

IRIN Africa (2007). "ZIMBABWE: Opposition Leaders Picked up by Police", 28 March; available at ⟨http://www.irinnews.org/Report.aspx?ReportId=71013⟩ (accessed 22 January 2009).

Keeley, J. and I. Scoones (2003). "Seeds in a Globalized World: Agricultural Biotechnology in Zimbabwe". IDS Working Paper 189, Institute of Development Studies, Brighton.

Kinsey, B. H. (2004). "Zimbabwe's Land Reform Program: Underinvestment in Post-Conflict Transformation". *World Development* 32(10): 1669–1696.

Marcus, R. and J. Wilkinson (2002). "Whose Poverty Matters? Vulnerability, Social Protection and PRSPs". Childhood Poverty Research and Policy Centre Working Paper 1, Institute of Development Policy and Management, University of Manchester, Manchester.

Masakure, O. and S. Henson (2005). "Why Do Small-Scale Producers Choose to Produce under Contract? Lessons from Nontraditional Vegetable Exports from Zimbabwe". *World Development* 33(10): 1721–1733.

Mijumbi, P. and J. Okidi (2001). "Analysis of Poor and Vulnerable Groups in Uganda". Occasional Paper 16, Economic Policy Research Centre, with support from DFID, Kampala.

Moser, C. (1998). "The Asset Vulnerability Framework: Reassessing Urban Poverty Reduction Strategies". *World Development* 26(1): 1–19.

Murray, C. (2002). "Livelihoods Research: Transcending Boundaries of Time and Space". *Journal of Southern African Studies* 28(3): 489–509.

Murshed, S. M. (2006) "Turning Swords to Ploughshares & Little Acorns to Tall Trees: The Conflict–Growth Nexus & the Poverty of Nations". Mimeo, The Birmingham Business School, Birmingham; available at ⟨http://www.un.org/esa/policy/backgroundpapers/conflict_growthnexus_murshed.pdf⟩ (accessed 22 January 2009).

Potts, D. (2006). "'Restoring Order?' Operation Murambatsvina and the Urban Crisis in Zimbabwe". *Journal of Southern African Studies* 32(2): 273–291.

Proudlock, K. (2007). "Zimbabwe Media Digest". Overseas Development Institute, London.

Prowse, M. (2003). "Towards a Clearer Understanding of Vulnerability in Relation to Chronic Poverty". CPRC Working Paper 24, Chronic Poverty Research Centre, Manchester.

Rohrbach, D., R. Charters and J. Nyagweta (2004). "Guidelines for Emergency Relief Projects in Zimbabwe: Seed and Fertilizer Relief". ICRISAT, Bulawayo.

Sachikonye, L. (2003). "Land Reform for Poverty Reduction? Social Exclusion and Farm Workers in Zimbabwe". Paper presented at the IDMP conference on Staying Poor: Chronic Poverty and Development Policy, April, Manchester.

Scarnecchia, T. (2006). "'The Fascist Cycle' in Zimbabwe, 2000–2005". *Journal of Southern African Studies* 32(2): 221–37.

Shepherd, A. and M. Prowse (2007). "Agricultural Growth, Poverty Dynamics and Markets". Background paper for Second Chronic Poverty Report, Overseas Development Institute, London.

Sinha, S. and M. Lipton (1999). "Damaging Fluctuations, Risk and Poverty: A Review". Background Paper for the World Development Report 2000/2001, Poverty Research Unit, University of Sussex, Brighton.

Tibaijuka, A. K. (2005). "Report of the Fact-Finding Mission to Zimbabwe to Assess the Scope and Impact of Operation Murambatsvina". UN Special Envoy on Human Settlements Issues in Zimbabwe; available at ⟨http://www.unhabitat.org/downloads/docs/1664_96507_ZimbabweReport.pdf⟩ (accessed 22 January 2009).

Torres, M. M. and M. Anderson (2004). "Fragile States: Defining Difficult Environments for Poverty Reduction". PRDE Working Paper 1, Poverty Reduction in Difficult Environments Team Policy Division, DFID, London.

Tschirley, D., C. Poulton and D. Boughton (2006). "The Many Paths of Cotton Sector Reform in Eastern and Southern Africa: Lessons from a Decade of Experience". MSU International Development Working Paper 88, Department of Agricultural Economics and the Department of Economics, Michigan State University, East Lansing.

Warrener, D. and C. Loehr (2005). "Working Effectively in Fragile States:

Current Thinking in the UK". ODI Synthesis Paper 7, Overseas Development Institute, London.

Woelk, G., S. Mtisi and P. J. Vaughan (2001). "Prospects for Tobacco Control in Zimbabwe: A Historical Perspective". *Health Policy* 57(3): 179–192.

Zimbabwe Independent (2007). "Mugabe Faces Dilemma", 26 February.

ZimOnline (2007). "Traditional Leaders Say 'Will Not Feed the Enemy'", 31 January; available at ⟨http://www.zimonline.co.za/Article. aspx?ArticleId=808⟩ (accessed 22 January 2009).

6

Vulnerability dynamics and HIV risk in the semi-arid tropics of rural Andhra Pradesh

B. Valentine Joseph Gandhi, Ma. Cynthia Serquiña Bantilan and Devanathan Parthasarathy

1 Introduction

In life, the only certainty is death. The uncertainty in this is only when and how it occurs. Human beings have always striven to delay the occurrence of death and to improve the ways in which they live by adopting different livelihood options or strategies. These often involve risk. The risks can be natural or human made, some within our control and some not. The success or failure of these mechanisms largely depend on social, cultural, economic and even natural factors. The context for this chapter is the onset of the HIV/AIDS epidemic in an already fragile natural environment of the semi-arid tropics, where the people are predominantly dependent on agriculture for their livelihoods.

2 The semi-arid tropics of India

India's semi-arid tropics (SAT), like most regions in the developing world, are affected by the low productivity of rain-fed agriculture, the changing globalized environment, scarcity of water and degradation of productive resources (land and biodiversity). They are also characterized by incomplete insurance markets, fragmented rural financial markets and a rudimentary or non-existent future price market. This leads to production risks and a heavy toll on the welfare of the people of SAT (Walker and Ryan 1990). The semi-arid tropics are plagued by uncertain rainfall,

Vulnerability in developing countries, Naudé, Santos-Paulino and McGillivray (eds), United Nations University Press, 2009, ISBN 978-92-808-1171-1

on which agricultural production is largely dependent, infertile soils, poor infrastructure, extreme poverty, rapid population growth and high risks. Natural resource base degradation, poor infrastructure and changes in demand and production patterns aggravate the already high levels of risk. Despite numerous determined efforts, poverty and hunger persist (Rao et al. 2005). The SAT regions have yet to benefit from the agricultural transformation process of the green revolution. Given the complexity of the problems and the vastness of the task, more innovative and effective approaches are urgently needed, especially in targeting the poor sectors. It is important to recognize that the poor have developed unique coping strategies to secure their livelihoods. These vary from household to household, and depend on factors such as socioeconomic status, education and local knowledge, ethnicity and the life-cycle phase of the household (Walker and Ryan 1990). In terms of livelihood risks, people adapt a set of mechanisms to cope with these risks, with migration being the major alternative, because it is available to people at all income levels (Bantilan and Anupama 2002). The dynamics of the semi-arid tropics, particularly on the vulnerability of rural households in the semi-arid region of south India to aggregate and idiosyncratic risks, were discussed in Chapter 2, which was based on the longitudinal panel data for 1975–1984 of the village-level studies of the International Crops Research Institute for the Semi-Arid Tropics (ICRISAT). This chapter is an update of the current scenarios pertaining to risk and vulnerability in these fragile lands.

2.1 HIV/AIDS in India's SAT

South Asia is home to the second-largest number of HIV/AIDS-infected people and has one of the fastest infection rates in the world. HIV prevalence rates are still rather low, but the huge population of the region translates these into large numbers. India accounted for half a million new infections in 2003. All over South Asia there are concentrated epidemics among vulnerable groups, closing fast the window of opportunity that exists for its prevention. Globally, India ranks second in terms of the percentage of infections and first in absolute levels. The National AIDS Control Organization of India's sentinel surveillance has shown that the high-prevalence zones of HIV are in the states of Andhra Pradesh, Tamil Nadu, Maharashtra and Karnataka – the heartland of the semi-arid tropics. Among these, Andhra Pradesh has the highest prevalence of HIV, with 2 per cent of the population infected (NIHFW and NACO 2006: 12). The epidemiological surveillance estimates that, on a national level, the infection rate in the rural areas is 57 per cent, or 5.2 million people, representing 0.91 per cent of India's population. AIDS statistics may be a poor indication of the severity of the epidemic, as in many cases the patient will die without being diagnosed with HIV and with the cause of death attributed to an opportunistic infection, such as tuberculosis.

2.2 Migration and HIV/AIDS

As the epidemic spreads, the link between migration and HIV is emerging more strongly than ever before. A study by the United Nations Development Programme in partnership with PLWHA (people living with HIV/AIDS) groups in the Asia Pacific region shows that nearly 67 per cent of the respondents said that migration was the main factor leading to their HIV vulnerability and that better access to information and services could have helped to protect them (UNDP 2005). Studies on South Africa have documented migration as an independent individual risk factor for acquiring HIV in a wide range of settings (Boerma et al. 2002). Although there are no nationally representative data sets on seasonal migration and other kinds of short-term mobility, rough estimates put the number of seasonal workers in India at about 30 million (Deshingkar 2006). This, however, is likely to be a gross underestimate. The International Labour Organization, for instance, estimates that there are up to 50 million males working in brick kilns across India. If their female partners (workers are often recruited in couples) are included, the number doubles. There are many other important sectors and subsectors (construction, stone quarries, diamond polishing, salt panning, rickshaw pulling, restaurants/cafes, road construction, crop transplantation and harvesting, plantations and prawn processing) that attract large numbers of transitory workers.

Similar patterns are also seen across the Asian countries, with high growth rates, marked regional inequalities and limited prospects for diversification in rural areas. Permanent rural–urban migration has also increased, but the recent trend definitely indicates an increase in seasonal migration from the marginal areas (semi-arid, drought prone, degraded forest areas, etc.) to the "hot spots" of high productivity (Deshingkar 2006).

According to UNAIDS (the Joint United Nations Programme on HIV/AIDS), "being mobile in and of itself is not a risk factor for HIV infection. It is the situations encountered and the behaviours possibly engaged in during mobility or migration that increase vulnerability and risk regarding HIV/AIDS" (UNAIDS 2001). Living and working away from home and apart from one's regular sexual partner, as well as the uprooting and the movement of so many migrant men and women in their primary, sexually active age, have undoubtedly created conditions that are conducive to sexual promiscuity and commercial sex. Gelmon et al. (2006) say that migration does not necessarily change an individual's

sexual behaviour, but it leads them to take their established sexual behaviour to areas where there is a higher prevalence of HIV. For some individuals, however, migration does change their sexual behaviour. Long
working hours, isolation from their family and movement between different locations may increase the likelihood of casual relationships, which in
turn increase the risk of HIV transmission. Cultural and language bar-
riers can also make it harder for workers to access information and sexual health services when they are away from their home communities.

2.3 The impact of HIV in rural households

The consequences of HIV infection range from having to give up the cultivation of remote fields or cash crops, to the sale of assets to cover medical and funeral expenses. Typically, the effect of the HIV impact occurs
when a migrant worker falls ill while away, uses his savings for medical
treatment and then returns to the farm household to be cared for and to
die. By attacking able-bodied, active adolescents and adults, HIV/AIDS
undermines the security of the farm household through the direct loss of
farm labour and of the time available for farm and household tasks. To
cope with this, the farm household has to reallocate both available labour
and the time of other household members. The welfare of the farm
household is also threatened through unexpected costs of caring for the
sick and the loss of remittances, which can lead to the sale of assets, animals or land. Documented evidence on the effects of HIV on agriculture
by the Regional Network on HIV/AIDS, Rural Livelihoods and Food Security (RENEWAL) highlights the following:
- promiscuous sexual relations and mobility;
- infection increases nutritional demands;
- the loss of agricultural knowledge resulting from the death of parents is
  creating the so-called "missing generation";
- poverty affects people's ability to respond to the consequences of
  AIDS;
- illness and death push households into deeper poverty, creating additional burdens;
- community safety nets become strained;
- information networks do not extend to the most seriously affected sectors (Gillespie and Kadiyala 2005).
  The role of farming systems and/or agricultural communities is also reviewed in ICRISAT's studies on Africa (Alumira et al. 2005). A few findings are summarized below:
Vulnerability to HIV/AIDS: Of the households under review, 65 per
  cent in Tsholotsho were HIV/AIDS infected and 58 per cent in Kezi.
  Women-headed families accounted for 46 per cent of households in
  Tsholotsho (where the mean number of resident household members

was six) and 45 per cent in Kezi (mean of seven resident members). In all, 30 per cent of Tsholotsho households and 41 per cent of Kezi households had taken in at least one orphan.

Poverty: When poverty was assessed in terms of relative wealth, with cattle ownership as the main denominator, 70 per cent of the households in each study district were classified as poor. The wealth categories were: the poor owned 0–4 head of cattle; the medium rich owned 5–10 head of cattle, and the rich or very rich owned over 11 head of cattle. Poverty was widespread.

Food production: Both cereals and legumes were produced. Generic crops (maize, sorghum, millet, groundnuts, bambara nuts) were cultivated by most households. Vulnerable households relied heavily on subsistence production for their livelihood.

Livestock production: HIV/AIDS-afflicted households tended to have fewer livestock than other households. Close to half of the HIV-infected households had no cattle. Smaller animals, mainly goats, sheep and chickens, followed a similar distribution. In Tsholotsho, 32 per cent of the households had no goats, 41 per cent owned a few goats (1–5) and 27 per cent owned more than 6 goats. These results show that targeted restocking for these households is essential.

Farm labour and draught power constraints: The lack of draught power was a key constraint: 56 per cent of the rich households in Tsholotsho owned at least two draught animals (78 per cent in Kezi), whereas only 19 per cent of the poor in Tsholotsho owned at least two draught animals. Although most households owned ploughs, many were not functional because the paucity of cash income prevented repairs. The mean number of adults over the age of 14 years was used as a proxy for labour: the mean number of adults per household was three in Tsholotsho and four in Kezi; the mean number of children under 14 years was three in both villages. Human labour was constrained by household health status.

Disease prevalence: There was a high incidence of illness in the communities, mainly HIV/AIDS-related opportunistic infections. In Tsholotsho, illnesses in order of importance were malaria (45 per cent), tuberculosis (26 per cent) and herpes and rheumatism (6 per cent); in Kezi, the corresponding occurrences were malaria (21 per cent), tuberculosis (34 per cent) and herpes and rheumatism (26 per cent). Ill health constrained farm production.

Dependency ratios: The dependency burden was assessed using dependency ratios as a proxy. The majority of vulnerable households (94 per cent in Tsholotsho and 86 per cent in Kezi) had up to three dependants per active adult and thus belonged to the moderate to high dependency categories. Dependency ratios were also calculated on the basis of gender (of the household head). Most female-headed households had high dependency ratios in both locations, whereas most male-headed households belonged to the moderate dependency category.

ICRISAT's comprehensive research in sub-Saharan Africa offers the potential to learn from these generic lessons, which could be of great value in India too in devising suitable development policy. A similar comprehensive strategy is needed for India. Even though national HIV infection levels in India are low compared with Africa, the country's vast population size translates even low national HIV prevalence into large numbers of infected people.

2.4 The risk-to-risk framework

In this context, the study explores the linkages between livelihood diversification and health, specifically with regard to the nature of risk behaviour pertaining to HIV infection, by attempting to identify who is most vulnerable and why. The study develops a theoretical framework from existing studies to guide the research process (see Figure 6.1).

This broad framework was formulated from a review of the literature on semi-arid tropics, migration and HIV/AIDS in India and Africa. It encompasses the broad linkages in rural SAT, where the dominance of agriculture as the major livelihood option has decreased, and discusses

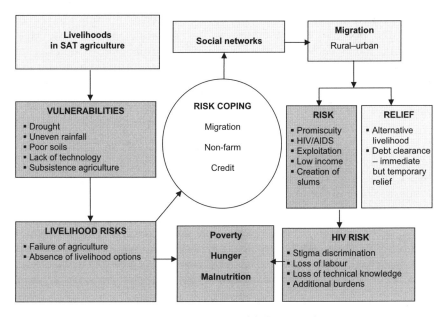

Figure 6.1 The risk-to-risk framework.

the dynamic interplay between these components and their outcomes. In the rural semi-arid tropics of Andhra Pradesh, livelihoods have predominantly been, and still are, based on rain-fed agriculture. Over the last three decades, agriculture in SAT has been threatened by persistent drought. The semi-arid tropics are home to the poorest people on the Indian subcontinent (Rao et al. 2005). Despite efforts by national and international organizations and the adoption of scientific research to develop a grey to green revolution, India's SAT has been largely ignored. This has caused livelihood insecurity for the rural households living in these areas. Agricultural failure leads to a loss of livelihood for the farmers and labourers working in farming. This, in turn, leads to poverty and hunger in an already fragile zone. According Walker and Ryan (1990), Bantilan and Anupama (2002) and Gandhi (2003), the major coping mechanism of the farming communities confronted by drought and the absence of livelihoods is migration. Migration offers immediate relief and a steady income, but it is not a permanent solution because it exposes the migrants to risks. Seasonal workers in India are not required to register in their destination locations; they are an unorganized sector, so they cannot claim benefits other than what has informally been agreed with them. This paves the way for exploitation. In addition, migration intensifies the risk of contracting HIV and sexually transmitted infections (Gelmon et al. 2006).

The impacts of HIV infection on rural households are many: agriculture is particularly threatened by the pandemic, given the implications of diminished labour power for the ability of affected households, particularly the poor, to feed themselves. A large-scale influx of the HIV epidemic might cause the already fragile environments to deteriorate further. Studies from Africa (which is comparable to India) highlight the strong linkages between HIV and migration. Studies examining this phenomenon are lacking for the SAT and are urgently needed. The vast size of the SAT in India makes it difficult to examine the effects of HIV or the nature of HIV risk behaviour, because the majority of Indian states have larger populations than most African countries. So, as an exploratory attempt, this study will examine these broad linkages from a micro perspective with a case study of Doruk, one of the SAT villages in Andhra Pradesh. Some of the findings are presented here.

3 Methodology

3.1 Approach and objectives

Theorists have previously tried to find an explanation for the rapid spread of HIV/AIDS in (southern) Africa. For example, Hunt (1996) distinguishes between theories based on *biological explanations* and those based on *social explanations*. The first category emphasizes a biological determination of the HIV/AIDS epidemic, whereas the second category has a historical, materialist or cultural nature. Webb (1997) further distinguishes between different approaches within social epidemiology. The structuralist approach emphasizes the importance of structures or macro issues, as these economic and political processes (e.g. the debt crisis, poverty, urbanization and government policy) influence the AIDS epidemic (Webb 1997: 31). This approach places epidemiology in a historical, economic-political context and has a strong focus on the power relations within society. According to the structuralist approach, individual human behaviour is partially determined by global economic and political structures that have an impact at the international and national levels, but also at the local level (Webb 1997; Lurie 2001). At the opposite end of the spectrum is the *anthropological approach*, which examines the heterosexual spread of HIV from a bio-anthropological point of view, in which cultural variables are the main objects of study (Webb 1997: 29) and the focus is on sexuality and the psychology of individual (sexual) behaviour. It is in this context that some theorists refer to the promiscuity of African men and the tolerance of African societies towards multiple sexual partners.

The danger inherent in the structuralist and anthropological approaches, however, is that both have the same deterministic nature. The former implies that, in any given area with the same structures, people develop similar behaviour patterns (for example, an individual migrating alone may be more promiscuous than the seasonal worker who migrates with his wife). The latter approach can easily lead to ethnocentrism and universalism that will over-simplify real life situations or deny the heterogeneity of societies. Moreover, the biased focus on the cultural and psychological elements of society ignores the importance of political and economic structures and their impact on the spread of HIV/AIDS. Neither approach on its own is able to explain the local and regional diversity in sexual behaviour (Webb 1997: 30–32).

There are no such theoretical studies in the context of the Indian SAT, however. From the African context (which is quite similar and comparable to the Indian SAT in terms of poverty and agro-ecological climate), it can be noted that the spread of HIV is determined not only by psychological factors but also by sociological, economic, political and historical factors. Webb conceptualizes the social epidemiology of HIV as the study of the constantly changing interrelationship between culture, the actions of the individual and sociopolitical factors. Thus the methodology for this study was formulated by exploring the interplay of the different factors that facilitate the spread of HIV and not merely by examining the numbers infected.

The objective of analysis in this chapter was to understand the interaction between livelihood insecurities, HIV infection risk and migrant vulnerability. This chapter is part of a larger study that seeks to find answers to the following questions:
(i)   To what extent do livelihood insecurities in the semi-arid tropics lead to migration?
(ii)   What are the risk behaviours of migrant workers in the context of livelihood insecurity?
(iii)   What are the implications of the migration and risk behaviour nexus for rural households?

The migration and risk behaviour nexus will be presented in this chapter.

3.2 Data

The study used three sources of primary data in analysing the vulnerability of rural livelihoods in risk-prone regions of Andhra Pradesh, India. The first source was longitudinal panel data developed by ICRISAT for the period 1975–2001 covering two villages in the semi-arid tropics. In particular, the modules on sources of income, livelihoods and measures of welfare were covered for the period 1975–1984, and census data from 2001 were also used. These data assisted our understanding of the changes in livelihoods from 1975 to the present day. The second primary data source was the hospital records of the Voluntary Counseling and Testing Centre (VCTC) in Bhongir, Nalgonda. The hospital receives patients from the surrounding semi-arid villages. The data consisted of 6,000 hospital records of individual patients spread over a period of four years (2002–2005). These data were used to draw inferences about the risk behaviour of individuals from farming communities. The third data source was the case study: one village in Dokur was selected based on the preliminary analysis, which highlighted the relatively high level of HIV/AIDS and migration in this village. A random sample of 30 per cent of the entire village comprising 497 households was chosen. In addition, extensive qualitative data were also used in the case study.

3.3 Area of study

Located in the heartland of the semi-arid Andhra Pradesh, Mahbubnagar is the most backward district of the state. It has a population of 3.5 million, and is perennially plagued by drought, resulting in a high incidence of seasonal migration. Dokur village, in particular, has a high incidence of poverty-related mobility and a number of HIV/AIDS cases were observed earlier (Gandhi 2004). The presence of the Institute for Rural

Health Studies (IRHS) in Dokur provided an additional advantage to studying health factors in the village. In 2003, the "lab", as the villagers popularly call it, reported eight HIV-positive cases among the migrant workers. Given the increase in migration and HIV cases being reported, Dokur was ideal for studying the dynamics involved within this context.

3.4 Sampling method in Dokur

Dokur was one of the villages included in the ICRISAT longitudinal data sets, known as the village-level studies or VLS, and was studied during 1975 to 1989 and revisited in 2001. This led to Dokur's household census in 2001, which we updated, and a stratified random sample obtained from this population census. The stratification was based on the holding of land, the transitory status of the people and gender.

The sample covered 30 per cent of the total population of Dokur village. The village had 497 households, of which 149 were selected for the quantitative survey. These were further stratified according to their migration status and gender, so that 30 per cent from each household group – the migrating and non-migrating families – were identified for the sample.

In addition to the quantitative survey, 21 key informant interviews were conducted, and 4 focus groups plus 2 social mapping exercises were carried out. These provided the basis for gathering qualitative data to complement the formal surveys.

3.5 Research tools

Quantitative and qualitative tools were used to elucidate the data, namely: (i) formal surveys (13 modules broadly covering aspects of socio-demography, livelihoods, asset base, general/sexual health status and practices, HIV awareness, the impact of migration and the effect of external interventions); (ii) focus group discussions and interviews with key informants (covering wealth perception ranking, livelihood ranking, HIV/AIDS awareness, the impact of interventions, migration and risk behaviour); and (iii) social mapping.

3.6 Ethical problems in field research

Consent from the respondents is considered to be an important aspect of conducting ethical research (Wang and Huch 2000; Holmes-Rovner and Wills 2002). Bearing this in mind, prior to the discussions, interviews and questionnaire the respondents were clearly advised of the reasons for the research. It was emphasized that the questionnaire was for research purposes only and that the information would on no account be shared with a third party. The research process was outlined and the consent of the respondents was requested before proceeding to the questionnaire phase. Respondents were cooperative and answered patiently, although at times the pre-interview explanations took as long as the actual process of the interview. ICRISAT had established a rapport with the villagers of Dokur that had spanned 30 years. During the course of the study, additional efforts were made to maintain that rapport. The research team organized a review camp, which was open to all village households but targeted the poorest families in particular. This was done to assure the villagers that it was a question of their health and that they should answer honestly.

4 Results and discussion

The results of the hospital data provided an insight into rural livelihoods and HIV linkages in the SAT. The primary data from the VCTC were analysed to determine the nature of the prevalence in the SAT areas and the types of risk behaviour people were exposed to. The results are presented here, followed by the observations from the Dokur case study.

4.1 Results from the analysis of the VCTC data for Bhongir

Two sets of data were gathered from the VCTC in Bhongir: one set was from the case records and the other constituted the ethnographic case-study data for each HIV-positive patient as recorded by the local HIV counsellor. To ensure confidentiality and protect the identities of the patients, no names were revealed and only the batch identification numbers were utilized. The majority of the patients were from the rural region even though the area hospital was located on a semi-urban site. A large number of the patients were farmers, agricultural labourers and migrant workers, and the wives/widows and children of migrants.

The VCTC case studies recorded by the counsellor revealed a new dimension of rural livelihoods in the surrounding areas. In India, intimate relations are a taboo subject and are not discussed in public, even less so in the rural areas. Discussing them in public would mean being shunned by society. However, a review of the VCTC case studies from the Bhongir area hospital changes one's perception of rural society – old assumptions fade and new dimensions emerge. The cases under review all concerned HIV-1 reactive or HIV-positive individuals. The counsellor at the centre recorded the patients' quantitative data according to a guide for collecting ethnographic data. Questions were largely related to the patients' sexual behaviour and their knowledge of the epidemic and of the treatment procedures available. These were collated by the researcher and categorized according to social group, sexual behaviour, perceptions of HIV/AIDS, nutritional status and stigma. The aim of this pilot study was to understand the nature and prevalence of HIV in the SAT.

Sexual behaviour

Seasonal migrants: Migrants generally constituted those villagers who reported agriculture as their primary occupation but who had been forced to migrate because of the difficulties of farming being able to provide them with a reliable source of livelihood. The group also included a few lorry drivers or tractor drivers and their spouses as well. The pattern of sexual networks among migrants was evident from the Bhongir VCTC cases. All of the HIV-1 reactive migrants had had regular/irregular partners outside their marriage; some had even had relations prior to their marriage (extramarital and premarital). Women were also actively involved in premarital and extramarital affairs but to a lesser degree than men. The infected women were mostly housewives or agricultural labourers; very few were actually involved as commercial sex workers. It was mainly the men who transmitted the disease: all the infected men had been involved with at least two regular partners other than their wife. However, there were a few incidents in which the wife had been the one with extramarital affairs and had transmitted the disease to her husband despite warnings by the counsellor. There were also cases where men who had tested positive got married, not heeding the advice given by the counsellor to postpone the marriage. Soon their wives tested positive as well. They reported that this was done to avoid community stigma. Both men and women kept silent about their HIV status, letting the other suffer.

Non-migrating residents: In the case of non-migrating respondents, sexual partners had usually been co-workers in the fields or neighbours. Most of the non-migrating but HIV-infected people were agricultural labourers. Some were shopkeepers.

Although some of the patients reported that they had had multiple intimate partners and had not used condoms, the majority said that they had acquired the disease through shared needles. According to the counsellor, this was an attempt to disguise extramarital affairs, because of the social stigma and taboo attached to HIV/AIDS. People felt more comfortable declaring that they shared needles rather than confessing to extramarital relationships. Most of the infected women claimed that they had shared needles, which is interesting because in the rural areas of India there are not many cases of users injecting drugs; these are primarily in urban markets or in the states of Manipur and Assam.

Perceptions and misconceptions about HIV/AIDS

Most of VCTC patients were aware or had at least heard of the epidemic, and were also knowledgeable about its modes of transmission. There were very few people who actually had not heard of HIV/AIDS, but some believed that it was punishment by the gods for a misdeed in their previous life. A few considered it to be sorcery or witchcraft. Some others said that it had been transmitted when they had cared for an HIV/AIDS patient. A few women expressed fears that they might have contracted the disease because they had been in close contact with an infected relative. Astrologers and ayurvedic practitioners were misleading people by claiming, first, that the disease was a phase that would eventually pass, and, second, that it was curable. They treated gullible patients with "Kerala medicine".

Perceptions about condoms

Among the respondents who had been tested reactive, condoms were scarcely ever used for the following reasons:
- they had no knowledge about using them;
- they thought their pleasure would suffer;
- the wife was suspicious about the behaviour of the husband each time he suggested a condom (she would ask: why do you want to use a condom? have you had sex with another woman? why are you afraid?);
- the opportunity of a sexual partner could not always be planned for because it happens by chance, and condoms were not available all the time;
- the social structure in India prevents women from having a say with regard to their husband's sexual habits – most wives were afraid to insist on a condom;
- men did not bother to use a condom when intoxicated.

Nutritional status

Almost all of the HIV-positive respondents were very poor and came from farming or agricultural backgrounds. According to the counsellor's records, the respondents lived in dire poverty, unable to pay even the minimal fee of Rs10 for the HIV test, so the area hospital did the test free for them. They also lacked access to sufficient food, not to mention a nutritious diet. In HIV-infected households, a sick member meant a push into deeper despair.

Stigma

It was evident from the respondents' answers that HIV/AIDS-infected people were not well looked after. On the contrary, they were stigmatized and isolated from society – the husband throwing out his wife, or the wife having to move back to her parents' house after discovering her spouse's infection. There were cases where the husband had died and the wife fell prey to the wrath of the in-laws; her children were mistreated in school and on the street while she struggled to find a job. The phenomenon of the "missing generation" observed in Africa is also emerging in rural India, where entire families have been wiped out by HIV/AIDS, perhaps leaving a small child as the sole survivor to live with the grandparents, who may themselves be too old to take care of themselves, let alone the child. This leads to further exploitation and loss of agricultural knowledge and labour power, which in turn affects the agriculture base of that particular area.

In the rest of this section we explore the HIV issue further, i.e. the number of people visiting the centre, the social group of the patients and the types of risk behaviour, as analysed from the VCTC quantitative records. During 2002, there had been 428 visitors to the centre, but this figure more than tripled in the following year (Figure 6.2). Among these visitors, the number of HIV-reactive cases for the entire year of 2002 was 25, but had gradually and consistently increased to 200 reactive patients as of September 2005 (Figure 6.3).

Even though the VCTC was in a peri-urban locality, visitors were predominantly from the agricultural labour population (Table 6.1). This corresponds to the findings of the National AIDS Control Organization's sentinel surveillance, which observes that the epidemic spreads faster in rural areas. As detailed in Table 6.2, the most common explanation given for the VCTC visit was multiple intimate partners, followed closely by shared needles. However, as explained by the counsellor, the report of

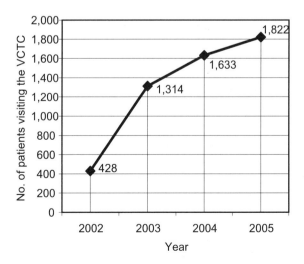

Figure 6.2 Total number of visitors to the VCTC, 2002–2005.

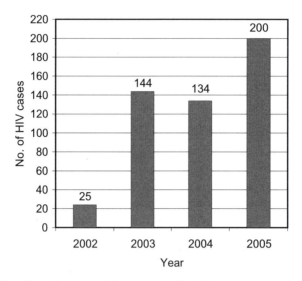

Figure 6.3 Number of HIV-positive cases, 2002–2005.
Source: Computed by the authors based on data collected during field research.

shared needles was an attempt to disguise the reality of multiple sex partners and was considered to be less damaging to the reputation.

From the VCTC study in Bhongir, it was possible to get an understanding of the prevalence of HIV among the rural population. In addition, it
was also possible to gain insights into the nature of risk behaviour. However, developments at the village level could be observed only through
an in-depth analysis aimed at bridging the gaps between rural livelihoods
and HIV linkages. The results from the primary data collected in connec-
tion with the case study for the Dokur village provide additional information on these dynamics.

4.2 Dokur village case study

Evolution of livelihoods, risks and coping strategies

Two decades ago, the major livelihood in Dokur was agriculture and
related farm labour (Jodha et al. 1977). Based on an examination of
the 1975 ICRISAT panel data set, Jodha et al. argued that small farm
households were likely to have more than one source of income. They
suggested that, where landholdings were small, households were more
vulnerable to the exigencies of drought and unreliable yields. Diversification of resource use, particularly family labour use, was one way to
supplement risky returns from the land. In terms of operational land-

Table 6.1 Patients visiting the VCTC, by occupational group, 2002–2005 (per cent)

Occupational group	2002				2003				2004				2005			
	Male	Female	Reactive male	Reactive female	Male	Female	Reactive male	Reactive female	Male	Female	Reactive male	Reactive female	Male	Female	Reactive male	Reactive female
Migrant labourer	42	22	29	0	20	15	21	14	37	13	28	16	27	18	24	9
Agricultural worker	24	41	57	57	42	30	46	42	36	31	61	37	33	30	47	47
Business	24	7	14	0	10	1	9	0	0	0	0	0	12	0	8	3
Dependant	0	0	0	0	8	2	9	2	0	0	0	0	8	2	16	5
Housewife	0	29	0	29	0	51	0	38	0	55	0	40	0	46	0	27
Student	9	0	0	14	20	2	15	4	28	2	11	7	20	3	5	9

Source: Compiled by the authors.

Table 6.2 Risk behaviour of visitors to the VCTC, 2002–2005 (per cent)

Declared risk behaviour	2002	2003	2004	2005
Multiple sex partners	83	50	41	49
Sharing needles	14	32	29	10
Child of HIV-infected parents	0	8	9	12
Blood transfusion	0	7	11	9
Others	3	3	10	20

Source: Compiled by the authors.

Table 6.3 Livelihood diversification in Dokur, 1975 and 2001 (per cent)

	2001	1975
Agricultural income		
Net crop income	10.40	46.10
Net livestock income	9.25	2.00
Farm/casual labour	6.52	46.30
Regular farm worker	1.21	–
Rental	–	2.20
Total agricultural income	27.38	96.60
Non-farm income		
Non-farm wages	1.33	–
Net migration labour	25.34	–
Remittances	0.20	–
Salaried jobs	4.75	–
Caste occupation	6.15	–
Business/trade and handicrafts	7.58	1.10
Other	27.27	2.30
Total non-farm income	72.62	3.40

Sources: Deb et al. (2002) for 2001; Jodha et al. (1977) for 1975.

holdings, households in all landholding groups, including the landless, diversified between 1975 and 2001. But, beyond this broad trend, it is difficult to discern any other pattern with respect to levels of diversification. If Jodha et al. are correct in their observation that diversification is a response to risk, then it becomes apparent from the 2001 census that all households, and not just small farmholdings, faced risks in agriculture and diversified in order to reduce their vulnerability. Table 6.3, showing the difference in livelihoods between 1975 and 2001, indicates that migration has gained importance as a major livelihood option in Dokur. As Table 6.4 indicates, the migration trend over the next five years did not decrease but, rather to the contrary, increased from 36 per cent of the

Table 6.4 Migration in Dokur, 2001 and 2006

	Migrating households		Non-migrating households		Total households
	No.	%	No.	%	No.
Census 2001	185	36	330	64	515
Census 2006	208	42	289	58	497[a]

Source: Compiled by the authors.
Note:
[a]The total number of households in the village dropped because 14 families moved permanently to Hyderabad and 4 households consisted of elderly people who had passed away.

Table 6.5 People's perception of how livelihood options have changed in their village

Occupation two decades ago	Present occupation
Agriculture	Migration
Farm labour	Agriculture
Livestock	Business (shops, real estate, labour contracts, etc.)
Caste occupation	Farm labour
Migration	Livestock
Business (shops, etc.)	Caste occupation

Source: Compiled by the authors.

households having at least one migrating member in 2001 to 42 per cent in 2006. Usually, the migrating member was the head of the household and his or her spouse.

During the focus group discussions and key informant interviews, the study concentrated on elucidating people's own perception of how livelihoods had changed and the reason for the change. The responses are grouped in Table 6.5. The villagers considered migration to be a livelihood option that is easily available to all. Given the semi-arid climate of Dokur, livelihoods had been dominated by the effects of persistent drought. Migration became a regular alternative strategy two decades ago with the onset of successive drought seasons. However, people had migrated as early as 30 years ago, particularly lorry drivers, those with contract jobs in the city, or army personnel. Large-scale organized migration began in Dokur only during the last 15 years. As Figure 6.4 indicates, migration increased considerably after 1993 and has continued to expand since then. This signifies the absence of livelihood options in the village and opportunities for better income offered by migration.

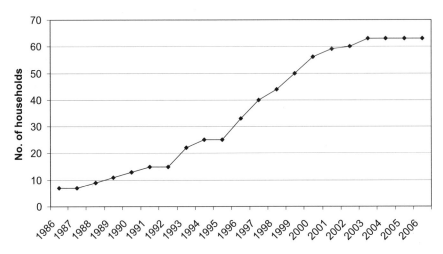

Figure 6.4 First-time migration of respondents, 1986–2006.

Drought began to affect Dokur in the late 1980s, but the village managed to survive because of its water tanks and reservoir. In the early 1990s, the tanks dried up, and this was followed by a decade of drought, leading to a sharp increase in migration, particularly among the landless labour class. Exit from the area continued to rise, mainly as a result of the push factors within the village. The recent trend, however, has been a combination of both pull and push factors, as was observed in this study.

According to the villagers, reliance on agriculture has decreased over recent decades because the continued scarcity of rainwater made agriculture impractical. The demand for caste occupations dropped, the cost of maintaining livestock increased and there was a paucity of capital available for business. In these circumstances, the only realistic option was migration to the city for work. In order to understand the push or pull factors behind the move, respondents were asked to relate the reasons why they had originally migrated and why they were now leaving. As Figure 6.5 shows, 70 per cent of the respondents stated that the drought and absence of a livelihood had been the main reason for their initial departure from the village. In 2005–2006, in contrast, 77 per cent had moved because of better income opportunities in the migration destinations, while 8 per cent felt that in addition to the improvement in income they also had more respect in the village (Figure 6.6).

In Indian society, caste determines relations within the power structure, but these can be weakened through class. As an individual's wealth increases, most of the issues or problems arising from his or her caste cease to exist or become mitigated. The continuing expansion of urban

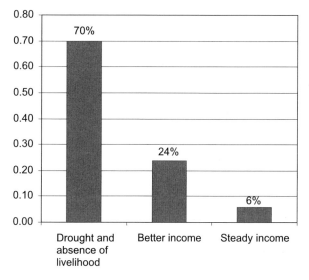

Figure 6.5 Reasons for migrating the first time.

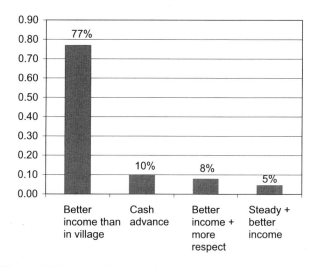

Figure 6.6 Reasons for migrating the second time, 2005–2006.

centres with the construction of new complexes, apartments and high-rise buildings by the private sector as well as of infrastructure such as roads by the public sector ensures the steady availability of urban jobs. This also means steady money. Furthermore, 10 per cent of the respondents had migrated because of the cash advance facility in the rural area.

Table 6.6 Reasons for migration (based on focus group discussions)

Men	Women
Better income	Equal income
Temporary escape from money lenders	More respect
Future investments	Remittances
More respect	

Source: See text.

Discussions with the focus group revealed interesting insights into why people migrated; the responses are summarized in Table 6.6. According to the men, better income opportunities were the main incentive for migration, whereas for the women the main incentive was equal income earning: for example, in the village, male farm labourers were paid Rs 65–80 whereas the rate for a female was Rs 35–50. At migration locations, both men and women earned equal wages of Rs 9,000–10,000.

The qualitative research tools also gave an insight into how migration occurred. Discussions with the key informants, many of whom were labour contractors, revealed that, in the first few years of the severe drought, upper-caste men of the village went to the cities to seek work from their urban relatives or friends. During these visits, they met civil contractors involved in government projects, and for a commission started to recruit labourers from their village. These social networks both within and beyond the village helped to trigger the migration process, which expanded from a few families in the initial stages to a large-scale phenomenon. The respondents ranked migration as the preferred occupation at present. However, they indicated that they would eventually like to return to agriculture. As Figure 6.7 shows, 37 per cent of the migrant respondents had invested their remittances in agriculture – buying or leasing land, digging bore wells, and so on. Land has traditionally been a source of status for villagers in India. According to discussions with the focus group and key informants, despite the paucity of rain, it was the ambition of every labourer to own land. Even if they migrated regularly, they would buy land in the hope that it would be used later, at least by their children if not themselves. Land, in lieu of cash, was also given as a dowry at the marriage of a migrant's daughter.

During discussions on the various uses of remittances, several interesting observations emerged. For example, according to the migrant respondents, 22 per cent had used their remittances for investing in livestock. Traditionally, very few households had owned livestock because Dokur was unsuitable for this purpose. However, migrants were now buying livestock for dairy and resale purposes (meat) to neighbour-

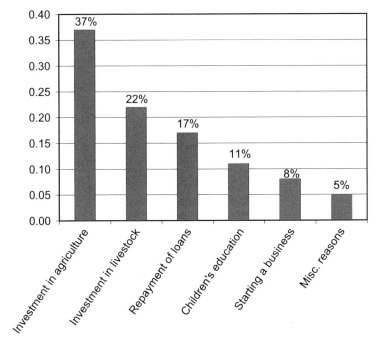

Figure 6.7 How remittances were used in Dokur, 2006.

ing villages. Loan repayment (17per cent) and children's education (11 per cent) were the next priorities; and 8 per cent had started new businesses, ranging from a tea stall or a wineshop to chicken and mutton centres. Although migration was initially triggered as a response to drought, which also generated "distress migrants", it offered certain benefits as well. The use of remittances is clear testimony to how resourceful these households had become. If it were not for migration, these people probably would have remained as casual labourers and landless peasants for their entire lifetime. Now, even though the changes were not great, there was opportunity through labour mobility for these villagers to achieve a higher socioeconomic standing. Although it was apparent that migration was increasingly becoming a major livelihood option in Dokur, it is also important to note that the majority of villagers did not migrate. The non-migrating respondents were asked to explain how they had coped with drought and to give their reasons for not leaving. Figure 6.8 summarizes their responses.

The majority of non-migrants were from "forward" communities and from landholding "backward" communities, which traditionally have

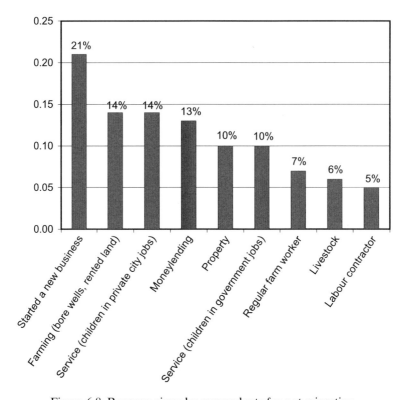

Figure 6.8 Reasons given by respondents for not migrating.

been resource rich and powerful. So, even during extreme drought, these villagers were able to cope without being forced to leave their homes. Of the non-migrating respondents, 21 per cent said that during drought periods they had started new businesses. It is interesting to note that the "new business" was usually related to migration – setting up real estate operations by buying plots in the nearby district headquarters, construction of housing with migrant labourers, or shops selling iron and other building materials. This enabled the non-migrating people to make money and, at the same time, to maintain their hold over lower-caste villagers.

The non-migrating villagers also mentioned moneylending and remittances from their children who were employed in government or private company jobs in Mahbubnagar, a nearby district, or in Hyderabad. Informal moneylending, particularly by upper-caste landlords, is a common practice in almost all villages in India, and Dokur was no exception. Moneylenders charged a 3 per cent interest rate compared with 1 per cent by the formal banking institutions. Despite this, village money-lenders were patronized because they were members of the community and could be relied upon for a loan in the event of an emergency.

Social groups

The results so far have shown that migration was indeed the most sought-after alternative livelihood strategy. It is also true that, although some individuals migrated to overcome unfavourable conditions, others did not. At this point it is important to understand who the migrating villagers were and who the non-migrating villagers were, and to identify the socio-economic conditions that caused this distinction.

The caste and landholding distribution of the migrant and non-migrating households can be determined from the 2006 census (see Table 6.7). Overall, the breakdown of village households was as follows: the landless constituted 26.0 per cent; small landholders 38.0 per cent; medium land-holders 19.9 per cent; and large landholders 16.1 per cent. It is interesting to note that 96 per cent of households among the scheduled caste migrated and a mere 4 per cent stayed behind. Caste has played an important role in the migrating process, because traditionally Dokur has been under the control of the upper-caste groups and the relatively powerful backward caste groups. This observation was confirmed during the focus group discussions and key informant interviews: the non-migrating villagers were usually the upper-caste members or their friends. It was the poorest of the poor who migrated; the landed and higher-caste groups had been able to diversify their livelihood options within the village.

Educational status of migrants

The role of education in enhancing a person's bargaining power and boosting self-confidence has been well documented in both sociology and psychology studies. Given the fact that it was the ultra-poor who migrated and that they had no assets, it is important to examine their educational status, because education is a necessity for life in urban centres and even for bargaining power. As has been recorded by many sociologists, three characteristics account for the respect an individual is accorded in rural India: first, caste; then, wealth; and, finally, education. As Table 6.8 shows, 60.4 per cent of migrant respondents with no schooling, 17.3 per cent of those with primary education and 3.2 per cent with high school level were employed as casual labourers.

Among the respondents who were employed as labour supervisors, 11.1 per cent had primary schooling and 3.2 per cent had middle school education. All of these respondents were from the scheduled caste and backward class communities. Labour contractors accounted for 4.8

Table 6.7 Migrants and non-migrants, classified by caste and land

	Migrating HH			Non-migrating HH				
	No. of households	% of total HH in Dokur	% among same social group	No. of households	% of total HH in Dokur	% among same social group	Total no. of HH	% among total HH
Landless households								
Scheduled caste	36	7.2	92.3	3	0.6	7.7	39	7.8
Backward caste	37	7.4	43.0	49	9.9	57.0	86	17.3
Forward caste	0	0.0	0.0	4	0.8	100.0	4	0.8
Total landless HH	73	14.7	56.6	56	11.3	43.4	129	26.0
Small landholding households								
Scheduled caste	37	7.4	74.0	13	2.6	26.0	50	10.1
Backward caste	62	12.5	56.9	47	9.5	43.1	109	21.9
Forward caste	0	0.0	0.0	30	6.0	100.0	30	6.0
Total small HH	99	19.9	52.4	90	18.1	47.6	189	38.0
Medium landholding households								
Scheduled caste	5	1.0	83.3	1	0.2	16.7	6	1.2
Backward caste	26	5.2	49.1	27	5.4	50.9	53	10.7
Forward caste	1	0.2	2.5	39	7.8	97.5	40	8.0
Total medium HH	32	6.4	32.3	67	13.5	67.7	99	19.9
Large landholding households								
Scheduled caste	0	0.0	0.0	1	0.2	100.0	1	0.2
Backward caste	1	0.2	3.4	28	5.6	96.6	29	5.8
Forward caste	3	0.6	6.0	47	9.5	94.0	50	10.1
Total large HH	4	0.8	5.0	76	15.3	95.0	80	16.1
Total households	208	41.9	41.9	289	58.1	58.1	497	100.0

Source: See text.
Notes: Castes or communities are government classifications based on religious stratification. Landless farmer = ownership of 0.2 ha or less of land. Small landholding farmer = ownership of 0.2–0.9 ha of land. Medium landholding farmer = ownership of 0.9–2.1 ha of land. Large landholding farmer = ownership of more than 2.1 ha of land.

Table 6.8 Educational status of migrant respondents and their occupations (per cent)

Educational status of respondent ($n = 63$)	Type of occupation		
	Labour contractor	Labour supervisor	Casual labourer
No schooling	–	–	60.4
Primary education	–	11.1	17.3
Middle school education	–	3.2	3.2
High school education and above	4.8	–	–

Source: See text.

per cent of the respondents, all of whom were from the forward class community (the upper-caste Reddys). Education offered the migrants the opportunity to move up the social ladder in terms of acquiring a relatively better job, as confirmed by the observation that none of the non-educated respondents were labour supervisors. The key informants from the scheduled caste community reported that they had not had the time to study because they were always working, and that their parents had needed their help at a very early age to assist the impoverished household and to repay debts. Education, or the lack thereof, had a direct impact on the occupation or position that they landed. In view of the observation from this study that migrants without education worked in the migration destinations as casual labourers at considerably lower wages than a labour supervisor, we need to examine the status of education of their children. Several education schemes are provided in the rural areas, such as the *Sarva Siksha Abhiyan*, and the midday meal programme, which was available for the village children. Village data indicated that 78 per cent of the migrants' children were not in school and 22 per cent were. This is based on the migrants with school-aged children; unmarried migrant respondents or those with no or infant children were excluded.

The study indicated that, despite the fact that migration provided an immediate alternative to the no-employment situation of the home district, one of its negative aspects was the long-term deterrent to livelihood enhancement. This has long-term implications – children remaining trapped in poverty just as their parents had been, being left out from various development schemes with no hope of alleviating deep-rooted poverty. Education, among other benefits, is known to give the confidence to be outspoken and to encourage resourcefulness. One of the conclusions from the participant-observation technique was that the respondents with some schooling, even if only lower-level education, were much more open to discussion or questions compared with the non-educated villagers, who were shy, reserved and highly insecure in dealing with new people or situations. Among the respondents with school-aged children not attending school, 49 per cent reported that children accompanying parents had been the main reason for lack of attendance, and 16 per cent cited lack of interest. A typical situation in many destination communities was one of parents working but children playing in the surroundings. Given that the interviews had been designed to support an ethnographic-type study, questions relating to the reasons their children migrated were added at the time of data collection: 58 per cent of the respondents whose offspring migrated with them reported that the children also worked for extra income, and 42 per cent said that their children had accompanied them because there was no one to take care of them in the village. From the focus group discussions and key informant interviews, it was learned that the children carried stones and cement and were paid an advance of Rs 3,000 if the child was 12 years or younger, and Rs 6,000 if younger than 18. This was justified on the basis that the children could not do work other than carrying loads or walking on cement to smoothen it. This raises the issue of child labour and the exploitation of children. According to the focus group, some of the parents were not interested in sending their offspring to school because they felt it was a waste of time: the children would end up being labourers and, if they learned the trade early, there might at least be a chance of becoming a supervisor or a contractor.

Moving on from the sociodemographic aspect of the study, the following section discusses the link between migration and health and is based on data collected from both the quantitative and the qualitative research.

Migration, health and risk behaviour

Dokur village is classified as high risk by national and international organizations and civil societies. Therefore it is imperative to have an understanding of risk behaviour and the health status of migrant and non-migrating villagers. Table 6.9 summarizes the risk behaviour of the migrant and non-migrant respondents. Of the total migrant households, 41 per cent of the married and 3 per cent of the unmarried respondents had visited a commercial sex worker (CSW) at the migration destination. Another 10 per cent of the married migrants had had intimate relations with both CSW and non-CSW partners; and 3 per cent had engaged in relations with non-CSW partners. These findings contradict earlier studies (UNAIDS 2001), which assumed that lonely married men migrating alone or single migrants were the ones to engage in risky behaviour. In the case of Dokur, the migrants travelled as couples, unless the wife was pregnant or sick. The non-migrant respondents exhibited less risky

Table 6.9 Types of risk behaviour of migrant and non-migrating respondents (per cent)

	Married	Unmarried	Total
Migrants ($n = 63$)			
Engaged in relations with:			
Commercial sex worker	41	3	44
Non-CSW partner other than spouse	3	0	3
No visits to CSW or non-CSW	40	3	43
Visits to both CSW and non-CSW other than spouse	10	0	10
Total	94	6	100
Non-migrating respondents ($n = 86$)			
Engaged in relations with:			
Commercial sex worker	4	3	7
Non-CSW partner other than spouse	10	0	10
No visits to CSW or non-CSW	73	7	80
Visits to both CSW and non-CSW other than spouse	3	0	3
Total	90	10	100

Source: See text.

sexual behaviour, although 10 per cent of the married non-migrant respondents reported having sexual liaisons with non-CSW partners and 4 per cent with a CSW. One key informant, who was the resident paramedic at the IRHS, mentioned that it was mostly the migrants who came for sexually related check-ups but that there were a lot of non-migrants as well. He added that the non-migrants were normally upper-caste men who kept traditional concubines as a status symbol. This group was also more aware of HIV and related risks, and used the condoms distributed by ASHA, a project of the Andhra Pradesh government. Figure 6.9 summarizes the reasons given by the migrant respondents for indulging in risky behaviour.

Social norms or cultural taboos of the village prohibited people from indulging in acts that they might otherwise have found tempting but, given the opportunity, they succumbed to temptation. Whereas epidemiologists argue that a person who indulges in risk behaviour – or, for that matter, does not indulge – will do so irrespective of the surroundings, the Dokur case study finds contrary evidence. People are sociable creatures and they adapt to different circumstances. Of the migrants exhibiting risk behaviour, 68 per cent reported that they had not been involved in promiscuous behaviour before migration. The long working hours without rest in the heat and dust added to the stress of the migrants and, as one of the key informants noted, a sexual relation was the cheapest entertainment available to them in the migration destination. Work sites attracted workers from numerous villages, making each a stranger, and

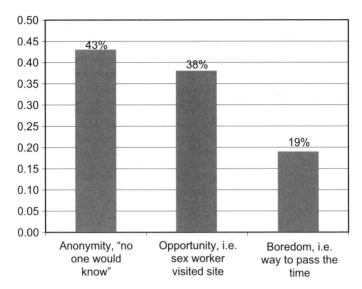

Figure 6.9 Reasons for risky behaviour in migration destinations.
Source: Computed by authors.

when a CSW visited the location it was much easier to resort to high-risk behaviour than would have been the case in the home village.

One of the major strategies used to combat HIV/AIDS in India has been to increase awareness among high-risk groups as well as the general population. This includes educating the people with regard to their awareness of HIV, including knowledge of the modes of transmitting and/or preventing the disease. Among the migrant respondents, 56 per cent were knowledgeable, 25 per cent had never heard of HIV, and 19 per cent, although aware of HIV, were not sure how it spread, was transmitted or could be prevented. For those who reported relations with a CSW or partners other than their spouse, condoms were not used in 76 per cent of the cases, nor had they used condoms with their spouse either. Even in the case of respondents knowledgeable about HIV/AIDS, condom use was limited. According to comments from members of the focus group, migrant life, or even rural life for that matter, was very different from life in the urban centres, where people could plan their sexual relations and condoms could be easily purchased at pharmacies. In villages, and particularly in the migration sites, "deals" were done very quickly; opportunities were unexpected or spur of the moment and condoms were not available. This attitude reflects high-risk behaviour on the part of migrant workers, because they endangered not only their own life but that of their spouse as well. This was evident also in Dokur village. In

2003, the IRHS reported 8 HIV cases, referring them to the local VCTC in Mahbubnagar. At the time of writing, there were 55 HIV-positive individuals in Dokur, 49 of whom were migrants. If this rate continues, Dokur will soon have to confront the effects of the poverty–HIV nexus that has plagued southern Africa, and this phenomenon will spread rapidly to other nearby towns and villages.

The quantitative and qualitative data on Dokur show that risky sexual behaviour was high among migrants, and that the majority of these people were not aware of HIV/AIDS. The local doctor at the primary health centre in Devarakadra Mandal pointed out that migrants generally were absent from the village when AIDS prevention officials visited and, even if they had been present, they were not interested in the programmes because they preferred to rest, call on relatives or engage in social events during their brief visit home. This was not surprising as the respondents spend nine months working outside the village.

The implications of risk behaviour

HIV risk behaviour compromises the health of the migrants and weakens their work efforts, particularly with respect to hard physical labour. Table 6.10 gives a comparison of the general and sexual health status of migrants and non-migrants. Compared with non-migrating villagers, the general health of the migrants was relatively poor, with 36 per cent of the respondents complaining of ill health and of considerable difficulties in handling daily tasks, especially at the migration sites.

The majority of the migrants experiencing ill health were from scheduled-caste or backward-class communities. Only two households from the forward-class community reported poor health, and this was due to the fact that they had suffered a recent accident. The health of

Table 6.10 Health status of the respondents (per cent)

	Migrants ($n = 63$)	Non-migrants ($n = 86$)
General health status		
Very good: able to do daily tasks easily	12	48
Good: generally able to do daily tasks	44	38
Poor: substantial problems with daily tasks	36	11
Very poor: unable to do any tasks	8	3
Sexual health status		
Suffering from sexual health-related illness	27	11
Recovering from sexual health-related illness	17	2
Never had problems with sexual health	54	71
Declined to comment	2	16

migrants is important and assumes considerable significance because a lump-sum advance payment of Rs 9,000 is made between contractor and worker when the migrant is recruited. This implies a work contract for nine months with the contractor, but were the migrant to become sick and unable to work this amount becomes a debt incurred by the migrant and he/she would have to work extra days to compensate for those lost owing to illness. This means a loss in pay for sick days plus costs for medicine and treatment of the disease. The IRHS reported that the migrants were mostly diagnosed with allergies, injuries and foot infections, as well as a high rate of sex-related illnesses.

The bottom panel of Table 6.10 summarizes the status of migrants and non-migrants with regard to their sexual health: 27 per cent of the migrants suffered from sex-related illnesses, compared with 11 per cent of non-migrants (gonorrhoea and syphilis being the common illnesses in Dokur), and another 17 per cent of the migrants and 2 per cent of non-migrants were reportedly recovering from similar problems. No sexual health problems were reported by 54 per cent of the migrants and 71 per cent of the non-migrating villagers; 2 per cent and 16 per cent of migrants and non-migrants, respectively, declined to comment on their sex-related illnesses. With regard to both general and sexual health, the migrants were the ones most seriously affected. The reasons are many and varied. As the focus groups revealed, seasonal workers lacked access to healthcare at the migration destination because they were not permanent residents. This was particularly true for road construction gangs, whose campsite would be at the mid-point of the connecting roads, and, as they finished in one area, they moved to the next. Only when their work was concentrated within the cities did they have access to healthcare. For non-migrant villagers, there was the clinic in Dokur for emergencies, the Mandal primary health care centre was a mere 4 kilometres away and the district general hospital was a half-hour bus ride from Dokur village.

Implications: From livelihood risk to HIV risk

As was observed in Dokur, migration is the response to livelihood risks and, in turn, paves the way for HIV risk. The issue of labour migration has two sides. On the one hand, it brings prosperity, enabling the purchase of land, debts to be cleared and bore wells to be dug, and helping the individual in general to move up the social ladder. On the other hand, transitory work exposes the migrant to high-risk practices because of a lack of awareness or education and makes rural households vulnerable to further livelihood deterioration. Extensive review and analysis of the empirical data helped to gain insights into the prevalence of HIV in the semi-arid tropics and the nature of risk behaviour. This can be traced back to the conceptual framework, confirming that livelihood risk translates into health risk with implications for the security of livelihood.

The structural link between the farm household and the outside world, established through the migratory movement of household members, creates the channel for the flow of both cash and HIV. Although migration fulfils the household's income needs, it can also cause the destruction of the household if it introduces HIV. This is a cyclical *risk-to-risk* phenomenon, where the livelihood risk leads to the HIV risk and the HIV risk leads to a further livelihood risk, and so the cycle continues. If left unchecked, it will not be long before the SAT of India begins to exhibit similar effects to those identified in Africa and other developing nations. The study adds new dimensions to the framework wherein the movement of migrants is not always a push factor caused by the absence of livelihoods, as was seen in Dokur. Migration in Dokur developed from being a risk response to becoming a regular way of life. The comparison of the 2001 and 2006 censuses shows that permanent migration has been steadily increasing, taking on proportions that can transfer rural poverty into urban poverty. This calls for a multisectoral, targeted approach for tackling the issue before it is too late.

5 Conclusions and future direction

The purpose of this chapter was to understand the linkage between livelihoods, migration and HIV, and to examine these broad connections in a micro perspective. The study confirmed the link between rural vulnerabilities, which is often the effect of being "traditionally poor" or rather, in the name of caste, being "born to be poor". This means great disadvantages in all aspects of wellbeing: not owning assets and not having access to education, which even affects migration as a coping mechanism with regard to the type of job available to the transitory worker. The wellbeing of individuals in a community is a good general indicator of human development. To be precise, in an agrarian community such as the Indian SAT, the state of health at the individual level cumulatively determines the health (or wellbeing) of the community. This in turn reflects the wellbeing of the state or nation. As is shown by the evidence, there are direct benefits from migration such as provision of income, but it is also a channel for the spread of the HIV epidemic in the SAT, causing a further deterioration of livelihoods and leading to household insecurity and social and economic imbalances.

The case study, the review of the literature and the attendant secondary studies have suggested that a linkage exists between livelihood insecurity, migration and risk behaviour in the SAT. The results presented in this chapter are the insights from a preliminary analysis. But further re-search is needed to understand HIV-infected households in order to de-termine how they cope with the added burden of medical costs and the loss of labour arising from the illness. Research so far has focused on the prevalence of HIV/AIDS in the SAT of Andhra Pradesh and the type of risk behaviour; understanding the coping mechanism of house-holds with HIV-infected members could provide a holistic picture and should be the direction of future research. From previous analysis and re-view, it is obvious that migrants lack a voice and, because of their transi-tory lifestyle, are often excluded from government HIV programmes or interventions. This calls for an amendment to the intervention strategies, be they on HIV awareness or employment guarantee schemes, so as to explicitly include migrant populations. Since migration is no longer just a risk-response mechanism but has become a way of life, policymakers should develop a multisectoral, well-informed intervention strategy at the village level if the goal is to alleviate poverty and achieve sustainable development at the grassroots level.

Note

This study is part of a doctoral dissertation study by B. Valentine Joseph Gandhi, aimed at understanding livelihood insecurities in rural Andhra Pradesh and their impact on farm and labour households. The study is being undertaken in collaboration with the Indian Institute of Technology (IIT), Mumbai, and the International Crops Research Institute for the Semi-Arid Tropics (ICRISAT).

References

Alumira, J. D., M. C. S. Bantilan and T. Sihoma-Moyo (2005). "Evolution of Social Science Research at ICRISAT and a Case Study in Zimbabwe". Work-ing Paper 20, ICRISAT, Bulawayo.

Bantilan, M. C. S. and K. V. Anupama (2002). "Vulnerability and Adaptation in Dryland Agriculture in India's SAT: Experiences from ICRISAT's Village Level Studies". Working Paper 13, ICRISAT, Patancheru.

Boerma, J. T., M. Urassa, S. Nako, J. Ng'Weshemi, R. Isingo and B. Zaba (2002). "Sociodemographic Context of the AIDS Epidemic in a Rural Area in Tanza-nia with a Focus on People's Mobility and Marriage". *Sexually Transmitted Infections* 78 (Suppl.1): 97–105.

Deb, U. K., G. D. N. Rao, Y. M. Rao and R. Slater (2002). "Diversification and Livelihood Options: A Study of Two Villages in Andhra Pradesh, India 1975–2001". ODI Working Paper 178, Overseas Development Institute, London.

Deshingkar, P. (2006). "Internal Migration, Poverty and Development in Asia". ODI Briefing Paper 11, Overseas Development Institute, London.

Gandhi, B. V. J. (2003). "A Descriptive Study on the Migrant Workers of the Lambadi Tribe". Master's thesis, University of Madras, Chennai.

Gandhi, B. V. J. (2004). "Social Capital and Migration". ICRISAT Internship Report, ICRISAT, Patancheru.

Gelmon, L., K. Singh, P. Singh, P. Bhattacharjee, S. Moses, A. Costigan and J. Blanchard (2006). "Sexual Networking and HIV Risk in Migrant Workers in India". Paper presented at the XVI International AIDS Conference, Toronto, 13–18 August.

Gillespie, S. and S. Kadiyala (2005). "HIV/AIDS and Food and Nutrition Security from Evidence to Action". *Food Policy Review* 7 (International Food Policy Research Institute, Washington DC).

Holmes-Rovner, M. and C. E. Wills (2002). "Improving Informed Consent: Insights from Behavioral Decision Research". *Med Care* 40(9 Suppl): V30–V38.

Hunt, C. W. (1996). "Social versus Biological: Theories on the Transmission of AIDS in Africa". *Social Science and Medicine* 42(9): 1283–1296.

Jodha, N. S., M. Asokan and J. G. Ryan (1977). "Village Study Methodology and Resource Endowments of the Selected Villages in ICRISAT's Village Level Studies". Economics Programme Occasional Paper 16, ICRISAT, Hyderabad.

Lurie, M. (2001). "Migration and the Spread of HIV in South Africa". PhD dissertation, Johns Hopkins University, Baltimore.

NIHFW and NACO (2006). *HIV Sentinel Surveillance: India Country Report, 2006.* New Delhi: National Institute of Health and Family Welfare, and National AIDS Control Organization.

Rao, K. P. C., M. C. S. Bantilan, K. Singh, S. Subrahmanyam, P. Deshingkar, P. Rao, P. Parthasarathy and B. Shiferaw (2005). *Overcoming Poverty in Rural India: Focus on Rainfed Semi-Arid Tropics.* Patancheru: ICRISAT.

UNAIDS [Joint United Nations Programme on HIV/AIDS] (2001). "Population Mobility and AIDS". UNAIDS Technical Update, UNAIDS, New York, February.

UNDP [United Nations Development Programme] (2005). "Migration and HIV in South Asia". Delhi: UNDP Regional HIV and Development Programme, South and North East Asia.

Walker, T. S. and J. G. Ryan (1990). *Village and Household Economies in India's Semi-Arid Tropics.* Baltimore, MD: Johns Hopkins University Press.

Wang, C. E. and M. H. Huch (2000). "Protecting Human Research Subjects: An International Perspective". *Nursing Science Quarterly* 13(4): 293–298.

Webb, D. (1997). *HIV and AIDS in Africa.* London: Pluto Press.

7

Vulnerability to hunger: Responding to food crises in fragile states

Colin Andrews and Margarita Flores

1 Introduction

This chapter examines the imperative for improved classification and analysis of food crises in different fragile contexts. Recognizing the continued persistence and protracted nature of food crises, the chapter questions how prevention and response mechanisms could be improved to help decision makers better address the determinants and the dynamic nature of hunger at both national and regional level.

The starting point to the chapter looks at vulnerability to hunger and the challenges raised by the increasing number of food crises, particularly in the African context. Drawing from the recent literature, the study brings into focus a number of operational bottlenecks that decision makers face in addressing food crisis situations. In particular the chapter looks at the implications of the absence of system-wide frameworks to compare the severity of different crises. In this context, the constraints raised by competing methodologies, institutional buy-in and the heterogeneity of different crisis situations emerge. Of particular interest is the case-study information presented, based on the early application of a food classification system named the Integrated Food Security Phase Classification (IPC). Originally developed by the Food and Agriculture Organization's Food Security Analysis Unit (FSAU) Somalia, the potential utility of this tool has emerged in a number of different contexts to provide a comparable situation analysis based upon technical consensus. The chapter examines emerging lessons from this common classification

Vulnerability in developing countries, Naudé, Santos-Paulino and McGillivray (eds),
United Nations University Press, 2009, ISBN 978-92-808-1171-1

framework, covering institutional adaptation, technical approaches and questions on data and analysis.

The chapter is organized as follows. Section 1 examines the context and challenges arising for decision makers tasked with responding to food crises across diverse crisis contexts. Section 2 presents an emerging framework for food security classification and response, based on the joint efforts of a number of UN and international agencies, including the Food and Agriculture Organization of the United Nations (FAO), the World Food Programme (WFP), the Famine Early Warning Systems Network (FEWSNET) and Oxfam GB. Section 3 presents emerging country-level analysis based on the initial adaptation of the IPC framework in the East African context. Main conclusions and recommendations for future consideration are presented in a final section.

2 Context and challenges

The imperative to better understand the nature and severity of food crises is reflected by the persistence and protracted level of hunger in different fragile contexts. The total number of chronically undernourished in the world is estimated at 854 million. As of February 2008, 36 countries faced food crises and required emergency assistance (FAO 2008a). Within this group, the protracted nature of crises reflects unsettling trends. According the FAO, the number of food emergencies has risen from an average of 15 a year in the 1980s to more than 30 since 2000, with the majority of crises reflecting continuous vulnerability rather than one-off crisis events. Of further concern is the persistence of crises in the African context. In sub-Sahara alone, the annual number of food emergencies has tripled during this period.

Although many African countries have the potential to reduce national levels of hunger, the persistence of hunger is further threatened by increasing food prices, potentially tighter grain markets, conflict, diseases and climate change (FAO 2007a). The lack of progress in reducing hunger and the increasing number of food crises indicate that, among other things, risk management, prevention and response mechanisms need to be improved to address the determinants and the dynamic nature of food insecurity at household, national and regional levels. The inadequacy of prevention and response mechanisms has been highlighted in key literature in recent years. Darcy and Hoffmann's study "According to Need" (2003) highlights system-wide issues facing agencies and donors at national and international level. Emerging strongly within this critique was the absence of system-wide frameworks for defining the relative severity of crises and for aligning responses accordingly. The study marks a departure from narrow methodological debates towards the policy, management and process issues underlying response. In turn it also focuses attention on the need to strengthen simultaneously a number of short-, medium- and long-term needs assessment and responses mechanisms.

To understand the challenges faced by decision makers in responding to different crisis scenarios, it is useful to consider how hunger and vulnerability are understood amongst practitioners and within the literature. This chapter defines hunger through a food security perspective. In 1996, the World Food Summit defined food security as a situation that exists "when all people at all times have physical and economic access to sufficient, safe and nutritious food to meet their dietary needs and food preferences for an active and healthy life" (FAO 1996). The now widely accepted World Food Summit definition reinforced the multidimensional nature of food security incorporating food access, availability, biological food use and stability:

- *food availability* refers to the physical presence of food at various levels from household to national level, whether from own production or through markets;
- *food access* refers to the ability to obtain an appropriate and nutritious diet; it is linked to resources, assets and income at the household level;
- *biological utilization* relates to the ability of the human body to convert food into energy effectively.

The stability dimension of food insecurity underlines the importance of temporal dynamics, where crisis situations are understood not only as a static or one-off event but also in terms of likely future changes, or susceptibility to particular risk factors. In this regard the concept of vulnerability can be instructive. Vulnerability refers to the full range of factors that place people at risk of becoming food insecure, including those factors that affect their ability to cope. Whereas much of the disaster management literature uses vulnerability with reference to a natural hazard, the food security literature and, more recently, part of the social risk management and poverty literature define vulnerability in terms of an unfavourable future outcome. Concerning food security, this could include the propensity to fall, or stay, below a given threshold within a certain timeframe (Lovendal and Knowles 2007).

As a measure of deprivation, vulnerability is appealing because it takes into account not just fluctuating standards of living but also the resilience of subsets of households (e.g. the landless, smallholders) against covariate (e.g. weather or crop changes) and idiosyncratic risks (e.g. unemployment or illness). It is, however, more difficult to identify the vulnerable not only because there are different measures (e.g. *ex ante* versus *ex post* vulnerability) but also because tracking the wellbeing of a particular household over time and after a shock event requires reliable data, which are seldom available (Gaiha and Imai 2008).

Box 7.1 Experience from the Horn of Africa drought, 2005–2006

A study undertaken by the UK's Overseas Development Institute (Pantuliano 2006) examines the inadequacy of the emergency response during the Greater Horn of Africa drought in 2005–2006, when at least 11 million people were in crisis in Djibouti, Eritrea, Ethiopia, Kenya and Somalia. The analysis questions why accurate and credible early warning (e.g. FEWSNET, FAO-FSAU Somalia) first emerging in October did not lead to a rapid and appropriate response and highlights how inadequate contingency planning, limited capacity in livelihood programming and inflexible funding mechanisms resulted in delays and deficiencies in livelihood interventions and the predominance of food assistance in the emergency response. Drawing on secondary data and interviews, the analysis points to the misunderstood nature of pastoralism, particularly across the Ethiopia–Kenya–Somalia borders, reporting malnutrition levels far beyond emergency thresholds, livestock losses of up to 70 per cent and the mass migration of pastoralists in search of water, food, jobs and relief aid. As argued within the study, the crisis reflected a context of chronic food insecurity where emergency alerts were signalled repeatedly, yet humanitarian and development actors found it difficult to distinguish the symptoms of chronic destitution from those of a critically unstable situation. As argued, the chronic vulnerability of pastoralists in East Africa was seen as an indicator of unsustainable livelihoods, without reference to a range of external political and economic factors perpetuating marginalization. Few national governments or external actors recognized this by appropriate policy responses, e.g. addressing access to natural resources such as land and water. Eventual funding appeals and contributions across Ethiopia, Kenya and Somalia were mobilized only around March 2006 and were eventually orientated to food aid responses – 77 per cent in Ethiopia, 46 per cent in Kenya and 40 per cent in Somalia.

Addressing vulnerability is also complicated by a range of limitations on the response side. Managing risks goes beyond assisting those affected by a particular shock in addressing their immediate food needs. Appropriate responses include long-term interventions to address chronic vulnerabilities. Box 7.1, for example, considers the inadequacy of response strategies in addressing vulnerabilities during the Horn of Africa drought crisis in 2005–2006. Here, despite the availability of credible and accurate early warning information, national governments, international agencies and donors were unable to address the crisis effectively in its early stages. Emergency operations did not reach full capacity until March or April 2006, at which time the crisis had evolved into one of the worst faced by the region in a decade. According to UN estimates, at least 11 million people were at risk in Djibouti, Eritrea, Ethiopia, Kenya and Somalia.

The case-study and wider literature serve to highlight a number of pertinent challenges in understanding and responding to food crises. First, food security is multidimensional, and this presents difficulties for decision makers in prioritizing and interpreting different information components. Although basic asset categories and livelihood strategy categories are well defined, the interplay with different sectors (e.g. health, water, sanitation and nutrition) is less well so. To this end, the setting of warning thresholds can be problematic, since increased understanding is often required to assess the vulnerability context – for example to consider institutional and policy constraints.

The Niger crisis of 2005 also provides an interesting case study. Here, it has been argued that the rationale for the food security strategy undertaken – subsidized cereal sales, agricultural inputs, cereal banks and public works programmes – was not analysed or adequately monitored despite the availability of information that might have promoted different strategies for target groups (ODI 2005). The Horn of Africa drought crisis in 2005–2006 also points to the misunderstood nature of pastoralism, despite clear and credible information sources. In both cases, it can be concluded that the analysis of complex situations and the interpretation of technical subject areas require additional support.

Second, the temporal aspects of hunger and food security are a challenge. The increased frequency and severity of crises, coupled with difficulties in disentangling acute and chronic underlying factors, raise complexities for both analysts and decision makers (Maxwell and Watkins 2003). The distinctions between temporary and longer-term food insecurity as well as seasonal changes suggest that a range of policy responses is required. Yet there is often a bias in policy response, marked by the provision of food aid and a narrow range of agricultural inputs (e.g. seeds and tools). By way of illustrative example, Figure 7.1 highlights the financial allocations afforded to different sectors in the UN Consolidated Appeals Process (2008), a mechanism aimed at streamlining the approach taken by UN institutions and their partners in appealing for funding to emergency relief operations.

The bias towards short-term response options reflects the separation of relief and longer-term interventions where the responses are compromised, *inter alia*, by short-term funding horizons in donor budgets and the earmarking of donor funds for specific UN or other international agencies (Levine and Chastre 2004).

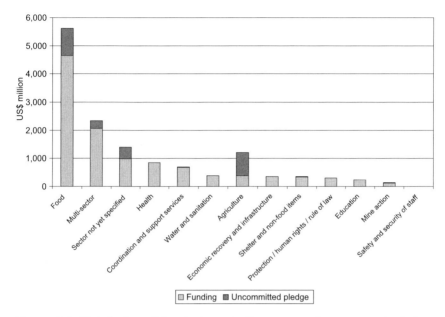

Figure 7.1 Global Consolidated Appeals Process requirements and pledges across main sectors, 2008.
Source: Financial Tracking Service (United Nations Office for the Coordination of Humanitarian Affairs), ⟨http://ocha.unog.ch/fts/reports/daily/ocha_R16_Y2008___0902021426.pdf⟩ (accessed 11 February 2009).
Notes: Funding = contributions + commitments. A pledge is a non-binding announcement of an intended contribution or allocation by the donor. A commitment is the creation of a legal, contractual obligation between the donor and the recipient entity, specifying the amount to be contributed. A contribution is the actual payment of funds or transfer of in-kind goods from the donor to the recipient entity.

3 A framework for food security classification and response

Until the widely influential "According to Need" analysis, the linkages between assessments, decision-making and response were relatively unexplored. The study, however, marks a departure from narrow methodological debates on measurement and definitions towards the policy, management and process issues underlying response. This focuses attention on the need to strengthen simultaneously a number of short-, medium- and long-term needs and response mechanisms. Arising from these concerns, in recent years international actors have pushed to strengthen analysis and decision-making on food crises through a range of different initiatives. In particular, there has been a focus on improving assessment methodologies; for example, WFP's Strengthening Emergency Needs Assessment Capacity Project; the World Health Organization's Health and Nutrition Tracking Service. More broadly, the question of system-wide reform and aid effectiveness has also come into increased focus through, for example, the Paris Declaration on Aid Effectiveness, the Good Humanitarian Donorship initiative, and the Development Assistance Committee's initiative on Managing for Development Results.

From the food security perspective, the IPC has emerged as a potentially innovative approach for improving food security analysis and informing decision-making (Maxwell 2006). The IPC is a standardized scale that integrates food security, nutrition and livelihood information into a clear statement about the severity of a crisis and the implications for food security and humanitarian response (FAO/FSAU 2006). Developed originally in Somalia by the FAO's FSAU, the IPC is now being adapted in the wider Horn of Africa region and beyond by a number of international agencies and national governments. Figure 7.2 illustrates an IPC outlook developed for the Central East Africa region during the Horn of Africa drought crisis from October 2005 to March 2006. The map (cartographic protocol) highlights the potential utility of food security classification through its disaggregation of different crises and handling of trends, whether they are underlying, seasonal or likely future outcomes established through early warning mechanisms. Although the main output of the IPC approach is this cartographic protocol, the analysis is also safeguarded by a number of supporting tools. In particular, a set of reference outcome indicators are identified with each phase, including threshold values referenced against internationally accepted cut-off points where available. These are matched against appropriate response interventions, summarized in Table 7.1 (see later). Some of the main opportunities foreseen within the IPC framework are as follows.

First, the analysis provides an organizing framework upon which to promote technical consensus amongst a range of stakeholders. By bringing together a set of diverse information variables, the IPC approach contributes to moving beyond a discussion on methodologies (e.g. anthropometric, biological measurement) towards improved contextual analysis. Although the IPC is not an information system in itself, the resulting process of analysis can help to highlight related upstream information requirements concerning data availability, data sources, monitoring and evaluation. The process of analysis can also help streamline information requirements and promote strategic information use.

Second, the approach promotes evidence-based analysis, which is particularly relevant given international initiatives around the effectiveness and efficiency of response (e.g. Good Humanitarian Donorship; the Central Emergency Response Fund). The emphasis further placed on

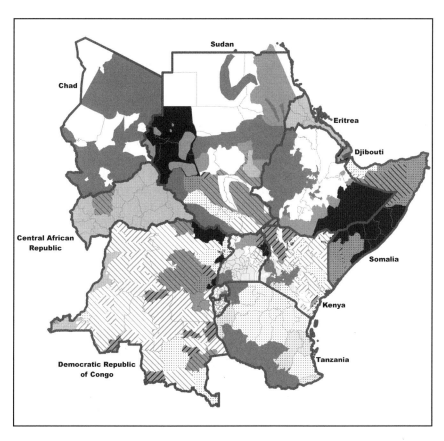

Current or Imminent Phase

- 1A Generally Food Secure
- 1B Generally Food Secure
- 2 Moderately/Borderline Food Insecure
- 3 Acute Food and Livelihood Crisis
- 4 Humanitarian Emergency
- 5 Famine/Humanitarian Catastrophe

Risk of Worsening Phase

- Watch
- Moderate Risk
- High Risk

Figure 7.2 Current Central and Eastern Africa food security situation, October to December 2008.
Source: Regional Food Security and Nutrition Working Group Analysis.
Note: This map is a compilation map: Chad, Djibouti and Ethiopia are FEWS-NET maps; Somalia, Kenya, Uganda, DRC and Burundi are national IPC maps with updates done at an IPC Regional Technical Meeting.

197

variable "situation analyses" also responds to many controversies over response strategies that are negotiated around perception, political implications and expected resources rather than evidence-based need. In this context, particular controversy has concerned the reliability and objectivity of agency needs assessment processes. As Darcy and Hofmann (2003: 16) assert, "needs assessment is often conflated with the formulation of responses, in ways that can lead to resource-led intervention and close down other (perhaps more appropriate) forms of intervention".

Finally, the IPC approach has been viewed as an entry point for institutionalizing country-level ownership and buy-in around food security issues. Institutional aspects within a country need to be considered in food security analysis to ensure ownership and transparency of approach and ultimately the translation of food security objectives into national programmes and poverty reduction strategies, where they exist (Pingali et al. 2005). This involves the early identification of relevant decision-making, as well as coordination structures (Flores et al. 2005). A recent review of Early Warning Information systems in Africa identified that information was often not linked to decision-making processes as an early priority, which often resulted in the separation of short- and long-term policy responses (Tefft et al. 2006). The typically diffuse nature of coordination structures at national level often poses complications. Amongst national authorities the responsibility for crisis response and food insecurity may rest across a number of different ministries with different sub-working groups also informing decision-making processes.

Section 3 examines recent country-level experiences in the implementation of the IPC approach, examining the opportunities and emerging challenges with particular attention to institutional aspects, the technical framework and data/analytical requirements.

4 Initial experiences in Central and East Africa

The IPC is in the early stages of adaptation outside of the original Somalia context, but has already been introduced in over 15 countries. A number of national governments, international agencies and donors have pledged their commitment and interest in developing and implementing the IPC further, particularly in the African context. At international level, a number of agencies have committed to devising a common approach for the longer-term development of the IPC, including Care International, the European Commission Joint Research Centre, FEWSNET, Oxfam GB, Save the Children UK and US, the FAO and the WFP.

Although modalities to support longer-term IPC development are being finalized, implementation exercises continue at country level and have been most concentrated in East and Central Africa owing to the region's strong humanitarian imperative, coupled with existing information and institutional structures. The following examines these early implementation activities to determine how identified challenges are being met, i.e. (i) national ownership and buy-in; (ii) adaptation of the IPC framework; and (iii) data availability and analysis.

4.1 National ownership and buy-in

The IPC aims to provide a platform to broker technical consensus amongst a broad range of stakeholders including government authorities and international agencies. National ownership and buy-in are, therefore, critical to ensure the inclusion of relevant information and decision makers and to ensure that the IPC complements rather than duplicates existing information and institutional structure. Initial implementation exercises within East and Central Africa have been based on a *system-based approach* to IPC development, involving the promotion of the IPC through existing information structures and institutional frameworks. Central to this approach is the need to ensure that IPC analysis is nationally owned and supported across relevant decision-making and coordination structures to ensure future sustainability. In this sense, nationally supported food security and nutrition networks provide the primary entry point to facilitate IPC development. Implicit in this approach is that the IPC draws upon existing information structures, instead of launching duplicative approaches.

The initial experiences of Kenya and Southern Sudan – presented to delegates at the Committee on World Food Security 33rd session in May 2007 – illustrate the way in which national ownership and buy-in are being achieved in contrasting contexts (FAO 2007b). Kenya has detailed institutional structures to support food security requirements (see Box 7.2). Within these structures, in March 2007 the IPC was employed as the analytical framework for the 2007 Short Rains Assessment under the management of a subcommittee through a process facilitated by the FAO and the Arid Lands Resource Management Project (KFSSG 2007). Despite the detailed institutional structure, it is significant to note that the IPC appeared to address a number of specific information and institutional requirements recognized by national authorities – for example, enabling consistency in terminology and technical consensus; providing a framework to integrate early warning information and situation analysis thereby capturing dynamic aspects of a crisis; providing definition on the relevance and cut-offs of various outcome indicators related to food security, nutrition and livelihoods.

Box 7.2 Kenya's food security institutional structure

Kenya's food security institutional structure includes (i) the Kenya Food Security Meeting (KFSM), the main coordination body, which acts as an open forum of high-level presentation of a broad grouping of organizations at the national level with an interest in food security; (ii) the Kenya Food Security Steering Group (KFSSG), a restricted group of stakeholders that acts as a technical "think-tank" and advisory body to all relevant stakeholders on issues of drought management and food security; and (iii) the Data and Information Subcommittee of the KFSSG (DISK), which focuses on improving the quality, quantity and timeliness of food security and disaster management information through increased data sharing, through coordinated investments in developing capacity and systems, and through continuous improvements in methodologies and techniques. The institutional structure points to advanced information collection and early warning analysis, also under the Arid Lands Resource Management Project (ALRMP).

Institutional lessons emerging from the Kenyan IPC adaptation include the following. First, the analysis was notable for the participation of a cross-section of government representatives including the ministries of water, agriculture, livestock and health. This provided a platform to discuss and refine analysis also with international agencies, specifically the FAO, FEWSNET, the WFP and World Vision. Second, the potential for decentralization is being exploited, with 32 districts trained and 16 districts fully involved in food security assessments. This will require significant investment in capacity-building and safeguards to ensure accuracy of analysis.

The government of Southern Sudan has endorsed the IPC based on its potential utilization for improving food security and livelihood analysis, disaster preparedness and information management (FAO 2007b). The value added in the Southern Sudan context is particularly relevant after the Comprehensive Peace Agreement (2004), where initiatives to strengthen, *inter alia*, food security institutional structures have been made. Within Southern Sudan, initial activities have focused mainly on awareness-raising and consultation around the IPC.

Efforts have largely focused on the identification of stakeholders and institutional structures to facilitate an IPC analysis. Sensitization and capacity-building efforts have taken place with government officials, including ministries of agriculture and forestry. Stakeholder groups from the Livelihood Analysis Forum (LAF) and other international agencies including CARE, the FAO and the WFP have also been involved in initial training exercises. The introduction of the Sudan Institutional Capacity Programme: Food Security Information for Action (SIFSIA) points to the formalization of improved food security mechanisms with national support, which points to future opportunities in developing the IPC further. After a round of training sessions under the auspices of LAF, the first official IPC map was produced in April 2008 and vetted by the authority of Southern Sudan.

The experiences of Sudan and Kenya highlight that institutional factors are part of the prevailing conditions upon which the success of the IPC will rest. Appropriate institutional support can ensure that the IPC is responding to legitimate demands and complementing existing information systems and structures. Institutional structures will also be critical in resolving the areas of technical debate detailed shortly. The identification of appropriate structures involves detailed awareness-raising and consultation, which have been seen in both case studies to result in improved dialogue and coordination.

4.2 Data and analysis

The IPC framework prescribes a set of key reference outcomes and the adoption of a number of supporting analytical tools, including cartographic maps, analysis templates and population tables. From a data perspective the approach raises a number of questions concerning the adequacy and coverage of reference indicators and data availability to meet these requirements. The utilization of data to enable a "convergence of evidence" analytical approach is a related issue. In this context the measures to safeguard credible analysis, interpretation and judgement arise. Initial field-based exercises have assuaged many of these concerns. Table 7.1 (the IPC Reference Table) presents a "golden standard" of data requirements that may be reached when different stakeholders pool and merge their analysis. The point is to provide guidance on appropriate information inputs, which may vary depending on the context-specific nature of a crisis.

Within Kenya, the Short Rains Assessment followed the key reference outcome indicators outlined in Table 7.1 and recommended in the IPC technical manual. Despite robust information structures, supporting data were found to be weak with regard to key food access and availability indicators, including markets (prices, food stocks), livestock and cross-border information. The possible scope of dietary diversity tools as a proxy measure for food access emerged in terms of harmonizing the tool with other approaches. Although nutrition and mortality indicators were perceived as widely available, their convergence and interpretation were

Table 7.1 IPC reference table

Key reference outcomes	Strategic response framework
Current or imminent outcomes on lives and livelihoods, based on convergence of direct and indirect evidence rather than absolute thresholds: not all indicators must be present	Objectives: (i) mitigate immediate outcomes (ii) support livelihoods (iii) address underlying causes

Phase classification 1:	Generally food secure	
Crude mortality rate	<0.5/10,000/day	Strategic assistance to pockets of food insecure groups
Acute malnutrition	<3% (W/H < −2 z-scores)	Investment in food and economic production systems
Stunting	20% (H/age < −2 z-scores)	
Food access/availability	Usually adequate (>2,100 kcal ppp day), stable	Enable development of livelihood systems based on principles of sustainability, justice, and equity
Dietary diversity	Consistent quality and quantity of diversity	
Water access/availability	Usually adequate (>15 litres ppp day), stable	
Hazards	Moderate to low probability and vulnerability	Prevent emergence of structural hindrances to food security
Civil security	Prevailing and structural peace	
Livelihood assets	Generally sustainable utilization (of 6 capitals)	Advocacy

Phase classification 2:	Chronically food insecure	
Crude mortality rate	<0.5/10,000/day; U5MR < 1/10,000/day	Design and implement strategies to increase stability, resistance and resilience of livelihood systems, thus reducing risk
Acute malnutrition	>3% but <10% (W/H < −2 z-score), usual range, stable	Provision of "safety nets" to high-risk groups
Stunting	>20% (H/age < −2 z-scores)	Interventions for optimal and sustainable use of livelihood assets
Food access/availability	Borderline adequate (2,100 kcal ppp day); unstable	Create contingency plan
Dietary diversity	Chronic dietary diversity deficit	Redress structural hindrances to food security
Water access/availability	Borderline adequate (15 litres ppp day); unstable	Close monitoring of relevant outcome and process indicators
Hazards	Recurrent, with high livelihood vulnerability	Advocacy
Civil security	Unstable; disruptive tension	
Coping	"Insurance strategies"	
Livelihood assets	Stressed and unsustainable utilization (of 6 capitals)	
Structural	Pronounced underlying hindrances to food security	

Table 7.1 (cont.)

Phase classification 3:	Acute food and livelihood crisis	
Crude mortality rate	0.5–1/10,000/day, U5MR 1–2/10,000/day	Support livelihoods and protect vulnerable groups
Acute malnutrition	10–15% (W/H < -2 z-score), greater than usual, increasing	Strategic and complementary interventions to immediately ↑ food access/availability and support livelihoods
Disease	Epidemic; increasing	
Food access/availability	Lack of entitlement; 2,100 kcal ppp day via asset stripping	Selected provision of complementary sectoral support (e.g. water, shelter, sanitation, health)
Dietary diversity	Acute dietary diversity deficit	
Water access/availability	7.5–15 litres ppp day, accessed via asset stripping	Strategic interventions at community to national levels to create, stabilize, rehabilitate or protect priority livelihood assets
Destitution/displacement	Emerging; diffuse	
Civil security	Limited spread, low-intensity conflict	Create or implement contingency plan
Coping	"Crisis strategies"; CSI greater than reference; increasing	Close monitoring of relevant outcome and process indicators
Livelihood assets	Accelerated and critical depletion or loss of access	Use "crisis as opportunity" to redress underlying structural causes
		Advocacy

204

Phase classification 4: Humanitarian crisis

Indicator	Humanitarian crisis	
Crude mortality rate	1–2/10,000/day, >2x reference rate, increasing; U5MR > 2/10,000/day	Urgent protection of vulnerable groups
Acute malnutrition	>15% (W/H < −2 z-score), greater than usual, increasing	Urgently ↑ food access through complementary interventions
Disease	Pandemic	Selected provision of complementary sectoral support (e.g. water, shelter, sanitation, health)
Food access/availability	Severe entitlement gap; unable to meet 2,100 kcal ppp day	Protection against complete livelihood asset loss and/or advocacy for access
Dietary diversity	Regularly 3 or fewer main food groups consumed	Close monitoring of relevant outcome and process indicators
Water access/availability	<7.5 litres ppp day (human usage only)	Use "crisis as opportunity" to redress underlying structural causes
Destitution/displacement	Concentrated; increasing	Advocacy
Civil security	Widespread, high-intensity conflict	
Coping	"Distress strategies"; CSI significantly greater than reference	
Livelihood assets	Near complete and irreversible depletion or loss of access	

Phase classification 5: Famine/humanitarian catastrophe

Indicator	Famine/humanitarian catastrophe	
Crude mortality rate	>2/10,000/day (example: 6,000/1,000,000/30 days)	Critically urgent protection of human lives and vulnerable groups
Acute malnutrition	>30% (W/H < −2 z-score)	Comprehensive assistance with basic needs (e.g. food, water, shelter, sanitation, health)
Disease	Pandemic	Immediate policy/legal revisions where necessary
Food access/availability	Extreme entitlement gap; much below 2,100 kcal ppp day	Negotiations with varied political-economic interests
Water access/availability	<4 litres ppp day (human usage only)	Use "crisis as opportunity" to redress underlying structural causes
Destitution/displacement	Large scale, concentrated	Advocacy
Civil security	Widespread, high-intensity conflict	
Livelihood assets	Effectively complete loss; collapse	

Source: FAO/FSAU (2006).
Notes: W/H = weight-for-height; H/age = height-for-age; U5MR = under-five mortality rate; CSI = Coping Strategies Inventory.

highlighted as a challenge. Concerning omitted variables, attention was devoted to water quality and income measures, and the need to improve coping strategy information was highlighted.

Overall, key data challenges pointed to weakness in data utilization rather than information availability. A comparative review of existing information sources (including the FAO, the Arid Lands Resource Management Project, FEWSNET, the WFP, different line ministries and steering groups) in Kenya was recently undertaken to identify the type of data, frequency of collections, constraints, level of enquiry (household, district, national, facility-based), geographical coverage and format (KFSSG 2007). Through this analysis it was concluded that existing data mechanisms are largely sufficient to meet identified data gaps; however, concerns relate to the analysis and processing of data. Effort is required to improve the use and analysis of indirect evidence, to clarify the indicator formatting required (e.g. trends, levels) and to standardize data reporting formats.

Within Southern Sudan, the preliminary introduction of the IPC points to familiar trends (FAO 2007b). Although it is in the early stages of application, the IPC approach is pulling together information from a number of key sources, including agricultural production output analysis undertaken by the FAO with the ministry of agriculture, Comprehensive Food Security and Vulnerability Mapping Survey (WFP) and analysis from the LAF. The analysis is helping different stakeholders to share information, identify information gaps and streamline future data collection and analysis. In all cases – and based on wider experiences at regional level – the challenges posed by data availability and analysis highlight that greater guidance is required on the overall process of analysis supporting the IPC. This brings into focus the need for more detailed guidance notes and information on the composition of technical teams.

4.3 Adaptation of IPC framework

The IPC framework has been applied at country level in Kenya and informally through a number of regional outlook training and awareness exercises targeted at country experts and representatives. Initial country experiences have led to a number of technical revisions that are currently being tested and are likely to form the basis of future revised technical manuals. This section summarizes the key technical issues to date, based on the original version of the technical manual (FAO/FSAU 2006). Further review of these issues is being conducted by an international technical working group.[1]

An overriding technical challenge has related to the applicability of the framework in non-crisis scenarios and in particular the sensitivity at the lower end of the IPC scale to distinguish between diverse crisis contexts. Three technical issues are related closely to this overriding concern:

- *Chronic factors.* The phase classifications and general descriptors of the original IPC framework include chronic aspects only in the second phase. This raises comparison problems because it introduces chronic factors in an apparently imbalanced manner across the classification. It also raises some possible ambiguities in terminology given the confusion that relates to the conceptualization of chronic food insecurity to describe both temporal and severity aspects (Devereaux 2006).
- *Analysis–response continuum.* The IPC distinguishes between situation and response analysis, as the first two steps in a response–analysis continuum. The separation of situation and response analysis is designed to safeguard the neutrality of the analysis and recognizes that response analysis and planning are part of wider negotiated processes. The underdeveloped nature of response analysis raises questions as to whether the IPC could (or should) be tailored to inform response.
- *Early warning aspects.* An understanding of the current situation and its likely evolution is required in order to plan appropriate responses. The combination of both functions under the IPC framework raises methodological and conceptual challenges, for example concerning the linkage between outcome and process outcomes.

4.4 Chronic factors

Initial experiences, particularly from Kenya, Rwanda, South Sudan and Tanzania training exercises, highlight some challenges and early progress in dealing with chronic factors (FSNWG 2007). In considering that the term "chronic" relates to the *duration* of food insecurity, the labelling and definition of the phase classifications may be problematic. Phase classification 2 (chronically food insecure) is the only category to introduce a temporal component. To this end, for countries confronted with persistent or long-term food insecurity, the overall utility of phase classifications 1 and 2 in distinguishing diverse sets of interventions to address structural factors may be a relative area of weakness in the framework.

Early experiences have led to the re-labelling of the second phase classification as "moderately/borderline food insecure" (FAO 2008b). This makes the framework more consistent in classifying severity. It also maintains the sensitivity amongst classifications and the relevance of current reference outcome indicators. As argued by Devereaux (2006), such information is more important and urgent in an emergency programming context than the duration of food insecurity. It also helps to defuse ambiguity on terminology.

Initial experiences in Kenya have also led to a number of additional technical revisions to introduce greater sensitivity into the IPC scale. First, it has been proposed to split the first phase into separate upper and lower categories to distinguish different food security contexts. Second, it has been suggested that temporal factors could be considered through the introduction of a more systematic "chronic ranking". For example, a simplified ranking could indicate the number of years all phases have been in a given crisis (e.g. <3 years, 4–7 years, 8–10 years). This may also draw attention to the more detailed analytical templates concerning chronic factors.

4.5 Situation and response analysis

In the recent Kenyan Short Rains Assessment, the team that developed the IPC situation analysis went a step further to develop a response analysis by phase and livelihood zone. The government of Kenya and the WFP incorporated a food sector response including beneficiary numbers and food requirements through the food estimates subcommittee of the Kenya Food Security Meeting. The latter, while using the IPC situation analysis, is necessarily a negotiated process. The central question is, therefore, "where does the IPC stop?" For some critics the IPC falls short. Lawrence and Maunder (2007) argue that, since the situation analysis includes the magnitude of the problem, it should also encompass needs assessment more thoroughly, the outputs of which include estimates of the number of people in need and the deficits they face. The IPC approach purposely delineates between both situation and response analysis in order to promote the importance of a neutral and multidimensional analysis of food insecurity. To this end, the IPC focuses only on estimating the severity and magnitude of the problem as reflected through phase classifications and population estimates. By defining the problem and identifying its multidimensional nature, the IPC as envisaged is designed to set the parameters of a response analysis. This is informed by evidence-based templates and further supported by a strategic response framework. The response analysis that follows would then most probably include a needs assessment to inform policy formulation and targeting based upon the identified problem.

For the above reasons, the emerging lessons from Kenya highlight the importance of *bridging* situation and response analysis – as distinct from introducing a more refined response analysis into the IPC framework. Already the generalized strategic response framework provides a series of non-prescriptive recommendations that can provide a bridge to response analysis. The Kenya experience also highlights that active measures need to be taken to convene appropriate stakeholders in a response analysis forum after a given IPC analysis. Within Kenya this recommendation underpins the continued importance of institutional factors.

5 Conclusions

The chapter highlights the imperative for improved analysis to enable more appropriate responses to crises. In particular, there is significant potential for food security analysis to be more systematic, using common standards and reference criteria that will enable more comparable analysis and foster minimal standards of rigour. Here, the value added of the IPC is explored as a mechanism to promote more comparable and transparent analysis with the aim of ensuring a more strategic, timely and needs-based response. The case-study evidence highlights the initial stages of IPC development outside of the original context in Somalia. This points to the unique field-based nature of the tool and the iterative lesson learning that is envisaged to support its more systematic development in the coming years by a range of national and international partners. Based upon initial experiences in developing the IPC, early evidence points to the following conclusions concerning the development of classification systems to understand food crises and vulnerability. The IPC applications point to the importance of national buy-in in the analysis of food security and vulnerability matters. Institutional aspects within a country need to be considered to ensure ownership and transparency of approach and ultimately the translation of food security objectives into national programmes and poverty reduction strategies where they exist.

The value added of the IPC is to bring consistency to the early stages of analysis, particularly through the separation of situation from response analysis. Too often, immediate responses to crises tend to prioritize needs assessments, largely based on a predetermined set of response options. The bridge between situation analysis, the underlying causes and risk and the analysis of response options has proven to be more accurate in providing a broader basis for policy framework. From the vulnerability perspective, this suggests that the IPC helps to illustrate underlying elements of vulnerability, such as whether certain hazards are of a covariate or an idiosyncratic nature. From here the analysis can be used to determine the potential severity and magnitude of a crisis event, with the early warning providing a valuable signal about future vulnerability patterns.

Acknowledgements

The designations employed and the presentation of material in this information product do not imply the expression of any opinion whatsoever on the part of the Food and Agriculture Organization of the United Nations concerning the legal status of any country, territory, city or area or of its authorities, or concerning the delimitation of its frontiers or boundaries. Content and errors are exclusively the responsibility of the authors and do not necessarily reflect the position of the FAO. Special thanks for comments received from Luca Alinovi, Gunter Hemrich, Luca Russo, James Tefft, Nick Haan, Zoe Druilhe and Denise Melvin.

Note

1. The IPC Global Partners prepared Version 1.1 of the Technical Manual (FAO 2008b); updates of the manual are available at ⟨http://www.ipcinfo.org/tech.php⟩ (accessed 23 January 2009).

References

Darcy, J. and C.-A. Hofmann (2003). "According to Need? Needs Assessment and Decision Making in the Humanitarian Sector". HPG Briefings 15, Overseas Development Institute, London.

Devereaux, S. (2006). "Desk Review: Distinguishing between Chronic and Transitory Food Insecurity in Emergency Need Assessments". SENAC/WFP, Rome.

FAO [Food and Agriculture Organization of the United Nations] (1996). "Rome Declaration on World Food Security and World Food Summit Plan of Action". Rome, 13–17 November.

FAO (2007a). "Assessment of the World Food Security Situation". FAO document CFS 2007/2, Committee on World Food Security (33rd Session), Rome, 7–10 May; available at ⟨ftp://ftp.fao.org/docrep/fao/meeting/011/J9455e.pdf⟩ (accessed 27 January 2009).

FAO (2007b). "Special Event: Perspectives on a Common Approach for Food Security Analysis and Response: The Contribution of the IPC". Committee on World Food Security (33rd Session), Rome, 9 May; available at ⟨http://www.ipcinfo.org/attachments/CFSmtg_IPC_specialevent_draftreport.doc⟩ (accessed 27 January 2009).

FAO (2008a). *Crop Prospects and Food Situation*. No. 1. Rome: FAO's Global Information and Early Warning Service; available at ⟨http://www.fao.org/docrep/010/ah881e/ah881e00.htm⟩ (accessed 23 January 2009).

FAO (2008b). *Integrated Food Security Phase Classification: Technical Manual Version 1.1*. Prepared by the IPC Global Partners. Rome: FAO; available at ⟨ftp://ftp.fao.org/docrep/fao/010/i0275e/i0275e00.pdf⟩ (accessed 27 January 2009).

FAO/FSAU (2006). *Integrated Food Security and Humanitarian Phase Classification: Technical Manual Version I*. Nairobi: FAO/FSAU Technical Series IV.

Flores, M., Y. Khwaja and P. White (2005). "Food Security in Protracted Crises: Building More Effective Policy Frameworks". *Disasters* 29(S1): S25–S51.

FSNWG [Food Security and Nutrition Working Group] (2007). Regional IPC Technical Workshop: Working Group Session. Nairobi, 1–3 February.

Gaiha, R. and K. Imai (2008). "Measuring Vulnerability and Poverty: Estimates for Rural India". WIDER Research Paper 2008/40, UNU-WIDER, Helsinki.

KFSSG [Kenya Food Security Steering Group] (2007). "Report on the IPC Learning Workshop, 23–26 April". KCB Management Centre, Nairobi.

Lawrence, M. and N. Maunder (2007). "A Review of the Integrated Food Security and Phase Classification (IPC)". RHVP Report, Regional Hunger and Vulnerability Programme, Johannesburg; available at ⟨http://www.sarpn.org.za/documents/d0002538/index.php⟩ (accessed 26 January 2009).

Levine, S. and C. Chastre et al. (2004). "Missing the Point: An Analysis of Food Security Interventions in the Great Lakes". Network Paper 47, Humanitarian Practice Network, Overseas Development Institute, London.

Lovendal, C. R. and M. Knowles (2007). "Tomorrow's Hunger: A Framework for Analysing Vulnerability to Food Insecurity". In B. Guha-Khasnobis, S. Acharya and B. Davis (eds), *Food Security: Indicators, Measurement, and the Impact of Trade Openness*. Oxford: Oxford University Press for UNU-WIDER.

Maxwell, D. (2006). "Global Trends in Food Aid". Paper presented at the WFP Meeting, Jakarta, 6–8 June.

Maxwell, D. and B. Watkins (2003). "Humanitarian Information Systems and Emergencies in the Greater Horn of Africa: Logical Components and Logical Linkages". *Disasters* 27(1): 72–90.

ODI [Overseas Development Institute] (2005). "Humanitarian Issues in Niger". HPG Briefing Note, Overseas Development Institute, London; available at ⟨http://www.odi.org.uk/hpg/papers/HPGBriefingNote4.pdf⟩ (accessed 26 January 2009).

Pantuliano, S. (2006). "Saving Lives through Livelihoods: Critical Gaps in the Response to the Drought in the Greater Horn of Africa". HPG Briefing Note, Overseas Development Institute, London; available at ⟨http://www.odi.org.uk/hpg/papers/RAPID_HornAfricaBriefing.pdf⟩ (accessed 26 January 2009).

Pingali, P., L. Alinovi and J. Sutton (2005). "Food Security in Complex Emergencies: Enhancing Food System Resilience". *Disasters* 29(S1): S5–S24.

Tefft, J., M. McGuire and N. Maunder (2006). "Assessment of Food Security Early Warning Systems in Sub-Saharan Africa". Policy Brief, FAO, Rome; available at ⟨ftp://ftp.fao.org/es/ESA/policybriefs/pb_04.pdf⟩ (accessed 26 January 2009).

Part II
Natural hazards and macroeconomic shocks

8

Vulnerability of small-island economies: The impact of "natural" disasters in the Caribbean

Martin Philipp Heger, Alex Julca and Oliver Paddison

1 Introduction

The Caribbean region is characterized by great diversity.[1] This manifests itself not only in the population size, ranging from less than 50,000 to close to 9 million, but also in the dispersion of income per capita, ranging from approximately US$500 to over US$17,000 (see Table 8.1). Similarly, alongside linguistic diversity – with Dutch, French, Spanish and English, as well as Papiamento, Maroon and Creole, being spoken in the region – there are also notable cultural influences stemming from Western Europe and North America, as well as Africa and Asia. Despite this diversity, by and large economies in the region face common challenges. For instance, as small countries they must overcome many disadvantages resulting from their small-island developing states (SIDS) nature. These include, for example, exhibiting a high degree of specialization because of the narrow range of resources available to them as well as the inability to take advantage of economies of scale owing to small domestic and regional markets. They also include being overly dependent on international trade and thereby particularly vulnerable to global trade developments, as well as coping with the pressures that high population density (despite having relatively small populations) exerts on the limited resource supply. These challenges are in fact well accepted and were acknowledged at, *inter alia*, the Global Conference on SIDS in Barbados in 1994, which resulted in the Barbados Programme of Action (BPoA) and set forth procedures

Vulnerability in developing countries, Naudé, Santos-Paulino and McGillivray (eds),
United Nations University Press, 2009, ISBN 978-92-808-1171-1

Table 8.1 Population size, GDP and sectoral composition of economies

Country	Total population, 2005	GDP per capita (current US$), 2005	Sectoral composition (per cent of value added)			
			Agriculture	Industry	Services, etc.	Manufacturing
Antigua and Barbuda	82,786	10,578	3.7	20.3	76.0	2.1
Bahamas	323,063	17,497[a]	2.3	10.4	81.9	5.4
Barbados	269,556	11,465	3.6	16.5	80.0	6.9
Belize	291,800	3,786	16.5	17.7	65.8	9.1
Dominica	72,000	3,938	18.6	24.0	57.3	8.1
Dominican Republic	8,894,907	3,317	11.7	29.6	58.7	15.5
Grenada	106,500	4,451	8.5	23.1	68.4	5.5
Guyana	751,218	1,048	31.3	27.0	41.7	9.6
Haiti[c]	8,527,777	500	27.9	17.0	55.1	8.4
Jamaica	2,654,500	3,607	5.6	32.7	61.7	13.7
Puerto Rico	3,912,054	17,685[b]	1.0	45.0	54.0	40.4
St Kitts and Nevis	48,000	9,438	3.2	27.5	69.3	10.1
St Lucia[c]	164,791	5,007	5.3	18.1	76.6	5.2
St Vincent and the Grenadines	119,051	3,612	8.2	24.6	67.2	5.5
Suriname	449,238	2,986	11.2	23.5	65.3	5.4
Trinidad and Tobago	1,305,236	11,000	1.1	55.1	43.9	6.9

Source: World Bank (2006).
Notes:
[a] 2002
[b] 2001
[c] Sectoral figures relate to 2003.

for governments and national, regional and international organizations to realize the sustainable development objectives defined in Agenda 21 of the Rio Declaration.[2]

A further common feature of particular relevance to the majority of Caribbean economies is that they are particularly vulnerable to natural and environmental disasters owing to their dependence on agriculture and tourism. This too is explicitly emphasized in the BPoA (see United Nations 1994: 30). In this view, the concept of vulnerability needs, however, first to be placed into context and to be properly defined, not only when dealing with SIDS and their susceptibility to suffering adverse impacts of natural hazards in particular, but also because there is no generally accepted, universal definition of vulnerability.[3]

Typically, the concept of vulnerability to natural hazards relates to two factors. On the one hand, vulnerability is determined by the frequency (incidence) and severity (intensity) of natural hazards. The second factor relates to the ability to deal with the impact of natural hazards, be it to withstand the potential negative consequences they may have on an affected region/country or to cope rapidly with the resulting damage. Vulnerability is therefore the outcome of the interaction between exogenous factors determined, e.g., by hydro-meteorological or geological characteristics that drive the incidence and intensity of hazards and the ability of a country/region to deal with the impact, which is in turn a function of endogenous elements. For the purposes of this chapter, an appealing definition of vulnerability may therefore be that of the United Nations International Strategy for Disaster Reduction (UN-ISDR): the conditions determined by physical, social, economic and environmental factors or processes that increase the susceptibility of a community to the impact of hazards (UN-ISDR 2004). Therefore, a high degree of vulnerability may be the result of a high incidence and intensity of natural hazards (i.e. physical and environmental factors); it may equally be the result of a lower incidence and intensity coupled with a lower ability to deal with the impact (weaker social and economic factors). This recognition is important insofar as it emphasizes the fact that vulnerability and poverty should not be conflated. Although there may be a link between vulnerability and poverty (or an alternative measure of wellbeing in general), it is not true that all poor are necessarily vulnerable or that the non-poor are either invulnerable or less vulnerable. Moreover, when relating the concept of vulnerability to SIDS, one must recognize that the "ability to bounce back" from the negative impact of natural hazards is particularly hampered by the characteristics that define them as small-island developing states. In particular, owing to their smallness (in relation either to their geographical size, their population size or indeed their relatively undiversified economic structure), there is an important structural component inherent in the concept of vulnerability in relation to SIDS. Hence, the low degree of resilience to natural hazards in the region results from the frequent occurrence of natural disasters, defined here as a situation or event that overwhelms local capacity, necessitating a request to the national or international level for external assistance (UN-ISDR 1992).

The impact of such disasters is often significant and has profound consequences for the economies affected, because disasters can undo years of development. For instance, a particularly active hurricane season in 2004 caused damage amounting to approximately US$3.1 billion, which translated into significant proportions of gross domestic product (GDP), ranging from approximately 10 per cent in Jamaica to more than 200 per cent in Grenada. Moreover, such monetary aggregates of the cost of damage capture only a small element of the actual impact of the event. What such figures do not convey is the impact on the economy and on society resulting, for example, from the loss of human life, from the disruption of public services and the adverse impact thereof on human well-being (break-up of families owing to migration, increased risk of disease, lack of access to health and education facilities, worsened public infrastructure available, etc.), and consequently from the impact of increased poverty owing to the loss of livelihoods, to name but a few channels. Although damage and losses arising from natural hazards are in principle not an obstacle to development, it may well be that the impact of such damage and losses poses a major stumbling block to development for many SIDS. Repeated setbacks resulting from the destruction of economic and social capital through natural disasters perpetuate the poverty cycle and can act as a catalyst for turning natural hazards into natural disasters per se.

This chapter aims to analyse the impact of natural disasters on SIDS, focusing on the Caribbean region in particular. Although all countries in the Caribbean region are particularly vulnerable to natural disasters, the aim is to identify factors that may mitigate their impact because this must be considered an important component of economic policy in the region to reduce vulnerability to natural hazards. The chapter is structured as follows. Section 2 presents a typology of countries in the Caribbean region, underlining their differences in terms of economic structure as well as highlighting their similarity with regard to vulnerability to natural hazards. Section 3 presents an econometric analysis of natural disasters in the region and analyses additional factors that may be important in determining the destructive power of a disaster. Section 4 concludes.

2 Caribbean economies

The Caribbean is composed of many diverse, small countries. The populations of the countries referred to in this study range from 8.9 million inhabitants in the Dominican Republic to 48,000 in St Kitts and Nevis. Similarly, there is a large degree of variability in income in the region, with an income per capita of over US$17,000 in the Bahamas being more than twenty times that of Haiti, at US$500.[4]

Moreover, this diversity is reflected in the underlying economic structure of countries in the region. Although most are constrained by the narrow resource base of their economies, the single dominant sectors that have merged in these economies differ, resulting in a bipolar structure that distinguishes between *service-based* economies on the one hand (Antigua and Barbuda, Grenada, St Kitts and Nevis, St Lucia, St Vincent and the Grenadines, the Bahamas, Barbados and the Dominican Republic) and *resource-based* economies such as Trinidad and Tobago (petroleum), Guyana (rice, timber, sugar and gold) and Suriname (rice, gold, and diamonds) on the other hand. Moreover, whereas Jamaica can be considered bipolar, with a significant extraction sector as well as strong services, Dominica and Haiti are generally considered to be agricultural economies owing to their relatively important agricultural sectors (contributing 18.6 per cent and 27.9 per cent of value added, respectively; see Table 8.1), despite having a dominant services sector (ECLAC 2006).

Even with these differences within the region, all countries share some important similarities. First, all Caribbean economies are very open, with the sum of import and export ratios (relative to GDP) exceeding 100 per cent for all Caribbean countries. Likewise, given their geographical constraints and the challenges arising from their smallness, taking advantage of economies of scale is limited for most countries. This in turn has translated into a dependency on imports for the majority of goods consumed within countries as well as the emergence of a relatively limited export base. In addition, increased specialization to compensate for the lack of economies of scale and to remain competitive in an increasingly global environment has contributed to high degrees of export concentration. In fact, in only five countries do the five main export goods account for less than three-quarters of overall exports, and in five others they represent more than 90 per cent of overall exports (see Table 8.2). Moreover, this percentage has increased in five countries (Belize, Haiti, Jamaica, St Kitts and Nevis, and Trinidad and Tobago) during recent years, signalling greater specialization rather than diversification.[5] This lack of economic diversification represents one of the sources of the inherent structural vulnerability common to all SIDS, especially regarding vulnerability to

Table 8.2 Top five export commodities as a percentage of overall export revenues, 1970–2005

Country	1970	2005	Single top commodity
Antigua and Barbuda	94.5 (1973)	91.7	69.9
Bahamas	97.0 (1974)	72.9 (2001)	19.2
Barbados	73.5	62.9	31.6
Belize	78.1 (1972)	90.1	26.2
Dominica	95.0 (1977)	89.8	42.7
Dominican Republic	88.1 (1972)	60.8 (2001)	17.6
Guyana	93.1	82.3	29.1
Grenada	95.3 (1977)	72.1 (2004)	40.3
Haiti	78.8	80.6 (1977)	47.7
Jamaica	83.0 (1972)	88.3	63.6
Puerto Rico	n/a n/a	86.5	46.3
St Kitts and Nevis	89.8 (1981)	97.6	87.2
St Lucia	85.0 (1973)	73.6	24.8
St Vincent and the Grenadines	95.2 (1976)	76.4	43.7
Suriname	97.1 (1974)	96.2	77.7
Trinidad and Tobago	89.3	92.1	45.7

Source: Authors' calculations based on the UN Comtrade database (United Nations n.d.).

natural hazards. To name but one channel, the impact of natural hazards on trade – in particular, the reduction in exports owing to decreased production capability and the increase in imports responding to reconstruction efforts – spills over to a worsening in the fiscal balance since many Caribbean countries derive a significant proportion of their revenues from the taxation of international trade, exceeding more than 50 per cent of total tax revenues in most cases (see ECLAC 2006).[6] Natural hazards therefore place a particular strain on the ability of the public sector to undertake reconstruction and can potentially lead to higher debt stocks to overcome the shortfall in revenues and the necessary increase in expenditure.[7]

In fact, all Caribbean economies are highly susceptible to natural hazards. Hydro-meteorological disasters such as hurricanes and wind storms are the most common natural hazards in the region, accounting for more than half of all natural disasters, but there is also a sizeable occurrence of flooding in the region, part of which is related to the after-effects of hurricanes and wind storms. In addition, the occurrence of disasters of geological origin (earthquakes and volcanic eruptions) was not insignificant in the region over the last four decades (see Figure 8.1).

The high vulnerability of the region is also owing to a combination of high frequency of natural hazards as well as high intensity of natural

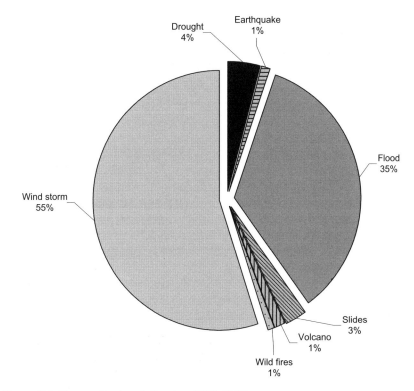

Figure 8.1 Types of natural disaster, 1970–2006.
Source: Based on data from CRED (2007).

hazards in the region. Figure 8.2 suggests that the occurrence of natural disasters is increasing; overall, an average of six natural disasters occurred in the region per year over the period 1970–2006. Economies such as Haiti, the Dominican Republic and Jamaica have experienced more natural disasters than many of the smaller economies (see Figure 8.3). However, being geographically larger, this outcome is not surprising. Taking the population size of each country into account, a rather different picture emerges: with more than one natural disaster per 10,000 inhabitants, St Kitts and Nevis, Dominica, and St Vincent and the Grenadines recorded the highest relative number of natural disasters over the period 1970–2006. In larger countries such as Haiti, the Dominican Republic, Trinidad and Tobago, and Suriname, the figure was less by a factor of more than 10.[8]

In addition to the high frequency of natural disasters, their high intensity is a key aspect in explaining the region's vulnerability to natural hazards. This, together with the fact that the spatial concentration of

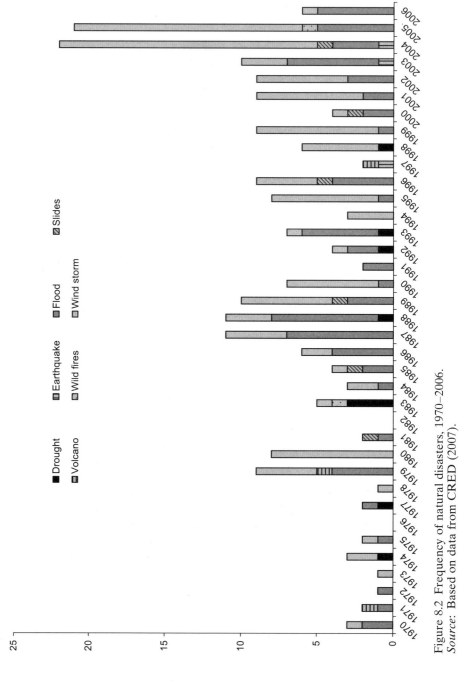

Figure 8.2 Frequency of natural disasters, 1970–2006.
Source: Based on data from CRED (2007).

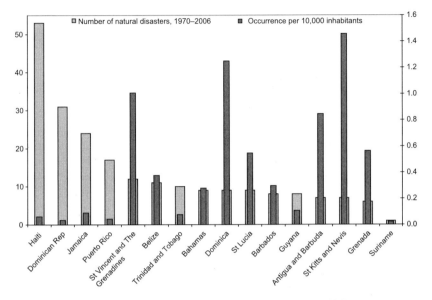

Figure 8.3 Occurrence of natural disasters by country, 1970–2006.
Source: Based on data from CRED (2007) and United Nations (2005).

economic activity in general, and productive capacity in particular, is higher in smaller countries, contributes to the significant damage that can occur – exceeding 50 per cent of GDP in individual countries (see Table 8.3). Moreover, this impact is particularly relevant because it is precisely smaller economies that, owing to the lack of a hinterland, are in general less likely to be able to recover rapidly from a natural disaster

Table 8.3 The destructive impact of natural disasters in the region

Country	Year	Event	Damage (% of GDP)
St Lucia	1988	Hurricane Gilbert	365
Grenada	2004	Hurricane Ivan	203
Dominica	1979	Hurricanes David and Fredrick	101
St Kitts and Nevis	1995	Hurricane Luis	85
St Lucia	1980	Hurricane Allen	66
Antigua and Barbuda	1995	Hurricane Luis	61
Guyana	2005	Floods	59

Source: Authors' calculations based on data from World Bank (2006) and CRED (2007).

without external assistance. Whereas larger economies can spread the burden over time as well as over space, thereby more ably absorbing the overall impact, coping strategies for smaller countries are more limited and reliance on post-disaster financing (taking the form of grants and loans from external sources) is likely to be more relevant.

2.1 The economic impact of natural hazards

Understanding the economic impact of natural hazards is important for implementing corrective policy action to lessen the hardship resulting from natural hazards that have turned into disasters. The impact of natural events on the economic fundamentals of economies essentially takes three forms: damage, indirect losses and secondary effects. As these have been well documented elsewhere (see ECLAC 2003), they are only briefly mentioned in the following.[9]

Damage and indirect losses

First, natural hazards cause damage to assets and to productive capital, i.e. stocks of capital such as infrastructure. Such damage usually occurs at the time of the hazard and will include items such as the damage (partial or total) sustained by physical assets such as buildings, machinery and infrastructure (roads, utility supply equipment, etc.).

In addition to damage, the economy in general, and agents in particular, incur indirect losses, such as losses in flows of income resulting from the impact of the event and costs incurred such as teachers' salaries and the repair of shelters used as emergency places for evacuation. Higher operational costs, such as higher transportation costs resulting from the damage sustained by roads and transport infrastructure, form part of the indirect losses because they are a direct consequence of the damage caused by the natural disaster. Moreover, shortfalls in harvests, for example, or in the provision of services resulting from the impact of the natural disaster also contribute towards indirect losses. In short, losses are a consequence of the impact of the event in general, and of the damage following the hazard in particular.

The overall impact of a disaster varies depending on its nature. Geological disasters such as earthquakes usually cause greater damage to assets and less indirect damage, particularly in economies based on agriculture. Hydro-meteorological disasters, on the other hand, such as severe wind storms, flooding or drought, usually have a more significant impact on indirect losses. In any event, the total impact of disasters, as measured by the sum of indirect losses and damage, can be substantial: the 2004 hurricane season for instance caused more than US$3 billion in damage in the countries considered in this chapter (see Table 8.4).

Table 8.4 The economic impact of the 2004 hurricane season in the Caribbean

Country	US$ million
Bahamas	1,000.0
Barbados	5.0
Dominican Republic	297.0
Grenada	889.0
Haiti	22.0
Jamaica	895.0
St Lucia	0.5
St Vincent and the Grenadines	5.0
Trinidad and Tobago	1.0
Total	3,114.5

Source: Authors' calculations based on data from World Bank (2006) and CRED (2007).

Secondary effects

Damage and indirect losses on stocks and flows, respectively, in the economy resulting from natural disasters are reflected in changes in the main economic variables, which are termed secondary effects. Such secondary effects are a result of the impact of the natural event: (i) by affecting an economy's production and distribution channels and thus depressing its overall rate of growth; (ii) through the loss of aggregate income and employment and spillovers onto consumption profiles; (iii) through increased imports resulting from the need to purchase intermediate goods and raw materials for repairs; (iv) by increasing insurance flows, and (v) through lower government revenue. Thus, the damage and indirect costs and the impact spill over to the external balance (the balance of payments, the level of indebtedness) and the internal balance of the affected economy (inflation, growth and income, the fiscal balance, employment, etc.).

Analysis of the impact of natural disasters is often undertaken on a case-by-case basis to obtain financial assistance to mitigate the impact. In contrast, the aim of a more encompassing analysis of natural disasters, spanning a larger set of countries, is to elicit overall patterns of impact and to derive policy recommendations based upon general observations that may not be identified on a case-by-case basis. Several studies have taken a broader look at the impact of natural disasters. For instance, looking at 16 countries in Latin America and the Caribbean, Auffret (2003) finds that the impact of natural disasters in the region is, in fact, so significant that the volatility of consumption in the Caribbean is higher than in any other region in the world.

In contrast to the unambiguous effects on consumption volatility, the evidence on the impact of disasters on growth is conflicting, particularly in the case of long-term growth. For example, whereas Benson and Clay (2003) argue that the impact of natural disasters on long-term growth is negative, Skidmore and Toya (2002) claim that disasters may *positively* impact long-term growth because the effect of a natural disaster may be to reduce the return on physical capital and thereby increase the relative return to human capital. Consequently, this may *induce* growth in general. How far this result remains valid for the Caribbean region, however, is not clear. For one thing, there are only a few Caribbean countries in Skidmore and Toya's sample. Moreover, there is a significant brain drain in the Caribbean, which reduces the benefit of higher levels of human capital in the region and potentially casts doubt on the applicability of these results to the Caribbean region.[10]

Making a more comprehensive assessment of impacts for a larger group of economies in the Caribbean region (in this case members of the Eastern Caribbean Currency Union, i.e. Antigua and Barbuda, Dominica, Grenada, St Kitts and Nevis, St Lucia, St Vincent and the Grenadines, and two dependent territories of the United Kingdom, Anguilla and Montserrat), Rasmussen (2004) finds, for instance, that a short-term impact of disasters is an immediate contraction in output, as well as a significant worsening of external balances, with a median increase in the current account deficit of approximately 10.8 per cent of GDP. He also points to a worsening of the fiscal balance, resulting from higher expenditures and lower receipts, which is argued to contribute to a cumulative increase in the median public debt (measured as a percentage of debt) of approximately 6.5 percentage points over three years.

Overall, we find that there is only limited work on the impact of natural disasters on international trade in general, especially in relation to smaller economies. For instance, although Gassebner et al. (2006) investigate the impact of major disasters on international trade flows and find that the level of democracy and the area of the affected country are key forces driving the impact of these events, their analysis essentially excludes all smaller Caribbean countries owing to the definition of large-scale disaster that is applied.[11] Easterly and Kraay (2000), in contrast, look at the issue of the volatility of small states, but they question whether vulnerability to external shocks such as those arising from the impact of natural disasters is caused by the more specialized trade patterns of smaller economies relative to larger economies, and they suggest that the greater degree of openness is likely to be a more applicable source of the greater volatility in terms-of-trade shocks that these countries experience.

3 Analysis of natural disasters in the Caribbean

This section deals with and reports on the assessed effects of natural disasters on economic performance and trade. Following a description of the data and the applied estimation procedure and a discussion of conceptual issues, we present the actual empirical estimations and draw conclusions from the results.

3.1 Data

The empirical analysis uses data from three sources. Data relating to the incidence of natural disasters, such as frequency, damage incurred and people affected (as measured by deaths, injured and affected in general), are drawn from the Emergency Events Database (EM-DAT) compiled by the Centre for Research on the Epidemiology of Disasters (CRED). This database contains data pertaining to over 16,000 natural disasters from 1900 to the present from various sources (including UN agencies, non-governmental organizations, insurance companies, research institutes and press agencies) and as such is considered to be one of the prime databases for such information.[12]

We use a number of disaster variables in order to capture the various effects that are hypothesized to result from a disaster. By doing so, we hope to distinguish between the different channels through which a disaster affects economic output. We also want to distinguish between distinct and latent effects, i.e. between the *direct* and *indirect impacts* of environmental hazards. Our variables of choice after applying our transformations are:

Dummy disaster: indicates whether a country was struck by a natural disaster during the year of observation;

Disaster count: nominal number of natural disasters per country and per year;

Deaths: number of persons either confirmed as dead, or presumed to be dead or missing, relative to the total population of the country;

Injured: number of people whose physical or psychological injuries are severe enough to require medical treatment, relative to the total population of the country;

Homeless: people needing immediate assistance with shelter, relative to the total population of the country;

Affected: people requiring immediate assistance during an unidentified period of emergency, which may in some cases include displaced or evacuated people;

Disaster cost: estimated costs resulting from the damage caused by a disaster, expressed in US dollars as a share of GDP and taken from several institutions.[13]

In our analysis we focus only on natural disasters, ignoring, for example, "technological" disasters, although it has been argued (Gassebner et al. 2006) that the medium that triggers the disaster might not be relevant for its particular form and hence a disaster can be regarded interchangeably, whether it stems from a technological malfunction or from an environmental crisis.[14] We believe, however, that there are distinct differences, which was in fact confirmed by a Chow breakpoint test.

The data used to calculate the Herfindahl–Hirschman index (HHI) were drawn from the United Nations Comtrade database, while the economic indicators that form our outcome variables were taken from *World Development Indicators 2006* (World Bank 2006). These include mainly measures of economic performance and trade that are of interest: *GDP/capita* (purchasing power parity) is expressed in international dollars for the year 2000; *Imports* and *Exports*, respectively, represent the percentage share of imports and exports in annual GDP; *Debt* measures total external debt in current US dollars relative to current GDP. The variables that we use later as either controls or intermediating variables are as follows:

Agri1: agricultural raw material exports, as a share of commodity exports as a whole;

Agri2: the value added of agriculture, as a percentage of GDP;

Agri3: agricultural raw material imports, as a share of commodity imports as a whole.

Our analysis covers 15 Caribbean states over the period 1970–2006: Antigua and Barbuda, the Bahamas, Barbados, Dominica, Dominican Republic, Grenada, Haiti, Jamaica, the Netherlands Antilles, Puerto Rico, St Lucia, St Kitts and Nevis, St Vincent and the Grenadines, Trinidad and Tobago, and the US Virgin Islands.[15] There are no missing observations for the disaster variables and the economic explanatory variables are characterized by very few missing observations for the period selected. The summary statistics are presented in Table 8.5.

3.2 Conceptual issues

Several conceptual issues need to be addressed. One emerges from the usual unit root considerations, in that we cannot simply regress natural disaster variables on trended variables such as GDP and other economic indicators. Hence, we experiment with a number of options to eliminate this potential bias, i.e. including year dummies, country-specific time trends and differentiated estimators. Furthermore, we do not expect our

Table 8.5 Summary statistics, 1970–2005

Variable	Mean	Median	Maximum	Minimum	Std dev.	Obs.
Disaster count	0.39	0.00	8.00	0.00	0.81	540
Disaster cost	0.08	0.00	8.41	0.00	0.59	540
Deaths	0.00	0.00	0.01	0.00	0.00	540
Affected	0.02	0.00	1.22	0.00	0.09	540
GDP/capita	7,347.11	5527.65	24,320.14	1,471.45	4,671.41	363
Imports	62.46	64.70	107.14	11.66	20.06	350
Exports	50.97	51.15	96.22	5.43	17.17	350
Debt	0.40	0.35	1.96	0.03	0.27	316
Import specialization: HHI imports	0.06	0.03	0.88	0.00	0.13	378
Export specialization: HHI exports	0.23	0.20	0.94	0.00	0.22	398
Agri1	0.45	0.20	8.07	0.00	0.88	289
Agri2	10.44	7.98	39.12	0.58	8.25	282
Agri3	1.86	1.94	4.90	0.07	0.93	278
Population density	233.71	222.87	626.87	16.96	137.71	468

Source: See text.

regressions to yield a high R^2 because it is unlikely that one can perfectly estimate economic output equations with natural disaster occurrences.

We apply a time dimension to our analysis not only to take advantage of a bigger data set but also to be able to analyse lag structures. The impacts of natural disasters will not only be felt immediately but also manifest themselves through time.

A final conceptual issue is reverse causality. It is possible that an ever-growing GDP triggers more natural disasters (see Figure 8.3) in absolute numbers, as well as more destructive ones owing to the environmental drawbacks that are associated with a growing economy.

3.3 Estimation and results

In our attempt to identify the decisive disaster variables, a simple OLS estimation (Table 8.6) including a full set of fixed effects and country-specific linear time trends revealed that our variables of choice for the purpose of assessing the impacts of natural disasters on economic performance and trade are: *Disaster count*, *Deaths* and *Cost* (in order of importance).[16] We shall use the *Cost* variable to illustrate the economic dimension of disasters and the *Death* variable to capture the social dimension affecting society after a disastrous event.

As seen in Table 8.6, the *F*-statistic testing the joint significance for the collection of explanatory variables is significant at every level, which indicates that our disaster variables are capable of explaining a significant

Table 8.6 Selection of proxies for natural disasters (OLS estimation), 1970–2005

	GDP/capita		Trade (% of GDP)		External debt (% of GDP)	
	(1)	(2)	(3)	(4)	(5)	(6)
Dummy variable						
Disaster dummy	-252.73		3.62		0.07*	0.02
	(219.28)		(2.28)		(0.03)	(0.02)
Disaster count		**-333.65**		2.50**		
		(120.12)		(1.41)		
Disaster cost/capita	461,843.1	351,292.2	3.86*	4.02*	-0.01	-0.01
	(453,085.0)	(447,848.8)	(1.95)	(1.95)	(0.03)	(0.03)
Disaster deaths/population	-4,734,286.0*	-3,952,312.0**	-28,287.63	-27,286.98	-155.11	-147.73
	(2,290,320.0)	(2288550.0)	(43,041.67)	(42,802.77)	(489.91)	(495.53)
Affected/population	-18.08942	77.61	-13.25	-13.30	**0.92**	**1.03**
	(1,042.668)	(1,021.925)	(10.72)	(10.69)	**(0.35)**	**(0.34)**
Injured/population	62,349.36	50,804.87	705.93	707.14	-114.58	-183.85
	(76,265.83)	(75,604.23)	(996.62)	(993.88)	(622.50)	(625.37)
Homeless/population	12533.04	14,022.72	169.90	172.24	-5.08	-4.07
	(14,586.19)	(14,432.90)	(164.40)	(163.98)	(5.24)	(5.24)
Obs.	363	363	350	350	316	316
R^2	.90	.91	.84	.84	.05	.04
F-statistic	**61.28**	**62.61**	**29.05**	**29.12**	**2.76**	**2.18**
	(0.00)	**(0.00)**	**(0.00)**	**(0.00)**	**(0.01)**	**(0.04)**

Source: See text.
Notes: Includes a full set of fixed effects and country-specific linear time trends. The table reports coefficients, with the related standard errors in parentheses; p-values: bold indicates a coefficient that is significant at the 1% level; *, ** represent significance levels of 5% and 10%, respectively. The unit of observation is a country-year.

part of the variation occurring in a country, across time, in GDP and trade. The R^2 indicates a range from .84 to .91, signalling a markedly better overall fit than we had expected.

However, the impact of natural disasters cannot properly account for annual and cross-country deviations in external debt, given the low R^2 of .04 to .05. Whereas most of the coefficients measuring the impact of natural disasters on debt are statistically insignificant, we nonetheless find that the coefficients on total affected population (column (6)) and the dummy variable for disasters (column (5)) show statistical significance at $\alpha = .1$ and $\alpha = .05$, respectively.[17] Thus, although the explanatory power is relatively low, signalling that other factors are the primary cause of measured debt fluctuations, natural disasters do contribute to the region's overall high level of indebtedness.

The point of the exercise so far has been to identify the most appropriate measure for the particular outcome variable of interest. The main result is that disasters do affect economic and trade activity significantly. Moreover, a disaster negatively affects GDP per capita, not only through its mere occurrence but also through the impact on its victims (the *Deaths* variable is significant in column (1) of Table 8.6). The trade activity and debt variables are in turn positively affected by the selected disaster measures. Because the *Count* variable is the most significant explanatory variable, it will form the point of origin and core of our impact analysis, while the other two variables will serve as auxiliary variables when analysing the effects on *GDP*. The *Cost/capita* variable will be our measure of choice when assessing the impacts on the trade variables (*Exports* and *Imports*) and the *Total affected* variable will be our cardinal explanatory measure for *Debt* as an outcome variable. All three indicators capture a different dimension and yield an overall good fit of the model.

Dynamic analysis

So far, the analysis has remained at the snapshot method of a moment in time. Clearly, given the nature of the data, we must turn to dynamic inspection. To do this, we include lagged versions of the explanatory variable to detect any persistent tendencies that may be present (see Table 8.7). Using panel data to estimate the time-varying independent variables, we correct for the unwanted but possible presence of time-constant omitted variables by using fixed effects estimation techniques and first differencing, with which we eliminate time-constant explanatory variables. The orthogonality condition should have been regained after proper differentiation of the variables.

Column (1) in Table 8.7 confirms that losses from disasters occur mainly contemporaneously rather than with a lagged influence for economic performance. The results suggest that the selected disaster variables

Table 8.7 The impact of catastrophic events on selected economic variables (OLS estimation), 1970–2005

Dummy variable	log[∂(GDP/capita)] (1)	∂ Exports (% GDP) (2)	∂ Imports (% GDP) (3)	∂ Debt (% GDP) (4)
$Disaster_t$	−0.24*	1.07*	**1.99**	0.10
	(0.10)	(0.45)	**(0.50)**	(0.11)
$Disaster_{t-1}$	0.11	−1.04**	1.14**	−0.07
	(0.12)	(0.59)	(0.65)	(0.11)
$Disaster_{t-2}$	0.19	−0.16	**−2.54**	−0.22*
	(0.12)	(0.58)	**(0.66)**	(0.11)
$Disaster_{t-3}$	0.13		−0.49	−0.03
	(0.12)		(0.64)	(0.08)
AR(1)	0.00	−0.14*	**−0.25**	
	(0.00)	(0.06)	**(0.06)**	
AR(2)	0.00	−0.13*	**−0.20**	
	(0.00)	(0.06)	**(0.06)**	
AR(3)	0.00		**−0.18**	
	(0.00)		**(0.06)**	
Obs.	212	306	228	294
R^2	.50	.08	.21	.21
F-statistic	3.70	1.50	3.93	1.47
	(0.00)	(0.09)	(0.00)	(0.03)
DW	1.9	2.00	2.03	2.09

Source: See text.
Notes: Includes a full set of fixed effects and country-specific linear time trends. The table reports coefficients, with the related standard errors in parentheses; p-values: bold indicates a coefficient that is significant at the 1% level; *, ** represent significance levels of 5% and 10%, respectively. The unit of observation is a country-year. Specification (1) uses the *disaster count* variable, specifications (2) and (3) use the *disaster cost/capita* variable, and specification (4) uses the *affected/population* variable as the disaster outcome variable(s). AR(1), AR(2) and AR(3) denote the first-, second- and third-order autoregressive variable respectively.

exert a positive influence on *GDP/capita* in the three periods following the disaster. Although these results are not significant at common levels, they still indicate the pro-cyclical movement that a disaster triggers after its occurrence. As such, the pattern emerges that, following a 23.7 per cent decline in GDP/capita in the period during which the disaster occurs, GDP/capita increases by approximately 11 per cent, 19 per cent and 13 per cent, respectively, in the three subsequent periods.

Interpretation of the results for *Exports* suggests counterintuitively that there is an increase in export performance relative to GDP as a consequence of a natural disaster during the transition period *t*, followed by a decrease for the following two years. Here we point to the following issues: (i) this result may be accounted for by the argument that the relative export rate has to increase owing to the decrease in GDP following the impact, which is the denominator of the term; the negative lags in the following periods can be explained through the subsequent recovery of GDP along its growth path; and (ii) taking into consideration the rather broad frame of observation, which extends across a range of 365 days, the phenomenon of an initial increase in export rates and a subsequent decline can also be accounted for through the long-term production process, whereby the commodities to be exported are already in stocks and depots but the future means of production are harmed.

Imports, on the other hand, react differently following the occurrence of a natural disaster: they increase in the year of the impact as well as the following year but decrease in the second and third years after the impact (column (3) of Table 8.7). This finding confirms that, in response to a natural disaster, the import demand of countries increases, responding, for example, to reconstruction needs.

The results from specification (4) are as counterintuitive as those from specification (3) are straightforward. External *Debt* as a share of GDP decreases in the years following a natural disaster. This may, however, be explained through the flows of aid and remittances to countries and the subsequent relief of external debt that is granted in the course of reconstruction.

To verify that the results reported above are not the outcome of the selected estimation method, a different estimation strategy was performed to verify the independence of the results from the methodology. The results of the complementary generalized method of moments (GMM) dynamic panel data estimation are presented in Table 8.8. The tendencies and phenomena detected in the OLS regression appear to be invariant in the regression method.

3.4 Intermediating factors defining the impact of natural disasters

As Yang (2006) argues, it is likely that additional factors are important in determining the destructive power of a hurricane other than its mere destructive existence. Thus, whereas we have so far fleshed out evidence that an individual disaster disrupts trade and economic performance, we need to analyse nuances of economies that may make the difference between a devastating natural disaster and one that is less harmful in terms of the damage and harm caused. We therefore introduce intermediating factors, i.e. factors that we hypothesize to be decisive in affecting the degree of a disastrous event and that occur in the findings of other authors.[18]

Table 8.8 Robustness check: The impact of disastrous events on selected economic variables (GMM dynamic panel data estimation), 1970–2005

Dummy variable	$\log[\partial(GDP/capita)]$ (1)	∂ Exports (% GDP) (2)	∂ Imports (% GDP) (3)	∂ Debt (% GDP) (4)
$Disaster_t$	−0.42	1.88	5.08**	0.62
	(0.27)	(2.85)	(2.73)	(0.91)
$Disaster_{t-1}$	0.28	−1.10**	0.64	−0.87*
	(0.16)**	(0.61)	(0.79)	(0.41)
$Disaster_{t-2}$	0.19	−0.19	**−2.78**	−0.20
	(0.16)	(0.60)	**(0.74)**	(0.46)
$Disaster_{t-3}$	0.26		−0.71	−0.34
	(0.18)		(0.72)	(0.47)
AR(1)	−0.03	−0.13	**−0.23**	0.06
	(0.12)	(0.08)**	**(0.068)**	(0.25)
AR(2)	−0.04	−0.13	**−0.21**	0.03
	(0.13)	(0.06)*	**(0.06)**	(0.19)
AR(3)	−0.13		**−0.20**	0.16
	(0.12)		**(0.06)**	(0.21)
Obs.	104	306	228	39
R^2	.43	.07	.09	.50
Durbin–Watson statistic	1.82	1.99	1.94	1.70

Notes: See Table 8.7. Includes a full set of country-specific linear time trends.

Heterogeneity in the effects of disaster damage may for instance be related to physical factors of the affected country. We therefore analyse whether characteristics typical of the Caribbean form a significant quantitative explanatory mark-up by interacting the disaster impact measure with these characteristics. More specifically, we hypothesize that the economic and human impacts of natural disasters will be affected by:

Population density of the island: it is likely that both the absolute number of people living in a selected area and the absolute size of the area they live in alter the degree of devastation: thus, recovery from a "theoretically equally intense and targeted" hurricane should be quite different for e.g. the Bahamas than for Barbados, which is more than 20 times more densely populated.

Trade diversification versus trade specialization: A country that specializes in the production of a single good or a few goods should find it more difficult to recover from an event that affects the means of production. This implicitly assumes that the possibility to switch to an alternative means of production should be beneficial.

Low dependence on the agricultural sector versus high dependence: A country that is more reliant on the agricultural sector is more vulnerable to natural disasters originating from hydro-meteorological hazards.

Low dependence on tourism versus high dependence: We hypothesize that an economy that is more reliant on tourism is more affected by a natural disaster owing to the required reconstruction of amenities and features that customarily attract tourists. *Tourism1* thus measures the number of arrivals on the island in a given year, and *Tourism2* measures the share of international tourism expenditures in current US dollars relative to GDP.

Import and export concentration: the more dependent a country is on imports and exports, the more vulnerable it may be to natural hazards and the trade disruption that these may bring about.

To determine the best-fit models for our outcome variables *GDP/capita*, *Imports*, *Exports* and *Debt*, we scale our disaster measures with the above-mentioned interaction terms. We present the coefficient estimates along with the standard errors of the *Count disaster* variable with the interlinked factors in Table 8.9 to check which interaction terms significantly alter the impact magnitude and in which direction.[19]

The results reveal that the inclusion of the re-scaled disaster measures leaves only a few variables virtually unchanged, indicating an insignificant interaction with that term. In fact, in most cases an evident alteration of the coefficient estimates of origin is discernible. For instance, our agglomeration measure *Population density* (measured in people per square kilometre) delivers the expected results in that, the more densely an island is populated, the larger will be the impact of natural disasters on output (*GDP/capita*). Similarly, our indicator of agricultural dependency and the measures for trade specialization (i.e. the Herfindahl–Hirschman indices) significantly add explanatory power to the disaster measure and alter the magnitude of the disastrous impact: countries with more agricultural exports and with more value added resulting from the agricultural sector will see higher imports following a natural disaster, as will those with a less diversified export and import structure.[20] The results also indicate, however, that there is no significant interaction between *GDP/capita*, *Exports* or *Imports* and dependence on tourism. Moreover, none of the intermediating factors has a significant impact on a country's debt stock.

Core model specification

Taking the results of the trial-and-error selection procedure of the interaction terms outlined above and recalling that none of the interaction

Table 8.9 The interaction of impacts of storms with other variables: IV estimation in the framework of dynamic panel data (GMM)

Dummy variable	GDP/capita (1)	Exports (% GDP) (2)	Imports (% GDP) (3)	Debt (% GDP) (4)
Count disaster, interaction with:				
Population density	−4.33**	−0.03	0.03	0.00
	(2.42)	(0.02)	(0.02)	(0.00)
Agriculture1	7,778.75	1.20	10.03*	0.06
	(364.31)	(2.89)	(4.53)	(0.09)
Agriculture2	8.17	−0.16	0.64**	0.01
	(44.32)	(0.28)	(0.35)	(0.01)
Agriculture3	−73.55	0.32	0.49	−1.36
	(156.09)	(0.80)	(0.87)	(3.98)
Tourism1	0.00	0.00	0.00	−3.54
	(0.00)	(0.00)	(0.00)	(0.00)
Tourism2	−10,189.24	−166.33	45.67	0.58
	(10,461.06)	(151.39)	(119.22)	(0.75)
HHI exports	−482,291.2	10,542.35**	**23,119.02**	−8.32
	(1293094.0)	(6,088.393)	**(7,196.59)**	(35.02)
HHI imports	−5,389,527.0	115,690.3	**273,822.90**	10.49
	(15,402,207)	(70,370.45)	**(84,967.89)**	(37.89)
		p-value of 11%		
GDP/capita		−0.00	0.01**	
		(0.00)	(0.00)	
Imports	−3.80			
	(9.91)			
Exports	−4.27			
	(14.96)			

Source: See text.

Notes: The table reports coefficients, with the related standard errors in parentheses; *p*-values: bold indicates a coefficient that is significant at the 1% level; *, ** represent significance levels of 5% and 10%, respectively. The unit of observation is a country-year.

terms in Table 8.9 provides significant coefficients for *Debt*, we present three formal model specifications – (1), (2) and (3) – to represent the core of our analysis of intermediating factors on the outcome variables of interest – *Imports*, *Exports* and *GDP/capita*:

$$IMP_{nt} = \alpha + \beta Dis_{nt} + \delta ExpSpec_{nt} + \theta IMPSpec_{nt}$$

$$+ \sum_{z} \delta_z Agr_{z,n} + \phi_n + \varphi + \mu_{nt} \qquad (1)$$

$$Exp_{nt} = \alpha + \beta Dis_{nt} + \delta ExpSpec_{nt} + \phi_n + \varphi_t + \mu_{nt} \qquad (2)$$

$$GDP_{nt} = \alpha + \beta Dis_{nt} + \tau PopDens_{nt} + \phi_n + \varphi_t + \mu_{nt} \qquad (3)$$

Henceforth our analysis is based on these three equations, in which n denotes the country and t the time. Dis_{nt} is the natural disaster measure of choice. $ExpSpec_{nt}$ and $IMPSpec_{nt}$ are measures that capture export and import diversification/concentration of goods and services, respectively. We use the normalized Herfindahl–Hirschman index to indicate the extent to which a country is dependent on a specific or a broad range of merchandise and services (imported or exported, respectively). Agr is a vector of z auxiliary interacting variables. In total, there are three ways of expressing the values of agricultural imports and exports for the economy, all of which have been introduced and elaborated upon above. ϕ_n and φ_t are included to mitigate institutional and cultural influences, as well as global shocks that occur during any particular year, with ϕ_n being the country fixed effect and φ_t being the year fixed effect. The estimated country and year fixed effects are included for the sake of capturing shifts in the mean of the underlying distribution over time in each country. μ_{nt} captures the unobservable and is assumed to be random and uncorrelated with the observable explanatory variables. It is the remainder from the general error term ε_{nt} from which we extracted the country and period fixed effects.

The estimation results of specifications (1)–(3) are given in Table 8.10. Specification (1) indicates that the physical damage caused by a disaster increases a country's imports. This decreasing effect on imports is likely to be even more pronounced the more specialized is a country's import base and the less specialized is its export base.

After controlling for import and export concentration, we find that the cost of a disaster no longer exerts a significant influence on the relative export rate. In fact, whereas the degree of export specialization/concentration does not significantly alter the export rate, a more narrow import range (i.e. greater "import concentration") will, *ceteris paribus*, lead to larger exports (specification (2) in Table 8.10). Moreover, we find that an additional disaster – given that it fulfils the inclusion specifics introduced at the beginning – reduces GDP by 5 per cent (specification (3) in Table 8.10). The negative coefficient estimate (significant at the 1 per cent level) for the population density measure indicates that the impacts of the disaster affect GDP even more with greater agglomeration of the population in the particular area.

Subsamples

We consider again the three best-fit specifications to describe the outcome variables of *GDP/capita*, *Exports* and *Imports* and split the data

Table 8.10 Most precise model specifications for the different outcome variables (OLS estimation), 1970–2005

Dummy variable	$\log(IMP_{nt})$ (1)	$\log(Exp_{nt})$ (2)	$\log(GDP_{nt})$ (3)
Dis_{nt}	0.02*	0.01	**−0.05**
	(0.01)	(0.01)	**(0.02)**
$ExpSpec_{nt}$	−0.21**	−0.10	
	(0.11)	(0.10)	
$IMPSpec$	**2.62**	**1.32**	
	(0.53)	**(0.23)**	
$Agr_{1,n}$	−0.05		
	(0.03)		
$Agr_{2,n}$	0.00		
	(0.00)		
$Agr_{3,n}$	−0.00		
	(0.02)		
$PopDens_{nt}$			**−0.01**
			(0.00)
Obs.	176	261	332
R^2	.86	.76	.93
F-statistic	16.06	13.51	90.17
	(0.00)	(0.00)	(0.00)

Source: See text.
Notes: Includes a full set of fixed effects and country-specific linear time trends. The table reports coefficients, with the related standard errors in parentheses; p-values: bold indicates a coefficient that is significant at the 1% level; *, ** represent significance levels of 5% and 10%, respectively. The unit of observation is a country-year. The disaster proxy used for specifications (1) and (2) is *Disaster cost/capita*; for specification (3) it is *Disaster count*.

set into two subsamples, above and below the median measure, to shed more light on the intermediating factors.[21] The results indicate that the subsamples are not homogeneous for most specifications (Tables 8.11–8.13) but that the coefficient estimates for the explanatory variables differ markedly, more in some cases than in others. The discrepancies between the two ends of the distribution are potentially important for policy recommendations.

Our results indicate, for instance, that although disasters have a significant negative impact on GDP as a whole (Table 8.11) they do not seem to discriminate between levels of agricultural specialization or population density. Their impact does, however, vary between different trade regimes. Whereas countries characterized by a high diversity of exports (hence reflecting a broad set of production possibilities and possible substitutions between the different productive sectors) will not see a statisti-

Table 8.11 Differences in the impact of natural disasters on GDP for specified subsamples (OLS estimation), 1970–2005

		$\log(GDP_{nt}$ per capita$)$								
Dummy variable	Entire group	High population density	Low population density	Import specialization	Import diversity	Export specialization	Export diversity	Strong dependence on agriculture	Low dependence on agriculture	
	(1)	(2)		(3)		(4)		(5)		
Dis_{nt}	**−0.05**	−0.02	−0.04	−0.05**	−0.00	**−0.04**	−0.04	−0.02	−0.04	
	(0.02)	(0.02)	(0.04)	(0.02)	(0.02)	**(0.03)**	(0.03)	(0.03)	(0.03)	
$PopDens_{nt}$	**−0.01**									
	(0.00)									
Obs.	332	173	159	147	90	154	94	122	97	
R^2	.93	.96	.94	.95	.99	.94	.97	.96	.97	
F-statistic	90.17	86.36	54.72	51.20	121.50	42.91	45.28	43.00	44.26	
		(0.00)	(0.00)							

Source: See text.

Notes: Includes a full set of fixed effects and country-specific linear time trends. The table reports coefficients, with the related standard errors in parentheses; p-values: bold indicates a coefficient that is significant at the 1% level; *, ** represent significance levels of 5% and 10%, respectively. The unit of observation is a country-year. The disaster proxy is *Count disaster* for the GDP/ capita estimation in Table 8.11 and *Disaster cost/capita* for the *Export* and *Import* estimations in Tables 8.12 and 8.13. The samples are divided into two groups based on their deviation from the median. A country whose reported measure lies below the median value will be subcategorized into one group; the rest into the opposite group.

cally significant decline in their GDP/capita following a disaster, those with more specialized export structures will witness a 4 per cent decrease in GDP per capita (with an α of .01) per additional disaster. Likewise, a country with a high import concentration (importing few different goods) suffers approximately a 5 per cent decrease in GDP per capita after a disastrous event, whereas a country with high import diversity remains literally unaffected by the event. A key finding thus emerges that more diversified economies are less vulnerable to natural disasters.

To analyse why this is the case, we take a closer look at the composition of imports and exports (see Table 8.12 and Table 8.13). We find that the costs resulting from the damage caused by a disaster do not lead to significant changes in imports and exports in countries that are more specialized in their imports, yet do lead to significantly greater imports and exports in economies that have a more diverse import structure. This may explain why the impact of disasters on GDP/capita is less in more diversified economies because these are able to offset greater import expenditure through higher export receipts. In fact, the argument also cuts in the opposite way in terms of export diversification: whereas countries with more diverse export structures do not see statistically significant increases in imports or exports following greater costs resulting from the damage caused by a disaster, those with greater export specialization witness a statistically significant increase in imports. However, they are unable to offset the higher import bill through greater export receipts because no significant change is recorded in the exports. Consequently, they see a significant decline in GDP/capita. This therefore enables us to conclude that both import and export specialization are a disadvantage for countries in terms of resilience to negative external shocks taking the form of natural disasters.

To further analyse the impacts of disasters, we stratify across income and the importance of agriculture. Relating to GDP, we find that low-GDP countries have significantly higher levels of exports following a disaster (Table 8.13) whereas high-GDP countries curb their exports in times of disaster (though not to a significant level). The higher export rate in less wealthy countries caused by a disaster could result from a greater need for foreign exchange, and hence greater export efforts, especially as imports in these countries increase significantly following a disaster (Table 8.12 and Table 8.13).

Disasters do not affect GDP/capita differently amongst the binary groups of strong and low dependence on agriculture. However, we find that economies less dependent on agriculture see a significant increase in imports following a disaster. These countries apparently depend more on imports (including agricultural commodities) in the aftermath of a disaster to cover their domestic demand relative to those that are more

Table 8.12 Differences in the impact of natural disasters on relative imports for specified subsamples (OLS estimation), 1970–2005

		IMP_{nt}							
Dummy variable	Entire group	Import specialization	Import diversity	Export specialization	Export diversity	Strong dependence on agriculture	Low dependence on agriculture	High GDP/ capita	Low GDP/ capita
	(1)	(2)		(3)		(4)		(5)	
Dis_{nt}	**1.78**	0.33	2.52*	1.66**	0.50	0.80	2.03**	0.35	2.68*
	(0.63)	(0.81)	(1.17)	(0.91)	(1.12)	(0.86)	(1.22)	(0.56)	(1.30)
$ExpSpec_{nt}$	−11.08	−18.69**	−9.87			**−22.70**	2.10	−22.73*	25.47
	(7.13)	(11.11)	(18.46)			**(7.56)**	(15.28)	(9.82)	(16.11)
$IMPSpec$	**130.90**			**142.14**	113.58	7.29	−88.14	51.33*	674.03**
	(32.26)			**(36.39)**	(432.49)	(13.35)	(71.95)	(25.41)	(333.64)
$Agr_{1,n}$	−3.537286**	−4.83**	−3.06	4.33	−8.66*			−6.42*	−2.29
	(2.115412)	(2.60)	(6.12)	(3.14)	(3.59)			(2.65)	(3.85)
$Agr_{2,n}$	0.09	0.41	−0.98	−0.24	1.09			0.51	−0.77
	(0.26)	(0.63)	(0.68)	(0.40)	(1.32)			(0.76)	(0.75)
Obs.	176	102	74	122	54	116	113	88	71
R^2	.83	.89	.82	.86	.92	.86	.90	.95	.88
F-statistic	13.07	11.30	4.06	12.93	4.26	9.00	12.61	18.06	6.68
	(0.00)	(0.00)	(0.00)	(0.00)	(0.00)	(0.00)	(0.00)	(0.00)	(0.00)

Notes: See notes to Table 8.11. Includes a full set of fixed effects and country-specific linear time trends.

Table 8.13 Differences in the impact of natural disasters on relative exports for specified subsamples (OLS estimation), 1970–2005

				Exp_{nt}			
	Entire group	Import specialization	Import diversity	Export specialization	Export diversity	High GDP/capita	Low GDP/capita
Dummy variable	(1)	(2)		(3)		(4)	
Dis_{nt}	0.78	−0.95	**3.06**	1.38	−0.01	−0.93	2.45*
	(0.64)	(0.87)	**(1.18)**	(0.90)	(1.23)	(0.79)	(1.09)
$ExpSpec_{nt}$	−2.69	−10.68**	44.65			16.34*	**9.44**
	(4.80)	(5.84)	**(13.23)**			(6.22)	**(10.02)**
$IMPSpec$	**60.33**			**64.32**	27.03	**73.07**	161.81
	(11.00)			**(11.78)**	(161.55)	**(14.15)**	(54.28)
Obs	261	156	105	164	97	127	97
R^2	0.76	0.78	0.77	0.75	0.86	0.95	0.87
F-statistic	13.51	7.96	4.72	7.50	7.80	18.06	9.40
	(0.00)	(0.00)	(0.00)	(0.00)	(0.00)	(0.00)	(0.00)

Notes: See notes to Table 8.11. Includes a full set of fixed effects and country-specific linear time trends.

dependent on agriculture. In particular, countries less dependent on agriculture are likely to have more developed economic structures; this may consequently contribute to the greater damage that disasters cause in them (partially confirmed in Table 8.11, though not significant) and may therefore contribute to the higher import bill for reconstruction.

The main aim of our analysis was to focus on the impact of disasters in the Caribbean. However, Tables 8.11–8.13 yield a number of interesting results regarding the control variables. Although these are specifically related to disasters, and one should proceed carefully with their interpretation, some are nevertheless of interest. For instance, Table 8.12 suggests that, whereas for the overall sample a larger agricultural sector depresses imports, this impact is not significant in countries that import a larger range of goods or in those that have a less diverse export base. It is possible that countries with a wider domestic production base, and hence more diversified exports, are able to satisfy local demand more, and therefore have lower import bills. Moreover, Table 8.12 suggests that a more important agricultural sector significantly lowers import bills only in relatively more wealthy countries; possibly a more important agricultural sector in their less wealthy counterparts will not offset imports because a basic import demand still needs to be met.

Turning to export specialization, Table 8.13 suggests that, for the sample as a whole, greater export specialization does not have a significant impact on exports. However, it seems that greater export specialization contributes to greater export revenue in countries that import a relatively broad range of goods. It is possible that highly specialized economies, i.e. those that need to import a broader range of goods because of their narrow domestic production base, benefit from their specialization by exporting relatively more than countries with a relatively wide production base. This suggests that moving towards greater specialization of exports is worthwhile only for those countries that are already relatively specialized. Indeed, Table 8.12 also suggests that greater specialization of exports will lead to lower import bills.

4 Conclusions

This chapter has examined the impact of natural disasters in the Caribbean – a region considered to be the most vulnerable to natural hazards even on a global scale (Rasmussen 2004). Although our chapter shows that the structure of the economies in the region – whether they are relatively more dependent on agriculture or not – is, in fact, irrelevant in considering the impact of disasters on wealth, it identifies why some countries in the region are more resilient to natural disasters than others.

Specifically, it highlights that the extent to which economies have diversified exports and imports is of fundamental importance in defining vulnerability to natural hazards. We therefore show that countries with a relatively more specialized export structure are more vulnerable to disasters; in particular, their vulnerability operates through trade because, in contrast to their less diversified counterparts, more diversified economies are more able to offset greater import expenditure in the aftermath of a disaster through higher export receipts.

These results are important considering that countries in the region have traditionally focused on monoculture. Although acknowledging that this in part is a legacy of the colonial era, which contributed to the emergence of dominant primary agricultural sectors (such as sugar and bananas), it is nevertheless important to note that greater specialization has specifically been fostered in the region as a result of the credo that small economies must specialize in niche markets to compete in global markets and to compensate for the lack of economies of scale available to them (Arjoon 1996; Downes 2000). Our findings however lead us to question whether this approach is the best option for a region as vulnerable to natural hazards as the Caribbean. Rather, with all indications that climate change will increase the incidence and intensity of hydro-meteorological hazards, reducing vulnerability to hazards through mitigation and adaptation must be considered paramount and should represent the core component of economic policy in the region.

Mitigation can in principle take two possible forms, either *after* the occurrence of a natural disaster (*ex post*), or *before* (*ex ante*), with a view to decreasing the overall impact of any likely event. To date, the focus has been on *ex post* mitigation, which, to varying degrees, relies on post-disaster assistance, taking the form of grants and loans from external donors. However, the process of securing and obtaining such funds is time consuming and usually requires individual negotiation between partners whose willingness to commit funds can be negatively affected by the occurrence of natural disasters and/or other emergencies elsewhere. Consequently, interest in disaster insurance has increased. In fact, in 2007 the first multi-country catastrophe insurance pool, the Caribbean Catastrophe Risk Insurance Facility (CCRIF), was created to provide immediate liquidity in the event of a significant natural disaster.[22] Nevertheless, the lack of economies of scale, insufficiently developed domestic insurance markets and the fact that providing coverage for large-scale systemic risks, rather than idiosyncratic risks, can often be prohibitively expensive to the provider imply that disaster insurance is either unavailable or often unaffordable in the Caribbean. It can therefore not be the solution to the region's vulnerability. Rather, *ex ante* mitigation and adaptation must be put at the forefront. As analysed in this chapter, diversification will form an important pillar in reducing vulnerability.

Acknowledgements

Comments and suggestions received from participants at the UNU-WIDER Conference on Fragile States – Fragile Groups: Tackling Economic and Social Vulnerability, Helsinki, 16–17 June 2007, and from Esteban Perez, Ana Cortez, Richard Kozul-Wright and Rob Vos are greatly appreciated. The opinions expressed in this chapter are those of the authors alone. The usual disclaimers apply.

Notes

1. In the context of this chapter, "the Caribbean" refers, unless otherwise noted, to the following island economies: Antigua and Barbuda, the Bahamas, Barbados, Dominica, Dominican Republic, Grenada, Haiti, Jamaica, St Lucia, St Kitts and Nevis, St Vincent and the Grenadines, Trinidad and Tobago. It also includes Suriname, Belize and Guyana, which, although not islands, are usually considered as small-island developing states (SIDS) because they have "island-like" features. Cuba was excluded from the sample owing to a lack of available data. The same holds true for a number of islands that are non-independent (such as the US Virgin Islands, the British Virgin Islands, Martinique), although Puerto Rico and the Netherlands Antilles have been included owing to the general availability of data.
2. The problems and constraints of the BPoA have since been reviewed; see, for example, ECLAC (1997).
3. The concept of vulnerability has often been defined according to the needs and goals of the various authors. Thywissen (2006) presents 29 definitions of vulnerability that have been identified in the literature.
4. See note 1 for the list of countries covered in this chapter.
5. In fact, the importance for small economies of specializing in "niche markets" is in many cases the result of the realization that competing in global markets without access to economies of scale is likely to fail (see Arjoon 1996; Downes 2000). However, the extent to which this may be detrimental in an environment prone to natural hazards must be discussed – one of the aims of this chapter.
6. Although the actual deterioration in the trade balance may in fact be offset by positive effects on the capital account owing to reinsurance flows. Moreover, as Pelling et al. (2002) point out, any potential period of increasing import capacity should not be interpreted as a genuine economic upturn but rather must be recognized as a temporary boom resulting from the period of reconstruction.
7. This may well have contributed to the high indebtedness of some countries in the region; in fact 14 Caribbean countries (referring to the region as a whole, not just the sample considered here) rank amongst the world's 30 most indebted emerging market countries, with 7 ranking among the top 10 (Sahay 2005).
8. This mirrors Rasmussen (2004), who finds that eastern Caribbean countries are among the most disaster prone in the world.

9. ECLAC (the Economic Commission for Latin America and the Caribbean) has been working since the early 1970s on assessing the socioeconomic impact of natural disasters in Latin America and the Caribbean, with an emphasis on macroeconomic indicators. It has undertaken numerous assessments of natural disasters within the Latin American and Caribbean region (ECLAC various years), as well as outside the region, because its methodology is recognized as a consistent, continuous and usable method for better recovery and reconstruction needs.

10. Docquier and Marfouk (2004) find that almost half of the 30 countries with the highest emigration rates are member states of the Caribbean region.

11. Using the Munich Re Foundation's (2006) classification of disasters, only events that either kill or injure at least 1,000 persons, cause at least US$1 billion in damages and/ or affect at least 100,000 persons are considered.

12. To be classified as a disaster, an event has to meet at least one of the following criteria: (i) 10 or more people must have been killed by the occurrence, (ii) 100 or more people must have been affected, injured or made homeless, (iii) a state of emergency must have been declared or (iv) an appeal for international assistance has been made. See EM-DAT at ⟨http://www.emdat.be/⟩ (accessed 27 January 2009).

13. Where the cost estimation was expressed in local currencies, CRED converted it into US dollars using the exchange rate on the day the disaster struck.

14. Natural disasters thus include the following: hurricanes, wind storms, earthquakes, droughts, epidemics, extreme temperature events, floods, famines, (mud) slides, waves, wild fires and volcanic eruptions.

15. Some of the countries listed in note 1 were excluded owing to data concerns.

16. Use of a binary dummy variable signalling only the occurrence of a natural disaster contains too little information to have any explanatory power; see column (1) of Table 8.6. This result makes sense in that one would expect, *ceteris paribus*, a country hit by a number of disasters during the same year to suffer more than a country hit only once.

17. This is in contrast to Noy (2007), who does not find any significant impact of the total affected population.

18. For example, Gassebner et al. (2006) interact their disaster variable with the democracy rating of the selected country, and Yang (2006) introduces a democracy index, alliance similarities and GDP as heterogeneous factors.

19. The disaster variables' impact on the outcome variables might react in three different ways to the interaction with a demographic factor: magnified, decreased or unaltered.

20. Note that a higher Herfindahl–Hirschman index means a higher degree of import/ export specialization, i.e. a less diversified import/export structure.

21. We do so merely to obtain two samples with a roughly even number of observations, rather than out of any theoretical considerations.

22. The CCRIF was launched by the World Bank in 2007 and represents an important step towards rapid mitigation of damage. However, since payments from the facility depend on the intensity of the particular natural event/disaster, rather than on the damage inflicted, the extent to which they will be able to mitigate the damage incurred remains to be seen. Moreover, the CCRIF does not provide disaster insurance to the private sector in the region. Yet it is precisely the need to provide insurance to individual property owners that should be addressed in the region.

References

Arjoon, S. (1996). "Managing Risk and Uncertainty: The Use of Scenario Planning". *Bulletin of Eastern Caribbean Affairs* 21(2): 1–10.

Auffret, P. (2003). "High Consumption Volatility: The Impact of Natural Disasters". World Bank Policy Research Working Paper 2962, Washington DC.

Benson, C. and E. Clay (2003). "Economic and Financial Impacts of Natural Disasters: An Assessment of their Effects and Options for Mitigation". Overseas Development Institute, London.

CRED [Centre for Research on the Epidemiology of Disasters] (2007). "EM-DAT: Emergency Events Database". Université Catholique de Louvain, Brussels; available at ⟨http://www.emdat.be⟩ (accessed 27 January 2009).

Docquier, F. and A. Marfouk (2004). "Measuring the International Mobility of Skilled Workers, 1990–2000". World Bank Discussion Paper 19/8, Brussels.

Downes, A. (2000). "Long-term Planning: Institutional Action and Restructuring in the Caribbean". ECLAC Serie Gestión pública 10, Economic Commission for Latin America and the Caribbean, Santiago.

Easterly, W. and A. Kraay (2000). "Small States, Small Problems? Income, Growth, and Volatility in Small States". *World Development* 28(11): 2013–2027.

ECLAC [Economic Commission for Latin America and the Caribbean] (1997). "Way Forward. Review of the Implementation of the SIDS POA: Priorities for the Future". Document LC/CAR/G.519, ECLAC, Port-of-Spain.

ECLAC (2003). "Handbook for Estimating the Socioeconomic and Environmental Effects of Disasters". Document LC/MEX/G.5 and LC/L.1874, ECLAC, Port-of-Spain.

ECLAC (2006). "Fiscal Policy and Tax Reform in the Caribbean". Document LC/CAR/L.94, ECLAC, Port-of-Spain.

ECLAC (various years). "Disaster Assessments for Central America and the Caribbean". ECLAC, Port-of-Spain.

Gassebner, M., A. Keck and R. Teh (2006). "The Impact of Disasters on International Trade". WTO Staff Working Paper ERSD-2006-04, World Trade Organization, Geneva.

Munich Re Foundation (2006). *Topics Geo – Annual Review: Natural Catastrophes in 2005*. Munich: Münchener Rückversicherungs-Gesellschaft; available at ⟨http://www.munichre.org/publications/302-04772_en.pdf⟩ (accessed 27 January 2009).

Noy, I. (2007). "The Macroeconomic Consequences of Disasters". Mimeo, University of Hawaii, Manoa.

Pelling, M., A. Özerdem and S. Barakat (2002). "The Macroeconomic Impact of Disasters". *Progress in Development Studies* 2(4): 283–305.

Rasmussen, T. (2004). "Macroeconomic Implications of Natural Disasters in the Caribbean". IMF Working Paper 04/224, Washington DC.

Sahay, R. (2005). "Stabilization, Debt, and Fiscal Policy in the Caribbean". IMF Working Paper 05/26, Washington DC.

Skidmore, M. and H. Toya (2002). "Do Natural Disasters Promote Long-Run Growth?" *Economic Inquiry* 40(4): 664–687.

Thywissen, K. (2006). "Core Terminology of Disaster Reduction: A Comparative Glossary". In J. Birkmann (ed.), *Measuring Vulnerability to Natural Hazards*. Tokyo: United Nations University Press.

UN-ISDR [UN International Strategy for Disaster Reduction] (1992). *International Agreed Glossary of Basic Terms Related to Disaster Management*. Geneva: UN-ISDR.

UN-ISDR (2004). "Living with Risk: A Global Review of Disaster Reduction Initiatives". Geneva.

United Nations (1994). *Report of the Global Conference on the Sustainable Development of Small Island Developing States*. UN Doc. A/CONF.167/9; available at ⟨http://www.sidsnet.org/docshare/other/BPOA.pdf⟩ (accessed 27 January 2009).

United Nations (2005). *World Population Prospects: The 2004 Revision*. New York: United Nations.

United Nations (n.d.). United Nations Commodity Trade Statistics Database; available at ⟨http://www://comtrade.un.org/⟩ (accessed 27 January 2009).

World Bank (2006). *World Development Indicators 2006*. Washington DC: World Bank.

Yang, D. (2006). "Coping with Disaster: The Impact of Hurricanes on International Financial Flows, 1970–2002". NBER Working Paper 12794, Cambridge, MA.

9

Natural disasters and remittances: Poverty, gender and disaster vulnerability in Caribbean SIDS

Marlene Attzs

1 Introduction

This chapter has three objectives, namely to (i) highlight the vulnerability of Caribbean small-island developing states (SIDS) to natural hazards; (ii) review the poverty profile of Caribbean SIDS; and (iii) provide an overview of a gendered approach to effective disaster risk management. Additionally, I look at the levels of poverty in selected countries of the Caribbean Community (CARICOM)[1] and highlight the fact that existing economic vulnerabilities (manifested as persons living in poverty) are exacerbated when hazards affect countries – the result is the passage of a natural disaster.

2 Disaster, poverty and gender profile of the Caribbean

Caribbean countries are highly vulnerable to natural hazards.[2] What exacerbates the impact of these hazards and ultimately converts them into natural disasters[3] for this geographical region is the latent vulnerability of the area in terms of its economic, social and environmental circumstances. It is estimated that almost 4 million Caribbean citizens were affected by natural disasters during the period 1990 to 2006.[4] As Table 9.1 shows, the majority of those affected came from Haiti and Jamaica. It is also interesting to note that, although Jamaica had fewer people affected by disasters, it incurred the highest disaster-related economic costs, total-

Vulnerability in developing countries, Naudé, Santos-Paulino and McGillivray (eds),
United Nations University Press, 2009, ISBN 978-92-808-1171-1

Table 9.1 Socioeconomic impact of natural disasters on selected Caribbean countries, 1990–2006

Country	Total no. of disasters	Total no. of people affected	Total damage (US$ '000)
Anguilla	1	150	50
Antigua and Barbuda	5	93,261	360,000
Bahamas	7	13,700	500,000
Barbados	3	3,000	0
Belize	7	145,170	330,240
Dominica	4	3,991	3,428
Grenada	4	62,045	894,500
Guyana	3	347,774	630,100
Haiti	28	2,221,815	101,000
Jamaica	13	943,734	1,808,787
St Kitts and Nevis	4	12,980	238,400
St Lucia	3	950	0
St Vincent and the Grenadines	5	1,834	0
Suriname	1	25,000	0
Trinidad and Tobago	7	1,787	25,127
TOTAL	95	3,877,191	4,891,632

Source: EM-DAT (n.d.).

ling nearly US$2 billion. The region is particularly susceptible to wind storms and floods, with 70 per cent of the people affected by the former category of disaster and 27 per cent affected by the latter category. Earthquakes affect only 3 per cent of the total Caribbean population that suffered damage from disasters.

2.1 Exploring the poverty–disaster nexus

The impact of disasters is not limited to the stark evidence on damage costs or lost lives but also reflects the possible impact on the developmental trajectory of a particular country. On this score, the literature on disasters and development has increasingly recognized that disasters are not simply extreme events created entirely by natural forces; rather they are sometimes manifestations of unresolved problems of development.[5] There are also explicit linkages between disasters and other developmental challenges such as poverty. For example, poverty may lead to unsustainable livelihood practices that exacerbate inherent vulnerability, with the result being disasters. To cite two examples:
  (i) hillside farming and slash-and-burn techniques that remove soil cover could cause mudslides and flooding following heavy rains;

Table 9.2 Poverty profile of selected CARICOM countries

Country	Year of poverty assessment	% of population below poverty line
Barbados	1997	13.9
Belize	1996	33.0
	2002	33.5
Grenada	1999	32.1
Guyana	1993	43.0
	1999	35.0
Jamaica	1993	24.4
	1997	19.9
	2002	19.7
	2004	16.9
	2005	12.7
St Kitts and Nevis	2000	30.5
St Lucia	1996	25.1
	2006	28.8
St Vincent and the Grenadines	1996	37.5
Trinidad and Tobago	1992	21.2
	1997	24.0
	2005	16.7

Source: Various sources.

(ii) unsustainable forestry and deforestation to use trees for firewood and charcoal could have disastrous downstream effects, such as flooding and destruction of homes and infrastructure.

Based on the poverty assessment studies done for selected CARICOM countries in the 1990s, at least 5 out of 9 countries had more than 30 per cent of their population living below the poverty line (Table 9.2). This means that the inherent environmental vulnerability of these countries to natural disasters is exacerbated by socioeconomic circumstances, especially, in this case, the level of pre-existing poverty.

Cardona (2003, 2005) identifies four indicators of disaster vulnerability, focusing on economic, social and physical factors and the actual performance of a country in engaging in effective disaster risk reduction measures. Cardona's Prevalent Vulnerability Index (PVI) seeks to capture prevailing vulnerability based on: (i) exposure in prone areas (ES); (ii) socioeconomic fragility (SF), and (iii) lack of social resilience (LR) (see Figure 9.1; see also IADB 2005).

All of the above can be captured in the disaster–poverty nexus since they all include elements that may be exacerbated by the direct and indirect impacts from hazards. In the context of this research it is also

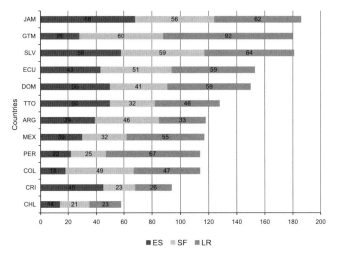

Figure 9.1 Prevalent Vulnerability Index: Ranking of countries, 2000.
Source: Cardona (2005).
Notes: The countries reviewed are Jamaica (JAM), Guatemala (GTM), El Salvador (SLV), Ecuador (ECU), Dominican Republic (DOM), Trinidad and Tobago (TTO), Argentina (ARG), Mexico (MEX), Peru (PER), Colombia (COL), Costa Rica (CRI) and Chile (CHL). ES = exposure in prone areas; SF = socioeconomic fragility; LR = lack of social resilience.

suggested that gender may be added as a cross-cutting indicator because the literature documents not only that the poor suffer the most in times of disasters but also that the poor tend to be female. Table 9.3 details all of the sub-indicators used in the composite index. Cardona's analysis of 12 countries in Latin America and the Caribbean[6] with respect to the PVI suggests that Jamaica is the most vulnerable country across all the contributing indicators: socioeconomic fragility, exposure in prone areas and lack of social resilience.

A study by the United Nations Development Programme (UNDP 1995) indicates that 1.3 billion people worldwide live in poverty, and 70 per cent of them are female. Data for selected Caribbean countries show that in some countries, Jamaica for example, at least 40 per cent of households are headed by females (Table 9.4 provides details). Given these data, it is not far-fetched to surmise that women tend to be very vulnerable to disasters. The World Bank's *World Development Report* on attacking poverty states, in its overview, that:

> Vulnerability to external and largely uncontrollable events – illness, violence, economic shocks, bad weather, natural disasters – reinforces poor people's sense of ill-being, exacerbates their material poverty, and weakens their

Table 9.3 Sub-indicators of exposure, resilience and socioeconomic fragility

Indicators of exposure/susceptibility
- Population growth, average annual rate (%)
- Urban growth, average annual rate (%)
- Population density, people per 5 km^2
- Poverty, population below US$1 per day PPP
- Capital stock, US$ million per 1,000 km^2
- Imports and exports of goods and services, % of GDP
- Gross domestic fixed investment, % of GDP
- Arable land and permanent crops, % of land area

Indicators of lack of resilience
- Human development index (HDI)
- Gender-related development index (GDI)
- Social expenditure: on pensions, health and education, % of GDP
- Government index
- Insurance of infrastructure and housing, % of GDP
- Television sets per 1,000 people
- Hospital beds per 1,000 people
- Environmental sustainability index

Socioeconomic fragility
- Human poverty index, HPI-1
- Dependants as proportion of working-age population
- Social disparity, concentration of income measured using Gini index
- Unemployment, as % of total labour force
- Inflation, food prices, annual %
- Dependency of GDP growth on agriculture, annual %
- Debt servicing, % of GDP
- Human-induced soil degradation (GLASOD)

Source: Cardona (2005).

bargaining position. That is why enhancing security – by reducing the risk of such events as wars, disease, economic crises, and natural disasters – is key to reducing poverty. And so is reducing poor people's vulnerability to risks and putting in place mechanisms to help them cope with adverse shocks. (World Bank 2000)

Wisner (2003) suggests that there is general agreement that risk is a part of the daily life of the poor and that comprehensive development (meaning some combination of human and economic development) should provide the conditions for increasing personal and social protection (UNRISD 2000).

2.2 Profile of Jamaica's female-headed households

There has been a debate in Jamaica on the increasing feminization of poverty based on the increasing number of female-headed households

Table 9.4 Percentage of households headed by women, by size of household, for selected Caribbean countries, 1990/1991

	All households	Size of household (no. of persons)			
		1	2–3	4–5	6+
St Kitts and Nevis	44	29	48	49	56
Barbados	43	41	45	39	52
Grenada	43	30	47	46	47
Antigua and Barbuda	41	33	46	42	47
St Lucia	40	33	45	42	39
Jamaica	40	–	–	–	–
Montserrat	40	36	42	39	44
St Vincent and the Grenadines	39	22	44	43	45
Dominica	37	27	44	39	36
Bahamas	35	–	–	–	–
Guyana	28	35	33	25	27
Trinidad and Tobago	28	34	34	22	25
Belize	22	27	26	21	18

Source: CCS (2003), Table 2.4.

that live in poverty. Data from the Jamaica survey of living conditions (1999) seem to suggest that the gender dimension of poverty is not as significant for that country as it may be in other regions. In 1999 for example, of the total number of individuals living below the poverty line, 50.7 per cent were males and 49.3 per cent females – an almost 50:50 distribution among men and women heading poor households.[7]

Louat et al. (1993) concur with the view that there is a weak link between poverty and female headship. Notwithstanding this seemingly even distribution, females and female-headed households are usually more disadvantaged compared with their male counterparts in terms of access to resources and the ability to ensure a decent standard of living. What is more worrisome than the 50:50 distribution is the policy implication that, as the authors note (1993: 6), "with female headship affecting nearly half of society, any disadvantage suffered by such households will have repercussions for the welfare of society as a whole, not just for a small, fringe group. Hence, the study of female headship is important."

Louat et al. (1993) further identify some of the defining characteristics of female-headed households in Jamaica as follows:
• Overall, 42 per cent of households in Jamaica are headed by women. Of these, three-quarters (or 31 per cent of all households) are headed by women who are the oldest generation present in the household and who do not have a spouse or partner in the household. These conform to the most common perception of female headship.

- In nearly all of the other quarter of female-headed households, the woman who heads the household belongs to the oldest generation in the household but does have a spouse or partner present.
- In only 3 per cent of all households are there members of a generation older than that of the head. Even within that group, the portion of female household heads with and without spouses/partners is similar.
- Of female heads of household, 25 per cent have a partner present in the household (in contrast, 59 per cent of male heads of household have a partner present).

2.3 A gendered approach to disaster risk management

In the disaster risk management literature, it is widely accepted that there are six stages in the disaster risk management lifecycle covering the pre- and post-disaster phases. Fothergill (1996) proposes a gendered approach to disaster risk management with the justification that men and women are likely to have different perceptions of the different disaster phases, and an understanding of their different responses to these phases could enhance the efficiency of disaster risk management. Table 9.5 is an

Table 9.5 Gender roles in disaster risk management

Stage of disaster risk management	Active participant
Risk perception	WOMEN: perceive natural and man-made disasters as more serious than do men.
Disaster preparedness	Both WOMEN and MEN: mixed levels of preparedness. Men pay more attention to technical aspects whereas women are more likely to ensure family members are all right.
Disaster risk warning and response	WOMEN: given their societal roles and networks.
Emergency response	MEN: reconstruction and recovery.
Post-disaster recovery	WOMEN: most likely to receive help from family members (Drabek et al. 1975); to get emergency payments and seek public assistance for the family (Morrow and Enarson 1996).
Reconstruction	WOMEN and MEN in different ways. Women, especially low-income women, manage fairly poorly in the reconstruction phase given that they have less insurance, less savings and less likelihood of long-term recovery (Bolin and Bolton 1986). Khondker (1996) suggests that women in the developing world are more adversely affected in the long run after the disaster.

Source: Adapted from Fothergill's table in Enarson and Morrow (1998).

adaptation of Fothergill's gendered risk management stages. In summary, Fothergill suggests that women are more likely to be the active risk respondent in the risk identification, risk warning (part of the risk mitigation phase), post-disaster and reconstruction phases. These tendencies arise, in part, out of the traditional roles of women as caregivers and also because of the social networks that women are more likely to be part of than men.

3 Remittances and natural disasters

3.1 The significance of remittances to Caribbean economies: The case of Jamaica

Attzs and Samuel (2007: 8) offer some stylized facts about the relationship between disasters and remittances in Central America and the Caribbean as follows:

• Migration increases in the aftermath of natural disasters. The passage of hurricane Gilbert (1989) in Jamaica and hurricane Mitch (1998) in Central America set off periods of higher migration.[8] A similar situation occurred after the 2000 earthquake in El Salvador. Many people seek temporary refuge after these events and never return to their home country.
• There is potential reverse causation between migration and the severity of the effects of natural disasters. Migration from a given area reduces economic opportunities in the area, and the infrastructure required to mitigate the effects of natural disasters, such as better drainage and flood control, is postponed, which exacerbates the effects of the next event. The occurrence of the next natural disaster prompts even more migration.
• Remittance flows to the countries of Central America and the Caribbean have been commensurately significant with the levels of migration. Remittances to Jamaica now account for approximately 19 per cent of GDP.

Remittances are transfers from earnings or stock of wealth by individual migrants to their country of origin (Figure 9.2). The reasons for remittances include support of dependants, repayment of loans, investment or other purposes. Of the English-speaking Caribbean countries, Jamaica has been the largest recipient of transfers, with remittances to that country increasing from US$184 million in 1990 to US$1,466 million in 2004 – growth of 697 per cent over the 15-year period or 46 per cent per annum. The main sources of remittances to Jamaica are the United States (60 per

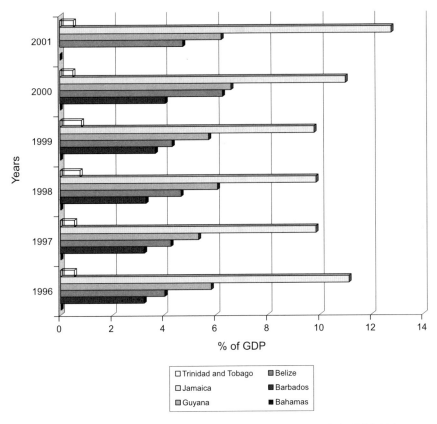

Figure 9.2 Remittances as a percentage of GDP in selected CARICOM countries, 1996–2001.
Source: Adapted from Kirton (2005).

cent), the United Kingdom (25 per cent), Canada (5 per cent) and the Cayman Islands (5 per cent).

Wisner (2003: 5) states that:

> remittances to rural and poor urban households from abroad are acknowledged to have become more and more a part of livelihood systems ... In the area of disaster risk reduction the transfer of funds from individuals abroad to assist recovery has been a notable feature of recent events such as the earthquakes in Gujarat and El Salvador.

A similar conclusion is drawn by Morduch (1994), who notes that remittances may play a significant role in smoothing consumption. Poor households that lack access to insurance and credit markets are vulnerable to severe declines in income from adverse shocks, and they may be forced to forgo income-generating, but risky, strategies. It is well documented that remittances also have had a special role in smoothing household consumption in the aftermath of disasters. As noted earlier, Jamaicans in the diaspora responded positively to the damage suffered in Jamaica after hurricane Gilbert. Specifically, as Clarke and Wallsten (2003: 5) record, "remittances increase when the household is hit by an exogenous shock ... and each additional dollar of hurricane damage led to an increase of US$0.25 in additional remittances".

In the case of the Philippines, Yang and Choi (2005) estimate that, for a sample of Filipino households, remittances replaced 60 per cent of income lost owing to weather-related shocks. The literature also identifies a distributive lagged effect of remittances. According to Yang (2006), an analysis of cross-country data showed that US$1 worth of hurricane damage led to roughly US$0.13 in additional remittances in the year of the hurricane and US$0.28 over five years after the damage. Kirton's (2005) commentary on the impact of remittances to Jamaica as supplemental income to poor households suggests that 26 per cent of total annual expenditure of the poorest decile is funded by remittances, representing 87 per cent of total support received by this group. This group is by far the most heavily reliant on remittances for economic support, followed by the second-poorest decile (see Table 9.6). Le Franc and Downes (2001) highlight a significant relationship between remittance flows and changing consumption-poverty levels in Jamaica.

Table 9.6 Importance of remittances by decile, Jamaica

Decile	Remittances as % of total annual expenditure	Total support as % of total annual expenditure	Remittances as % of total support
1	26	30	87
2	17	31	55
3	11	21	52
4	12	21	57
5	14	16	88
6	15	19	79
7	11	13	85
8	14	20	70
9	16	20	80
10	7	14	50

Source: Kirton (2005).
Note: Total support includes support from children, relatives, remittances, rental income, national insurance schemes, pensions, food stamps, interest income, dividend income and windfall.

4 Policy implications and conclusions

This section distils some policy responses from the discussion above.

- The literature suggests that remittances are a significant form of post-disaster financing and help to smooth consumption for affected households. The impact of remittances in this regard is seen as having both an immediate as well as a lagged effect. Many studies, including Fajnzylber and López (2007), show that remittances rise in the year following an economic shock. In the case of Central America and the Caribbean, the major disasters are hurricanes and tropical storms, which occur mainly during the third quarter of the year. Hence one would expect an increase in remittance flows during the year of the disaster, with some spillover into the following year for reconstruction purposes.

- The poor suffer the most, especially in times of a disaster. With women constituting 70 per cent of the world's estimated 1.3 billion poor, there is a need to have a gendered approach to disaster risk management. The PVI clearly points to Jamaica's lack of socioeconomic and environmental resilience to disasters and, given that country's poverty and gender profile, it is suggested that risk reduction policies should be implemented that bear the gender disparities in mind.

- A useful disaggregation of the remittances data would be information on the recipients of remittances by gender and by structure of household. There is no doubt that remittances play a significant role in smoothing consumption after a disaster. The data for Jamaica contained in Table 9.6 show that, for the poorest decile in that country, remittances constituted the lion's share of their supplemental income (87 per cent). Additional useful information would be about who these recipients are, whether the split in remittances is 50:50 between male- and female-headed households, or whether women receive more than men. Casual empiricism suggests that women receive the greater portion of these remittances.

Notes

1. Member countries of CARICOM are Antigua and Barbuda, the Bahamas, Barbados, Belize, Dominica, Grenada, Guyana, Haiti, Jamaica, Montserrat, St Lucia, St Kitts and Nevis, St Vincent and the Grenadines, Suriname, Trinidad and Tobago.
2. Hazards are defined here according to the Glossary of Terms of the Emergency Events Database (EM-DAT) as a "threatening event, or probability of occurrence of a potentially damaging phenomenon within a given time period and area" (see ⟨http://www.emdat.be/ExplanatoryNotes/glossary.html⟩, accessed 28 January 2009).
3. A disaster is defined as a "situation or event, which overwhelms local capacity, necessitating a request to national or international level for external assistance ...; an

unforeseen and often sudden event that causes great damage, destruction and human suffering. Though often caused by nature, disasters can have human origins. Wars and civil
disturbances that destroy homelands and displace people are included among the causes
of disasters" (EM-DAT Glossary of Terms, ⟨http://www.emdat.be/ExplanatoryNotes/
glossary.html⟩, accessed 28 January 2009).
4. In this document only the following disasters are covered: floods, earthquakes and wind
storms (hurricanes).
5. Former UN Secretary-General Kofi Annan (2004) is reported as saying that "poverty
and population pressure force growing numbers of poor people to live in harm's way –
on flood plains, in earthquake-prone zones and on unstable hillsides".
6. The countries reviewed were Jamaica, Guatemala, El Salvador, Ecuador, Dominican Republic, Trinidad and Tobago, Argentina, Mexico, Peru, Colombia, Chile and Costa Rica
(see also Figure 9.1).
7. It is interesting to note that the 1998 survey of living conditions for Jamaica shows that
66.1 per cent of single-parent households living in poverty were headed by females,
whereas only 33.9 per cent were headed by males.
8. The United States extended the temporary protective status programme to migrants from
Central America who left after the region was struck by hurricane Mitch.

References

Annan, K. (2004). Opening Remarks at the 4th Forum on the International
Decade for Natural Disaster Reduction. Available at ⟨http://www.unisdr.org⟩
(accessed 10 February 2009).
Attzs, M. and W. Samuel (2007). "Natural Disasters and Remittances in Central
America and the Caribbean". Mimeo, Department of Economics, University of
the West Indies, St. Augustine, Trinidad and Tobago.
Bolin, R. C. and P. Bolton (1986). *Race, Religion and Ethnicity in Disaster Recov-
ery*. Boulder, CO: Institute for Behavioral Science.
Cardona, O. D. (2003). "Indicators for Risk Measurement: Methodological Fundamentals". IDB/IDEA Disaster Risk Management Indicators Program. Uni-
versidad Nacional de Colombia, Manizales; available at ⟨http://idea.unalmzl.
edu.co/⟩ (accessed 28 January 2009).
Cardona, O. D. (2005). "Indicators of Disaster Risk and Risk Management".
Paper prepared for the World Conference on Disaster Reduction, Kobe, Japan,
18–22 January.
CCS [Caribbean Community Secretariat] (2003). *Women and Men in the Carib-
bean Community: Facts and Figures, 1980–2001*. Georgetown, Guyana: CCS
Statistics Programme and United Nations Department of Economic and Social
Affairs Statistics Division.
Clarke, R. G. and S. Wallsten (2003). "Do Remittances Act Like Insurance?
Evidence from a Natural Disaster in Jamaica". World Bank Policy Research
Paper, Washington DC.
Drabek, T. E., W. H. Key, P. E. Erickson and J. L. Crowe (1975). "The Impact of
Disaster on Kin Relationships". *Journal of Marriage and the Family* 37(3): 481–
494.

EM-DAT (n.d.). "The OFDA/CRED International Disaster Database". Available at ⟨http://www.emdat.be/Database/CountryProfile/countryprofile.php⟩ (accessed 27 January 2009).

Enarson, E. and B. H. Morrow (1998). "Perspectives on Gender and Disaster". In *The Gendered Terrain of Disaster: Through Women's Eyes*. Westport, CT: Praeger.

Fajnzylber, P. and J. H. López (2007). *Close to Home: The Development Impact of Remittances in Latin America*. Washington DC: World Bank.

Fothergill, A. (1996). "Gender, Risk and Disaster". *International Journal of Mass Emergencies and Disasters* 14(1): 33–56.

IADB [Inter-American Development Bank] (2005). *Indicators of Disaster Risk and Risk Management: Summary Report for WCDR*. Program for Latin America and the Caribbean. Study coordinated by Instituto de Estudios Ambientales (IDEA), Universidad Nacional de Colombia, Manizales.

Khondker, H. (1996). "Women and Floods in Bangladesh". *International Journal of Mass Emergencies and Disasters* 14(3): 281–292.

Kirton, C. (2005). "Remittances: The Experience of the English-speaking Caribbean". In D. F. Terry and S. R. Wilson (eds), *Beyond Small Change: Making Remittances Count*. Washington DC: Inter-American Development Bank.

Le Franc, E. and A. Downes (2001). "Measuring Human Development in Countries with Invisible Economies: Challenges Posed by the Informal and Remittance Sectors in Jamaica". *Social and Economic Studies* 50(1): 169–198.

Louat, F. M., E. Grosh and J. Van Der Gaag (1993). "Welfare Implications of Female Headship in Jamaican Households". World Bank Working Paper 96, Washington DC.

Morduch, J. (1994). "Poverty and Vulnerability". *American Economic Review*, 84 (2): 221–225.

Morrow, B. H. and E. Enarson (1996). "Hurricane Andrew through Women's Eyes: Issues and Recommendations". *International Journal of Mass Emergencies and Disasters* 14(1): 5–22.

UNDP [United Nations Development Programme] (1995). *Human Development Report*. New York: Oxford University Press.

UNRISD [United Nations Research Institute for Social Development] (2000). *Visible Hands: Taking Responsibility for Social Development*. Geneva: UNRISD.

Wisner, B. (2003). "Sustainable Suffering? Reflections on Development and Disaster Vulnerability in the Post-Johannesburg World". Paper submitted to *Regional Development Dialogue* 24(1).

World Bank (2000). *World Development Report 2000/2001: Attacking Poverty*. Oxford: Oxford University Press; available at ⟨http://go.worldbank.org/7KWQQ1WVT0⟩ (accessed 29 January 2009).

Yang, D. (2006). "Coping with Disaster: The Impact of Hurricanes on International Financial Flows, 1970–2002". Mimeo, University of Michigan, Ann Arbor.

Yang, D. and H. Choi (2005). "Are Remittances Insurance? Evidence from Rainfall Shocks in the Philippines". Mimeo, University of Michigan, Ann Arbor.

10

Growth-oriented macroeconomic policies for small-island economies: Lessons from Singapore

Anis Chowdhury

1 Introduction

One characteristic that small-island economies share is vulnerability. This arises from a number of factors, such as small size, remoteness, proneness to natural disasters and environmental fragility (see Briguglio 1995; Atkins et al. 2000). They are also very open economies with a high trade–GDP ratio, but their export base is very narrow, dominated by primary products and natural resources. They are largely dependent on external financial assistance, and their financial sector is extremely shallow. Thus, small-island economies are subject to external disturbances from the world goods and financial markets. As a result, small-island economies experience significant volatility in their economic growth.

Although most observers believe that small-island economies are structurally disadvantaged, some hold the view that they also have advantages. Kuznets (1960), for example, notes the advantage of a small and more cohesive population, which allows them to adapt better to change. Easterly and Kraay (2000) argue that the growth advantages of openness (trade and investment) outweigh the disadvantages in terms of trade volatility and, hence, small states do not necessarily have a poorer economic performance than larger countries.[1] Nevertheless, real per capita GDP growth tends to be much more volatile in smaller economies than in larger ones, and there is a growing consensus that high output or growth volatility adversely affects the poor. That is, the poor are more vulnerable to shocks and macroeconomic volatilities (see de Ferranti et al. 2000;

Vulnerability in developing countries, Naudé, Santos-Paulino and McGillivray (eds),
United Nations University Press, 2009, ISBN 978-92-808-1171-1

World Bank 2000). The poor have less human capital to adapt to down-turns in labour markets. They have fewer assets and less access to credit to facilitate consumption smoothing. There may be irreversible losses in nutrition and educational levels if there are no appropriate safety nets, as is usually the case in most developing countries. The *World Development Report 2000/2001* (World Bank 2000) finds asymmetric behaviour of poverty levels during deep cycles: poverty levels increase sharply in deep recessions and do not come back to previous levels as output recovers.[2]

This is an important observation in light of the orthodox macroeconomic policy package designed by the International Monetary Fund (IMF) since the early 1980s. The focus of such policies has been almost entirely on either price stability or external balance. The presumption is that price stability and external balance are prerequisites for sustained rapid growth. Using the macroeconomic experience of the Caribbean and Pacific island economies, this chapter will argue for a balance between the price and output stabilization goals of the macroeconomic policy mix. This chapter also takes a contrary view to the conventional wisdom that small, open island economies do not have much control over their macroeconomic instruments. The experience of Singapore shows that an island economy can successfully stabilize both employment and price levels by adopting innovative macroeconomic policy mixes. Drawing on the Singapore experience, this chapter will outline a framework for growth-promoting, pro-poor macroeconomic policies for small-island economies/micro states.

2 Economic characteristics of Caribbean and Pacific island economies

Table 10.1 presents some basic socioeconomic indicators of Caribbean and Pacific island economies. Table 10.2 lists their vulnerability index and output volatility index. As can be seen, despite their smallness and high vulnerability, their real GDP per capita (in purchasing power parity terms) is reasonably high when compared with larger developing countries. A number of Caribbean island economies also have a high human development index (HDI), while the rest are ranked as medium human development countries. Analysing the relative performance of small-island developing economies, Briguglio (1995: 1622) wondered "whether the economic fragilities of small-island developing economies are actually the reason for their relatively high GDP per capita and Human Development Index".

The high real per capita income and HDI may, therefore, give an impression that poverty in the Caribbean and Pacific islands is not as acute

Table 10.1 Size and socioeconomic indicators: Caribbean and Pacific island states, 2005

Economy	Area ('000 km²)	Population ('000)	Real GDP per capita (PPP$)	Human Development Index
Caribbean island states				
Antigua and Barbuda	0.44	82.8	12,500	0.815
Bahamas	14.00	323.1	18,380	0.845
Barbados	0.43	269.6	17,297	0.891
Belize	23.00	291.8	7,109	0.778
Dominica	0.75	72.0	6,393	0.798
Dominican Republic		8,984.9	8,217	0.779
Grenada	0.34	106.5	7,843	0.777
Guyana	216.00	751.2	4,508	0.750
Haiti		8,527.8	1,663	0.529
Jamaica	11.00	2,654.5	4,291	0.736
St Kitts and Nevis	0.27	48.0	13,307	0.821
St Lucia	0.62	164.8	6,707	0.795
St Vincent and the Grenadines	0.39	119.1	6,568	0.761
Suriname	164.00	449.2	7,722	0.774
Trinidad and Tobago	0.44	1305.2	14,603	0.814
Pacific island states				
Cook Islands	0.24	n/a	n/a	n/a
Fed. States of Micronesia	0.70	111.0	n/a	n/a
Fiji	18.27	848.0	6,049	0.762
Kiribati	0.69	99.0	1,475[a]	n/a
Marshall Islands	0.18	63.0	1,970[a]	n/a
Nauru	0.02	n/a	n/a	n/a
Palau		20.0	n/a	0.535[b]
PNG	462.24	6,000.0	2,563	0.530
Samoa	2.94	185.0	6,170	0.785
Solomon Islands	27.56	478.0	2,031	0.602
Tonga	0.75	102.0	8,177	0.819
Tuvalu	0.03	10.0	n/a	0.542[b]
Vanuatu	12.19	211.0	3,225	0.674

Sources: World Bank (2006); UNDP (various years).
Notes:
[a] 1999
[b] 2003

as in other countries. However, surveys of living conditions conducted between 1996 and 2002 in the Caribbean reveal a very different picture. These surveys used poverty measures in terms of the ability to buy a basic consumption basket of food and non-food items, such as education, housing and transportation. According to these surveys, Haiti and Suriname are at the high end of the spectrum, with an estimated poverty

Table 10.2 Composite vulnerability and output volatility index of Caribbean and Pacific island economies

Economy	Composite vulnerability		Output volatility	
	Index	Rank	Index	Rank
Caribbean islands				
Antigua and Barbuda	10.621	2	13.38	2
Bahamas	10.368	4	7.37	24
Barbados	5.780	38	4.34	73
Belize	6.854	25	9.63	14
Dominica	8.138	15	6.12	40
Dominican Republic	4.680	91	5.52	54
Grenada	8.232	14	6.89	30
Guyana	7.976	16	11.87	4
Haiti	4.366	97	5.86	51
Jamaica	7.426	19	3.43	90
St Kitts and Nevis	6.388	29	5.97	49
St Lucia	7.469	18	6.59	34
St Vincent and the Grenadines	4.736	89	6.08	42
Suriname	5.055	60	7.56	23
Trinidad and Tobago	5.358	49	8.75	17
Pacific islands				
Fiji	9.034	9	6.84	31
Papua New Guinea	6.182	31	5.03	64
Samoa	7.345	20	6.92	29
Solomon Islands	8.389	11	11.21	8
Tonga	10.470	3	13.18	3
Vanuatu	13.343	1	3.61	89

Source: Commonwealth Secretariat (2000).
Note: Ranks among 110 developing and island states.

incidence of 65 per cent and 63 per cent, respectively. Clustered in the 30–40 per cent range are Belize, Dominica, Grenada, Guyana, St Kitts and Nevis, and St Vincent and the Grenadines. The estimated poverty rates in Anguilla, St Lucia and Trinidad and Tobago range between 20 per cent and 29 per cent, and they are 14 per cent and 17 per cent, respectively, in Barbados and Jamaica (Bourne 2005).

The quality of life is equally dismal in the Pacific islands (Figure 10.1). For example, in Papua New Guinea (PNG) and Vanuatu 30–40 per cent of the population live below the National Basic Needs Poverty Line,[3] and about 61 per cent do not have access to safe water. Whereas 58 per cent of children are receiving education in Vanuatu, the figure is only 41 per cent in PNG. In Fiji, the percentage of the population living below the National Basic Needs Poverty Line is 25 per cent, and 53 per cent of the

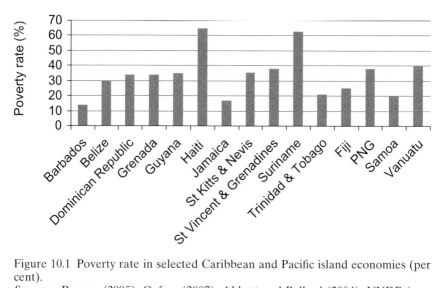

Figure 10.1 Poverty rate in selected Caribbean and Pacific island economies (per cent).
Sources: Bourne (2005); Oxfam (2007); Abbott and Pollard (2004); UNDP (various years).

population do not have access to safe water. The poverty rate in Samoa is about 20 per cent, and in the Solomon Islands only 52 per cent of children are enrolled in education.

What is more disturbing is the vulnerability of the population to poverty. For example, in Jamaica the poverty rate goes up from 3.2 per cent to 25.2 per cent when the international poverty line moves from US$1/day to US$2/day. In the Dominican Republic, the poverty rate jumps from 3.2 per cent to 16.0 per cent, and in Trinidad and Tobago it rises from 12.4 per cent to 39.0 per cent with the upward adjustment of the international poverty line.[4] This means a large number of people live just above the poverty line, and any sustained adverse shock to the economy can push them into poverty. Therefore, it is important to analyse the sources of volatility in order to stabilize income and employment growth at a high level.

3 Macroeconomic performance and sources of volatility

As can be seen from panels (a) and (b) in Figure 10.2, extreme volatility is the hallmark of both the Caribbean and the Pacific islands and, for most, growth remains subdued, averaging less than 4 per cent. This is despite the fact that most have been quite successful in containing the inflation rate at less than 4 per cent (Figure 10.3). This indicates that price

(a) Caribbean islands

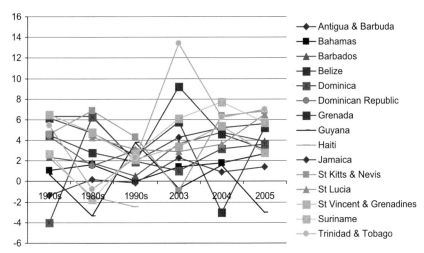

(b) Pacific islands

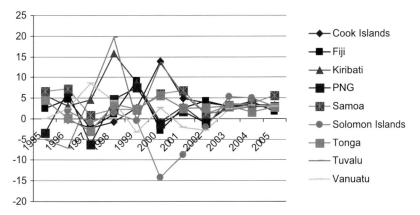

Figure 10.2 GDP growth in the Caribbean islands and in the Pacific islands (per cent).
Sources: World Bank (2002b) and ECLAC (2006) for the Caribbean Islands; ESCAP (2006) for the Pacific islands.

stability or low inflation may be a necessary but not a sufficient condition for sustained economic growth.[5] Volatility of growth itself may affect growth, because economic instability tends to skew investment towards short-run gains in a non-optimal way (Perry 2003).

Importantly, economic volatility affects more adversely the employment and incomes of less skilled workers who do not have adequate

(a) Caribbean islands

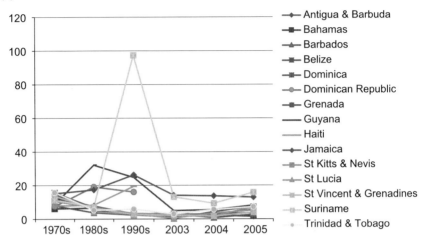

(b) Pacific islands

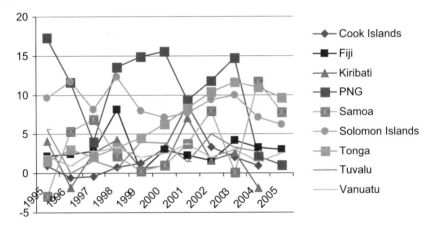

Figure 10.3 Inflation in the Caribbean islands and in the Pacific islands (per cent). *Sources*: World Bank (2002b) and ECLAC (2006) for the Caribbean islands; ESCAP (2006) for the Pacific islands.

coping mechanisms. The absence of publicly funded well-targeted safety nets accentuates the problem. Thus, in addition to the persistently poor, a large number of people remain vulnerable to shocks to the economy. Hence, macroeconomic policies should aim not just at price stability but also at output and employment stabilization, especially when shocks originate from the supply side.[6]

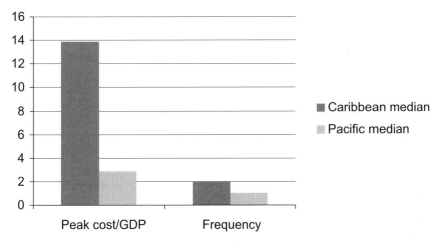

Figure 10.4 Frequency (per year) and costs of natural disasters, 1970–2000.
Source: World Bank (2002a).

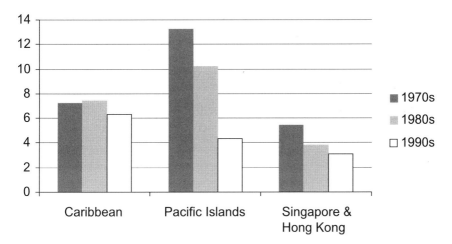

Figure 10.5 Volatility of terms of trade.
Note: Terms-of-trade shocks are defined as (trade/GDP)x(change in terms of trade).
Source: World Bank (2002a).

It is well accepted that the island economies are particularly prone to natural disasters (Figure 10.4).[7] As Figure 10.5 shows, Caribbean and Pacific island economies have also suffered larger terms-of-trade shocks than two successful island economies, Singapore and Hong Kong.[8] A relatively favourable disposition certainly has played a role in Singapore's and Hong Kong's better macroeconomic and growth performance. Nonetheless, their economic condition was not hugely different in the 1950s and 1960s from that of the Caribbean and Pacific islands, with widespread unemployment and poverty.[9] Economic policies and the activism of the government, especially in Singapore, have been largely responsible for the turnaround in their fortunes. In addition, both Singapore and Hong Kong are better able to absorb shocks owing to the depth of their financial sector.

Although the island economies are subjected to mostly adverse supply shocks, nearly all of them followed conservative macroeconomic policies, as required by their adjustment package with the IMF.[10] This is evident from Figure 10.6, which shows the growth rates of domestic credit to the private sector. As can be seen, domestic credit grew at a much faster rate in Singapore and Hong Kong. In the case of the Caribbean countries, domestic credit to the private sector remained more or less stagnant since the 1980s. That is, the monetary policy stance in these countries has been by and large contractionary.

There is a consensus that fiscal policy in most poor countries with a weak revenue base tends to be pro-cyclical.[11] Government revenues in the Caribbean and Pacific small-island economies depend excessively on trade taxes and foreign aid. Thus, trade shocks and aid volatility are a major source of instability in government revenues. If foreign aid flows do not match the loss of revenue during adverse shocks, governments are forced to cut investment expenditure, since it is politically difficult to cut non-development expenditure, such as civil servants' salaries or various

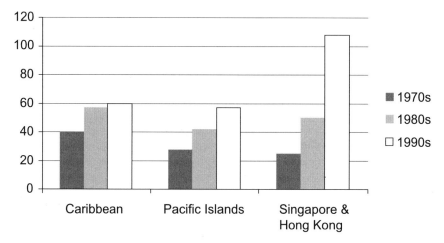

Figure 10.6 Domestic credit to the private sector (per cent of GDP).

subsidies and welfare programmes. This exacerbates the impact of shocks, as well as harming long-term growth potential. This kind of adjustment was observed particularly in the Pacific island economies, where development expenditure was already too low as a percentage of public spending. However, there have been some differences in the fiscal policy response of the Eastern Caribbean Currency Union (ECCU) governments:

> [They] dedicated a large share of their spending to public investment, particularly during the 1980s, when external assistance was abundant. In the late 1990s and early 2000s, these countries raised public spending, including for investment, trying to offset exogenous shocks on growth and declining private investment. (Fichera 2006: 50–51)

As a result, the ECCU countries grew at a faster rate. Even the worst-performing ECCU country experienced positive growth (2.5 per cent on average) in per capita income during 1995–2004.

Figure 10.7 shows that public consumption growth has been highly volatile in both Caribbean and Pacific island economies. Perry (2003) has found that fiscal volatility accounts for 15 per cent of excess volatility in Latin America and the Caribbean. This excessive volatility in the growth of public consumption is largely owing to the boom/bust nature of revenues, and results in pro-cyclical fiscal policy. Thus, one can reasonably conclude that pro-cyclical fiscal policy and tighter monetary policy aimed solely at price stability in the wake of exogenous supply shocks exacer-

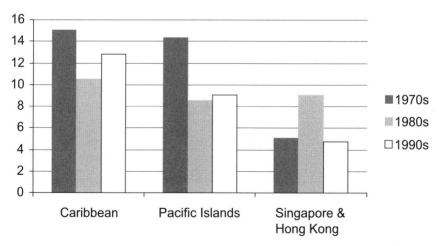

Figure 10.7 Volatility of public consumption growth (percentage change).
Source: World Bank (2000).

bated the impacts of shocks.[12] This brings us to the critical issue of the role of macroeconomic policies.

The recent empirical growth literature has shown that there is a strong negative correlation between pro-cyclical fiscal behaviour and the long-term growth rate. On the other hand, counter-cyclical fiscal policy enhances growth possibilities by providing fiscal relief (tax cuts and subsidies) to the struggling private sector during economic downturns, as well as by boosting government investment in key economic and social sectors.[13]

The restrictive monetary and pro-cyclical fiscal policy stance not only accentuates the depth of economic contraction and harms long-term growth, but also has an asymmetrically adverse impact on the poor. To begin with, a tighter credit policy affects smaller and medium-size enterprises, which depend mostly on bank financing, more than it affects larger firms. This has adverse employment impacts for low-skilled workers, as evidenced by the negative correlation between the volatility of nominal GDP and the income growth of the poor (see Chowdhury 2006). Studies have also found that social expenditures are, at best, kept constant as a percentage of GDP during downturns, and the more targeted social expenditures tend to fall as a percentage of GDP, when they should expand as the number of poor and unemployed increases.[14]

4 The role of macroeconomic policies

4.1 Conventional macroeconomic models for small open economies

What role can macroeconomic policies play in very open small-island economies? Khatkhate and Short (1980) believe very little. According to them, the degree of policymakers' control over macroeconomic target variables (e.g. output, inflation and external balance) is inversely proportional to the degree of openness of the product market ("by its [mini state's] exposure to foreign trade such that the economic targets of its economy are largely beyond its control" – Khatkhate and Short 1980: 1018).[15] Given that mini states are price takers in the international market, the volume of exports, and therefore output, is determined by the mini state's productive capacity, which is influenced more by such factors as weather than macroeconomic policies. At the same time, being highly import dependent, their inflation is, by and large, determined by their trading partners.

Corden (1984), on the other hand, using the example of Singapore, developed a model of a small open economy in which all products are tradable and demonstrated that exchange rates can be used to target inflation and wages policies can be used to target competitiveness and, hence, employment. Since the aggregate demand for output is perfectly price elastic, domestic demand and, hence, monetary policy and fiscal policy do not have any direct effects on the price level or employment.[16] To the extent that the monetary authority pegs the exchange rate to a predetermined level, money supply becomes endogenous. Thus, monetary policy works only through its effects on the exchange rate. When the exchange rate is allowed to float, perfect capital mobility renders fiscal policy ineffective owing to induced exchange rate effects.[17]

Treadgold (1992) provided a critique of Khatkhate and Short, and extended Corden's model to suit the conditions of small Pacific island economies. To begin with, a number of Caribbean and Pacific island economies do not have separate currencies; they use either US, Australian or New Zealand dollars. Thus, they cannot have the exchange rate instrument as suggested by the Corden model, but they can still use wages policy for employment targets. Secondly, even for those economies that have their own currencies, the assumption of perfect capital mobility is not relevant, because this would require perfect substitutability between domestic and foreign bonds. However, even when the assumption of perfect capital mobility is replaced with incomplete capital mobility, Treadgold shows that, under different labour market conditions, the policy implications of the basic Corden model remain relevant. When money wages are inflexible downward, the achievement of the employment target would require abandoning an independent inflation target. That is, the exchange rate should be varied to achieve the domestic inflation needed to reduce real wages for the employment target. On the other hand, downward real wage inflexibility excludes the possibility of achieving any independent employment target, and macro policy (i.e. exchange rate policy) should be directed to controlling the price level only. Finally, the micro states that experience a high degree of labour mobility with larger economies essentially face a given real wage determined in the larger economies. Their labour market mimics a competitive labour market and, hence, employment is determined endogenously. As in the case of downward real wage inflexibility, these micro states should use the exchange rate to achieve the inflation target.

In sum, fiscal and monetary policies cannot play stabilizing roles in any of the three theoretical models reviewed above. In the Corden model and its modified version, the stabilization (price level and employment) role is assigned to the exchange rate and wages policies. The fact that some Caribbean and Pacific island economies were able to successfully maintain very low inflation rates by using conventional demand management policies proves Khatkhate and Short's conclusion wrong. To the extent that the effectiveness of policy instruments (exchange rates) in the Corden–Treadgold framework depends on falling real wages, it does not offer much hope in economies where poverty is high and real wages are at subsistence level. In these countries, real wage resistance does not have to be an outcome of a centralized wage-setting mechanism and/or the nature of labour market institutions. Real wages are already so low that they cannot be reduced any further.[18]

All three models focus on the demand-side role of fiscal and monetary policies and ignore the fact that, in developing countries, these policies are used predominantly for economic growth and hence enhancing aggregate supply. Thus, employment creation in these models implies movement along the labour demand curve (i.e. a reduction in real wages). They also assume symmetry in both capital inflows and outflows and consider only short-term portfolio investment, not long-term foreign direct investment. Most developing countries, especially the small Caribbean and Pacific island economies, do not attract much in the way of capital flows. As noted earlier, vulnerability risks outweigh the expected gains from interest rate differentials, and these economies are more prone to capital flights than to capital inflows. For their long-term economic growth, they need foreign direct investment and foreign aid, which are not sensitive to interest rate differentials. Once these considerations are taken into account, fiscal and monetary policies assume radically different roles from what can be derived from the Mundell–Fleming model and its variants. In particular, when the direct long-term (growth) and short-term (demand) aspects of macroeconomic policies are juxtaposed or treated simultaneously, employment creation does not depend on lower real wages (movement along the demand curve); instead, employment is created by shifting the labour demand curve. That is, what is needed in fragile economies such as the Caribbean and Pacific islands is state-led development strategies.

4.2 Lessons from Singapore

The conventional wisdom is that Singapore pursues conservative macroeconomic policies, as evidenced by its large foreign reserves and budget surpluses. However, close observers of Singapore believe that the government budget surplus is a misleading indicator of the government's fiscal stance owing to the presence of various statutory boards and a large public sector. By the mid-1980s, prior to the start of privatization, there were about 490 government-linked companies (GLCs) and 30 statutory boards, which had substantial monopoly power. Governments often used these GLCs and statutory boards to pump-prime the economy whenever there was any sign of an economic downturn. These measures do not show up in the budget of the government. Profits from GLCs and statutory boards subsidized deficits in government priority areas such as housing, which kept up effective demand. Thus, Toh (2005: 43) points out:

> Far from non-intervention, the government believes in short-term discretionary measures to even out adverse impacts caused by the international business cycle and changing economic trends. Fiscal policy is a key instrument for aggregate demand management.

In a rigorous study using the IMF methodology of fiscal stance, Nadal-De Simone (2000) found that, contrary to the common view, fiscal policy in Singapore during 1966–1995 was not contractionary most of the time. Although the fiscal policy multiplier is found to be small, owing to the openness of the economy, the government did not shy away from using it, because it relied on the crowding-in factor of infrastructure and social investment. Fiscal policy in Singapore is used predominantly to promote non-inflationary economic growth – supporting investment, entrepreneurship and job creation. GLCs and statutory boards were created in the late 1960s to jump-start industrialization. The government also owned the largest bank, the Development Bank of Singapore. Huff (1995) notes that government expenditure on infrastructure, accounting for 38 per cent of all gross capital formation, played a large role in Singapore's annual real GDP growth of 5.7 per cent during the early phase of its development (1960–1966).

Singapore was able to undertake public sector investment on a massive scale without incurring unsustainable debt and inflationary pressures owing to its savings policy. There are three aspects to its national savings policy. The first is strict adherence to the principle of achieving a surplus (or at least not running a deficit) on the current account of the government. Second, the government followed the commercial principle of profit generation for the GLCs and statutory bodies. Thus, the primary budget surplus and profits from GLCs and statutory boards contribute substantially to public sector savings. Finally, the scheme of compulsory contributions to the Central Provident Fund (CPF) forces every employee to save. Combined contributions by both employees and employers rose to 50 per cent of the payroll at its peak in the mid-1980s. These measures raised national savings from about 12 per cent of GDP in 1965 to close to 45 per cent of GDP in 2004.

The CPF scheme has been instrumental in non-inflationary development financing. First, the government could access a large pool of funds and did not have to borrow from the monetary authority, which is inflationary. Second, the compulsory contributions to the CPF dampened demand pressure coming from public investment. They acted as an automatic stabilizer for inflation. Critics argue that GLCs, together with the public sector, crowd out private enterprise. However, there is little evidence of that in Singapore: "Every $1 increase over the preceding decade in public sector capital formation was associated with an increase in private sector capital formation of $3 during the 1970s and $2.8 for 1980–1992" (Huff 1995: 747).

For Singapore, being highly dependent on external trade, its management of the exchange rate has been crucial. The Singapore dollar exchange rate is based on a managed float system. The Monetary Authority of Singapore (MAS) manages the float within a target band based on an undisclosed trade-weighted basket of the currencies of Singapore's major trading partners. Given the openness of Singapore and its high import content, this seems to be a very sensible policy; because contractionary monetary or interest rate policies can have only a limited effect on inflation, domestic inflation was kept low by allowing the exchange rate to appreciate in line with foreign inflation (Huff 1995: 752). Furthermore, reduction in the volatility of the exchange rate arising from exchange rate targeting may reduce uncertainty and hence promote trade. In order to retain some control over monetary policy while following a managed exchange rate, Singapore deployed a number of measures. They included withholding tax on interest earned by non-residents on Singapore dollar holdings and preventing banks from making Singapore dollar loans to non-residents or to residents for use outside Singapore, except to finance external trade. These amounted to restrictions on short-term capital flows, while Singapore always welcomed foreign direct investment.

Finally, Singapore used wages policy to complement its growth-oriented fiscal and monetary policies. Through the regulation of the labour market (partly by legislation barring activist trade unionism and partly by regulating the foreign labour supply) and tripartite wage determination at the National Wages Council, Singapore ensured that its unit labour cost remains internationally competitive.

5 State-led development strategy

This section outlines some basic features of state-led development strategy.

5.1 Fiscal policy

Given the poor state of infrastructure, human resources and other critical factors for economic growth, as well as the lack of private investment in these areas (owing to market failure or inadequate markets), the government has to play a leading role. This means a predominant role for fiscal policy for both the development and the stabilization of economic cycles. This is, indeed, the recommendation of an IMF-sponsored study of the Pacific island economies.

> In the Pacific, the discouraging effects on private investment of high-cost, low-quality utilities are aggravated by poor infrastructure. The region's governments, together with donors, need to strengthen public investment efforts and ensure that such programs focus on developing physical and human capital that complement rather than substitute for private sector investment. (Fichera 2006: 53)

Obviously the question arises as to the financing of deficits and its implications for inflation and the external balance, as well as the sustainability of government debt. First, we should note the "golden rule": borrow to finance investment and balance recurrent/routine expenditure. If borrowing is done to invest productively, then debt will remain sustainable – economic growth will generate revenues to repair the budget deficit. Second, the aim should be to maintain debt sustainability over the cycle; that is, to have the political will to offset higher deficits incurred during downturns with higher revenues during the upswings. This may also mean adjusting the back of the safety net and reducing expenditure designed to jump-start the economy, as well as expanding the revenue base.

It is to be noted that a number of Caribbean and Pacific island economies have a fiscal stabilization fund. Reserves are accumulated in these funds during commodity booms to be used during the downswings. However, there are considerable doubts about the robustness of the political system and elites in the Caribbean and Pacific island economies needed to prevent a pro-cycle bias in fiscal measures. Nonetheless, a number of institutional measures can be suggested to ensure the viability of counter-cyclical fiscal measures. For example, Perry (2003) believes that legislation regarding the government's fiscal behaviour during upswings and downswings of the economy can potentially remove the pro-cycle bias of fiscal policy.[19] However, fiscal rules face a dilemma between flexibility and credibility. Too rigid rules to achieve credibility may lead to high costs in forgone flexibility. Fiscal rules to support counter-cyclical fiscal measures must also ensure long-term debt sustainability. Designing rules to achieve a balance between flexibility, credibility and sustainability may not be an easy task. Reviewing a number of countries that have some kind of fiscal rules, Perry finds the rule adopted by Chile requiring structural balance or a modest structural surplus most useful.[20] However, given the development needs of the small-island economies, the fact remains that the governments will have to borrow in the short to medium term. Owing to a poor credit rating in the international capital markets and the lack of a well-developed domestic capital market, the governments have two options for borrowing: (a) borrowing from central banks and (b) foreign aid. Foreign aid, indeed, has been a significant source of government financing in both Caribbean and Pacific island economies.

Borrowing from central banks

Borrowing from central banks will increase money supply.[21] The endogeneity of money supply will prevent interest rates from rising; hence there will be no possibility of a crowding-out effect. On the contrary, government investment in infrastructure and human resource development is likely to crowd-in private investment.[22] Whereas improved infrastructure reduces business costs, subsidized provision of public health and education can be regarded as a social wage, which dampens wage demand. Both factors enhance the investment climate.[23] Additionally, since the productive capacity of the economy is likely to expand with public investment, the increase in the money supply will not be as inflationary. In any case, a moderate level of inflation is not found to be harmful for economic growth (see Chowdhury 2006). In the absence of a well-developed taxation system, inflationary tax (or seigniorage) becomes an important source of government revenue for financing development (see Kalecki 1976).

Foreign aid

Foreign aid is a non-inflationary source of finance for governments. Foreign aid already plays a significant role. Pacific island economies are among the highest aid recipients in the developing world. There is a general perception, however, that the large aid flows have failed to spur rapid economic growth.[24] However, a comprehensive study of seven Pacific island economies has found a statistically significant positive relationship between aid and growth, with diminishing returns (Pavlov and Sugden 2006).[25] This finding is consistent with findings elsewhere and is not sensitive to either the policy environment or institutions. A World Bank study also reported a positive relationship between foreign aid and economic growth in the Caribbean region study (World Bank 2002a). Thus, the findings imply that the lessons learnt in other countries are largely applicable to the Caribbean and Pacific island economies.

The apparent lack of aid effectiveness or diminishing returns to aid can be traced to a number of confounding factors. First is the uncertainty of disbursements and the divergence between commitments and disbursements. Aid volatility can cause significant problems for project implementation and government budgets. Second, aid is fraught with principal–agent problems. The recipient countries not only renege on commitment to reforms, but also divert aid funds to undesirable uses, such as government consumption or development projects chosen purely on political grounds. Third, diminishing returns to aid could result from the lack of absorptive capacity. Finally, large aid flows can cause real appreciation of local currencies to the detriment of the tradable sector, known as the "Dutch disease syndrome".[26]

The key element for addressing the above issues is the predictability of aid flows and confidence in the donor–recipient relationship. The Caribbean and Pacific island economies experience high volatility of fiscal revenues owing to their heavy reliance on trade. Aid is needed to smooth out fluctuations in revenues and should not be another source of shocks to the budget. Perhaps a "fiscal insurance scheme" could be developed for the respective regions, with donor funds to address volatility in fiscal revenues.[27] That is, donors can contribute a certain portion of aid to a regional common pool to be drawn by the country facing unforeseen declines in fiscal revenues. The recipient countries should also contribute to this regional common pool a certain portion of their revenue windfalls.[28] A jointly managed regional common pool or a fiscal insurance scheme as suggested above can play a positive role in improving donor–recipient relations. Donors can help overcome some of the absorptive capacity problems by not requiring counter-funding and by providing technical assistance in aid management and administration. Other measures can also be considered to monitor aid administration. For example, aid may be used in helping national governments to strengthen democratic institutions designed to provide checks and balances on government expenditure.

Finally, the possibility of Dutch disease is remote, because these countries do not operate at full employment (a vital assumption of the Dutch disease hypothesis). Moreover, the Dutch disease syndrome can be avoided in a number of ways. First, if aid is used for direct imports and/or technical assistance, then there is no need for real appreciation for resource transfer to occur. Second, if aid is used for productivity-enhancing investment, then that offsets the impact of the real exchange rate on competitiveness (see Chowdhury and McKinley 2006).

5.2 Monetary policy

Growth-oriented monetary policy has two features. First, as noted in the discussion about fiscal policy, monetary policy has to be accommodative to governments' investment needs. This is premised on the large body of empirical evidence that moderate inflation does not harm economic growth, and may even be necessary. Furthermore, an accommodative monetary policy is needed to ease the counter-funding problem for the utilization of aid and hence enhance the absorption of aid.[29] Second, the monetary authorities should use low-cost directed credits to support labour-intensive small and medium enterprises (SMEs). Subsidized special credit programmes, of course, distort the credit market as well as run the risk of being infected with rent-seeking behaviour. However, the costs of distortions and rent-seeking have to be weighed against the costs of market failures in the credit market, which result in discrimination against SMEs and the agriculture sector.[30] One may have concerns about the impact of low-interest policies on savings and financial sector development. To begin with, low real interest rates must not mean negative real deposit interest rates, which, in fact, has been the case in a number of Caribbean and Pacific island economies. Second, empirical evidence shows that, in low-income countries, financial development is mainly demand led; that is, it follows growth. This is consistent with the observation that current income plays a more dominant role in household savings decisions than the interest rate. Additionally, as the experience of Singapore shows, rapid mobilization of domestic savings depends more on non-market measures such as compulsory savings schemes and public sector surpluses than on real interest rates. Finally, a low-interest-rate policy has advantages for both public debt sustainability and low inflation. It reduces interest payments on public debt as well as the business cost on account of working capital. Both factors contribute to low inflation.

5.3 Exchange rate and capital account policies

The Caribbean and Pacific island economies have exchange rate systems ranging from currency union to dollarized and floating regimes. As expected, the dollarized economies have inflation rates close to the rates in the country of the currency they use, and the countries with an independently floating system have higher inflation rates. The economies with a pegged exchange rate system have mixed experiences with inflation.

In contrast to the IMF's suggestion of freer and more flexible currency regimes, some observers have argued for a dollarized regime for the Pacific region and the use of the Australian dollar in the Pacific economies (De Brouwer 2002; Duncan 2002).[31] The argument is based on the depth of domestic financial and foreign exchange markets being insufficient to support the liquidity necessary to maintain a freely floating exchange rate, and the lack of skilled personnel to run a central bank. The adoption of a strong foreign currency is also likely to impose fiscal discipline in economies where maintaining central bank independence is difficult. Some have also examined the possibility of forming a currency union like the East Caribbean Currency Union (Jayaraman et al. 2005). Although dollarization improves macroeconomic stability, the main objection to it may arise from the vastly different types of shocks facing the Pacific island economies compared with the country of the strong currency (Australia, New Zealand and the United States). Thus, responses to these shocks require some macroeconomic policy independence, which would be lost if dollarized. Very low inflation rates in the strong currency country may be too constraining for these economies, which are prone to supply shocks and need to undergo structural change. Furthermore, dollarization would deprive them of seigniorage, an important source of revenue for countries with a poor domestic revenue base.

Currency unions are also not without problems, especially when there is a lack of significant convergence of macroeconomic indicators. At the same time, when the members' trade structure and partners are very similar, they are likely to suffer from the same terms-of-trade shocks almost simultaneously. This can place enormous pressure on the fiscal balance and monetary situation of all member countries trying to adjust to the shock. Considering the pros and cons of various exchange rate regimes, it seems reasonable that the small-island economies should follow an adjustable peg exchange rate system. As mentioned earlier, Singapore has been quite successful in using an adjustable peg exchange rate system to contain inflation.[32] However, an economy (or economic union) cannot have macroeconomic policy independence and an open capital account under a pegged exchange rate system. This means there should be some restrictions on capital mobility. Neither the Caribbean nor the Pacific region receives much short-term private capital. Their main source of outside capital is foreign aid and workers' remittances, which are not sensitive to interest rates. Their main problem is capital outflow, and it makes sense to have some controls on capital flight. Restrictions on short-term capital outflows do not necessarily create any disincentives to long-term foreign direct investment.

6 Concluding remarks

This chapter has reviewed the macroeconomic performance of Caribbean and Pacific island economies. Given the high volatility of their output growth and its adverse impacts on long-term growth as well as on the poor, the chapter argued for the output stabilization role of macroeconomic policies. Drawing on the experience of Singapore, the chapter also argued that, contrary to the conventional wisdom, macroeconomic policies can play both stabilization and directly growth-promoting roles in highly open small economies. However, it requires some appropriate institutional frameworks to regulate the labour market, mobilization of savings, movements of short-term capital (capital flights) and the government's fiscal behaviour. Given high aid-dependency, there also needs to be improvement in aid delivery and aid management.

However, no one country is identical to another, and there are considerable differences among groups of countries. Thus, small-island states need to be innovative in designing their own institutions based on their own history and context. Furthermore, given their size, remoteness and other constraints, it seems they would be better off by pooling regional capacity and resources. This would entail opening up their own markets to inflows of goods, services, capital and labour from the region, something akin to a currency union.

Notes

1. In a cross-country regression with 157 countries, Easterly and Kraay (2000) found that "[m]icrostates are 50 percent richer than other states, controlling for location". In a sample of 48 countries, Milner and Westaway (1993) did not find significant evidence of the effect of country size on economic growth. Armstrong et al. (1998) also did not find in their cross-country regressions any significant effect of population size on economic growth. Srinivasan (1986) and Streeten (1993) argue that small may be beautiful. Singapore and Hong Kong are examples of two highly successful yet small economies.
2. Scatter plots of a large number of cross-country data reveal that the variability of nominal GDP growth has a negative correlation with the growth of the average income of the poorest fifth of the population, and a positive correlation with inequality (measured by the Gini coefficient). See Chowdhury (2006); Glewwe and Hall (1998).
3. The National Basic Needs Poverty Line is a measure of the minimum income needed to buy sufficient food and meet basic needs such as housing, clothing, transport and school fees (Oxfam 2007).
4. These figures are from *Human Development Report 2002* (UNDP 2002).
5. Fichera (2006: 51), in reviewing the macroeconomic performance of the Pacific islands and the Eastern Caribbean Currency Union countries, remarked: "policies ... although effective at maintaining relative macroeconomic stability over 1995–2004, have not been effective at promoting growth. Clearly, while macroeconomic stability is a necessary condition for growth, it is not sufficient."
6. Interestingly, contrary to what has become known as the "Washington consensus" as pursued by the international financial institutions, which aimed solely to stabilize nominal variables (e.g. inflation), the originator of the Washington consensus, John Williamson, did include the need to stabilize the real economy *à la* Keynes in his list of "good policies" (see Williamson 2004).
7. See Chapter 8 in this volume for discussion of the factors causing vulnerability.
8. See Chapter 8 in this volume for the econometric estimation of the economic cost of natural hazards.
9. Singapore's poverty rate was nearly 25 per cent in the mid-1950s, and even in 1970 the unemployment rate was over 8 per cent.
10. See Worrell (1987) for the experience of Caribbean economies. For the Pacific islands' experience, see Siwatibau (1993).

11. Eslava (2006) surveys the literature on the determinants of pro-cyclicality of fiscal policy. Also see Gavin et al. (1996) for the Latin American and Caribbean context.

12. ECLAC (2006: 36), in its *Survey of Latin America and the Caribbean, 1999–2000*, commented: "The priority given ... to fighting inflation and restoring credibility of stabilization policies had given a procyclical bias to macroeconomic policy."

13. United Nations (2006: Chapter IV) provides a brief summary of the literature on the economic and social consequences of pro-cyclical macroeconomic policies.

14. See the World Bank study by de Ferranti et al. (2000).

15. Caram (1989) holds a very similar view: "Under the conditions now prevalent in small developing countries, it is not to be expected that monetary financing and the ensuing increase in effective demand will result in an appreciable increase in domestic production. The domestically generated supply of goods is insufficiently diversified and, as a result of physical and organizational bottlenecks, has barely any short-term elasticity. Owing to this and to the ample opportunities for imports, despite the exchange controls in force, the additional demand will focus largely on the supply from abroad. The so-called monetary approach to the balance of payments ... proves to be highly topical for these countries."

16. In an economy (closed or open) with downward aggregate demand, expansionary monetary and fiscal policies work by raising the price level. The increased price level reduces real wages and hence increases employment and output. But when an economy faces perfectly price-elastic aggregate demand, the domestic price level cannot differ from the world price.

17. This follows from the standard Mundell–Fleming IS–LM–BP model with flexible exchange rates and perfect capital mobility.

18. Lodewijks (1988) exhaustively dealt with the limitations of real wage cuts in the context of PNG.

19. Singapore has legislation barring the current government's access to accumulated reserves to prevent politically motivated expenditure.

20. Application of Chilean-type fiscal rules requires improvements in fiscal accounting, reliable estimation of potential output and revenue elasticities. Countries would also have to develop ways to adjust for the cyclical components in interest rates.

21. This option is available only to countries with their own currencies, controlled by a monetary authority. The option is also limited for countries with a currency board that links domestic money strictly to the availability of foreign currencies.

22. The World Bank (1998: xii) notes that, in Pacific island economies, "[b]asic education, health care, and physical infrastructure are the highest priorities to improve living standards for the widest group of poor people, and to lay the foundations for sustained, broad-based income growth."

23. This is, in fact, the experience of the successful East and Southeast Asian economies.

24. See, for example, Feeny (2007). However, a negative correlation between aid flows and economic growth could be just a statistical artefact. It may be due to the fact that, in most cases, aid flows respond to natural disasters and other negative supply shocks that retard growth. None of the studies that report a negative aid–growth relationship conducted any counter-factual analysis. That is, what would have happened in the absence of aid? If aid responds to negative supply shocks, then the non-availability of aid is likely to exacerbate the impact of negative supply shocks and there would be a deeper drop in income.

25. The seven Pacific island economies studied are Cook Islands, Fiji, Kiribati, Samoa, Solomon Islands, Tonga and Vanuatu.

26. For evidence of the Dutch disease syndrome in Pacific micro states, see Laplange et al. (2001).

27. Dos Reis (2004) highlighted the usefulness of a fiscal insurance scheme for the countries of the Eastern Caribbean Currency Union. Such a scheme can alleviate problems of policy coordination within a currency union.
28. Some Pacific countries already have a fiscal stabilization fund. The regional stabilization fund can supplement the national fund.
29. The traditional rationale for aid is to fill the savings–investment gap and the current account gap. The savings–investment gap is generally related to government budget deficits. Aid funds are converted into domestic currency to be spent by the government, which causes inflationary pressure leading to real appreciation. The real appreciation, in turn, causes higher imports to be financed by foreign currencies made available through aid in the first place. This is the normal channel through which aid gets *spent* and *absorbed*. Conservative fiscal and monetary policies thus lead only to the accumulation of foreign reserves and defeat the purpose of aid. See Chowdhury and McKinley (2006).
30. See Chowdhury (2006) for an illustration of various monetary policy instruments for achieving both employment and moderate inflation targets.
31. Jayaraman (2005) did not find much support for using the Australian dollar. Based on trade flow statistics, he argued that there is a stronger case for adopting an Asian currency. Bowman (2006) concludes: "Dollarization to the US dollar, the de facto standard in Asia, or a move to a common currency may be preferable alternatives to dollarizing to the Australian dollar."
32. See Drake (1983) for a comprehensive discussion of exchange rate choices for small open economies. Drake suggests an intermediate regime between an absolutely fixed exchange rate regime with no monetary discretion and a fully flexible exchange rate regime with monetary discretion.

References

Abbott, D. and S. Pollard (2004). *Hardship and Poverty in the Pacific*. Manila: Asian Development Bank.

Armstrong, H., R. de Kervenoael, X. Li and R. Read, R. (1998). "A Comparison of the Economic Performance of Different Micro-States and between Micro-States and Larger Countries". *World Development* 26(4): 639–656.

Atkins, J. P., S. A. Mazzi and C. D. Easter (2000). "Commonwealth Vulnerability Index for Developing Countries: The Position of Small States". Economic Paper 40, Commonwealth Secretariat, London.

Bourne, C. (2005). "Poverty and Its Alleviation in the Caribbean". Lecture at the Alfred O. Heath Distinguished Speakers' Forum, University of the Virgin Islands, 14 March; available at ⟨http://www.caribank.org/titanweb/cdb/webcms. nsf/AllDoc/20A2B5DCFD56F79E0425740F0068F1EB/$File/BournePoverty.pdf⟩ (accessed 28 January 2009).

Bowman, C. (2006). "The Governor or Sheriff? Pacific Island Nations and Dollarization". Mimeo, Asia Pacific School of Economics and Government, Australian National University.

Briguglio, L. (1995). "Small-Island Developing States and Their Economic Vulnerability". *World Development* 23(9): 1615–1632.

Caram, A. (1989). "Guidelines for Monetary Policy in Small Developing Countries". In J. Kamanarides, L. Briguglio and H. Hoogendonk (eds), *The Economic Development of Small Countries: Problems, Strategies & Policies*. Delft: Eburon, in conjunction with the Foundation for International Studies, University of Malta, and the Faculty of Economics, University of Amsterdam.

Chowdhury, A. (2006). "The 'Stabilisation Trap' and Poverty Reduction: What Can Monetary Policy Do?" *Indian Development Review* 4(2): 407–432.

Chowdhury, A. and T. McKinley (2006). "Gearing Macroeconomic Policies to Manage Large Inflows of ODA: The Implications for HIV/AIDS Programs". International Poverty Centre Working Paper 17. Also presented at UNU-WIDER Conference on Aid Effectiveness, Helsinki, 16–17 June.

Commonwealth Secretariat (2000). "Small States: Meeting Challenges in the Global Economy". Report prepared for the Commonwealth Secretariat/World Bank Joint Task Force on Small States, Washington DC.

Corden, M. (1984). "Macroeconomic Targets and Instruments for a Small Open Economy". *Singapore Economic Review* 29(2): 27–37.

De Brouwer, G. (2002). "Should Pacific Island Nations Adopt the Australian Dollar?" *Pacific Economic Bulletin* 15(2): 161–169.

De Ferranti, D., G. Perry, I. Gill and L. Serven (2000). *Securing Our Future in a Global Economy*. Washington DC: World Bank.

Dos Reis, L. (2004). "A Fiscal Insurance Scheme for the Eastern Caribbean Currency Union". Mimeo, Intergovernmental Group of 24 (G24).

Drake, P. (1983). "Monetary and Exchange Rate Management in Tiny Open Underdeveloped Economies". *Savings and Development* 7(1): 4–19.

Duncan, R. (2002). "Dollarising the Solomon Island Economy". *Pacific Economic Bulletin* 15(2): 143–146.

Easterly, W. and A. Kraay (2000). "Small States, Small Problems? Income, Growth, and Volatility in Small States". *World Development* 28(11): 2013–2027.

ECLAC [Economic Commission for Latin America and the Caribbean] (2006). *Economic Survey of the Caribbean 2005–2006*. Santiago: ECLAC.

ESCAP [United Nations Economic and Social Commission for Asia and the Pacific] (2006). *Economic and Social Survey of Asia and the Pacific, 2006*. New York and Bangkok: United Nations.

Eslava, M. (2006). "The Political Economy of Fiscal Policy: Survey". Inter-American Development Bank, Working Paper No. 583.

Feeny, S. (2007). "Growth Impacts of Foreign Aid to Melanesia". *Journal of the Asia Pacific Economy* 12(1): 34–60.

Fichera, V. (2006). "The Pacific Islands and the Eastern Caribbean Currency Union: A Comparative Review". In C. Browne (ed.), *Pacific Island Economies*. Washington DC: International Monetary Fund.

Gavin, M., R. Hausmann, R. Perotti and E. Talvi (1996). "Managing Fiscal Policy in Latin America and the Caribbean: Volatility, Procyclicality and Limited Credit-worthiness". Inter-American Development Bank Working Paper 326.

Glewwe, P. and G. Hall (1998). "Are Some Groups More Vulnerable to Macroeconomic Shocks Than Others? Hypothesis Tests Based on Panel Data from Peru". *Journal of Development Economics* 56(1): 181–206.

Huff, W. (1995). "What Is the Singapore Model of Economic Development?" *Cambridge Journal of Economics* 19(6): 735–759.

Jayaraman, T. (2005). "Dollarisation of the Pacific Island Countries: Results of a Preliminary Study". Department of Economics, University of South Pacific Working Paper 2005/1.

Jayaraman, T., B. Ward and Z. Xu (2005). "Are the Pacific Islands Ready for a Currency Union? An Empirical Study of Degree of Economic Convergence". Department of Economics, University of South Pacific Working Paper 2005/2.

Kalecki, M. (1976). *Essays on Development Economics*. Brighton: Harvester Press.

Khatkhate, D. and B. Short (1980). "Monetary and Central Banking Problems of Mini States". *World Development* 8(12): 1017–1025.

Kuznets, S. (1960). "Economic Growth of Small Nations". In E. A. G. Robinson (ed.), *The Economic Consequences of the Size of Nations*. Proceedings of a Conference held by the International Economic Association. Toronto: Macmillan.

Laplange, P., M. Treadgold and J. Baldry (2001). "A Model of Aid Impact in Some South Pacific Microstates". *World Development* 29(2): 365–383.

Lodewijks, J. (1988). "Employment and Wages Policy in Papua New Guinea". *Journal of Industrial Relations* 30(3): 381–411.

Milner, C. and T. Westaway (1993). "Country Size and the Medium-term Growth Process: Some Cross-country Evidence". *World Development* 21(2): 203–211.

Nadal-De Simone, F. (2000). "Monetary and Fiscal Policy Interaction in a Small Open Economy: The Case of Singapore". *Asian Economic Journal* 14(2): 211–231.

Oxfam (2007). "Poverty in the Pacific", ⟨http://www.oxfam.org.nz/index.asp?s1= what%20we%20do&s2=where%20we%20work&s3=pacific&s4=Poverty%20in %20the%20Pacific⟩ (accessed 28 January 2009).

Pavlov, V. and C. Sugden (2006). "Aid and Growth in the Pacific Islands". *Asian-Pacific Economic Literature* 20(2): 38–55.

Perry, G. (2003). "Can Fiscal Rules Help Reduce Macroeconomic Volatility in Latin America and the Caribbean Region?" World Bank Policy Research Working Paper 3080, Washington DC.

Siwatibau, S. (1993). "Macroeconomic Management in the Small Open Economies of the Pacific". In R. Cole and S. Tambunlertchai (eds), *The Future of the Asia-Pacific Economies: Pacific Island Economies at the Cross Roads?* Canberra: Pacific Development Centre and the National Centre for Development Studies, Australian National University.

Srinivasan, T. N. (1986). "The Costs and Benefits of Being a Small Remote Island, Land-Locked or Ministate Economy". *World Bank Research Observer* 1(2): 205–218.

Streeten, P. (1993). "The Special Problems of Small Countries". *World Development* 21(2): 197–202.

Toh, M. (2005). "Singapore". *Pacific Economic Outlook, 2005–2006*. Singapore: APEC Centre.

Treadgold, M. (1992). "Openness and the Scope for Macroeconomic Policy in Micro States". *Cyprus Journal of Economics* 5(1): 15–24.

UNDP [United Nations Development Programme] (various years). *Human Development Report*. New York: Oxford University Press.

UNDP (2002). *Human Development Report 2002: Deepening Democracy in a Fragmented World*. New York: Oxford University Press.

United Nations (2006). *World Economic and Social Survey 2006*. New York: United Nations.

Williamson, J. (2004). "The Washington Consensus as Policy Prescription for Development". World Bank Lecture Series Practitioners of Development, 13 January.

World Bank (1998). *Enhancing the Role of Government in the Pacific Island Economies*. Washington DC: World Bank.

World Bank (2000). *World Development Report 2000/2001: Attacking Poverty*. Washington DC: World Bank.

World Bank (2002a). "Development Assistance and Economic Development in the Caribbean Region: Is There a Correlation?" Caribbean Group for Cooperation in Economic Development, World Bank Report 24164-LAC.

World Bank (2002b). "Caribbean Economic Overview, 2000: Macroeconomic Volatility, Household Vulnerability, and Institutional and Policy Responses". Concept Paper, Caribbean Group for Cooperation in Economic Development, World Bank, Washington DC.

World Bank (2006). *World Development Report 2006*. Washington DC: World Bank.

Worrell, D. (1987). *Small-Island Economies: Structure and Performance in the English-Speaking Caribbean Since 1970*. New York: Praeger.

Part III

Conclusion

11

Vulnerability in developing countries: Implications and conclusions

Wim Naudé, Amelia U. Santos-Paulino and Mark McGillivray

1 Introduction

Recognizing the multidimensional and complex nature of households and countries' vulnerability to various hazards is a core issue in economic development and policy. This book purposely adopted a multifaceted approach to illustrate how a better understanding of vulnerability is essential if progress is to made in global development. This approach consisted of dealing with the concept of vulnerability from different viewpoints and in relation to different hazards, so as to consider the relationship between vulnerability, poverty and other hazards such as natural hazards, ill health, famine and macroeconomic shocks. It also consisted of exploring vulnerability in a variety of developing country settings: from some of the largest and most successful developing countries (such as China) to some of the smallest and most struggling developing countries (such as Zimbabwe). The book also contains studies based on a multitude of methodologies, from theoretical constructs to quantitative as well as qualitative studies of vulnerability.

Having approached vulnerability in developing countries from these perspectives, it is appropriate that we pause and take stock in this final chapter. We will therefore now attempt to generalize and place in context some of the implications from this book, in particular implications for further research into the concept and measurement of vulnerability (section 2) and for the policies and measures to deal with vulnerability in developing countries (section 3).

Vulnerability in developing countries, Naudé, Santos-Paulino and McGillivray (eds), United Nations University Press, 2009, ISBN 978-92-808-1171-1

2 Implications for the concept and measurement of vulnerability

We will now draw some implications for understanding and measuring vulnerability, and identify some areas for further research. Before we do so, however, it is useful to summarize the concept and measurement of vulnerability as used in this book, and to do so within the context of the poverty literature. We showed in Chapter 1 that vulnerability can be applied to different levels (e.g. households, countries) and to different outcomes (poverty, natural hazards, etc). At the household (micro) level, vulnerability is most commonly defined as the probability that a household will remain in, or fall into, poverty in future. At a higher level, it is the probability that a country or region will experience a negative shock or perturbation.

At the household level, the concept and measurement of vulnerability should not be seen in isolation from the more general concern with the concept and measurement of poverty. In fact, further progress in conceptualizing and measuring vulnerability is likely to come from various initiatives to define and measure poverty better. We briefly discuss these aspects in section 2.1 below. In a related manner, there is likely to be further progress in measuring vulnerability to various types of hazard, as the availability of data permits. In section 2.2 we discuss the possible directions this could take and summarize a number of requirements for a good measure of vulnerability. At a higher level, concerns about the vulnerability of countries or regions should not be seen in isolation from concerns about state capacity and fragility and the institutional prerequisites for country resilience. It is also important to take into consideration the relationship between country-level vulnerability and fragility and household-level vulnerability. We briefly discuss these aspects in section 2.3.

2.1 Vulnerability and poverty

At a micro level, concern about vulnerability is essentially a concern about poverty. This reflects the fact that there has been significant progress in the understanding of poverty in recent years. However, much of this progress still needs to be fully taken into account by policymakers. Traditionally, poverty was taken to refer to "income poverty" and was measured statically, e.g. as the percentage of people at a particular point in time earning less than the (arbitrarily chosen) poverty line. This is still the measure used in the Millennium Development Goals to measure progress in the fight against poverty.

More recently, and greatly inspired by Amartya Sen's capabilities view of poverty, it is seen as a multidimensional concept extending beyond mere income measures. Hulme and McKay (2005) discuss the shortcomings of being concerned only with income poverty in the context of vulnerability. There is also agreement in academic circles that poverty is not a static concept but a dynamic one (Addison et al. 2008). Two main lines of research into the dynamics of poverty are multi-period poverty and uncertainty. Multi-period poverty refers to the fact that households can move into and out of poverty, as was shown in the case of Tajikistan in Chapter 4. Here the notions of chronic and transient poverty have been put forward to give a time dimension to poverty – thus the chronically poor are those who persist in poverty over a long time period. It is estimated that there are 320–443 million people currently living in chronic poverty (for an overview, see *The Chronic Poverty Report 2008–09* – CPRC 2008).

In the context of poverty, concern with uncertainty arose because a household that is currently not poor may become poor in future – in other words, such a household may be vulnerable to poverty. Thus, the concept of vulnerability to poverty as it is studied in this book can now be seen in its proper context: it is an attempt to expand the concept of poverty from a static to a dynamic one. In this perspective, extensions to the concept and measurement of vulnerability to poverty are likely to be driven by further research into refining the concept and measurement of poverty. One aspect that stands out immediately is the distinction between chronic and transitory poverty, which has implications for household vulnerability. It is recognized, for instance, that there might be path dependency in poverty – the longer a household is in poverty, the more difficult it may find it to escape (Bossert et al. 2008). This implies greater vulnerability to falling into poverty and remaining in poverty. A key result in this book, contained in Chapter 4, is that the factors that explain a household's likelihood of falling into poverty are different from those that explain moving out of poverty. Amongst the latter factors, the extent and persistence of poverty matter. In addition, the causes of chronic and transitory poverty differ. Chronic poverty often has multiple causes, and the chronically poor are often deprived across multiple dimensions. This means that vulnerability to poverty needs to take into account other forms of vulnerability and suggests that poverty, especially chronic poverty, is in itself a fundamental cause of vulnerabilities in other domains. Chronic poverty very often has a geographical/spatial pattern, where pockets of poverty persist in certain geographical regions over time. Chapter 4 has shown how important the geographical dimension is in determining the likelihood that households will escape from poverty.

Another aspect that stands out is that current measures of vulnerability generally treat household vulnerability as time invariant. Current efforts to achieve greater integration between the lines of research on multi-period poverty and uncertainty are therefore likely to spill over and inform research on vulnerability (Günther and Maier 2008).

Finally, although this book has made a distinction between micro- and macro-level vulnerability, there is a need to integrate the levels across which vulnerability is measured. This would require a consideration both of how household-level vulnerability to poverty adds up to the aggregate vulnerability of a whole region or country, or even perhaps across the world, as well as of how country-wide or region-wide vulnerability to hazards translates into household-level vulnerability to poverty. Dutta et al. (2008) discuss such a potential measure of household vulnerability to poverty that can be aggregated. There remains, however, plenty of scope for further research into integrating the micro and macro levels of vulnerability. In section 2.3 we sketch further linkages between these levels of vulnerability. But first we deal with further extensions of vulnerability to various others hazards.

2.2 Multidimensional vulnerability

The various contributions in this book support the notion of vulnerability as a multidimensional concept, even though most contributions have come from either an economics or a social science background.[1] Given that vulnerability can exist on different levels and in reference to a wide variety of potential hazards, and is studied across various disciplines, there are many ways in which to define and measure vulnerability. As the availability of data in developing countries improves, so will the various ways of measuring vulnerability. A potential danger is that this will see a proliferation of vulnerability measures or "vulnerability indices". There have already been warnings in the literature that the term "vulnerability" is in danger of being used too loosely, or that its understanding is marred by a proliferation of definitions. To minimize this danger it is perhaps necessary in this conclusion to suggest a number of criteria that a good measure of vulnerability should ideally satisfy. As we point out, satisfying these criteria is not trivial. Given the current situation we also suggest a number of avenues for further research.

The first criterion for a good measure of vulnerability is to bear in mind that vulnerability is an *ex ante* notion, so that any measure of vulnerability should have a "predictive quality" (Cannon et al. 2003). Yuan and Wan (2008) deal with the prediction of vulnerability and find that not all measures of vulnerability have equally good predictive qualities.

Moreover, measures of vulnerability to poverty are sensitive to the poverty line used.

Second, measures of vulnerability should define vulnerability in relation to a socially acceptable level of outcome (Alwang et al. 2001: 33). What is deemed socially acceptable may of course differ across contexts. For example, in the case of vulnerability to poverty the socially acceptable level of outcome is generally taken to be some "poverty line", expressed in terms of income or assets (see Chapters 2, 3 and 4). Not only is the choice of poverty line often controversial but, as Yuan and Wan (2008) have recently shown, measures of vulnerability to poverty are sensitive to the choice of poverty line. Similarly, in economic vulnerability indices at a country level, arbitrary cut-off levels are used below which countries are deemed to be vulnerable. A major difficulty here is that there will be countries very close to the cut-off levels that may in reality be either vulnerable or not vulnerable but not identified accurately. To overcome this problem, fuzzy set theory has been proposed (see e.g. Baliamoune-Lutz and McGillivray 2008), which allows for a gradual transition from one condition to another. Clearly, more research is needed into the reference points for vulnerability measures.

Third, measures of vulnerability should ideally contain information on the causes of vulnerability and the relative importance of idiosyncratic and covariate risk (Günther and Harttgen 2006). How this is applied will differ between micro- and macro-level measures. In Chapter 2 of this book it was shown how to identify the relative importance of idiosyncratic and covariate risk at a household level. We have not dealt with this at a macro level in this book. However, we can mention in this regard that Guillaumont (2008) has argued that countries face two main sources of vulnerability: (a) environmental or natural shocks, such as natural hazards; and (b) external shocks related to trade and international prices. How vulnerable a country is to these would depend on (a) the size and frequency of these shocks, (b) the degree of exposure to these shocks, and (c) the capacity of the country to react to these shocks. From this he suggests that one should distinguish between structural economic vulnerability (which is exogenous) and state fragility (which is vulnerability resulting from inappropriate policies and institutions and weak governance). Thus, in dealing with vulnerability it is often most useful to address state fragility. We will return to this aspect in section 2.3 below.

Fourth, a good measure of vulnerability should refer to a specific cause of vulnerability: a single indicator measuring "total" household or country vulnerability is unlikely to be meaningful (Cannon 2008). Thus we have emphasized in this book that we are concerned with vulnerability "to" some hazard, and the various chapters have studied vulnerability bearing this requirement in mind.

Finally, a useful criterion for a vulnerability measure to meet would be the ability to capture the dynamics of vulnerability. Thus an ideal vulnerability measure should be able to measure vulnerability (say, to poverty) not only before a hazard occurs but also during and after. Birkmann (2007) argues in this regard for measuring the vulnerability of households before, during and after a natural hazard has occurred. This is an important consideration when we want to use vulnerability measures to track the impact of policies and measures. Thus, if for instance after a flood people are left more vulnerable to ill health (owing to a greater incidence of water-borne diseases) or more vulnerable to poverty (owing to lost assets), it would be useful to have measures that could capture these changes in multidimensional vulnerability over time. Measuring the dynamics of vulnerability remains an important area for further research.

2.3 Vulnerability, resilience and state fragility

A number of chapters in this book have discussed the importance of understanding how a household or a country copes with risks. The implication is that vulnerability cannot be properly assessed without considering a system's ways and means of coping with risk. The term "resilience" is often used to denote a household's or a country's coping mechanisms. It has been studied in this book both at a household level and at a country level. At the household level, there is indeed a growing body of work that studies household resilience. Both *ex ante* and *ex post* coping strategies have been distinguished. *Ex ante*, households often attempt to diversify their sources of incomes, and, *ex post* a negative event, they often rely on various forms of insurance (see e.g. Fafchamps 2003; Dercon 2005). In section 3 we will deal in greater depth with the issue of insurance as an *ex post* coping strategy. For present purposes though, an important message in this book is that household capabilities, household assets and the fragility of their contexts (including state fragility and fragility of the natural environment) play an important role in vulnerability. The role of household capabilities (characteristics) and assets has been particularly stressed in Part I of this book. We can note that the role of assets in coping has also been studied in other disciplines, and is especially prominent in the sustainable livelihoods approach (e.g. Moser 1998). There is also a growing concern with fragile states and fragility of the natural environment, as the chapters in Part II of this book in particular have shown. Given the scope of this book, we are now in a position to draw these two strands together.

Figure 11.1 is a conceptual framework that summarizes and generalizes the linkages between Parts I and II of this volume. The figure aims to

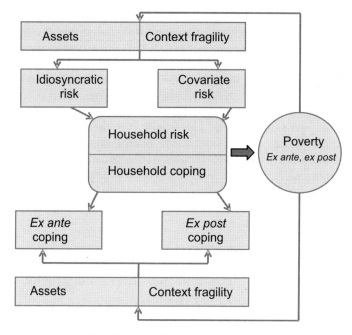

Figure 11.1 Vulnerability, resilience and fragility.

illustrate the integrated nature of vulnerability, resilience and fragility. It shows household vulnerability centrally as being determined by household risk and household coping (resilience). The extent to which vulnerability interacts with idiosyncratic and covariate hazards/shocks (including natural hazards and macroeconomic shocks) determines the outcome in terms of current or expected states of poverty, whether poverty is defined in income, consumption or broader wellbeing terms. Both the extent of and sensitivity to hazards, and the coping strategies adopted, are functions of a household's endowments or assets and the fragility of the external context, be it local, regional, national or global. The type of hazard shock also influences a household's coping strategy, with covariate shocks being more difficult for individual households to manage or insure against, calling for national or international support (Dayton-Johnson 2006: 7).

Often, the fragility of the context will determine the extent of household assets or endowments. For instance, in fragile states public infrastructure provision is often lacking. However, as the arrows in the figure imply, household assets and endowments can also influence the extent of fragility at the regional or national level, through for instance non-tangible assets such as trust, social networks and cohesion. The figure also shows that poverty has a feedback effect to household assets and the fragility of the external context. This reflects the fact that poverty is in itself a cause of vulnerability at the household level and of fragility at the national level (Hulme et al. 2001). This fact has been amply demonstrated in the chapters in this book, where adverse coping mechanisms have been emphasized. Elsewhere in the literature, adverse forms of coping have been shown to impact negatively on the fragility of the macro environment, most notably in the case of sustainable livelihoods and natural hazards where poor people often have no alternative but to over-exploit scarce natural resources, in the process also increasing their vulnerability to natural hazards. For example, deforestation is often a significant contributing factor to flooding and mudslides, which claim significant numbers of lives in developing countries.

3 Implications for policies and measures to deal with vulnerability

Vulnerability can never be eliminated. However, a number of suggestions for dealing with vulnerability in a manner that will contribute towards a reduction in household poverty can be drawn from this book. Our conceptual framework as presented in Figure 11.1 suggests that, in order to deal with vulnerability, policymakers and development institutions need to focus primarily on households (their risks and resilience), on assets (including insurance) and on the fragility context. In focusing on these, at least three basic requirements need to be met.

3.1 Basic requirements

First, households cannot be left on their own to deal with the hazards they face, even though they are remarkably inventive and resilient. Their efforts at insuring themselves against risk need to be complemented by community, government and international actions. There are three reasons for external assistance to mitigate household vulnerability. One is that the sheer impact of shocks is often overwhelming for individual households. This has been amply illustrated in this book in the chapters dealing with vulnerability to natural hazards in small-island states. A second reason is that many of the goods needed to strengthen household resilience are public goods. Several of the chapters in this book have emphasized the importance of basic goods and services, including education, health services, public infrastructure and protection of property rights, as essential determinants of household vulnerability. A third reason is that the consequences of vulnerability can have negative spillover effects on other households and countries through adverse coping.

Second, policymakers and development institutions need to acknowledge that poverty is a multidimensional, dynamic and forward-looking concept. As is clear from our conceptual framework in Figure 11.1, poverty is the outcome of the relative impacts of risk and resilience, both of which are affected by policies. It would therefore be very useful if performance indicators related the success of poverty reduction strategies and policies to their impact on risk and resilience.

Third, based on the discussion of Figure 11.1, it is clear that the nature of vulnerability will differ from household to household and from country to country. Local knowledge is therefore vital in addressing vulnerability. This is an important lesson from Chapter 4. It is unlikely that a one-size-fits-all approach will be useful in addressing vulnerability.

Fourth, as implied by the previous requirement, vulnerability and resilience need to be measured and measurements need to be continually improved. As has been shown in this book, this applies to various levels and outcomes of vulnerability. The proper and useful measurement of vulnerability and resilience will require much better data than are currently available. It is especially in the most vulnerable countries, for instance those in sub-Saharan Africa, where data constraints are often the most serious. Investing in sound, reliable, timely and regular data to capture poverty/vulnerability/resilience will in itself be an investment in resilience.

3.2 Appropriate responses

How can vulnerability be reduced or managed? Here we propose an approach that aims to reduce risks, to mitigate risks and to assist risk coping, through three broad classes of interventions: (a) strengthening resilience, (b) building bulwarks, and (c) ensuring quality institutions. The approach is outlined in Figure 11.2, which argues, based on the various contributions in this book, that vulnerability should be dealt with by governments, donors and development institutions by focusing on household capabilities, on assets and insurance, and on the fragile context facing households in developing countries. The aim is to reduce risks, mitigate risks where they exist, and help households to cope in a positive manner with risks. This could be achieved in a number of ways, as described under "Policies & measures" in Figure 11.2.

The first is by strengthening household resilience. The various chapters in this book have identified a number of ways in which this can be done. For instance, raising incomes (Chapters 2, 7 and 9), providing education

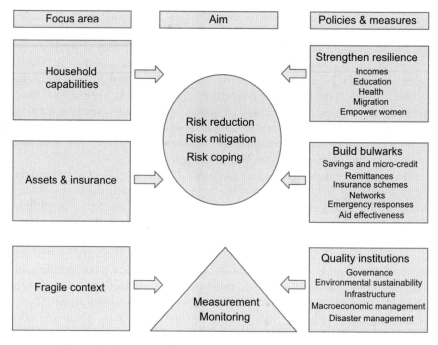

Focus area	Aim	Policies & measures

Figure 11.2 Responding to vulnerability: A generic approach.

and health (Chapters 4, 6 and 7), addressing the challenges faced by migrants (Chapters 6 and 9), and empowering women (Chapters 5 and 9) are all crucial means through which to improve household resilience.

The second way is to build bulwarks. Bulwarks are primarily intended to help households to manage risk *ex post*. Thus, from the contributions in this book we can identify a number of measures, such as raising household saving and providing access to micro-credit (Chapter 3), facilitating remittances (Chapters 6 and 9), strengthening networks (Chapters 2, 3, 6 and 9) and improving emergency responses and aid (Chapters 7, 9 and 10). Also, based on the assessment of the relative importance of idiosyncratic and covariate risks in this book (Chapter 2), we can stress the general importance of insurance (both formal and informal) for coping. For both households and countries, insurance mechanisms are essential in limiting adverse shocks to income from also causing adverse shocks in consumption. Insurance is thus said to be "consumption smoothing". Unfortunately, as many studies have found, households in developing countries tend not to have adequate insurance, as evidenced by the degree to which they cannot smooth out their consumption in times of crisis. We did not deal in depth with the issue of insurance in this book because the UNU-WIDER study on *Insurance Against Poverty* (see Dercon 2005) is devoted to the issue of insurance.

The third class of measures to deal with vulnerability relate to ensuring the establishment and functioning of quality institutions. Much has been written about institutions and development in recent times, and we do not wish to discuss this literature in detail here. Instead the reader is referred to the UNU-WIDER study on *Institutional Change and Economic Development* (Chang 2007). However, a few aspects from this book are worth stressing as far as the role of institutions in vulnerability is concerned. A number of chapters in Part II showed that covariate risks – for instance in relation to natural hazards and macroeconomic shocks – are high in developing countries, particularly in small-island developing states. Here, the requirement for risk reduction would necessitate appropriate policies and institutions to help these countries cope with the effects of both "structural" vulnerability and state fragility. In essence, such countries must put policies and institutions in place that strengthen their economic resilience. In the case of many developing economies, increasing economic diversification has been recommended as a strategy to reduce the risks from adverse external shocks (structural vulnerability). Furthermore, as was argued in Chapter 10, macroeconomic policies in these countries should aim not only at price stability but also at output and employment stabilization. The preconditions are however that countries build and strengthen appropriate labour market, financial and governance institutions.

Finally, the approach summarized in Figure 11.2 needs to be complemented by the finding in a number of chapters that household coping strategies need to be better understood. For instance, adverse forms of coping can exacerbate household poverty and vulnerability and can push households into chronic poverty. In the Zimbabwean case discussed in Chapter 5, adverse coping included children dropping out of school, soil degradation as a result of desperate but unsustainable farming methods, cutting down on healthcare and engaging in criminal activities. Also, although migration is a favoured coping strategy in developing countries – in the face of droughts or conflict for example – Chapter 6 in this book has shown that such a coping strategy is in itself not without risks. It is also important to bear in mind the call in Chapter 9 for a "gendered" approach to vulnerability. Women often comprise a disproportionate share of the poor, and women's traditional roles as caregivers and their often more extensive social networks make them important agents in the identification and mitigation of risks and in post-disaster assistance. The overall implication is that strategies and policies to deal with vulnerability should be careful not to introduce or cause new sources of vulnerability.

4 Concluding remarks

The chapters in this book have shown that great progress has been made in recent years in understanding and expanding the notion of vulnerability, and that these advances have important implications for the reduction of poverty. They have also shown that much remains to be done, in terms of refining, measuring and applying the notion of vulnerability, but also in tackling vulnerability through strengthening household resilience, building appropriate bulwarks against risk and creating and maintaining quality institutions. It is hoped that this book will stimulate further research and discourse on these aspects.

Note

1. De Léon (2006) contains an excellent summary of the development of the concept of vulnerability outside the field of economics, from the work of Chambers (1989), which focuses on sustainable livelihoods of households, to the work sponsored by the Department of Economic and Social Affairs of the United Nations, which focuses on the vulnerability of small-island states, and the work of the United Nations University's Institute for Environmental and Human Security.

References

Addison, T., D. Hulme and R. Kanbur (2008). *Poverty Dynamics: Interdisciplinary Perspectives*. Oxford: Oxford University Press.

Alwang, J., P. B. Siegel and S. Jorgenson (2001). "Vulnerability: A View from Different Disciplines". Social Protection Discussion Paper 0115, World Bank, Washington DC.

Baliamoune-Lutz, M. and M. McGillivray (2008). "State Fragility: Concept and Measurement". UNU-WIDER Research Paper RP2008/44, Helsinki.

Birkmann, J. (2007). "Assessing Vulnerability Before, During and After a Disaster of Natural Origin in Fragile Regions: Case Study: Tsunami in Sri Lanka and Indonesia". Paper presented at the UNU-WIDER Conference on Fragile States – Fragile Groups, Helsinki, 15 June.

Bossert, W., S. R. Chakravarty and C. D'Ambrosio (2008). "Poverty and Time". Paper presented at the UNU-WIDER Conference on Frontiers of Poverty Analysis, Helsinki, 26–27 September.

Cannon, T. (2008). "Reducing People's Vulnerability to Natural Hazards: Communities and Resilience". UNU-WIDER Research Paper No. RP 2008-34.

Cannon, T., J. Twigg and J. Rowell (2003). "Social Vulnerability, Sustainable Livelihoods and Disasters". Report to DFID, Conflict and Humanitarian Assistance Department (CHAD) and Sustainable Livelihoods Support Office, London; available at ⟨http://www.benfieldhrc.org/disaster_studies/projects/soc_vuln_sustlive.pdf⟩ (accessed 29 January 2009).

Chambers, R. (1989). "Vulnerability". *IDS Bulletin* 20(2): 1–7.

Chang, H.-J. (2007). *Institutional Change and Economic Development*. Tokyo: United Nations University Press.

CPRC [Chronic Poverty Research Centre] (2008). *The Chronic Poverty Report 2008–09: Escaping Poverty Traps*. Available at ⟨http://www.chronicpoverty.org⟩ (accessed 29 January 2009).

Dayton-Johnson, J. (2006). "Natural Disasters and Vulnerability". OECD Development Centre Policy Brief 29, Paris.

De Léon, J. C. V. (2006). "Vulnerability: A Conceptual and Methodological Review". *Source* 4/2006. Bonn: UNU-EHS.

Dercon, S. (ed.) (2005). *Insurance Against Poverty*. UNU-WIDER Studies in Development Economics. Oxford: Oxford University Press.

Dutta, I., J. Foster and A. Mishra (2008). "On Measuring Vulnerability". Paper presented at the UNU-WIDER Conference on Frontiers of Poverty Analysis, Helsinki, 26–27 September.

Fafchamps, M. (2003). *Rural Poverty, Risk and Development*. Cheltenham: Edward Elgar.

Guillaumont, P. (2008). "Design of an Economic Vulnerability Index and Its Use for International Development Policy". UNU-WIDER Research Paper 2008/99, Helsinki.

Günther, I. and J. Maier (2008). "Poverty, Vulnerability and Loss Aversion". Paper presented at the UNU-WIDER Conference on Frontiers of Poverty Analysis, Helsinki, 26–27 September.

Günther, J. and K. Harttgen (2006). "Estimating Vulnerability to Covariate and Idiosyncratic Shocks". University of Göttingen, Department of Economics.

Hulme, D. and A. McKay (2005). "Identifying and Understanding Chronic Poverty: Beyond Income Measures". Paper presented at the Many Dimensions of Poverty Conference, Brasilia, Brazil, 29 August.

Hulme, D., K. Moore and A. Shepherd (2001). "Chronic Poverty: Meanings and Analytical Frameworks". CPRC Working Paper 2, Institute of Development Policy and Management, Manchester.

Moser, C. (1998). "The Asset Vulnerability Framework: Reassessing Urban Poverty Reduction Strategies". *World Development* 26(1): 1–19.

Yuan, Z. and G. Wan (2008). "Can We Predict Vulnerability to Poverty?" UNU-WIDER Research Paper 2008/82, Helsinki.

Index